Peace Be upon You

Peace Be upon You

THE STORY OF MUSLIM, CHRISTIAN, AND JEWISH COEXISTENCE

Zachary Karabell

Alfred A. Knopf · New York · 2007

THIS IS A BORZOI BOOK
PUBLISHED BY ALFRED A. KNOPF

Copyright © 2007 by Zachary Karabell
All rights reserved. Published in the United States by Alfred A. Knopf,
a division of Random House, Inc., New York,
and in Canada by Random House of Canada Limited, Toronto.
www.aaknopf.com

Knopf, Borzoi Books, and the colophon are
registered trademarks of Random House, Inc.

Library of Congress Cataloging-in-Publication Data
Karabell, Zachary.
Peace be upon you : the story of Muslim, Christian,
and Jewish coexistence / by Zachary Karabell.
p.   cm.
Includes bibliographical references and index.
ISBN 978-1-4000-4368-2
1. Religions—Relations. I. Title.
BL410.K37 2007
201'5—dc22   2006031501

Manufactured in the United States of America
First Edition

CONTENTS

Peace Be upon You

Introduction

THERE IS KNOWN history and forgotten history, history that sup-
ports our sense of present and history that suggests other pathways. Here is the known: in A.D. 632, the Prophet Muhammad died in
Mecca. He left a vibrant set of teachings, nine wives, a number of children, and several thousand Arab followers who called themselves Muslims. Less than two decades after his death, the adherents of this new
faith had destroyed one empire and crippled another: the Persian shah
was hunted down and killed on the banks of the Oxus River after a
thousand-mile chase; Heraclius, the Byzantine emperor, who had only a
few years before retaken Jerusalem, saw his realm cut in half as the heirs
of Muhammad occupied Damascus, Antioch, Alexandria, and Jerusalem. The emperor collapsed and died when he learned that the city of
Christ had fallen, even though the Muslims had spared the inhabitants
the depredations normally inflicted by conquering armies.

With the Persians annihilated and the Byzantines crippled, the victorious Muslim armies were limited only by numbers and their own internal divisions. Had they stayed united, they might have continued on to
India in the east and Europe in the west. As it was, they paused to fight
two civil wars. Then the conquests began again, and Arab navies reached
the walls of Constantinople before they were halted by a mysterious
substance called Greek fire that set ships ablaze. Thousands of miles to
the west, the general Tariq ibn Ziyad crossed from North Africa into the
Iberian Peninsula and advanced to the Pyrenees. His armies might have
continued all the way to the English Channel had he not been recalled
by the caliph. He returned across the strait that now bears his name—

3

Jebel Tariq, the Mountain of Tariq, Gibraltar. Some years later, his vanguard met the stiff resistance of Charles Martel at the battle of Tours, in what would later become southern France, and the conquerors retreated from Europe, content with their new kingdom, al-Andalus, where they would remain for nearly a thousand years.

The sudden eruption of Islam left an indelible mark on Europe and established a template of conflict between Islam and the West. But conflict is not the only story: after the Muslims consolidated their gains, the Abbasid caliphate came to power in Baghdad in the middle of the eighth century. At its height, the Abbasid Empire stretched from present-day Morocco to the mountains of Afghanistan. The greatest of its caliphs was Harun al-Rashid, who ruled from Baghdad in a palace as ornate and romantic as subsequent imagination described it. He gathered the greatest musicians, poets, dancers, and, above all, theologians. Poets would appear at court and sing praises to the wonders of wine, while pious scholars, many of whom took the Quranic injunction against alcohol seriously, listened politely. A winning poem or a delightful song could earn a poet gold, or horses groomed in the caliph's stables, or a slave girl for the night.

On countless evenings, the court was transformed into an arena for theological debate. Muslim men of learning, schooled in sharia, the law derived from the Quran, offered their wisdom and drew on the philosophical tradition of the ancient Greeks. The works of Aristotle and Plato were translated into Arabic and used not only to enrich Islam but to create new science and new philosophy. And the caliph was not content simply to take the word of his learned men. He wanted to see how their ideas met opposing theologies, and he invited scholars and preachers of other faiths to his court. Jews, Christians, Buddhists, and Muslims engaged in spiritual and spirited jousts, and each tradition was enriched by knowledge of the others.

From the beginning of Islam, Muslims viewed Jews and Christians as distant, slightly errant, relatives. In honor of the fact that they worshiped the same God and had been given the same revelation as Muhammad, they were called *ahl al-kitab*, the People of the Book. Muslims were expected to treat them honorably. Though Harun al-Rashid went further than most to embrace different faiths, he was fully within the Islamic tradition.

But Harun al-Rashid soon passed into myth, known in the West and in the Muslim world mostly as a character in *A Thousand and One Nights,* along with Ali Baba, Sinbad the Sailor, and Scheherazade. Today, the notion that a Muslim ruler and a Muslim state might tolerate and even welcome other faiths is alien, not only to people in the Judeo-Christian West but to hundreds of millions of Muslims as well. The early-twenty-first-century world is polarized by the conflict between Muslims, Christians, and Jews. Many Americans and Europeans see Islam as a religion of violence, especially toward those who do not share the faith, and millions of Muslims understand the history of Islam to be one of conquest and victory over nonbelievers, followed by defeat and setbacks. On all sides, this lens distorts the past, constricts our present, and endangers our future.

In truth, each of the three traditions has a core of peace. In churches throughout the world, worshipers turn to one another and say, "Peace be upon you." Walk into any store, home, or mosque anywhere in the Muslim world, and you will be greeted with *salaam alaykum,* "Peace be upon you." And the response is always the same: "And upon you, peace." Jews in Israel will begin and end a conversation with the simple salutation *shalom,* "peace." Each of the faiths teaches its followers to greet friends and strangers with the warm open arms of acceptance. Peace comes first and last.

That is not the common view. Scholars have rarely lost sight of the legacy of coexistence, and a student at almost any university can take courses or read one of the thousands of books and articles that illuminate it. Yet somehow that awareness has remained locked away in university libraries or confined to college courses. As a result, in America and in Europe, all that most people hear is the echo of the Arab conquests that followed Muhammad's death. And in the Muslim world, the memory of imperialism and Western aggression obscures memories of cooperation.

I have spent much of my life asking why this is. The reason may be simple: perhaps times of death and war leave a more lasting impression than periods of peace and calm. Maybe turmoil and confrontation sear the memory more deeply. But there are consequences to our selective readings of the past, in both the Muslim world and the Western world. As much as we want history to say something definitive about the present, it does not. History is a vast canvas, where it is possible to find support for nearly every belief, every statement about human nature, and every possible outcome of the present. That doesn't make history any less important, but it is up to each of us to use it well.

My first political memories were shaped by growing up in the 1970s, when the Arab-Israeli conflict was a focus of American foreign policy and the cause of unending international tension. With the exception of the Cold War between the United States and the Soviet Union, the Arab-Israeli conflict seemed to be the most likely candidate for plunging the world into chaos, and the phrase "peace in the Middle East" was always met by a derisive laugh. But while the Israeli side of the story was well represented in the media and in classrooms, the Arab side was not. That was the side I wanted to learn about.

That led to more than a decade of study, first as an undergraduate in New York and then as a graduate student in England and in Boston. I studied Arabic, traveled throughout the Middle East, and began to teach the history of the region and the history of Islam. I found that my students usually viewed Islam through a dark prism of Muslim hordes threatening to deluge Christendom. The actual stories might have been blurry in their minds, but each time they saw a picture of a mosque or of an imam leading prayer, it struck a deep negative chord: Islam is a religion of war and violence, and Muslims have clashed with Christians and Jews forever. Those beliefs were hardly limited to my students. They are part of our culture.

Throughout the Middle East and North Africa, I encountered a similar prejudice toward the West. Well before the events of September 11, 2001, there was an entrenched belief that the West is the enemy of Islam. That has only intensified in recent years. Images of an aggressive, imperialist West from the time of the Crusades through the twentieth century animate angry Pakistani preachers in Peshawar, indignant Saudi clerics in Medina, and of course Osama bin Laden. Not only is the court of Harun al-Rashid forgotten, but so too is medieval Iberia, where the Jewish polymath Maimonides, the Sufi mystic Ibn 'Arabi, and a phalanx of Christian monks helped one another unravel the meaning of God and the universe; so too is the twelfth-century Levant, where the inhabitants of Crusader city-states and Muslim emirates traded, bartered, and intermarried; so is the Ottoman Empire, where each religious community, whether Greek Orthodox, Jewish, or Maronite Christian, was allowed almost complete autonomy save for the payment of annual taxes. The

Ottoman system, in fact, was a form of religious freedom nearly as expansive as what existed in the early United States.

But while anti-Western prejudice was part of the culture of the Middle East, it was only one part. The Islam I encountered barely resembled the images I grew up with and that continue to surround us today. The Islam of a cabdriver who helped me navigate Cairo, who stopped to pray and then played his bootleg Madonna cassette, who wanted to know about New York and looked at me as a good way to get a week's worth of pay to feed his family, didn't fit the narrow images that surround us in the West. The Islam of village mosques in Egypt or of a Saudi truck driver who gave me a lift in Jordan and then took an hour-long detour just so I could gaze over the Sea of Galilee; the Islam of Ahmed the hairdresser on a bus to Syria, who did his best to convince a twenty-something me to go to his salon in Damascus; and the Islam of the Kurdish family that sold me a kilim near Lake Van, in eastern Turkey—none of that was familiar.

But what was perhaps most unexpected was how infrequently I encountered Islam in the Muslim world. We have heard so often that there is no separation of church and state in Islam, and that religion is at the heart of everyday life. It is for some, but it shares space with the ebb and flow of daily existence. A man might pray at a mosque, spend a quiet moment submitting to God, and then be plunged into his workaday world, squabbling with neighbors, speaking with friends, watching the soccer game on television, going home to his children. The uneventful reality of everyday life should be obvious, so obvious that it shouldn't even bear mentioning. But what is so startling is that it isn't obvious to us, nor is the prosaic quality of our daily lives obvious to them.

That is true not just for our present but for the past. Today more than ever, bringing the panoply of the past into sharper focus is vital. That means clearing away the cobwebs and paying attention to the long periods where coexistence was more prominent, and also examining the reasons for war and violence that had little to do with religion, even when it was Muslims fighting Christians or Muslims fighting Jews.

Like any prejudice, the mutual animosity between Islam and the West is fueled by ignorance and selective memory. If we emphasize hate, scorn, war, and conquest, we are unlikely to perceive that any other path is viable. If we assume that religion is the primary source of conflict, we are unlikely to address factors that have nothing to do with religion. Unaware of the history of coexistence between Islam and the West, Americans tend to believe, though perhaps not say, that until the Muslim world becomes less Muslim and more Western, terrorism, nuclear pro- liferation, and war are inevitable. The same myopia about the past inclines Muslims from Rabat to Jakarta to dismiss talk of democracy and freedom as simply the latest Western, not to mention Christian and Jew- ish, assault on their independence and dignity.

Reclaiming the legacy of coexistence may not make the world whole, but it does show that Islam and the West need not be locked in a death dance. To the degree that each creed holds that it alone has the key to truth and salvation, there will always be a degree of tension. But rivalry and competition do not lead inexorably to war and violence. Christians, Jews, and Muslims have lived constructively with one another. They have taught one another and they have learned from one another. Judaism was central to the formation of Islam, and for a millennium and a half, until the end of World War II, Jews under Muslim rule enjoyed more safety, freedom, and autonomy than they ever did under Christian rule. Muslim states over the course of fourteen centuries have allowed for religious diversity and not insisted on trying to convert those who follow a different creed. From the beginning of Islam, Christian and Muslim states traded with one another. For fourteen centuries, Chris- tians fought as soldiers in Muslim armies, and in the twentieth century, Arab Christians were instrumental in creating the states of the modern Middle East.

Focusing only on conflict is like skipping every other page while reading a book. It isn't just incomplete; it is misleading to the point of incoherence. At the same time, it is important to avoid the opposite temptation and not replace one distorted reading of the past with another. Too often, those who attempt to rectify the imbalance provide the missing pages but delete the others. The result is just as skewed. The tolerance of Muslim society is praised and moments of concord are highlighted, but the violence and animosity are downplayed. Coexis- tence is treated as the norm and conflict as the anomaly, when in truth, both are threaded through the past and our present. Also overlooked is the fact that not all cooperation is good cooperation. Alliances between Muslim and Christian states were often the result of "the enemy of my enemy is my friend," concluded for the purposes of war, not peace. That should temper any optimism that we can all just get along.

So as not to substitute one skewed version of the past with another, the pages that follow present stories of both conflict and cooperation. This book is not meant to be a comprehensive history of the past fourteen hundred years, and most of the stories have been told elsewhere by others in more depth. However, because the periods of concord are less known to most people, the lesson for the present and the future naturally seems optimistic: there is a possibility of peace and constructive coexistence between Muslims, Christians, and Jews—and more to the point, between believing Muslims, Christians, and Jews who, in their heart of hearts, think that their creed and their creed alone reflects God's will. Given today's realities, that is a hopeful message.

This book is, of course, framed by the events of the early twenty-first century. Muslim societies have been their most tolerant when they have been secure. That is hardly unusual in human affairs, but for most of the past century, few Muslim communities have felt secure. One of the results of September 11 is that Western societies have also become insecure, rationally or not. The result is a rise of intolerance on all sides. Increasingly, more people throughout the world believe that Muslim and Western societies are destined to clash and that they will always clash until one or the other triumphs. That belief is poisonous, and one antidote is the rich historical tradition that says other paths are not only possible but have been taken time and again.

By historical standards, today's fissure between Islam and the West is not exceptional, but because of the technologies of death and because of weapons of mass destruction, that fissure has the potential to undo us. That is reason enough to take a look back and recognize that while the relationship between Islam and the West can be fratricidal, it can also be fraternal. Retrieving the forgotten history of relations between Islam and the West isn't a panacea, but it is a vital ingredient to a more stable, secure world. The story begins in the seventh century, on the western coast of the Arabian Peninsula, in the city of Mecca, where a man named Muhammad, born of the tribe of Quraysh, heard the voice of God. "Recite!" he was told, and he did. And the world changed forever.

❧ ❧

CHAPTER ONE

In the Name of the Lord

S OMETIME AROUND the year 570 in the Western calendar, Muhammad ibn Abdullah was born in the oasis town of Mecca, just off the western coast of the Arabian Peninsula. The town was separated from the Red Sea by a narrow, steep mountain range, and it sat at the edge of the vast desert that defined the Arabian Peninsula. The oasis was dominated by the Quraysh tribe, who controlled the camel trade that passed through Mecca. The trade route linked Yemen, in the south, to the settled agrarian regions hundreds of miles north, which were then divided between the Byzantine emperor and the Sasanian monarch of Persia.

Though Muhammad was a member of the ruling tribe, his clan was not particularly prominent. His father died when Muhammad was a boy, and his uncle Abu Talib became his protector. For most of the next forty years, Muhammad lived an anonymous life like that of many others in Mecca; he established himself as a merchant and married an older widow named Khadija. Had he died before the age of forty, his would have been one of the countless lives invisible to history, and Mecca itself would have remained a small provincial town no more important than thousands of others throughout the world. But around the year 610, Muhammad began to hear the voice of God, and for the first time, God spoke in Arabic.

Muhammad did not share these revelations with anyone other than his wife. Prophets were rarely welcome, and Muhammad did not have sufficient standing in the community to defend himself against adversaries who might not welcome the message he was being given. While the experience of receiving the revelations was physically wrenching for

Muhammad, the substance was socially wrenching for the Meccans. Rather than a system anchored by tribe, clan, and family, Muhammad announced a new order, anchored by God's will and human submission to it—hence the words *islam,* the Arabic word for "submit," and *muslim,* the Arabic word for one who does.

Muhammad began to share the content of what he was being told with a small circle of friends and family, and slowly the message spread. At first, the more powerful members of the Quraysh dismissed the sermons as irrelevant, but as more people started to listen, the Quraysh became concerned. From what they could glean, Muhammad's call represented a challenge to the social order that they dominated.

They were right to be concerned. In their Mecca of tribe and clan, they were supreme. Obeisance was given to the various gods and spirits known as jinn (the kindred English word is "genie"), but one's tribe was more consequential than any god. At the time, there was a nascent sense of monotheism, though not much more developed than a vague notion that there was one god more powerful than the others. But the Quraysh of Mecca were not prepared to embrace Him alone, because that would have upended the status quo. In their world, the tribe, not any god, determined social standing and marriage, and it was up to the tribe and the clan to avenge wrongs committed by others. Tribal authority was absolute—until Muhammad announced that it was not.

The core message was simple: there is one God, one messenger, and a choice. The God is Allah, who is the same as the God of Abraham, the God of the Hebrew prophets, the God of Jesus, and the God of the Christians. The messenger is Muhammad, a man like any other until he was chosen to convey God's word in Arabic. And the choice is to surrender to God's will and to the truth of Muhammad's recitations and thus be saved for eternity.

The initial revelations emphasized the extent of God's power and the degree of human powerlessness in the face of it. Later assembled in the Quran, these verses paint a vivid picture of a world destined to end in a final judgment, and they warn that only those who embrace the message conveyed by Muhammad will be blessed. Because the revelations unfolded over the course of many years, it took some time before they congealed into a coherent belief system. Within a decade, however, Muhammad began to challenge the system of the Quraysh directly.

The most prominent symbol of that confrontation involved the so-called Satanic Verses, which were an earlier version of a portion of the Quran that seemed to allow for the dual worship of Allah and of three of the gods of the Quraysh: al-Lat, al-Uzza, and Manat. The Satanic Verses may have been an attempt to strike a compromise with the increasingly hostile Quraysh, but the Quraysh were not placated. Instructed by the archangel Gabriel, Muhammad recanted the verses. He claimed that they had been a trick of the devil and issued an unequivocal condemnation of al-Lat, al-Uzza, and Manat. They were not gods, he declared, only mere names.

This assault on the prevailing religious system marked a dramatic turn away from conciliation with the rulers of Mecca. Initially, Muhammad had emphasized social justice, the mystery of life, and Allah's supreme power, and had hoped that the Quraysh would accept him. When it became clear that they would not, he indicted not just the religion of the Meccans but the Quraysh who upheld it.

As long as his uncle Abu Talib was alive, Muhammad could be criticized and marginalized but he could not be silenced or physically harmed. When Abu Talib died, in 619, however, Muhammad was placed in a precarious position. Faced with an antagonistic tribe and few options, he was responsible for the security and well-being of a community of followers, most of whom occupied the fringes of Meccan society, and he was beginning to attract adherents beyond the city.

As the position of the Muslims in Mecca deteriorated, it was not simply a problem of discrimination and intimidation. Without the protection that his uncle provided, Muhammad and his followers were in physical danger, and he began looking for a new home. He could not, however, simply pick up and leave. He had to find a tribe in another town willing to offer him protection and acceptance. In a world where resources were scarce and water, date palms, and trade were tightly controlled, there was no such thing as moving to another town to start a new life, and certainly not with eighty followers in tow.

After several false starts, Muhammad through his intermediaries negotiated an arrangement with several tribes in the oasis of Yathrib, later known as Medina, two hundred miles north of Mecca. They wanted Muhammad to become their chief. The tribes of Medina were at an impasse, and they were willing to turn to Muhammad because he could act as a neutral arbiter. Having secured a home in Medina, Muhammad and his followers then began to leave Mecca, quietly, in small groups, so that the Quraysh would not notice.

The move from Mecca to Medina in 622, known as the Hijra, was one of the defining moments in Islamic history. It led to the establishment of an independent and increasingly powerful Muslim community. It also put this community in direct contact with three Jewish tribes. Muhammad expected that they would embrace him as the last in a long line of prophets. They did not.

THE PEOPLE OF THE BOOK

THE WORLD of early-seventh-century Arabia was sparsely populated. Settlements centered on water sources, and these attracted traders and tribes. Some worshiped local deities; others not at all. But there were also a substantial number of Jews and Christians. The Christians were from several different sects, and few followed the doctrines established by the patriarchs in Constantinople. The Monophysite Christians of Egypt, believing that Christ's human nature had been absorbed by his divine nature, were deeply disenchanted with the Byzantine emperor and the official interpretation of the Trinity; the Christians of Syria and Palestine were only slightly less disaffected; and the Assyrian (Nestorian) Christians of what is now Iraq, who had their own view of the nature of Christ, had long been seen as heretics by the church fathers further west. But even though the Christians of Arabia were disparate, Muhammad and the Meccans would have been familiar with the outlines of their faith, including the life of Christ and the basic precepts of the New Testament.

The Jews had been in Arabia for centuries. Before Muhammad's birth, the Arabian king Dhu Nuwas had converted to Judaism and then launched what appears to have been a mini pogrom against the Christians. In many respects, Arabian Jews were indistinguishable from other tribes. The harsh realities of desert life and the way that people adapted and survived did not know from clan or creed. Jews dressed in the way everyone else dressed, and confronted the same challenges posed by nature. They traded with the Quraysh and other leading Arab tribes, and spoke a dialect of Arabic. Because of their God and certain aspects of diet, marriage, and law, they were culturally distinct. On the whole, however, they were more familiar than alien to Muhammad, and that may explain his initial hope that they would welcome him and his message. The Quran is quite clear that there is an unbroken line from the Hebrew prophets through Jesus Christ leading ultimately to Muhammad. When the Jews of Medina refused to acknowledge that, Muhammad and his increasingly powerful followers began to treat them as enemies.

Initially, when Muhammad arrived in Medina, an agreement was reached between the two non-Jewish tribes, the three Jewish tribes, and the new community of Muhammad and his followers. Whether this was a written document or a verbal understanding, it became known as the Constitution of Medina, and it was a model of ecumenism. It was also a necessity. Given the circumstances of Muhammad's arrival in Medina, it was essential that the various parties agree on how this new confederation would be governed. Without that, there would be no way to settle the conflicts that would inevitably arise.

Many of the constitution's clauses dealt with relations between the newly arrived Muslims and the major tribes of Medina. "The believers and their dependents constitute a single community [*umma*]" was the first clause, and in terms of later Islamic history, one of the most important. In that simple statement, the unity of Muslims everywhere was established. To this day, there is a deep sense in the Muslim world that all believers constitute one community. That means that state boundaries and doctrinal differences that separate Muslims are false and wrong.

Having established the principle of unity, the constitution laid out the responsibilities of the tribes: they would each police themselves and administer justice to their own members, and murder was forbidden. No individual Muslim was to act in a manner contrary to the will or needs of other Muslims, and believers were enjoined to take care of their dependents. And as for the Jews, they "belong to the community and are to retain their own religion; they and the Muslims are to render help to one another when it is needed." Intertribal alliances were hardly unknown in pre-Islamic Arabia, and tribes did not need to share a religious system in order to act in concert. In that sense, Muhammad and the other interested parties could draw on past precedent in drawing up the Constitution of Medina.[1]

For a brief moment, Medina became a unified Jewish-Muslim community. In the words of the constitution, "The Jews have their religion,
and the Muslims have their religion," and yet the two lived side by side
as equals and supported each other when and where support was
needed. Muhammad saw himself as the last in a series of Jewish
prophets, and he instructed his followers to face Jerusalem when they
prayed. In this hybrid community, Muhammad had the role of first
among equals and the arbiter of disputes. The Constitution of Medina
created a precedent for peaceful and cordial coexistence. Unfortunately,
it did not last long.

There were three powerful Jewish tribes, and the first that Muhammad confronted was the Banu Qaynuqa. The precise reason for the fissure isn't clear. The ninth-century chronicler al-Baladhuri reported
only that "the Jews of Qaynuqa were the first to violate the covenant and
the Prophet expelled them from Medina."[2] Al-Bukhari, also writing in
the ninth century, mentioned that as the Muslim community grew, the
Muslim immigrants needed more land and more date groves, and the
reluctance of the Jews to accede to Muhammad's authority made them a
legitimate target. Another aggravating factor was the refusal of the Jewish
tribes to come to Muhammad's aid during the battle of Badr, when the
Muslims of Medina, to the astonishment of the Quraysh, defeated a small
army sent from Mecca. Still others claim that hostilities erupted because
an Arab woman was the victim of a practical joke that resulted in her skirt
riding up too high, which led a Muslim man to kill the perpetrator, who
happened to be Jewish. Whatever the proximate cause, the Jews of the
Banu Qaynuqa refused to validate Muhammad's claims to prophethood.
After a standoff, they were expelled, and that led to a symbolic shift
in how Muslims prayed. Instead of facing Jerusalem, they now turned
toward Mecca. Jerusalem would remain a holy city for Muslims, but after
the banishment of the Banu Qaynuqa, Mecca became the focal point.

Over the next three years, the Muslims of Medina gained converts,
including some Jews. Events alternated between skirmishes with the
Quraysh and confrontation with the remaining Jewish tribes. After
Muhammad led his followers to a battlefield victory against the Meccans, he broke with the second Jewish tribe, the Banu Nadir. They were
expelled after a two-week siege, but unlike their predecessors, they were
not allowed to take their weapons.

The final tribe, the Banu Qurayza, having watched as Muhammad consolidated his power, made a fateful choice: they cast their lot with the Meccans, who were preparing a final assault on Medina. The Muslims had taken control of the trade caravans, and had cut Mecca off from the source of its wealth and strength. While the Banu Qurayza did not actually consummate an alliance with the Meccans, they did not support Muhammad, and may well have been in negotiations with his enemies. Either way, they were in a difficult position. A victory for the Meccans would reduce the autonomy and influence of Medina, and lessen the power of the remaining Jewish tribe even if it removed the threat of Muhammad. A victory for the Muslims was hardly much better, and indeed turned out to be much worse. After the Meccans failed to take Medina in 627 and were forced to retreat, Muhammad ordered an attack on the Qurayza, who succumbed after a siege that lasted nearly a month. This time, the penalty wasn't expulsion; it was execution.

The fate of Medina's Jews did not establish a good precedent for future relations, but subsequent history has magnified the conflict. Some of the animosity between the Muslims and Jews of Medina was about God and prophecy, but just as much was about power and who had it. After their flight to Medina, Muhammad and the Muslims struggled to build a viable state, and the Jews of Medina as well as the Meccans represented real threats. In seventh century Arabia, when tribes fought, expulsion was the typical consequence of defeat, and the execution of all adult males, while extreme, was not beyond the pale. In truth, it would not have been beyond the pale anywhere in the world at that time, and much greater acts of brutality were commonplace.

The Jews may have been a threat to Muhammad, but Muhammad was also a threat to the Jews. He offered a vision of the world that was at once similar to the Torah and yet not. Many of the stories in the Quran were part of the Jewish tradition and familiar to the Jews. But Muhammad's telling of those stories was different, in both subtle and significant ways. For instance, in the Quran, Joseph is imprisoned for refusing the advances of a powerful woman, but that woman is not Pharaoh's wife but rather a governor's wife, and in a scene not in the Bible she is then made to recant her accusations when Joseph is brought into Pharaoh's court. The theological consequences of these discrepancies may be minor, but the problem for both Jews and Muslims was the fact they existed at all. Moses, Noah, Jacob, and other biblical heroes figure prominently in the Quran, and while their stories are largely the same as in the Torah, they are not precisely the same. And that in itself opened a fissure between Muhammad and the Jews.

The reaction of the Jewish tribes was a mixture of bemusement and derision. They viewed Muhammad as a bumpkin, and assumed that he couldn't get the Bible right. At least that is the impression given by later sources. It's difficult to be sure of any of what happened in Muhammad's lifetime, given the long remove between the written record of what transpired and the actual events. While the gospels, for instance, were composed within decades after the death of Jesus, the most authoritative written biographies of Muhammad date from more than two centuries after his death. Even so, it is hard to imagine that the Jews of Arabia, believing themselves to be the heirs of two thousand years of tradition, would have rushed to embrace a man from Mecca claiming to wear the mantle of a prophet. Initially, they could stand apart from Muhammad, and still hope to use him to keep the peace in Medina. As his political and military power increased, and as he began to attract more converts, he became a threat. The Jewish tribes did what they could to undermine Muhammad. They failed, but the way they were then treated had little to do with their Jewishness.

To a considerable degree, how Muhammad confronted the Jews was little different from how his immediate successors dealt with Arabian tribes who refused to bow to the Muslim caliphs. In fact, it was little different from the way the warring tribes of Israel dealt with one another during the rise and fall of the kingdom of David and Solomon, recounted in the Bible. What was distilled and preserved in historical memory, however, was that from its founding days, Islam did not tolerate Judaism. That memory seeped into Muslim cultures and into Western culture, while the context evaporated.

THE PASSAGES from the Quran that speak about the Jews are often linked to passages that speak about Christians. Muhammad encountered fewer Christians than Jews, but Christians were also part of the theological landscape. To the north and across the Red Sea to the west, the Byzantine Empire was ruled by a Christian emperor, and while Muhammad and the other inhabitants of the west coast of Arabia were not immersed in the issues that troubled the Byzantines, bits and pieces of news made their way along the trade routes. So did bits and pieces of

Christian theology, which was lumped with Jewish traditions to form from Muhammad's perspective (and that of other Arabs as well) a single continuum, from Noah to Abraham to Joseph, leading inexorably to Jesus.

In the Quran, Jews and Christians are often treated as one people, related to each other but distinct from the new community of Muslims. Together, Jews and Christians were called the *ahl al-kitab*, the People of the Book; the "Book" is the Bible. The Quran is ambivalent about the People of the Book, and the verses that discuss them alternate between respect and scorn. On the one hand, the People of the Book, like the Muslims, had been chosen by Allah to receive his message. That entitled them to recognition and honor. According to Quran 28:63, "Those to whom we gave the Book before this believe in it, and when it is recited to them, they say, 'We believe in it; surely it is the truth from our Lord. Indeed even before we had surrendered.' These shall be given their wage twice over for what they patiently endured." Or 29:46: "Dispute not with the People of the Book, save in the fairer manner . . . and say, 'We believe in what has been sent down to us, and what has been sent down to you; our God and your God is One, and to him we have surrendered.'" These are two of many passages where Muslims are ordered to treat Christians and Jews with the utmost respect, because they answered God's call earlier and stayed true to their faith.

But other passages adopt a different tone and criticize the People of the Book for losing their way. "We sent Noah, and Abraham, and We appointed the Prophecy and the Book to be among their seed; and some of them are guided, and many of them are ungodly. Then We sent, following in their footsteps, Our Messengers; and We sent, following, Jesus son of Mary, and gave unto him the Gospel. And we set in the hearts of those who followed him tenderness and mercy . . . but many of them are ungodly" (57:26–27). Other passages drip with antagonism. "The Jews say, 'Ezra is the son of God'; the Christians say, 'The Messiah is the Son of God.' That is the utterance of their mouths, conforming with the unbelievers before them. God assail them. How they are perverted!" (9:30).[3]

It would have been much simpler for the early Muslim community to make a clean, harsh break from the Jews and the Christians. Rather than wrestle over whether they were entitled to special treatment, Muhammad and his immediate successors could have dismissed them as apostates and adversaries and presented them with the choice to convert or be eliminated. But that was not an option. Just as Christian societies, no matter how violently and harshly they persecuted Jews, were unable to arrive at a justification for ending Judaism, Muslim societies had to make room for the People of the Book.

The result was ambivalence. Jews and Christians were neither warmly embraced nor unequivocally condemned. The Quran frequently acknowledges that they were, in their time, chosen by God, and that initially they heeded his call. The message that Allah delivered to the Hebrew prophets and then to Jesus was pure, but according to the Quran and Muslim tradition, in the process of transcribing what God had said, Jews got the stories and the morals wrong, and Christians erred in thinking of Jesus as the Son of God rather than as a prophet and the son of Mary. The mistakes committed by the People of the Book made the revelations to Muhammad necessary. Just as God repeatedly sent messengers to the tribes of Israel when they strayed from the path, he sent Muhammad to the Arabs. The new revelations were addressed to the People of the Book as well, and the fact that most of them did not rush to follow Muhammad was taken as proof of how far they had strayed. The more they resisted, the more the later verses of the Quran railed against their ungodliness.

For Muslims, the great failing of the People of the Book was that they had distorted the message. That created anger and indignation, but rarely hatred. The Quran condemns the People of the Book for perversion but also commands Muslims to treat them differently than other nonbelievers. Jews and Christians were not the only ones to merit special treatment; Zoroastrians were later added to the mix. But Jews and Christians were the only ones linked so intimately to Islam. In fact, because of a shared tradition, Jews, Muslims, and Christians could all be considered People of the Book. They were all members of a family, a family created by God. And just as a brother cannot kill his brother no matter how misguided that brother is, Muslims had to find a way to tolerate Christians and Jews, no matter how lost, foolish, and sinful they were.

In looking for the foundation of relations between the faiths, it makes sense to focus primarily on how Muslims dealt with Jews and Christians rather than on how Jews and Christians dealt with Muslims. Judaism evolved over centuries before the emergence of Christianity, and early Christianity had to grapple with Judaism but not with Islam. Muslim identity, however, was tied to the People of the Book. There was never a time when Muslims did not have to grapple with Jewish and Christian arguments against Islam. From the start, they had to figure out how to deal with Jews and Christians living next to them and under them as conquered people. As a result, Muslims had to think through relations between the faiths far more than Christians and Jews ever did. The subsequent history of relations between the three, therefore, begins with how Muslims treated Jews and Christians. Only after the first wave of Muslim conquests were Jews and Christians forced to invent theologically acceptable compromises that would allow them to acquiesce to Muslim rule.

THE CONQUESTS

MUHAMMAD'S political achievements were impressive. What happened shortly after his death was astonishing. Between 627 and 632, Muhammad removed the Jews from Medina, defeated the last of the Meccan resistance, and extended the reach of Islam throughout the Arabian Peninsula and north toward the fringes of the Byzantine and Sasanian Empires. When Muhammad died, in 632, his father-in-law and one of the earliest and oldest converts to Islam, Abu Bakr, was chosen as his successor and given the title *khalif rasul Allah*. The title literally translates as "successor to the messenger of God," but what that meant in practice was anyone's guess. It clearly did not suggest that Abu Bakr was also a messenger of God, because Muhammad was heralded as "the seal of the prophets," and therefore the final emissary to be sent by Allah before the end of days. It also did not mean that Abu Bakr or any subsequent caliph had the same moral or religious authority that Muhammad had possessed.

The issue of religious authority raises a freighted question: what is the connection between church and state in Islam? Because of Muhammad's role as both prophet and leader, it is sometimes said that Islam was born as a theocracy. In some respects, that is true. The community of Medina was both a religious community of the faithful and a political community composed of Muslim emigrants, the Arab tribes of Medina, and for a time Jews, with Muhammad as the first among equals. But while Muhammad was blessed as a prophet and revered, he was not seen as infallible, at least not during his lifetime. His was, therefore, a theocracy that understood that distinction between an all-powerful God and an honored leader.

Though Medina under Muhammad is revered by Muslims as an ideal, it has never been a viable model for Muslim society. When Muhammad was alive, there was no church-state dichotomy. However, as the Muslim community took on a military character after his death, there was a clear sense that the political and military realms were separate from the spiritual and personal. That was supported by the Quran, which drew an unambiguous distinction between the spirit and the flesh, and between the earthly world and the world beyond. Some verses in the Quran speak to human history and worldly affairs; others speak to the mysterious power of God and man's insignificance in the face of that. Muhammad was both prophet and political leader, but while those roles were united in him, they were distinct.

The questions surrounding the parameters of the caliph's authority demonstrate that most Muslims understood the distinction. No one questioned that Abu Bakr, as caliph, would lead the armies. But most rejected the notion that he had inherited the doctrinal authority of Muhammad. Respected for his wisdom and acclaimed for his piety, Abu Bakr ordered his soldiers to attack the tribes who had used Muhammad's death as an excuse to break away from the community of Islam. The fragmentation of the community after Muhammad's death was a crucial test: if Abu Bakr had not been able to maintain the coalition that Muhammad had assembled, it is more than likely that Islam would have wilted before it had even bloomed and that the message would never have made its way out of the desert. The brief, bloody wars waged by Abu Bakr to reestablish the federation may have been couched in the religious terms of apostasy, but the political dimension was just as important.

These wars not only cemented the legacy of Muhammad, but also established a hierarchy of priorities that remain until today. Many of the Arab tribes that Abu Bakr defeated had only recently become Muslims; others had never truly converted in the first place. All were treated as enemies of the faith who deserved (and were given) no mercy. Ever since, apostasy has been the most severe offense against the Muslim community, greater by several orders of magnitude than anything that a non-Muslim can do. Only a Muslim can be a Muslim apostate, and only apostates are marked as unforgivable. Neither Christians nor Jews roused that level of animosity, not in Muhammad's lifetime and not for most of the next fourteen hundred years.

Within two years of Muhammad's death, most of the Arabian Peninsula was under the control of the caliph. In a few instances, there was slaughter, but Abu Bakr's greater aim was to subjugate and unite the tribes, not annihilate them. One of the best ways to ensure loyalty for the future was to reward the faithful in this world with material riches. Usually, tribal chieftains consolidated their authority by leading their followers on successful raids. But with Arabia more or less unified, and intertribal raiding no longer permissible, the caliph had to look elsewhere for booty, and the most promising targets were the rich empires of the Persians and the Byzantines to the north.

In the space of less than a decade, Arabs conquered the area now covered by Egypt, Israel, Syria, Lebanon, Jordan, Iraq, southern Turkey, western Iran, and the Arabian Peninsula. At the time, Iran and Iraq were controlled by the Persian Sasanian Empire, and the regions to the west of the Euphrates River were ruled by the Byzantine emperor in Constantinople. Both were elaborate, centralized states, with monotheistic state religions—Zoroastrianism in Persia and Christianity in Byzantium. Both had existed for centuries, and had inherited state structures, armies, and imperial traditions that stretched back centuries more. The Sasanians were the latest in a long line of dynastic potentates that had governed Persia, part of a heritage that included Darius and Xerxes and the armies that had nearly overwhelmed classical Greece five hundred years before the birth of Christ. For their part, the Byzantines were the direct offshoot of the Roman Empire, and Christianity had become the state religion after the conversion of Emperor Constantine in the first decades of the fourth century.

On the face of it, the fact that Arab nomads swept out of the desert and crushed these dynasties is difficult to fathom. But in history as in life, timing is everything. The Sasanians and Byzantines had just concluded an especially bitter and taxing war against each other. The Sasanians had taken Jerusalem and Damascus and penetrated deep into Asia Minor, cutting off Egypt and North Africa and jeopardizing the integrity of the Byzantine Empire. The emperor Heraclius had simultaneously been confronted with an invasion of Slavic tribes that threatened Constantinople from the Balkans. Only by virtue of his great skill as both a leader and a general did he manage to withstand these dual onslaughts. While the war between the Persians and the Byzantines wasn't a religious conflict per se, the Persian king treated Heraclius with contempt, and Jerusalem was singled out for humiliation. In turn, as Heraclius began to reverse the tide, he destroyed Zoroastrian fire temples in revenge.

Heraclius proved his mettle as a leader and a commander when he repelled both the Slavs and the Sasanians. The culmination was the liberation of Jerusalem. Having achieved an improbable victory, Heraclius made a point of going to the holy city in 630. To great fanfare, he personally restored the True Cross to its place in the Anastasis (later called the Church of the Holy Sepulchre) and proclaimed the recent triumph of the empire as a victory for Christ. "There was much joy at his entrance to Jerusalem," said a contemporary account, "sounds of weeping and sighs and abundant tears…extreme exaltation of the emperor, of the princes, of all the soldiers and inhabitants of the city; and nobody could sing the hymns of our Lord on account of the great and poignant emotion of the emperor and the whole multitude."[4]

But the war had taken a toll on both regimes, on their treasuries and their soldiers, and neither had recovered its full strength four years later when the successor to Abu Bakr, the caliph Umar ibn al-Khattab, ordered his forces to attack. The Persian Empire had descended into a brief but ruinous civil war, and Heraclius had withdawn in exhaustion from an active role in leading the Byzantine armies. In contrast to an emperor whose power was waning, the new caliph was a physical and military dynamo, an early convert known for his passionate, bristling persona and his unbridled allegiance to Muhammad. At some point during his rule, Umar acquired the title *amir al-mumin,* Commander of the Faithful, which became part of the moniker of all subsequent caliphs. Umar took the military dimension of his role seriously, and he executed it brilliantly.

Three battles essentially decided the fate of both empires. In 634, at Ajnadin, south of Jerusalem, and in 636, at Yarmuk, in Syria, the main Byzantine divisions in the region were wiped out by smaller, more mobile Arab forces. In 637, at the battle of Qadisiya, near the Euphrates, the Persian army led by General Rustam was annihilated. The Persian capital of Ctesiphon was occupied, and for the next decade and a half, the Sasanian emperor was pursued by Arab detachments across Persia until he was cornered and killed. To the west, in 639, the Muslim commander Amr ibn al-As invaded Egypt. The cities of Alexandria and Heliopolis (north of modern Cairo) quickly fell, and by 641, all of Egypt was under the control of the caliph.

As Arab armies fanned out across the Near East and North Africa, they were faced with a problem: how were they going to govern the conquered people? Would there be a mass exodus of Arabs from the peninsula into the major urban centers? Would they raid and then retreat with the spoils? Would they isolate themselves from the Christians, Jews, and Zoroastrians that comprised the population of the conquered lands? And how would they handle societies that were primarily agricultural, that required a different social organization to keep irrigation works intact, to ensure harvests? Some Arabs had settled in cities like Mecca, but others were primarily nomadic, and not accustomed to living in one location year-round. There was nothing in the Quran to provide an easy answer to these new and urgent questions, and the breathtaking speed of the victories meant that there was no luxury to sit back and deliberate over options.

Because the Quran had been so explicit about the People of the Book, however, there was some guidance about how to treat the Christian populations of Syria, Palestine, and Egypt. Zoroastrians, who made up a considerable portion of the Persian Empire, were also granted protections. Like the Quran, the Zoroastrian holy text, the Avesta, had initially been an oral revelation, but parts of it were eventually put in writing. That made it possible for the Arab conquerors to include the Zoroastrians as a People of the Book, simply because they had a book. But alongside *ahl al-kitab,* another category developed, the *ahl al-dhimma* (People of the Pact), which encompassed not only the Zoroastrians but a whole range of sects and local religions that were alien to the Arabs of Mecca and Medina.

The line between People of the Book and People of the Pact is hard to discern. The first "pact" was supposedly between the defeated Jews of Medina and Muhammad, but it's unclear whether such a pact existed or whether it was an invention of later theologians. Over the centuries, the legal distinctions between People of the Book and People of the Pact were the subject of countless treatises and debates. Muslim jurists, like jurists everywhere, parsed every conceivable angle, and probed every hypothetical issue they could imagine. By the middle to late seventh century, however, the idea of *dhimmis* (the term for someone who is entitled to the protections guaranteed to the People of the Pact) was ensconced in the Arab-Muslim empire.[5]

The People of the Book who lived under Muslim rule were *dhimmis*. They were set apart, favorably, by their possession of holy scripture inspired by revelations from God (Allah). That entitled them to a modicum of respect by Muslims. But to earn favored status, the People of the Book had to acknowledge the authority of their Muslim rulers, and they had to pay a poll tax. In return, they were allowed to govern themselves. They could worship freely in churches or synagogues or fire temples. They could eat pork and drink alcohol. They picked their own local leaders who had wide latitude over most aspects of daily life, from marriage to inheritance and estates, from petty crimes to crimes of passion. The People of the Book had no armies; they did not control any city or province; but most of the time, they were left alone.

This didn't mean that they were treated well, only that they were not treated as badly as conquered peoples usually were. Later traditions suggest that both Muhammad and Umar, for instance, were not willing to extend this tolerance to those Jews and Christians living in Arabia itself, and Umar is said to have carried out the last major expulsion of the Jews of Arabia when he removed the Jewish tribes from the Khaybar oasis. Outside the Arabian Peninsula, however, the treatment was more benign.

The Arab-Muslim invasions were significantly less violent and disruptive than the Persian-Byzantine wars that immediately preceded them, or than many of the previous wars of conquest undertaken by the likes of Alexander the Great and the Roman legions. Though there were a fair number of pitched battles, many cities fell without bloodshed. Damascus in the seventh century was a key part of the Byzantine Empire, but its inhabitants were disenchanted with the emperor and with the church leaders in Constantinople. The key issue was a long-simmering doctrinal dispute over the nature of Christ, and the bishops in Constantinople had little patience with the intransigence of churches in Damascus and throughout the Near East. As a result, when faced with an Arab army near its walls, Damascus put up only token resistance.

Besieged by five thousand horsemen commanded by Khalid ibn al-Walid, the citizens of Damascus were faced with a quandary: they had little enthusiasm for laying down their lives to defend the empire, but they did not want to surrender the city only to face slaughter. The bishops of the city's various sects entered into talks with Khalid to discuss a peaceful surrender. To assuage their concerns, Khalid wrote out a promise on a piece of parchment, stating,

> In the name of Allah, the compassionate, the merciful. This is what Khalid would grant the inhabitants of Damascus, if he enters therein: he promises to give them security for their lives, property and churches. Their city-wall shall not be demolished; neither shall any Muslim be quartered in their houses. Thereunto we give them the pact of Allah and the protection of his Prophet, the caliphs, and the Believers. So long as they pay the poll-tax, nothing but good shall befall them.

Having secured these promises from Khalid, the bishops unlocked the gates, let the Muslims enter the city, and doomed the Byzantine garrison to defeat.

Similar scenes were repeated throughout the Near East. The Christian inhabitants of the city of Hims, north of Damascus, were so infuriated with Heraclius that they chose to join the Arabs in order to fight against the Byzantines. The Arab commanders promised the people of Hims that they would be protected if they surrendered. Instead, they volunteered to help. "We like your rule and justice far better than the state of oppression and tyranny in which we were. The army of Heraclius we shall indeed repulse from the city." The Jews also joined the cause. "We swear by the Torah," they told the Muslim commanders, "no governor of Heraclius shall enter the city of Hims unless we are first vanquished and exhausted."[6]

In a similar vein, the Arab general who led the invasion of Egypt, Amr ibn al-As, went out of his way to assuage the fears of Egyptian Christians. Legend has it that before he became a Muslim, Amr had saved the life of a Christian deacon from Alexandria. In gratitude, the deacon purchased Amr's entire stock of goods, and Amr then began to do regular business in Egypt. The Nile Delta was the breadbasket of the Mediterranean, and Alexandria was a commercial hub. It was Amr ibn al-As who purportedly convinced the caliph Umar to authorize an invasion, and one of the reasons he gave was that the Christian population, like the Christians of Syria, was disaffected with the rule of Constantinople.

The rift between the Egyptian church and Constantinople had been growing for decades, and it was based on both politics and theology. The Coptic Church of Egypt adhered to the doctrine of Monophysitism, which stated that Christ had one nature, and that nature was divine. (Hence the term "Monophysite," from the Greek meaning "one nature.") This was in direct contradiction to the creed that had been established by the Council of Chalcedon almost two hundred years before, which held that Christ had both a human nature and a divine nature. Though these debates hardly seem worth fighting and dying for, in the early centuries of Christianity the exact nature of Christ was the most divisive issue. Wars were waged over whether Christ was equally divine and human, more human than divine, or more divine than human. The division between Egypt and Constantinople also had a political dimension. The bishop who had been sent by the emperor to keep the Copts in line succeeded only in intimidating the Egyptians with pogroms and inquisitions. By the time of the Arab conquests, the alienated populace was deeply resentful of Byzantine rule.

Amr ibn al-As took advantage of these strains in order to gain the allegiance of the Egyptians, and that may explain why Egypt fell so quickly to an army of less than five thousand soldiers. Later Arab chroniclers even claimed that the Coptic Church actively aided the Arabs and helped them defeat the Byzantine garrisons in the Delta, having been promised by Amr that their churches would be undisturbed and their tax burden manageable. For the Copts and their bishops, it was a tolerable trade-off. They knew they had to pay taxes to someone, and at least the Muslims would allow them to practice their faith the way they wished, free from the repressive, arrogant authority of Constantinople.[7]

In many respects, the conquests were swift and largely bloodless. Instead of the usual scenes of wanton death and destruction, the cities and towns occupied by the Arabs were treated almost gently, and seem to have welcomed the exchange of rulers. Given the disarray of both the Persian and the Byzantine armies in the region, and the absence of strong organized resistance, that makes sense. There was, in essence, no need for substantial violence. Yet that has not prevented other conquerors at other times from committing nauseating atrocities. Why, then, were the Muslim conquerors relatively benign? The paucity of sources makes it difficult to answer that question, but one thing is undeniable: the Quran instructed Muslims to respect the People of the Book, and that is precisely what they did. The early history of Islam, therefore, unfolded against the backdrop of toleration for the religions of the conquered.

There were also pragmatic reasons. Compared to the number of people spread across thousands of miles of territory, the percentage of Arabs and Muslims was tiny. The early caliphs grasped that there was no way for them to rule without the active cooperation of the conquered. In fact, unless the local administrative systems were left intact, the caliph would not be able to gather taxes; without the local officials, who would physically collect them? And while there was pressure on the caliph to allow his commanders to raid and pillage the occupied cities, that would have created further complications. Once that was done, what then? Many of the tribal leaders who led these armies also wanted the caliph to allow their troops to take land and replace the Byzantine or Persian administrators. But then the armies would have disbanded, leaving the newly acquired regions in a vulnerable and potentially chaotic state.

The solution was to create garrison cities, at Basra and Kufa in what is now southern Iraq, and to leave only a minimal number of troops in the older, established urban centers. The garrison settlements in southern Iraq, and later one at Fustat (Cairo), on the Nile, were a way to keep the armies intact, but that in turn meant that there were precious few soldiers to maintain control of formerly Byzantine cities such as Damascus, Jerusalem, and Antioch, or of Persian centers like Rayy and Merv. That made it imperative for the Muslims to do as little as possible to disrupt the status quo in the newly acquired lands. They removed the top layer of Byzantine and Persian administration, but initially they left the other layers untouched. In that sense, religious toleration was a pragmatic component of an overall strategy of staying separate from the conquered peoples.

Later accounts portray Muslim armies sweeping across the region. But while they did inflict crushing defeats on the legions of two different empires, and then occupied a large number of cities, many people in the lands now controlled by the Arabs were only vaguely aware of what had happened. In fact, for years, many had only sketchy details about the conquests. They knew that the Byzantine rule had evaporated, and that people dressing and speaking differently had appeared demanding tax payments. They learned that these were Arabs calling themselves Muslims, and slowly, they gleaned the basic precepts of Islam. But as late as 680, a Christian named John from the city of Fenek in the region of

Mosul wrote an account that was remarkably uninformed about Islam and about the Muslim conquests, although he praised the Arabs for respecting both ordinary Christians and Christian monks. Other Christians from different regions were similarly confused. This was partly a function of the isolation of most people and the time it took for news to spread from the metropolises to the provinces. But it was also the result of the particular nature of the conquests. As one scholar has noted, the Muslims left such a light footprint on the parts of the world they occupied that it took more than a century before many of the people under their rule began to adjust their lives significantly and figure out what had taken place between 630 and 640.[8]

The simple fact is that if you weren't in Damascus or central parts of Iraq, if you weren't in the Nile Delta or the old centers of Sasanian power, your life didn't change dramatically after the conquests. Once every year or so, a group of soldiers and a local governor might appear to demand payment, but that had also been the case under the prior regime. In time, a few soldiers settled in your town, and they might have been Muslim. Gradually, local governors appointed by the caliph set up their own commercial and cultural networks, which were tied to the larger world of Islam, but this happened so slowly that it would have been almost imperceptible to any one person living during these years.

Much of this is contrary to the imagined history of Arab warriors carrying the Quran in one hand and a scimitar in the other. Yes, they were driven by religion, and yes, they were magnificent fighters, mobile, unconventional, and fearless. They combined a pre-Islamic tradition of raiding with the solidarity and certainty of true believers. But they were also tribal, and tribes rarely admit converts. The message of Islam had been given to Muhammad in Arabic for an Arab audience, and while Arabs believed that the message was universally true, they did not go out of their way to convince non-Arabs. They sought to rule and to tax the peoples of the Near East and beyond, but they did not try to save their souls or show them the true light. If non-Arabs wanted to hear the message, it was there to be heard, but they were not embraced if they did. Non-Arab converts were initially treated not much better than the People of the Book, and in some circumstances they may have been treated worse. There were reports, shaded by later animosity no doubt, that the governor of Iraq in the late seventh century, Hajjaj ibn Yusuf, known as a brutal but effective administrator, rounded up all the non-Arab converts from Basra and Kufa, tattooed their foreheads, and sent them back to their villages and towns.

Eventually, the shabby treatment of converts would lead to a revolution, but for the first hundred years after the conquests, the empire was ruled by an Arab elite that only gradually became absorbed into the societies that they had conquered. While in Egypt and the Tigris-Euphrates region garrison cities were created, even in the far-flung corners of the empire, in Andalus to the west or in the remote corners of what is now northeast Iran and Afghanistan, the Arabs stood apart and separate, secure in their faith, uninterested in missionary work.

Scholars have long since disposed of the image of Islam being spread by the sword, but that has not altered popular imagination. The belief that the Arab conquests were wars of conversion has been stubbornly immune to the facts. Forced conversion would have been directly at odds with the Quran, which states in one of its least ambiguous verses, "No compulsion is there in religion" (2:256). This clear scriptural injunction was obeyed by the early conquerors.

In only one tenuous respect is the image of Islam as welded to the sword legitimate. Eventually, the vast lands that came under Muslim domination did become Muslim societies. The process of conversion took centuries, and happened peacefully and organically. But conversion did happen, and only because of those initial military victories followed by strong Muslim dynasties that managed, with some difficulty, to retain control. That was no small accomplishment. History is littered with victories that did not lead to new empires. Insofar as the sword and the Quran together removed Christianity as the dominant religion in North Africa, Egypt, the Near East, and, much later, Turkey, they did go hand in hand. But only by conflating centuries can it be said that Islam was spread by force, and it simply cannot be said that the initial conquests imposed Islam on the conquered.[9]

While there is ample documentation of these facts, not all accounts of the conquests convey an impression of Muslim tolerance, and the gap between what happened and what people think happened is partly the result of Christian chroniclers. At the time of the fall of Jerusalem, the patriarch, Sophronius, led the resistance to the Arabs and negotiated the surrender of the city. He also acted as Umar's tour guide in 638 when the caliph made a pilgrimage to receive the city personally. Though Jerusalem had been demoted by Muslims in favor of Mecca, it was still

considered a holy site, and Umar understood the significance of its passing into Muslim hands. Entering the walls, he rode his usual white camel
and wore his usual unpretentious bedouin garb. Umar was met by the
resplendent patriarch, wearing the rich robes of his office, and surrounded by his equally resplendent retinue. The caliph was taken on a
tour of the holy sites, after which he promised that he would leave the
Anastasis (Holy Sepulchre) untouched. He then ordered that a mosque
be built on the Temple Mount, which less than a century later was
replaced with Al-Aqsa.

The occupation of Jerusalem was among the least tumultuous that it
has ever known, and for a city that has been raided, sacked, and
destroyed so many times, that is saying something. Even so, that did not
endear the Arabs to the vanquished. The construction of a mosque on
the site of Solomon's Temple was seen by Jews and Christians as a sign of
God's severe displeasure. The patriarch interpreted the victory of the
Arabs as a punishment for the sins of Christians. "If we were to live as is
dear and pleasing to God," he told his congregation, "we would rejoice
over the fall of the Saracen enemy and observe their near ruin and wit-
ness their final demise. For their blood-loving blade will enter their
hearts, their bow will be broken and their arrows will be fixed in them."

Sophronius was a staunch defender of the two-nature creed enshrined by the Council of Chalcedon, and he used the triumph of the
Arabs as an excuse to berate dissident sects throughout the Near East,
especially the Egyptian Copts, for rejecting that formula. In retribution,
God had sent the Arabs to "plunder cities, devastate fields, burn down
villages, set on fire the holy churches, overturn the sacred monasteries,
oppose the Byzantine armies arrayed against them." Though acting as an
agent of God's wrath, Muhammad, continued the patriarch, was a
"devil," and his message a blasphemy. But the Christians had only themselves to blame for straying, and that had led to their utter defeat.[10]

The patriarch viewed the Muslim occupation as a tragedy on a cos-
mic scale. So did his master, the emperor Heraclius. For both men, the
defeat was mortally crushing. Having spent long years wresting control
of Jerusalem from the Sasanians, Heraclius had assumed that he had
found favor in the eyes of God, and when he replaced the True Cross in
the Church of the Anastasis in 630, he must have believed himself
blessed. When he heard that a desert chieftain with the strange title of
"caliph" had entered the holy city as a conqueror, he was stricken, emo-

tionally and physically. He had been in Antioch at the time, and as the Arabs advanced, he retreated to the coast of Asia Minor. In Constantinople, adversaries took advantage of the setbacks and began to plot. Ailing and despondent, Heraclius returned to a capital and a family conspiring against him. He died within months.

While the emperor and his patriarch in Jerusalem saw Muslim success as the result of Christian sin, some went even further and claimed that Islam was nothing more than a Christian heresy. So said John of Damascus, one of the last great Christian theologians of the Muslim Near East. Though he grew up in Damascus, he left the city sometime in the late seventh century and spent significant portions of his life penning angry rebuttals of Muslim theology. In contrast to the ecumenical portrait of the early Arab commanders left by medieval Muslim historians, John of Damascus condemned Islam as

> a people-deceiving cult of the Ishmaelites, the forerunner of the Antichrist.... It derives from Ishmael, who was born to Abraham of Hagar, wherefore they are called Hagarenes and Ishmaelites. And they call them Saracens, inasmuch as they were sent away empty-handed by Sarah.... These were idolaters and worshipers of the morning-star ... and until the time of Heraclius they were plain idolaters. From that time till now a false prophet appeared among them, surnamed Muhammad, who, having happened upon the Old and the New Testament and apparently having conversed with an Arian monk, put together his own heresy.

According to John, Muhammad then "composed frivolous tales," which were cobbled together by his followers to form the bare bones of a sect.[11]

In essence, John treated Islam as no different from the dozens of other heresies that had contaminated early Christianity. While his interpretation was harsh, his denunciation of Islam as Christian heresy is a powerful testament to the close connection between the two faiths. Christian polemicists never described Zoroastrianism as a bastardization of Christianity, nor did later Europeans link Hindus and Buddhists to Christianity. The schisms of the early Christian church represented alternate and opposed interpretations of the scripture. These schisms could last decades or even centuries, but eventually one side lost or was marginalized and was then labeled a "heresy" by the "orthodox." John of

Damascus, writing during a time when the strength of the church in the Near East was waning, was dismayed and angered by the success of Islam. He believed that Muslims had distorted the true word of God by denying the divinity of Christ, just as earlier heretics had. Unlike those earlier heresies, however, Islam had resisted efforts to quash it and now was a direct challenge to the legitimacy and survival of the Byzantine Church.

THE COMMUNITY DIVIDES

MUSLIM ATTITUDES toward the People of the Book were hardly the focus in these early years. Instead, the first generation of Muslims were occupied with defining a new political order. The initial wave of conquests paused in the middle of the seventh century because of internal divisions. The succession to Muhammad had been a problem even with the choice of Abu Bakr, but after Umar ibn al-Khattab, the issue became more acute. The third caliph, Uthman, was assassinated, and Ali ibn Abu Talib, who had married Muhammad's daughter Fatima and was also the Prophet's cousin, then became the fourth caliph. During Ali's brief reign, the tenuous unity of the Arab tribes collapsed. The central debate was over who should be the rightful heirs to Muhammad. Different clans of the Quraysh staked their claim. The Meccan aristocracy tried to seize the upper hand and were in turn challenged by the Medinese, who asserted that because they had joined Muhammad first, they should be preeminent. But even amongst the Medinese and Muhammad's immediate family, there were divisions.

If these political and tribal fissures weren't sufficient to create chaos, there was an added doctrinal dimension: did the caliph have to be connected to and descended from Muhammad by blood, or was piety the most important factor? In short, the question was whether the caliph would be a hereditary monarch, who would pass on his rule to his children, or a first among equals who would earn his authority through the respect of the community.

Ali was the most controversial of the first four caliphs. His elevation to the caliphate triggered a civil war. He had fiercely loyal followers who believed he had been Muhammad's favorite and was then unjustly denied the caliphate for more than two decades. At the same time, he was attacked not only by rival clans and other claimants but by groups who believed that the caliphate should be reserved for the pure of faith regardless of blood ties to Muhammad. The civil war that ended with Ali's assassination in 661 was a kaleidoscope of warring factions, and the partisan nature of subsequent sources makes it even harder to sort out what happened. Ali seems to have tried to negotiate with his enemies in order to keep the Muslim community intact, but that only alienated some of his followers. The purists who assassinated him felt that he had betrayed them and abdicated his responsibility by not vigorously campaigning against his adversaries. While the specifics are clouded, the outcome is not: the caliphate of Ali opened a religious chasm within the Muslim community. The *shi'a Ali,* or "party of Ali," became known as the Shi'a, and the rest became known as Sunni, or "traditionalists." Each of these in turn fragmented into multiple factions and sects, but the Sunni-Shi'a division has lasted to this day.

To subsequent generations of Muslims, Ali's death marked the end of the "Rightly Guided Caliphate." The first four caliphs had all been personally connected to Muhammad, by blood, friendship, or marriage. The caliph who replaced Ali, Muawiya, was one of the Quraysh and related to Uthman. He had been a superb general during the initial conquests, and then governor of Syria. But even with formidable backing of the garrison cities and of Cairo, only when Ali's eldest son, Hasan, agreed not to contest Muawiya's leadership was his hold on the caliphate secure.

The Umayyad dynasty founded by Muawiya lasted for nearly a century. The Muslim empire shifted from loosely organized, dynamic confederacies of tribes into a more structured state spanning thousands of miles and ruled from Damascus. Initially, the Umayyads tended more to internal affairs than to continuing the wars of expansion, but skirmishes with the Byzantines continued, especially given the proximity of Damascus to the heartland of the Byzantine Empire. The Umayyads built a navy, and seized Crete and Rhodes, but these were minor acquisitions compared with the territory conquered only a few years before. Muawiya's death and the ineptitude of his son triggered another civil war, which again featured the partisans of Ali and rebellion in Mecca and Medina. After, the victorious Umayyads initiated a new wave of conquests and more substantial attacks on Constantinople.

The Umayyads led the first Muslim empire that directly impacted the Christians of Europe. Advancing from Egypt, Arab armies took

Carthage (Tunis) toward the end of the seventh century, and then proceeded west along the Mediterranean coast. At the beginning of the
eighth century, Tariq ibn Ziyad, a freed Berber slave of the Muslim governor of North Africa, invaded Spain with an army that he led across
the narrow strait that would be named after him, Jebel Tariq, known in
the West as Gibraltar. The Iberian Peninsula at the time was ruled by the
Visigoths, a Germanic tribe that had seized the region during the last
days of the Roman Empire. As in Egypt, relations between rulers and the
ruled were tense and hostile, and the local populace did not go out of
their way to halt Tariq's advance. Cities such as Córdoba and Toledo fell
without a fight, and while the Goths did mount some resistance, the
entire peninsula, called by the Arabs al-Andalus, was soon under Tariq's
control. Only the Pyrenees stood between him and Europe. He might
have continued his advance had he not been recalled by the caliph, who,
it would appear, had never actually given his consent to the invasion of
Spain and was not clear what value it added to his empire.

The conquest of Spain had an incalculable impact on Europe and on
the evolution of Western civilization, but initially, it was a footnote for
the Umayyads. More important to the Muslims at the time was that the
success of the Umayyads was a defeat for those who believed the community should be ruled not by the most powerful dynasty, but by the
most pious and pure.

The relocation of the capital to Damascus cemented the new order,
and reduced the influence of Medina and Mecca. The result was that the
Umayyad Empire evolved like other empires. Its ruling class, and a small
but growing percentage of its subjects, were Muslim, but the state
was governed and organized much like the Byzantines, the Persians, or
medieval states in Christian Europe were. The caliph retained the title
Commander of the Faithful, and he was the ultimate arbiter of religious
disputes, but the same was true of the Byzantine emperor. The caliph
had supreme authority and a court, governors, and an army, but so too
did the Han emperor in China. And in matters of faith, law, and doctrine,
the Umayyads began to defer to religious scholars and judges.

For the caliph in Damascus, what mattered was control, order, and
income. Control was maintained by placing strong governors in each
province and making them responsible for collecting revenue. The garrison settlements evolved into thriving cities, and the armies of the
caliph were the ultimate keepers of the peace. But day to day, the

decentralized nature of the empire meant that its inhabitants enjoyed substantial autonomy. The overwhelming majority of those inhabitants were People of the Book, and autonomy meant toleration for their religious beliefs and institutions. While the conquerors were not above inflicting humiliations on the conquered, that was not the predominant experience. For the Copts of Egypt, for the peoples of Andalusia, and for the Christians of the Near East, the reign of the Umayyads was more benign and less intrusive than what had come before the arrival of Arabs and Islam. Communities were left to organize themselves, with minimal intrusion from the state. While the Copts, for instance, were second-class citizens relative to the ruling Arab elite, they had also been second-class citizens relative to the ruling Byzantine elite. At least under the Arabs they did not face religious persecution. They had to pay a poll tax, and were sometimes subjected to restrictions on travel, especially between villages and cities, but it wasn't as if most Egyptians had enjoyed personal freedoms under the Byzantines that were then denied by the Muslims.

Today, millions of people—especially in the Muslim world—still believe the myth that the caliph ruled the spirit as well as the flesh of his subjects and that the early Muslim empires represented a unique and potent synthesis of faith and power. This has troubling implications for how Islam has been defined in the modern world. Most people living under Muslim rule in the seventh and eighth centuries would not have recognized this picture of their world. Unless they directly and explicitly challenged the authority of the caliph and his deputies, they were allowed an extraordinary degree of latitude. No doubt there were examples to the contrary. People with power usually abuse that power, and governors overstepped. But those abuses were not systematic. Instead, the system was designed to maintain much of the status quo, and that meant a small Muslim ruling class that impinged as little as possible on a large Christian-Jewish populace.

By the early decades of the eighth century, the initial conquests were mostly complete. The Umayyads staged several more assaults on Constantinople, and one, led by the caliph's brother in 717, nearly succeeded. The Umayyads attacked from both land and sea and laid siege to the metropolis. A combination of famine, Bulgarian mercenaries, and Greek fire annihilated the Arab fleet and debilitated the army. It was the last time that the Umayyads came close to toppling Constantinople, and soon, the Byzantine emperor had reclaimed most of Asia Minor and pushed the Umayyads over the mountains and back into the river valleys and deserts of Syria and Iraq.

Within the Muslim world, Christians began converting to Islam, but in trickles rather than droves. As they moved out of the garrison cities, Arabs were slowly integrated into the societies that the first caliphs had tried to keep them separate from. They married, and their wives and children became Muslim. Arab soldiers found ways to settle and acquire land; Arab merchants began to trade; and men of religion started to carve out a special sphere of influence. Christians who hoped to advance found work with local governors or mayors or even at the court in Damascus, as scribes, translators, and advisers. And slowly, born of contact in both the cities and the surrounding countryside, a new, hybrid culture evolved that combined elements of Islam, Christianity, Judaism, and Zoroastrianism, and of Persian, Byzantine, Egyptian, Greek, and Arab society. In North Africa and Spain, Berber and Visigoth were added to the mix. Had the phrase existed, it would have been called a multicultural world.

The tolerance of Muslims toward the People of the Book unfolded in the context of unquestioned Muslim dominance. The conquerors could afford to be tolerant because the People of the Book posed little threat. During Muhammad's lifetime, that was not the case. The Jews of Medina could have jeopardized Muhammad's status as both Prophet and leader of the community, and the result was harsh treatment. But once the conquests began, and it became clear that the Christians of the Near East would not and could not resist Muslim domination, the Muslims adopted a policy of tolerance that was both sublime and mundane, sublime because it was grounded in the Quran and mundane because it allowed them to rule an empire with minimal manpower.

Muhammad's life and the subsequent conquests established a framework for the next millennium and a half. The seeds of both conflict and peaceful coexistence were sown, and however fascinating subsequent history has been, most of what followed has differed only in specifics. The same notes have been endlessly replayed, with variations on the theme, but no radical departures from the score.

For centuries after the initial conquests, coexistence was the norm, but not one whose echo can be heard today. The fall of Jerusalem, the expulsion and execution of the Jews of Medina, and the wars between the Umayyads and the Byzantines—those are remembered. What came after, in Damascus, in Iraq, Iran, and Andalusia, has become a mirage—glimpses of it appear in the modern world, flickering on the periphery of our collective vision, and then evaporate and disappear. Unlike a mirage, however, that past is real, and nowhere was it more real than on the banks of the Tigris at the court of the caliph in Baghdad.

≫ ⋘

CHAPTER TWO

AT THE COURT OF THE CALIPH

D URING THE REIGN of the caliph al-Mahdi, around A.D. 780, the Nestorian patriarch, Timothy I, was summoned to the palace in Baghdad to debate theology with the caliph himself. Al-Mahdi was a devout man, who spent most of his brief decade as Commander of the Faithful consolidating the realm recently taken over by his family, the Abbasids. Baghdad was a new city in an ancient land, but already it was bustling with the wealth, commerce, and knowledge that came with its status as the epicenter of an empire.

The Nestorian Christians of Iraq had long since broken with the bishops of Constantinople over those fraught questions of Christ's true nature and whether Mary should be thought of as the mother of God or instead as the mother of Christ. The Nestorians, like the Copts in Egypt, had been deeply disenchanted with Constantinople and had almost welcomed the Muslim conquest. But slowly, they came to see Islam as a threat to Christianity in the Near East, especially because it was the creed of the ruling class. With each passing year, more Christians defected to Islam. As Islam matured, its scholars developed more coherent arguments against Christianity. In an attempt to stem the tide, the Nestorians had to formulate an equally compelling defense.

Timothy was a learned man, befitting his station and status. He was schooled in Greek and in Arabic, and at the time of his audience with the caliph, he had overseen the translation of numerous works of Greek philosophy into Arabic, including scientific tracts by Ptolemy and political treatises by Aristotle. These had been commissioned by the caliph to enhance the wisdom of the Muslim community, and they had been preserved by the Nestorians because the tools of argument and philosophy were useful to them as well. Those deadly debates about the nature of Christ had been fought not just with swords but with the weapons of rhetoric and logic honed by the ancient Greeks.

It was Timothy's status as a translator of Aristotle's *Topics* that drew the attention of the caliph. Al-Mahdi was a man ripe for a challenge, especially a theological one. He had been ruthless in his pursuit of Persian Manichaeans and instituted a pogrom against them. Unlike Christians and Jews, and distinct from Zoroastrians, Manichaeans preached what Muslims took as a godless world defined by a war between Good and Evil. They also were accused of trying to prevent people from converting to Islam, and thereby undermining the legitimacy of the caliph. That made them anathema to the Abbasids, and evicted them from the protective shield that covered the People of the Book.

The brutal suppression of the Manichaeans casts Muslim tolerance for the People of the Book into even sharper relief. The Abbasids were capable of suppressing religious expression if they perceived a clear and present danger. Coexistence with Jews and Christians was therefore a deliberate choice. Unlike the Manichaeans, the Nestorian Christians did not explicitly challenge the legitimacy of Abbasid rule; they simply rejected the message of the Quran, as they had from the beginning of Islam. That was a challenge that al-Mahdi and his court enjoyed.

It was not the first time that the court was the scene of an elaborate debate pitting one faith against another, but it was the first time that the caliph had been one of the debaters. Al-Mahdi's motivations are lost to us. Perhaps he invited Timothy for a friendly joust simply for sport. After all, the court was the scene of revolving nightly entertainment, with ribald poetry one evening, love songs the next, and scholarly disquisition the evening after. Perhaps the reasons were more serious and sober. Al-Mahdi had a reputation for devotion, and he showered holy sites from Mecca to Jerusalem with his largesse. He was also a reader, and by the time Timothy was summoned, the caliph had studied the works of Aristotle and other philosophers. Just as al-Mahdi would not have gone into battle without a sword and the training to use it, he was not about to invite a Christian scholar to a debate without learning the arts of rhetorical war.

After more than a century of living in a predominantly Christian world, Muslims had analyzed Christian doctrine and found what they considered to be several glaring issues. Once Timothy had been ushered into the audience chamber, al-Mahdi confronted him with questions about the virgin birth and the nature of Christ, which were two of the hardest questions a Christian theologian could face. If Timothy had been wise, and we have every reason to suppose that he was, he would have anticipated these, but it must have been intimidating nonetheless to stand in front of the Commander of the Faithful and be told the following: "O Catholicus, it does not benefit someone like you, a man of learning and experience, to say about God Almighty that He took himself a wife and bore her a son." Timothy responded, reasonably enough, that God did not have a wife, and that anyone who said so was a blasphemer. The caliph, wearing the black garments of the Abbasids, sitting on an elevated, richly cushioned platform surrounded by retainers, then asked the patriarch to describe Christ and to explain how it was that God could have had a son. The debate continued in this vein for several hours, the tone courteous and the dialogue elevated.

Both men acknowledged the kinship of Islam and Christianity, though their perspectives could not have been more different. The caliph argued that the Muhammad's arrival was actually prefigured in the gospel of Saint John. John referred to the "Paraclete," to the guide or counselor who would come after the death of Jesus to lead his followers, and Muslims argued that the Paraclete was, in fact, Muhammad. The failure of the Christians to flock to the Quran was, said the caliph to Timothy, a failure to heed the prophecy of their own scripture. Timothy, naturally, disagreed. "If I found in the Gospel a prophecy concerning the coming of Muhammad, I would have left the Gospel for the Quran, as I have left the Torah and the [Hebrew] Prophets for the Gospel."

The caliph then asked Timothy whether he believed that the Quran was the word of God. This was, to say the least, a dangerous question. Timothy could not explicitly say no, because that would have crossed a perilous and possibly fatal line. Even in the court of the caliph, with the understanding that there would be freewheeling and open debate, a Christian could not attack one of the central tenets of Islam. Timothy adeptly sidestepped a direct answer but left no ambiguity about what he thought. "It is not my business to decide whether it is from God or not... but all the words of God found in the Torah and the Prophets, and those of them found in the Gospel and the writings of the Apostles have been confirmed by signs and miracles; as to the words of your book [the

Quran] they have not been corroborated by signs and miracles. Since signs and miracles are proof of the will of God, the conclusions drawn from their absence in your Book is well known to your majesty."[1]

THE GOLDEN AGE OF BAGHDAD

TIMOTHY'S MEETING with the caliph was one of many similar encounters between Muslim scholars and Christians in Baghdad and elsewhere. It is easy to overlook how astonishing these exchanges were, and how unusual. The previous centuries had been marked by acrimonious controversies between different Christian sects, which rarely ended with a cordial meal and usually resulted in the imprisonment, death, or excommunication of one or more of the parties. The internecine fighting among Christians, and between Christians and the pagans of Rome, stood in stark contrast to the relative comity between Muslims, Christians, and Jews under the first Muslim empires.

The exchange between al-Mahdi and Timothy took place at the height of the Abbasid power. Only thirty years before, the family of al-Mahdi had led a revolt against the Umayyads. The victory of the Abbasids shifted the locus away from Syria and Damascus and toward Iraq and Iran. The Abbasid revolution had been organized in distant Khurasan, in northeast Iran. It was a disparate coalition of non-Arab Muslims, followers of the party of Ali (Shi'ites), and provincial governors. The revolution had been planned for years, and was launched as a coordinate assault on the Umayyad state. Part of the appeal was the suggestion that the end of days was near, and that the Umayyads had betrayed the message of the Quran. Like the followers of Ali, the Abbasids also claimed that the Umayyads were not the rightful heirs to Muhammad and had unjustly seized the mantle of the prophet.

Buoyed by the eschatological fervor of their followers, the victorious Abbasids (who traced their lineage to al-Abbas, an uncle of Muhammad) soon distanced themselves from many of the allies that had helped them overthrow the Umayyads. Radical ideologies have a way of spinning out of control, and the Abbasids had no intention of relinquishing what they had fought so hard to obtain. If that meant executing erstwhile friends who were more motivated by the hereafter than the now, that was a price the first Abbasid rulers were willing to pay.

In later years, the early Abbasid Empire would be romanticized as the golden age of Islam, and for good reason. At their apex in the late eighth and early ninth centuries, the Abbasids controlled a vast realm. They faced few external threats, possessed immense wealth, exercised astute judgment in administering the empire, and exuded confidence. Their erudition, intellectual sophistication, and artistic creativity easily surpassed the Umayyads. Histories were written, poems composed, works translated, and cities built with graceful architecture and planning. Islamic jurisprudence caught up with the more established corpus of Jewish law, and Islamic mysticism borrowed from Christian monasticism and then flowered on its own. Successive caliphs relentlessly pressured the Byzantines and conspired with the Slavs and other enemies of Constantinople to undermine the power of the emperor. The island of Sicily fell to Muslim control at the beginning of the ninth century, and the Mediterranean became a Muslim lake. To the far east, only the mountains of Afghanistan and the Hindu Kush stood between the Abbasids and China.

Yet because of its sheer size, the empire was rarely stable and faced constant threats from within. The revolutionary genii unleashed against the Umayyads could not be so easily rebottled, and each one of the Abbasid caliphs was confronted with internal revolts and ideological challenges. Rarely did a year pass without some uprising in some town or province. These hardly jeopardized the regime, but they still required dispatching troops, fighting battles, and bringing the perpetrators to justice, usually be executing them in dramatic fashion. Dismemberment, gibbeting disfigured corpses, and other forms of ritual humiliation were common, in the hope that future rebels would think twice about mounting a challenge. Judging from how frequently the caliph and his representatives had to resort to such punishments, that hope was in vain.

These uprisings could be dealt with easily when they were within a few hundred miles of Iraq or Iran, but the farther away they were, the harder they were to suppress. The journey from the central regions to distant North Africa took months, and already the Abbasids had failed to retain Andalusia, which remained under the control of the last of the Umayyad princes. Even Khurasan, the seat of Abbasid power, was susceptible to rebellion, especially after the Abbasids turned their back on the more fervent believers in the end of days. But while the loss of Spain could be managed, the loss of Khurasan and the central lands could not.

The Abbasids understood this from the start. Having staged a revolution from Khurasan, they knew that distant provinces needed to be tethered to the center. But they also realized that the empire was too large and that it would be nearly impossible to govern both North Africa and Central Asia. The choice to tilt toward Iran and Central Asia was automatic. Sometime after 760, the caliph al-Mansur decided to build a new capital on the banks of the Tigris, which would become Baghdad. He needed to be closer to Khurasan but still near the heart of the Near East, and he wanted his base to be a city without entrenched factions that might undermine his authority. The location he chose was not far from the ancient Persian capital of Ctesiphon, and it was in the middle of the major agricultural provinces of the Fertile Crescent, connected by a canal to the Euphrates River to the west, and along the trade routes linking Egypt to Central Asia and China. By building a new capital, the caliph could also determine who would live there, further enhancing his power.

Baghdad was conceived as a round, walled city with four gates and circles emanating from the caliph's palace at the center. Markets, schools, and mansions filled the districts beyond the walls, and in the suburban outskirts, troops and retainers were rewarded with tracts of land irrigated by canals extending from the river. Baghdad was an artificial creation that soon became the only island of stability in a tumultuous, ever-disintegrating imperium, a place that the caliph and courtiers would retire to as a respite, to ponder the impenetrables of God, poetry, wine, and women.[2]

The move to Baghdad was more than geographic. With it, the empire shifted toward Persia and away from Arabia, toward an Islam that was more diverse and less Arab, and toward a culture that celebrated the divine right of kings and sybaritic pleasures. It was also a more urban and cosmopolitan society—which shaped the evolution of Muslim theology. Creativity, reason, and openness to new ideas were embedded in early Abbasid culture. "A city without peer in the world was Baghdad then," said one medieval historian, and for a time, Baghdad thrived as few cities ever have or ever will.

One of the hallmarks of that openness was the easy toleration of Christians and Jews, who still made up a majority of the population ruled by the Abbasids. That toleration ran the gamut from cool coexistence to fruitful dialogue and active collaboration. Muslim scholars studied the wisdom of the societies they had conquered and liberally borrowed and incorporated ideas and practices. In the two centuries after the Abbasids gained power, Islam took on most of the characteristics that were to define it for the next thousand years, and a fair number of those characteristics drew on the pre-Islamic traditions of Christians, Jews, and Persians. In those two centuries, the four major Muslim schools of law emerged, and judges and scholars placed their stamp on thousands of questions about how a Muslim should act and behave.

This openness to the wisdom of the pre-Islamic past stemmed in part from the regime's focus on maintaining power. Having overthrown one dynasty, the Abbasids were acutely aware that they too might be overthrown, and they were determined not to be. Any tool, technique, or philosophy that might help them govern was welcome, regardless of its provenance. In addition to studying the legacy of the Christian states that they had supplanted, they examined classical Greece and the imperial legacy of the Persian shahs. They were also utilitarian about people, and the Abbasid caliphs invited Christians, Jews, and Zoroastrians to serve the state.

As a result, non-Muslims held high administrative posts in the government bureaucracies (*diwans*). From the treasury to the department of public works to the department of war, the People of the Book and *dhimmi*s were employed as tax collectors, guards, and scribes. One of the most influential tax collectors under Caliph al-Mansur was a Jew, and many of the ninth-century viziers of the Abbasids were Nestorians or Nestorian converts, who had replaced the first family of viziers, the Barmakids, who were Buddhist converts from what would now be Afghanistan. These non-Arabs and non-Muslims had crucial skills that the caliphs needed. They were often multilingual, and knew Greek, Persian, and Arabic, as well as Syriac. The Byzantine administration of Syria and the Near East had been conducted in Syriac and Greek, and the Abbasids were able to maintain continuity and stability by drawing on individuals who knew those languages and were in some way connected to that legacy. Al-Mansur was aware, however, that he could not simply rely on their knowledge. That would give the People of the Book too much influence over the court and the empire. In order to build up a Muslim alternative, he ordered the translation of Syriac, Greek, and Persian texts.

The consequences of this state-sponsored translation movement were tectonic. The impetus may have been banal—how to govern an empire using a predecessor's tools. But the translation of Greek knowledge into Arabic eventually paved the way for the transmission of classical knowledge into Western Europe. It is not a stretch to say that the West as we know it could not have emerged had it not been for the translations commissioned by the Abbasids in Baghdad as well as in Basra. Similar efforts occurred in Egypt and later in Andalusia, but the movement began in the late eighth century under the caliph al-Mansur, his children, grandchildren, and great-grandchildren.

The range of translated works stretched from classical Greece through the early years of the Roman Empire. There was a particular focus on the Neoplatonists, who, beginning in the third century B.C., had combined the philosophy of Plato and Aristotle with the science of Hellenistic geniuses such as Ptolemy and the mysticism of later thinkers such as Plotinus. The subjects covered by these writers were eclectic and sometimes obscure, but the net effect for the Abbasids was a burst of theological discourse as complicated, arcane, and divisive as the debates over the nature of Christ had been in early Christianity.

Among the central concerns of the Neoplatonists was the divide between the material and the spiritual, between the body and the soul. That in part accounts for the almost obsessive concern in early Christianity over whether Christ was fully divine, fully human, or an alchemical combination of the two. It also explains the evolution of Muslim theology under the Abbasids, and the emergence of three distinct approaches to Islam.

Encouraged by successive caliphs, philosophers debated whether the Quran was the "uncreated" word of God or created by God. Those who believed that the Quran was created came to be known as the rationalists, as opposed to traditionalists, who believed that the Quran was the pure emanation of God. The traditionalists were not open to using Greek philosophy to illuminate the Quran, and they did not approve of debates with the People of the Book. For them, the Quran was part of God, and hence unquestionable, unalterable, and not subject to human interpretation. The rationalists (or *mu'tazali* in Arabic) disagreed. They felt that the idea of an uncreated Quran came perilously close to the Christian idea of the Trinity, which to their thinking meant worshiping more than one God. That was heresy. Not only was the Quran created by God, and hence separate from him, but it could, as one of God's creations, be examined by human reason in order to understand it better. It could be "interpreted," and humans were entitled to use their minds in order to become better acquainted with God's will.

This split between rationalists and traditionalists has continued in one form or another to the present day. At various points, rationalists, by whatever name, have had the upper hand. At other points, the traditionalists have. In the modern era, the rationalists have been the reformers, those who have argued for change and modernization in the Muslim world. The traditionalists have resisted science and innovation as contrary to God's will, and the most extreme have turned toward forms of radical fundamentalism. Over the course of centuries, however, the rationalists have been just as central, perhaps more so, and they were the guiding force in the heyday of Baghdad.

There was another group, loosely defined but still part of the warp and woof of society, that distanced itself from both factions and refused to enter the debate or serve as judges and officials. They were men, and not a few women, of quiet piety. At some point, they began to call themselves Sufis, named for the wool cloth they wore. They preferred to stay clear of the court and worship God as simply and purely as they could. They too borrowed from Christianity, but from the tradition of hermits and ascetics. Like the Desert Fathers and Saint Antony, they embraced physical extremes and practiced self-denial, isolated themselves in remote and unforgiving regions, and engaged in constant prayer.

These ninth-century divisions—between rationalists and traditionalists, between those who believed that reason, science, and philosophy were tools meant to be used for God's glory and those who looked to a literal reading of the scripture with minimal human innovation, along with the emerging Sufis and the ever-present Shi'ites—not only deepened over time, but became hydraheaded. Each one produced its own sects and splinter groups, until centuries later, Islam was as fragmented and varied as Christianity with its many sects and offshoots. The early fissures within the Muslim community are a guide to how Islam evolved in much the same way as the debates among the Founding Fathers in the United States are crucial to understanding the American soul.

These divides also shaped how Muslims related to the People of the Book. The rationalist approach that found favor at the Abbasid court welcomed discourse with Christians, Jews, Zoroastrians, Buddhists, and many others. The dialogue between Timothy and al-Mahdi was repeated nearly fifty years later, when the caliph al-Ma'mun invited

Theodore Abu Qurra, a Greek Orthodox bishop from Syria, to the court. Much like Timothy years before, Abu Qurra stood before the caliph to defend Christian theology. Al-Ma'mun, in turn, tried to expose what he saw as the inconsistencies of the Christian faith. Abu Qurra had written extensively about the competing religions of the Near East, and he had concluded that only Christians could lay claim to possessing the one true religion.

Rather than simply asserting the truth of the gospel, Abu Qurra used analogies, hypotheticals, and parables to prove his point. "Let's say that I grew up on a mountain ignorant of the nature of people," he wrote in one treatise, "and one day...I went down to the cities and to the society of people, and I perceived them to be of different religions." He would have noticed that most religions forbid some things and permitted others, and most "claimed to have a god." How then could he tell which was true? Well, God, in his wisdom, would have sent a messenger to inform people of the truth. But that person who came down from the mountain would also notice that different people had claimed to be messengers and put forth a set of teachings. How then to separate the wheat from the chaff? By studying each tradition, Abu Qurra claimed that he could identify inconsistencies and weaknesses in all of them except for the gospel.

Like Abu Qurra, Muslim scholars dissected competing scriptures, and the rationalists delighted in analyzing the Torah and the gospel to find errors of logic. Both sides could be mean-spirited. Abu Qurra frequently disparaged Muslims in subtle ways, calling them "those who claim to have a book sent down to them by God." Muslims responded by ridiculing the inconsistencies in the New Testament. They also excoriated the idea of virgin birth and the Trinity as inherently illogical and hence proof that Christianity was not the true religion. From the vantage point of the early twenty-first century, what is most striking about these debates is not just that they took place, but that such a premium was placed on logic rather than faith. An elite group of Muslims and Christians in the Abbasid ninth century relied on reason and philosophy, not personal piety or the strength of belief, in order to demonstrate the truth of their religions.[3]

What also stands out is how much common ground there was, not just between the philosophers, caliphs, and theologians, but between Sufis and Christian and Jewish hermits and monks. Those ascetics who recoiled from the imperial opulence that accompanied empire looked at the life of Muhammad and saw a man and a society characterized by piety uncluttered by materialism. Like the Jewish Essenes at the time of Christ and the Desert Fathers of Egypt in the fourth century, they were disgusted by the finery of the court, and they viewed the elaborate theological debates and the exquisite complexity of Greek philosophy as signs of decadence. Rather than fight to change the system, they retreated from the material world. These early ascetics were the precursors to the more organized Sufi movements of later centuries. They believed that the greatest good was unity with God, and that only with strict and arduous spiritual discipline could that unity be achieved.

The Sufi ascetics were a thorn for the ruling class, a reminder of how removed those rulers were from Muhammad's life. Though the Abbasid caliphs were diligent about leading the annual pilgrimage to Mecca as often as feasible, the frequency diminished. By the late ninth century, most caliphs went on the pilgrimage once or at most twice during their reign. That was only one example of the untethering from the early roots of Islam, and that disturbed the ascetics. They urged more attention to personal faith and less to the affairs of the world. They borrowed techniques from Christian monks, and from the Buddhists of Khurasan, and emulated their rituals. Often, communities would form around one holy individual, usually but not always male. That person would dictate how the group prayed, what verses of the Quran would be recited and when. In time, as Sufi movements proliferated, Sufis split into different camps, some stressing silent prayer and self-restraint, others emphasizing dancing and ecstatic rituals that would send the practitioner into a frenzy of faith.

What made Baghdad and much of Abbasid culture so vibrant, however, was that these opposed elements lived together in relative peace. Sometimes, that meant distinct and separate groups. But it was also true that individuals could seamlessly fit into different, and seemingly contradictory, categories. A caliph might be pious on Friday and deliver a sermon from the mosque pulpit and then be drunk Saturday night while listening to erotic poetry. A merchant attached to his material possessions might take two months for the pilgrimage, or spend one day a week praying under the leadership of a holy man or ascetic. A soldier might be a farmer when he wasn't fighting, and a government official could both serve a Muslim caliph and belong to one of several religions.

Even the line between Muslims and Christians blurred. Prayer and ritual were often a mix of Muslim customs and Christian. In Baghdad, Christians lived in the eastern districts, near a large Jacobite monastery that had been built on the banks of the Tigris. But Muslims took part in Christian celebrations like Palm Sunday, and Christians honored Muslim festivals such as Eid al-Fitr, which is the ritual breaking of the fast at the end of the month of Ramadan. According to a medieval Egyptian historian, this mixing and matching of festivals "was a sign of mutual respect and brotherhood between the religions.... Moreover, some of the converts to Islam, as Muslims, continued their old practices even after accepting Islam."[4]

Slowly, Muslim converts gained more acceptance, especially in the eastern parts of the empire, where Arabs were few and far between. Where some Umayyad governors had humiliated the converts, the Abbasids began to welcome them. The spread of Islam was facilitated by urbanization. As more people moved to urban centers, they left their old lives behind for new opportunities. In order to participate fully in society and in order to have more social mobility, many of these immigrants to the cities converted, especially as the stigma attached to conversion waned. The act of conversion, however, did not mean that all aspects of one's older identity suddenly disappeared. That took several generations, and even then, non-Muslim rituals, habits, and attitudes survived in different guise. Whether it was the way Sufis prayed or the way Abbasid judges approached questions of law and philosophy, elements of Byzantine, Christian, Jewish, and Persian culture were incorporated into Abbasid society.[5] In North Africa and Spain, there was even more of a synthesis, and Muslim culture took on attributes of the Berber and Roman culture that the Arabs had conquered.

Open religious debate was simply one facet of the Abbasid court. Until late in the ninth century, Muslim society was a messy mélange of philosophy, piety, politics, and passion. The caliph Harun al-Rashid, who succeeded his father, al-Mahdi, after the brief rule of his brother, is one of the few caliphs whose name in known in the West. That is because he figures prominently in *A Thousand and One Nights*, but his centrality in those fables in no accident. To later generations, his reign and those of his second son and grandsons were seen as the apex of Muslim greatness. Harun may have fostered learning, but he seems to have celebrated poetry and indulged in wine and women with at least as much enthusiasm.

It is too easy, in the harsh light of the modern world, to forget the complexity of these centuries. In the West, there is only the vaguest sense that Arabs, Persians, and Islamic society in general were once at the cutting edge of innovation, science, and creativity. The prevailing image is that Muslim history has been the story of stern orthodoxy, hostile to other creeds and foreign influences. Even within the Muslim world, the memory of the age of the great caliphs has been distorted and sanitized to fit the mold of today's traditionalists. It is remembered as a golden age, after which there was a slow, steady decline. But for many in the contemporary Muslim world, who equate power with moral and spiritual purity, the decadence of the Abbasid court might be hard to reconcile. The Abbasids were powerful, but they were not pure. In their daily lives, they were like other rulers from time immemorial. Islam was a distinguishing characteristic, but the caliphs shared more with Chinese emperors and Byzantine rulers than they did with the companions of Muhammad. They were cosmopolitan, erudite, and attached to the pleasures of wealth.

Even al-Mahdi, known for his piety, had a court full of eunuchs and female slaves. According to the ninth-century historian al-Tabari, "al-Mahdi had a profligate streak and was passionately fond of talking about women and sexual relations." He could also be cruel in his punishments, and was not above taunting his concubines, one of whom, a Christian slave girl, cried when he snatched a cross from her neck. Rather than giving it back to her, he ordered a poet to compose a song about her distress.

Poets and singers loomed large at the court. That was an artifact from pre-Islamic Arabia as well as a legacy of Persian culture. Songs were often paeans to the virtues of the ruler, occasionally parables about the right way to live and rule, and sometimes odes to sex and wine. One of the most celebrated poets was Abu Nuwas, who was a fixture at the court of Harun al-Rashid. Part jester, part comic, and part philosopher, Abu Nuwas regaled the caliph with the high and the low. Once, when Harun al-Rashid was overcome with one of his periodic bouts of melancholy, Abu Nuwas greeted him, "By God, I never saw a man so unfair to himself as the Prince of True Believers is. The pleasures of this world and the Other are in your hand; why not enjoy them both? The pleasures of the world to come are yours for the sake of your charity to the poor and the orphans, your performance of the Pilgrimage, your repairing of mosques.... As for the pleasures of this world, what are they but these: delicious food, delicious drink, delicious girls."[6]

The line between the holy and the profane was not as sharp as it became in later centuries. The poetic style of Abu Nuwas—who employed it for profane purposes—was also used by Sufis to describe the experience of approaching unity with God. Sufis appropriated the language of passion and wine to describe God as a lover, much as Christian monks and Jewish mystics did. Instead of that love culminating in sex, the apex was the union of the devout believer with God. Not all mystics approved of this approach, and some pious-minded found it as distasteful and immoral as they found the court. But at the height of its power, the Abbasid Empire was a mélange of contradictory elements, and thrived accordingly.

While there are considerable differences between now and then, the similarity to the contemporary West is hard to deny. In Europe and America of the twenty-first century, the language of pop culture makes its way into churches, rock music is appropriated by evangelicals to spread the word, and material extravagance is part and parcel of the lives of the rich and famous. Western society has been a mix of the holy and the profane for some time. Materialism and the pleasures of the flesh don't negate faith and piety. It may even be that the friction has been a source of creativity and dynamism, and that Abbasid culture flourished because of, not in spite of, this delicious stew of piety, intellectual curiosity, and decadence.

While Harun al-Rashid may be the most famous of the Abbasid caliphs, his son al-Ma'mun presided over an equally magnificent court, which surpassed his predecessors in both hedonism and erudition. Al-Ma'mun not only continued the translation movement begun by his grandfather; he expanded it. He funded an extensive group of scholars, physicians, and astronomers, and their works were assembled in a state-funded library known as the *bayt al-hikma,* the House of Wisdom. The library was a center for translations from Greek to Arabic, and it was said to be the intellectual hub of the empire. It is difficult to untangle the myth from reality, and it may be that the actual House of Wisdom was little more than an administrative office that coordinated the translation not of Greek works of philosophy, but of Persian works into Arabic.[7] But even if the actual, physical place were less than the legend, it is still a powerful symbol.

Al-Ma'mun was a man of contradictions. He initiated a theological inquisition over the createdness of the Quran, yet he also sent envoys to the Byzantine emperor asking for as many manuscripts as the emperor cared to share. The Abbasids and the Byzantines were in a constant state of war, with regular campaigns and frequent skirmishes. Yet that did not stop al-Ma'mun from politely requesting treatises ranging from Euclid the mathematician to the physicians Hippocrates and Galen. It's not known what the emperor said in response, but the manuscripts were obtained and added to the already considerable trove being assembled in Baghdad.

Al-Ma'mun's encounter with Theodore Abu Qurra was one of many similar debates staged between Christians and Muslims at the court. According to one account, the caliph held a salon every Tuesday afternoon where questions of theology and law were explored. Food and drink were served first. When everyone had relaxed at the end of a meal, the discussions began and lasted well into the evening. On one occasion, the chamberlain interrupted a debate to inform the caliph that a Sufi was at the gate, wearing a "coarse white frock," who asked to be admitted. Addressing the caliph, the Sufi did not mince words. "This throne here, on which thou sittest—dost thou sit thereon by common agreement and consent of the body of True Believers, or by abuse of power and the violent forcing of thy sovereignty upon them?" Few rulers in any century allow their legitimacy to be questioned. The usual response would have been to throw anyone who spoke in this fashion into a dark dungeon and then execute him. Instead, al-Ma'mun answered the challenger and replied that he had been chosen by his father, Harun al-Rashid, and that he held power only in order to protect all true believers and maintain order. If those believers found some other man more worthy, the caliph concluded, he would happily resign his position and bow to the new caliph's authority.[8]

This willingness to engage controversial issues created an environment where ideas could flourish. The historian al-Tabari described another incident, when al-Ma'mun hosted a debate on Shi'ism at the court. One of the debaters, who was hostile to the party of Ali, lost his temper and began shouting at his opponent, calling him "an ignorant peasant." The caliph admonished him, "Hurling insults is unseemly, and unpleasant language is reprehensible. We have allowed theological disputation to take place and have staged the open presentation of religious viewpoints. Now upon whoever speaks the truth, we bestow praise; for whoever does not know the truth, we provide instruction." Al-Ma'mun understood that only in an atmosphere where divergent views were welcome could knowledge advance, and that such advancement was to the greater glory of God. The Abbasids in their prime reaped the rewards of this openness.

For example, during al-Ma'mun's reign, a young man came to court looking for patronage. His name was Abu Yusuf Yaqub ibn Ishaq al-Kindi, and he became one of the great minds of his age. Al-Kindi was credited with more than 260 works on subjects ranging from philosophy to logic, music to astronomy, geometry to medicine, astronomy to the natural sciences. He believed that the only way to live as a true Muslim was to understand the meaning of the Quran and the life of the Prophet, and that the only way to understand either of those was to use the power of the mind to interpret what the Quran said. His defense of philosophy was simple and timeless: God gave man the power to think, and only by using that power could humans submit to God fully. Al-Kindi also believed, like the Neoplatonists before him, that the material world often prevented people from seeing the true nature of God and his creation. With reason and intellect, the truth could be discerned.[9]

The glories of his court may have sparkled, but al-Ma'mun had another, less noble side. Though he fostered debate and translations, he also conducted an inquisition against the traditionalists. He was, in short, tolerant of all except those who were intolerant of him. Granted, the traditionalists tended to be enemies of inquiry, reason, and philosophy, but al-Ma'mun was willing to violate his own principles of open disputation when that suited his interests. Abbasid culture was tolerant, but there were limits. As much as Christians, Jews, and others who did not share the faith were accepted, there were times when they were not.

For instance, in 806, during the height of Harun al-Rashid's power, violence erupted between Christians, Jews, and Muslims. This may have been triggered by a Byzantine attack on an Abbasid outpost, but the result was not good for the People of the Book. In retaliation, the caliph ordered his soldiers to destroy a number of churches. Rumors then spread that the churches had actually been burned down by Jews looking to stoke animosity between Christians and Muslims. Somewhat later, the writer, philosopher, poet, and jester al-Jahiz penned a lengthy exposition in which he mocked Christians and excoriated the Jews. He made a special point of ridiculing the Christians as unappealing to look at, and the Jews as downright ugly—which is ironic, given that al-Jahiz himself had a reputation as one of the most physically hideous, albeit intellectually luminous, men of his time. Also during Harun al-Rashid's reign, the chief judge of Baghdad issued an opinion that "no *dhimmi* should be beaten in order to extract payment of the poll tax, nor made to stand in the hot sun, nor should hateful things be inflicted upon their bodies, or anything of the sort. Rather they should be treated with leniency." However, according to the judge, they should be imprisoned for failure to pay the tax, and held in prison until they did.[10]

Discrimination increased later in the ninth century as the Abbasid Empire began to fray. Laws were passed that limited the ability of Christians and Jews to serve as officials, and edicts forbade the ringing of church bells and made it illegal for non-Muslims to ride horses. They were to ride donkeys or mules only. Both Jews and Christians were told to wear "honey-colored turbans" and their women were instructed to don "honey-colored scarfs." They were also ordered to wear wooden symbols around their necks that marked them as non-Muslims, and to nail wooden images of the devil to their doors.

Seen through a modern filter disposed to assume religious hatred, those actions are easily interpreted as signs of Muslim animosity toward other faiths. The Abbasids, much like the Umayyads before them, alternated between the noblesse oblige of tolerance and contemptuous indifference, with much more of the former than the later. The mid-ninth-century edicts against the People of the Book need to be placed in the context of an overall strategy to retrench and regain lost ground. The impetus was not animosity toward the People of the Book per se but rather the growing power of Turkish mercenaries, who had become the shock troops for the Abbasids and were becoming a threat to the caliph's authority. The persecution of the People of the Book was only one small element of a major effort to establish a new power base. That effort relied on traditionalists who would not question the caliph and on troops who would serve only him. Marginalizing the People of the Book and suppressing dissent were necessary, albeit cold-blooded, tactics.

The swing from tolerance in secure times toward intolerance in times of threat would be repeated for the next thirteen hundred years. At their apex, the Abbasids invited questioning, dialogue, and debate. They looked for knowledge wherever they could find it. As their power waned, as provinces started to break away and armies began to mutiny, toleration yielded to us versus them. Feeling that their authority and control were in jeopardy, the Abbasids resorted to predictable paranoid behavior by turning toward the conservative traditionalists, who were willing to rubber-stamp royal absolutism. Afterward, in the intermittent decades of calm, the court would again embrace philosophy and debate. But the pattern had been established: security and coexistence on the one hand, and insecurity and intolerance on the other.

THE CLASH OF CIVILIZATIONS?

THROUGHOUT THIS PERIOD, the Abbasids contended with a still powerful Christian empire emanating from Constantinople. After the failed sea assaults of the Umayyads, the war between the Byzantines and Abbasids reverted to the land. Just as the caliphs often led the annual pilgrimage to Mecca as a symbol of their authority, they also led armies to the frontier with the Byzantines to demonstrate their mettle. Young princes were sent to the front for their first taste of battle. In parts of what is now southeastern Turkey, there was a continuous state of war for more than a century, as cities like Malatya were seized and then retaken, seized and then retaken, until the inhabitants learned not to become too attached to one regime or the other. On both sides, there were instances of forced deportation and relocation, but these were not the norm. Rarely did the conquerors take revenge on the local populace, recognizing them for the pawns that they were. In the case of Malatya, famous for its delicious, sweet apricots, it was far wiser for both sides to keep production going and enjoy, in this case literally, the fruits of war.

Ever since Edward Gibbon penned his magisterial *Decline and Fall of the Roman Empire*, in the eighteenth century, the historical reputation of Byzantium has suffered in the West. Gibbon's literary skills are indisputable, but his choice of title is a bit odd. Constantinople was founded at the beginning of the fourth century, and the Byzantine Empire did not end until the fifteenth century, when the Ottoman Turks finally occupied the once-great city. It took more than one thousand years, an entire millennium, for the empire to "fall." Either this was the slowest, most drawn out collapse in human history or there was much more to that millennium than decline. Elsewhere in the world, entire civilizations rose, flourished, and evaporated while the Byzantines were supposedly falling apart.

Until well after the year 1000, Byzantium was *the* great Christian power, and the one that the Muslim world, with the possible exception of Andalusia, used to define Christianity. It was also a constant adversary, and relations between Muslim dynasties and the Byzantines shaped how later Muslims understood the relationship between Christian states and Muslim ones.

The Muslims called the Byzantines "Romans," which they were and were not. They were the heirs to the eastern part of the Roman Empire, but they spoke Greek. They represented a fusion of Greek and Roman society. They also developed a form of Christianity different from what evolved in the West. The Byzantine emperor was both a political and a religious authority, and he had the last word in matters of both doctrine and law. There was no division between church and state, though there were bitter disputes over theology that pitted the emperor against different factions.

The lack of separation between religion and state in Christian Byzantium helps explain why the war between the Abbasids and the Byzantines always had a religious component. Faced with an adversary that fused the church and the state, the Abbasids relied on the caliph as the defender of his faith. When the two empires fought each other, therefore, it became a war between Islam and Christianity.

The concept of holy war, jihad, is embedded in the Quran, but it is and always has been a word fraught with multiple meanings. Muslims speak of jihad as both a struggle to submit to God's will and a battle against unbelievers. It was not true, historically, that Muslims were obligated to wage war against those who refused to bow to Allah. As we have seen, Muslims were content to rule over a large population of non-Muslims without expending the slightest bit of effort to convert them or to challenge their beliefs. But when Muslims did face war with non-Muslims, they could draw on the concept of jihad as a source of strength and justification.

The modern West is uncomfortable with the notion that war might be sanctified by God, but the idea that war is something separate from God and faith would have been alien to Muslims, Christians, and Jews for most of recorded history. In the Old Testament, when the Israelites wage war, God is almost always a factor, either urging them on or admonishing them. From Constantine the Great through Justinian and Heraclius, the Byzantine emperor viewed war as a holy errand. Victory was a sign of God's pleasure, defeat indicative of moral weakness. And the Byzantines framed their wars against the Persians and then the Muslims as Christian struggles against those who had not seen the light of Christ.

The early Abbasid caliphs believed that war with the Byzantines was a religious obligation. Not all of them pursued it with equal vigor, but Harun al-Rashid relished the task. He got his first taste of battle as a teenage prince, and when he became caliph in his early twenties, he was so eager to fight against the Greeks that he often moved his court out of Baghdad and relocated to the garrison city of Raqqa, more than a hundred miles to the northwest on the Euphrates, so that he could be closer to the Byzantine front. When poets lauded his achievements, as court poets were supposed to do, they spoke of his victories over the "polytheists." One way that Muslims denigrated Christians was to accuse them of polytheism because of the worship of the Holy Trinity. It was easy enough for Muslim propagandists to portray the Trinity not as the three emanations of one God but as three separate Gods. That made the war against the Byzantines much more satisfying.

For Harun the outcome was also satisfying, because he was able to force the Byzantines to pay tribute in return for an end to hostilities. This was celebrated as proof that Islam was the true faith, but the triumph may have had less to do with his strength than with the disarray of his enemy. At the time, the Byzantine Empire was in the midst of a grave theological crisis that led to a near collapse of the state. The Iconoclast Controversy pitted those who believed that images of Christ were no better than idols against those who believed that icons were essential aids. During Harun's reign, power in Constantinople was seized by the icon-friendly Empress Irene, who had fought a war with her son and had secured the throne after she had him dragged in chains before her and ordered his eyes plucked out. But the victory had taken years, and she was wise enough to fight one fight at a time, even if that meant paying the Abbasid caliph to leave her alone.

She, in turn, was overthrown and exiled by her finance minister, Nicephorus, who discontinued the payments to Harun al-Rashid, saying, "the Queen who was my predecessor put you in the Knight's square and herself in the square of the pawn and sent you the sort of wealth that you should really have been sending her, but that was because of the weakness of women and their foolishness." Harun was not pleased. "In the name of God, the Compassionate, the Merciful. From Harun, Commander of the Faithful, to Nicephorus the dog of the Byzantines: I have read your letter, son of an infidel woman. You shall see my answer, and it will not be in words." True to his threat, in 806, Harun marched into central Anatolia and captured the city of Heraclea. Though that was still hundreds of miles from Constantinople, it was on the other side of the Taurus Mountains that separated the two realms and on the edge of an unguardable plateau that stretched nearly to the Byzantine capital. Nicephorus was forced to ask for peace and once again pay tribute.[11]

Not surprisingly, the campaign against Byzantium coincided with the harsh measures Harun took against Christians in 806. In the tense atmosphere of war, tolerance gave way to something akin to Abbasid nationalism, and the brief, intense persecution of Christians in Iraq was one manifestation of holy war. Once the battle was over and Nicephorus had sued for peace, the restrictions disappeared.

However, just because Harun al-Rashid was fighting a jihad against one Christian power did not mean that he was waging jihad against all Christians. During these years, he made multiple overtures to the Carolingian, and very Christian, Charlemagne, who had been crowned by the pope as Holy Roman Emperor in Rome on Christmas Day in the year 800. Charlemagne was just as much a Christian monarch as the Byzantine emperor, and had in fact set himself up as the Western alternative to the Byzantines. Members of his court even referred to him as "King David" as a way of linking him to the biblical tradition of rulers who owed their throne to God's will. But because Charlemagne was a rival of the Byzantines, and a sworn enemy of the remaining Umayyads in Spain, he was seen as a potential ally by Harun al-Rashid. The caliph wooed him with emissaries bearing fulsome praise and lavish gifts, including an elephant transported at great expense from North Africa.[12]

Harun's son al-Ma'mun was equally inconsistent. One moment he was dispatching envoys to Constantinople asking for original works of Aristotle; the next he was sending armies into Turkey looking to inflict as much harm on the Byzantines as possible. Toward the end of his life, al-Ma'mun seems to have become more ardent about waging jihad, and in 833, he too captured Heraclea, just as his father had. The emperor at the time was Theophilus, who was forced to ask for terms and wrote a conciliatory letter to the caliph:

It seems more sensible that the two opposing sides should come together over their respective shares of good fortune than adopt courses injurious to themselves.... I have written you inviting you to make a peace agreement... so that you may remove the burdens of war from upon us and so that we may be to each other friends and a band of associates, in addition to accruing the benefits and widened scope for trading through commercial outlets.... If you reject this offer... I shall penetrate into the innermost recesses of your land.

Al-Ma'mun responded in kind. He told Theophilus that he would not be fooled by a letter that combined honeyed words with threats. Instead, he would send his own armies forth. "They are more eager to go forward to the watering-places of death than you are to preserve yourself from the fearful threat of their onslaught.... They have the promise of one of the two best things: a speedy victory or a glorious return" to God as martyrs in battle. He offered the emperor a choice: pay a tribute, or be made to understand Islam by watching the caliph's armies eradicate his.[13] Not surprisingly, neither man was swayed, but al-Ma'mun died before he could carry out his retaliation.

These battles continued on and off for the next few centuries, but soon enough, both empires were more absorbed in fending off the Turks than in fighting each other. The Abbasids, by the end of the ninth century, had only nominal control over North Africa, and by the middle of the tenth century had lost Egypt. Powerful generals, backed by Turkish soldiers recruited or enslaved from Central Asian steppes and the regions surrounding the Caspian Sea, swore allegiance to the caliph but functioned as autonomous viceroys in distant provinces. Turkish tribes also began to pose a serious problem for the Byzantines, but like the Germanic tribes that had slowly sapped the energies of the Roman Empire, the Turks were anything but unified, and shared little in common except common linguistic roots. Their lack of cohesiveness made life even more difficult for the Abbasids and the Byzantines. Even when one tribe was defeated, others sprang up. And both empires tried, sometimes successfully but usually not, to use the Turks as a weapon against the other.

The Abbasids sank more quickly. Although the caliphate remained intact in Baghdad until the thirteenth century, after the mid-tenth century, the caliph's reach did not extend much beyond Iraq. At times, the irrelevancy of Iraq and the caliphate meant that the region was calm and stable. Central and southern Iraq were often the only places of peace in a thousand-mile radius. As a result, Baghdad remained a cultural hub where philosophy, science, and art survived. Throughout much of the tenth century, Baghdad was a center for inquiry, where Arab scholars probed ever more deeply into metaphysical questions that had once been the purview of the Greeks. Philosophers built on the work of al-Kindi and fused mysticism and rationalism. Yet, in relative terms, Baghdad did decline, and the creative flame relocated far to the west, to al-Andalus.

It is true that the glory of Baghdad was never quite as glorious as it looked through the misty eyes of later generations. By modern standards, it was hardly a model of law and order. The caliphs were men of their age, and that age did not know from the legal and moral niceties that the modern world demands. But during the height of the Abbasids, there was an eruption of intellectual and philosophical creativity that has rarely been exceeded. Wealth certainly played a part, but many societies have generated wealth without fostering thought. Simple curiosity was also a factor. One thing, however, is undeniable: this flowering of inquiry, this preservation of the knowledge of ancient Greece and the advancement of math, science, and philosophy took place in an environment where Muslim rulers welcomed and invited interaction with the People of the Book. They used Christian scholars and administrators as foils to hone their own arguments about Islam, and the interaction between the faiths—sometimes friendly, often competitive, occasionally contemptuous, and now and then violent—ignited a cultural renaissance.

The heated, passionate embrace of coexistence was central to a golden age whose prerequisite was a powerful Muslim state secure in its legitimacy. That was true when Harun al-Rashid ruled, and it was true when Abd al-Rahman, the last of the Umayyads, retreated to the Iberian Peninsula after most of his family had been massacred by the first Abbasid caliph. Insulated by the Pyrenees to the north and by the Strait of Gibraltar to the south, Spain was the last redoubt of the Umayyads, and it became a cultural mecca. Even after the Umayyads fell to dynasties from North Africa, Spain continued to be a place where Muslims ruled but the People of the Book thrived. Between them they created a jewel that shone every bit as bright as the golden light that emanated from the caliph's court in Baghdad.

CHAPTER THREE

The Sacrifice of Isaac

T HE CITY OF CÓRDOBA in the middle of the ninth century was blossoming. The Umayyads, exiled from Damascus, had carved out a kingdom, and Córdoba was their jewel. Though Spain had prospered under the Romans, under the Muslims it thrived even more. By the mid-ninth century, Andalusia was entering a period of nearly unrivaled prosperity. For a brief period, in fact, Muslim Spain was the most vibrant spot on earth, a place that saw a magical fusion of commerce, learning, and power that put it in the rarefied company of classical Greece, imperial Rome, Han China, and Renaissance Italy. But in 851, something happened that nearly ended its golden age before it had barely begun.

Except for the extreme north and west of Iberia, the whole peninsula was ruled from Córdoba, and the city matched Baghdad as a seat of culture, wealth, commerce, and learning. As in the eastern regions of the Islamic world, Muslims were significantly outnumbered by Christians. Spain was also home to a large Jewish population that had migrated there in the second century. While the rate of conversion to Islam in Spain may have been faster than in Iraq or Egypt, in the middle of the ninth century, Muslims were nowhere near a majority of the population. Both Christians and Jews occupied prominent positions in society, and they shared the rewards of Córdoba's increasing power and wealth.

One day in 851, a monk named Isaac, who had left the city three years before in despair as more Christians converted to Islam, returned. He entered the palace of the prince and was admitted to the chambers of one of the city's leading Muslim judges. Isaac was no stranger to the court, and he was no ordinary monk. He had been trained in both Latin and Arabic and had occupied an important position in the government before he resigned his office and retreated to a self-imposed exile. Having worked in the palace until his abrupt resignation, he was known there, and the judge received him warmly.

Claiming that he wished to learn more about Islam, he questioned the judge about Islamic law and theology. Happy to engage in the conversation, and perhaps hoping that Isaac had returned because he was contemplating converting, the judge began to speak. But before he could finish his answers, Isaac cut him off and denounced Islam as an evil religion, and Muhammad as a false prophet who had been consigned to hell for deceiving the Arabs. Now, there were things you could say about Islam as a Christian, and things you could not. You could have a heated dialogue with a Muslim about the finer points of theology. You could profess that you believed that Jesus was the Christ and the Son of God, and you could politely refrain from praising Muhammad and the Quran. But you could not, under any circumstances, say what Isaac said that day, and you certainly could not say it to one of the most prominent judges in the city.

Hearing Isaac's sudden outburst, the judge was both confused and outraged, confused because Christians had been living peacefully and prosperously under Muslim rule for more than a century, and outraged to hear Muhammad and the holy Quran spoken of in such vile terms. He struck Isaac across the face, and was about to do so again when one of his advisers reminded him that until guilt could be established beyond a reasonable doubt, religious law demanded that Isaac not be physically harmed. The judge offered Isaac a chance to recant what he had just said, and suggested that he must be drunk or in a temporary state of insanity. Isaac answered that he was of sound mind, knew exactly what he was saying, and meant every word of it. He was, he announced, "on fire with a zeal for righteousness." He had lived for too long amid the Muslims, and stayed silent. He had retreated from the world, but he could not shut it out. He had come to Córdoba to speak, and to die a martyr.

That gave the judge no alternative but to have Isaac arrested and brought before the ruler. Isaac then repeated his denunciation of Muhammad and of Islam. The sentence was automatic: death. He was decapitated, and his body was hung upside down across the river from the palace for public humiliation. After that, his corpse was cremated and his ashes scattered in the Guadalquivir River to deny him the consecration of a Christian burial and prevent others from using the body as a holy relic.

If the prince hoped he could keep the contagion from spreading, he was mistaken. Isaac's martyrdom set off a chain reaction that lasted for the next eight years. Within weeks, another half dozen Christians sought death by publicly condemning Islam as a false faith. Said one who appeared before the judge who had sentenced Isaac, "We abide by the same confession, O judge, that our most holy brother Isaac professed. Now hand down the sentence, multiply your cruelty, be kindled with complete fury in vengeance for your prophet. We profess Christ to be truly God and your prophet to be a precursor of the antichrist and an author of profane doctrine." Hearing this, the judge had little choice, and probably little hesitation, in granting their wish and sentencing them to death.

While there were lulls that lasted as much as six months, these outbursts continued on and off until 859. Some of the martyrs were women. Some were recent converts to Islam who repudiated their new faith, and thereby commited the dual capital crimes of blasphemy and apostasy. Some were married; some young; some old; but all met the same end.

The main chronicler of the Córdoba martyrs was the monk Eulogius, who after describing the fate of his fellow Christians, emulated their example and was himself executed in 859 in the same gruesome fashion. It was said by one contemporary that Eulogius presented his neck to the executioner's blade while making the sign of the cross and that when "his body was thrown from the upper level [of the palace] onto the riverbank, a dove of snowy whiteness, gliding through the air, in the sight of all flew down and sat on the martyr's body." It was also said that he told the executioner that he welcomed death. "Sharpen your sword, so that you can return my soul, freed from the chains of the body, to Him who gave it." His followers were so overcome by his death that the guards of the city took mercy and allowed them to retrieve his body so that they could give Eulogius a proper burial.

By the time the last of the Córdoba martyrs had been executed, more than fifty people had sacrificed themselves on the altar of their faith. They courted capital punishment, and they received precisely what they yearned for. Later generations embellished their stories, and added the poetic touches about doves and other symbols of sanctification. A number of them, including Eulogius, were canonized. They became for generations of Catholic Spaniards heroic symbols of resistance against Islam and against the Arab encroachment. The story of the martyrs was used by later Christian princes to rouse passions in their war to expel the Muslims from Spain. That feat was finally accomplished when the last Muslim kingdom fell to Ferdinand and Isabella in 1492, the same year that a Genoese merchant named Christopher Columbus sailed across the Atlantic, and in their moment of victory the victorious monarchs carried with them the memory of the martyrs who had perished more than six hundred years before.

CHRISTIANS AND CÓRDOBA

THE ACTIONS OF the martyrs were especially startling given the status of Christians in Muslim Spain. While the rapid spread of Muslim rule in the eighth century had hardly been a welcome development, it also was not as disruptive as early invasions had been. Before the Arab conquest, the peninsula had been wracked by wars. After, though Christians lost prestige and power, they were left to govern themselves. Some cities suffered during the wave of conquests after 711, but many others surrendered without violence when the Visigoth state disintegrated. As in Syria, Palestine, and Egypt in the seventh century, the Arabs promised the local inhabitants that their homes and land would not be seized and that their religious customs would not be curtailed.

For instance, in 713, one of Tariq's generals signed a treaty of capitulation with the notables of the city of Murcia. Under its terms, the Christians of the city and the surrounding towns would "not be killed or taken prisoner, nor ... separated from their women and children. They will not be coerced in matters of religion, will not be burned, nor will sacred objects be taken from their realm." In return for this leniency, the Christians vowed not to resist the conquerors, and not to assist their enemies. They also agreed to pay taxes on livestock and harvests, as well as a poll tax of one dinar per year. The Arab and Berber armies occupied the city, a handful settled down, and life for the local population continued with only minimal disruption.[1]

Córdoba became the seat of Muslim power in Andalusia after Abd al-Rahman, the last of the Umayyads, seized control in 756. His reign ushered in a long period of stability, and while there was often tension between the various Muslim principalities, Córdoba itself remained relatively calm and unscathed. The battle of Tours, near Poitiers, France, may have halted the Muslim advance into Europe, but it did nothing to undermine Arab control over the lands south of the Pyrenees. By the time that Isaac made his fateful visit to the palace in 851, Christians had been living side by side with Muslims for longer than anyone then living could remember.

However, as was happening thousands of miles away in the Abbasid heartland, Christians in Spain were gradually being coopted into mainstream Muslim society. Year by year, more of them were abandoning the faith and converting. The advantages were undeniable. Though a Christian could rise high, there was a limit. A Muslim lord might employ a Christian or a Jew as a minister, and the People of the Book could become rich and powerful, but they were never allowed to forget that their freedoms were at the mercy of the Muslims who controlled the armies and the treasuries. Marriage was one of the primary bonds that cemented alliances between rulers and elites, but the People of the Book could not marry Muslims. Even as they adopted Arabic as their primary language, Christians could not avoid the fact that they were second-class citizens in their own country.

In order to integrate themselves, young, ambitious Christian men began to emulate the manners and mores of the ruling Muslims. Paul Alvarus, who recorded the last days of Eulogius, lamented that

> the Christians love to read the poems and romance of the Arabs; they study Arab theologians and philosophers, not to refute them but to form a correct and elegant Arabic. Where is the layman who now reads the Latin commentaries on the Holy Scriptures, or who studies the Gospels, prophets or apostles? Alas! All the talented young Christians read and study with enthusiasm the Arab books...they despise the Christian literature as unworthy of attention.

Like so many conquered peoples throughout history, the Christians of Andalusia were drawn to the power and culture of those that had conquered them.

Though many resisted the urge to convert and lived quiet yet secure lives, they still benefited, even with their second-class status, from the success of Córdoba. That was why they were appalled when Isaac set off a chain reaction of martyrdom—not at the decision of the Muslim authorities to execute the Christians, but at the decision of the martyrs to provoke a response. In courting execution, the martyrs were jeopardizing the delicate balance that had evolved between Christians and Muslims, and most Christians sided with the Muslim authorities and denounced the martyrs as deluded fanatics.

While Paul Alvarus and Eulogius lauded Isaac and the others as saints equal to those who had suffered persecution at the hands of Roman emperors in the third century, other Christians vehemently disagreed. Where the Romans were pagans who had murdered Christian saints in order to prevent the spread of monotheism, the Muslims were believers. In fact, some Christians denied that Isaac and his followers even qualified as martyrs, because they had been killed not by pagans but by "men who worship God and acknowledge heavenly laws."

At the same time, that made Muslims a greater threat than the pagans ever were. Because they identified themselves as part of the heritage that began with Abraham, they were unlike previous adversaries. As some Syrian Christians had noted in the eighth century, Muslims posed the same challenge to mainstream Christianity that Christian "heretics" did. A Christian who would never be tempted by paganism might see Islam as a viable alternative. Not only did Muhammad place himself within the prophetic traditions that spanned the Old and New Testaments, but he carved out a special sphere for Christians and Jews as People of the Book. While that established a degree of tolerance, it also made it harder for Spanish Christians to resist the relentless pressure to assimilate.

In short, the real fight for Eulogius and the other martyrs of Córdoba wasn't between Christians and Muslims, but between Christians who were trying to stay true to the church and those who were falling away. It was an archetypal struggle that conquered peoples face: resist or assimilate. With each passing decade of Muslim rule, the pull of assimilation grew stronger. Whether or not they converted, Christians were adapting to a world governed by Muslims. They were learning Arabic, forgetting the scripture, and looking for ways to ingratiate themselves with the ruling class. Eulogius railed against Christians who collected taxes from other Christians on behalf of Muslim lords. Before his martyrdom, Isaac had been a classic case of the Christian who curried favor at the court of the prince. Like nineteenth-century Indians who donned English accents and morning coats in an effort to make themselves more acceptable to the British ruling class, many Christians took great pains to mimic the Muslim elites.

The martyrs stirred the pot, but their efforts backfired. The bishop of Seville condemned them, and after the death of Eulogius, the movement came to a halt. Spanish Christians were not prepared to rise up en masse, and if they had tried, they would have failed. They had numbers on their side, but no army and no organization. Besides, well into modern times, popular uprisings rarely took place and almost never succeeded. Rather than causing Christians to remain steadfast and resist Muslim rule, the martyrs may have had the opposite effect. By showing the futility of active defiance, they cemented the case for coexistence. Christian rulers in the northwest of Spain continued to fight against the kingdom of Córdoba, but the Christians who lived under Muslim rule became progressively more "Arabized." There was no repeat of the Córdoba martyrs.

THIS LAST GASP of defiance on the part of Spanish Christians was followed by a dazzling 150 years. Constructive relations between Muslims, Christians, and Jews was part of Córdoba's genius. The city grew to nearly a hundred thousand inhabitants, larger than Paris, London, and Rome combined, and nearly the size of Constantinople and Baghdad. The rulers of Córdoba adopted the title of caliph in the tenth century, after the Abbasids in Baghdad came under the domination of Turkish generals who had once served them. The caliphs of Córdoba, like their brethren in Baghdad, turned their city into a capital of commerce, learning, and architectural brilliance. They ruled with the certainty of power and wealth, and with the calm haughtiness that comes with knowing that you are blessed by God.

Córdoba became a cultural jewel, so beautiful and refined that it was dubbed by one Christian visitor "the ornament of the world." It was filled with wonders, crowned by the Mesquite, the Great Mosque, whose rows of seemingly endless columns—graceful, curved, perfectly geometrical—created a space at once huge and intimate. Drawing on the architectural legacy of Rome and Byzantium, it was in its day as awe-inspiring as any ancient wonder. The marvels extended beyond the metropolis itself. Near Córdoba, the caliph built a retreat of palace complexes, a symbol of wealth and power that crested only for a moment before the caliphate began a rapid decline in the eleventh century. The complex was constructed on the orders of Abd al-Rahman III; ten thousand laborers and artisans worked for decades crafting the inlaid buildings and courtyards replete with fountains and airy domes.[2]

With this opulence came arrogance. John of Gorze, the delegate of a German prince, was kept waiting for three years before he was at last ushered into the caliph's presence. He was awestruck by the rows of soldiers outside the complex, and he had never in his life seen what appeared before his eyes when he was actually admitted to the caliph's audience chamber. According to a contemporary account, when John "arrived at the dais where the caliph was seated alone—almost like a godhead accessible to none or very few—he saw everything draped with rare covering, and floor-tiles stretched evenly to the walls. The caliph himself reclined upon a most richly ornate couch, and as John came into his presence, the caliph stretched out his hand to be kissed." The contrast between the world John knew and the one he now witnessed could hardly have been greater. Germany in the tenth century was a jumbled mess of warring fiefdoms, and princelings were fortunate if they had a roof that didn't leak, a castle at least partly fortified with stone, and enough wood for heat. There was almost as much cultural distance between John and Abd al-Rahman as there was between Marco Polo and the court of Kublai Khan in the thirteenth century and between the tribes of the Amazon and the Spanish and Portuguese conquistadors in the sixteenth.[3]

John must have imagined that he was in the presence of a kingdom that would last centuries, but it would barely survive the new millennium. In retrospect, the eleventh-century collapse of the caliphate is less surprising than the fact that it endured for more than 250 years. There were sharp divisions among the Muslims who ruled Andalusia. The conquest of Spain had been accomplished by an uneasy alliance between Arabs from Syria and Arabia and Berbers from what is now Morocco. The Arabs treated the Berbers as second-class clients, and for the first centuries of Muslim rule in Spain, the Arab elites were able to control the fertile lands and prosperous cities and relegate the Berbers to less desirable and less profitable areas of the Iberian Peninsula. Although the princes of Córdoba were dominant, smaller cities frequently tried to escape the control of the Umayyads, and they often established alliances with Christian lords. Rarely was there a period without at least one active minor war. For a time, this constant state of war increased the power of the caliphate. The need to maintain a significant army was a spur for technical innovation and more effective administration. It also made commerce essential. Trade was a vital source of revenue. In essence, low-level warfare was part and parcel of Córdoba's success, and its undoing.

THE JEWS OF SPAIN

THE RELENTLESS DEMAND for more revenue benefited both Christians in the countryside and Jews in the cities. The Arabs who settled in Iberia shunned farming, and they needed the Christian peasantry to remain on the land. Agriculture was not only a source of food; it was also a source of income. The best way to maintain production was to cause as few interruptions as possible, and that meant leaving the Christians alone except for collecting taxes. Even here, Christians were often delegated to be the tax collectors on behalf of the Muslims, much to the chagrin of zealots like Eulogius but to the satisfaction of almost everyone else.

But while Christians often saw their relative status decline, Jews tended to benefit, both in Spain and throughout the Mediterranean world. In the towns and cities, Jews found themselves in a unique position as intermediaries between Muslim-dominated Spain and the rest of the world. Having suffered severe discrimination at the hands of the Visigoths, Jewish communities under the Muslims enjoyed more freedom, affluence, and social standing than any Jewish community would until the nineteenth century.

Jewish merchants established international networks. In the ninth and tenth centuries, no one Muslim state controlled the Mediterranean, but though there were pirates and raiders, the region was a much safer place and more open to trade than any part of Europe at the time. Because commerce was in everyone's interest, and because no ruler had the ability to control it, the Mediterranean evolved into a de facto free trade zone. Spain was its western anchor, and it produced textiles, paper, and leather, as well as spices, olive oil, and countless other products.

Jews acted as agents for Muslim rulers who wanted either to import luxury goods or to export for profit. Because of their close networks and international contacts, they were able to overcome the limitations that faced merchants everywhere: how to ensure that goods were paid for.

Without an international banking system, payment depended on a high level of trust, and such trust was usually a function of personal and family bonds, often cemented by marriage. Jews in Cairo married Jews from Spain; Jews from Spain married Jews from the Levant. The result was that there were Jewish merchants and moneymen in most major commercial centers in the Mediterranean, and they had counterparts throughout the Muslim world whom they trusted and were eager to do business with. While there were also powerful Muslim merchant families, who had their own networks and were more numerous than the Jews, it was easier for a Jew to trade with Christians in Europe than it was for Muslims, and it was far easier for Jews to trade with the independent Christian kingdoms in northern Spain.[4]

Because of a rare and precious discovery of a trove of documents buried in the basement of a Cairo synagogue, there is an unusual amount of information about the links between Jewish merchant families during these centuries. These merchants ventured well beyond the Mediterranean. They crossed the Turkish steppe and sailed the Indian Ocean. However, in those areas, they were simply one group among many, whereas in the northern Mediterranean and in northern Spain they alone were capable of acting as go-betweens. The independent Spanish Christian kingdoms were locked in constant battle with the Muslims, but Jews lived on both sides of the divide. North of the Pyrenees, Western Europe was an economic and cultural wasteland, with a few centers of commercial activity where Jewish merchants led the way. Graced with their connections to the rich and sophisticated Muslim cities of Spain and of the eastern Mediterranean, Jews were a bridge between the Muslim world and the Christian hamlets of Europe.

Two names stand out in these centuries: Hasdai ibn Shaprut and Samuel the Nagid. Born early in the tenth century, Hasdai served two of the Cordoban caliphs as a physician and counselor. Muslims had long debated whether Jews and Christians could act as doctors for Muslim patients, but in the end, pragmatism trumped theological concerns. The caliph expected the best medical treatment available, and he didn't particularly care what scripture his doctors read as long as they kept him and his family alive and healthy. Hasdai ibn Shaprut was born into a wealthy family and trained not just in Hebrew but in Latin and Greek. He was given Christian tutors, studied ancient physicians such as Galen and Hippocrates, and learned Arabic. As legend has it, he gained the notice of the caliph because of his studies of poisons and their antidotes. No ruler was secure enough not to need a skilled physician who might save him from the murderous inclinations of a courtier or rival, and antidotes for poison were coveted.

Having demonstrated his utility, Hasdai was rewarded with a position at the court. He flourished, and he became a patron not just of other Jews, but of anyone who could write an appealing poem or make a compelling argument. As the highest-ranking Jew in the caliph's court, he was treated as the leader of the Jewish community of Córdoba, and they seem to have embraced him as such. Within a short time, he had cemented both his position as a trusted adviser to the caliph and as the representative of the Jews. The caliph then turned to Hasdai for two delicate and unusual negotiations, one with the Byzantine Empire and the other with a distant tribe of Jews living in the land of the Khazars on the southern reaches of the Russian steppe.

The diplomatic exchanges between the Byzantine emperor and the Cordoban caliph were motivated by the same political calculations that had led Harun al-Rashid to reach out to Charlemagne more than a century before. Córdoba was competing not just with Baghdad, but with a new empire in Egypt that claimed leadership over the Muslim world. Very little of this competition was military, although as the new rulers of Egypt grew in power, they moved across North Africa and approached closer to the center of Cordoban power. But there was a competition over who could legitimately claim to be the successors to Muhammad as true rulers of the Muslim community. For their part, the Byzantines, who were enjoying something of a revival, had never accepted the presence of Muslim kingdoms in the Near East, and they took advantage of the bitter animosity between the Umayyads of Spain and the Abbasids of Iraq. Given that the caliph in Córdoba and the emperor in Constantinople both wanted to eliminate the Abbasids, they had a common cause.

The emperor, Constantine, sent a delegation to the caliph, which included not just the usual pleasantries, gifts, and fulsome words of praise, but also several manuscripts. One of these, by the Greek physician Dioscorides, was an encyclopedia of rare and valuable remedies, ointments, and other treatments for ailments. It had been partially translated in Baghdad, but from a corrupt and fragmentary manuscript. The one sent by the emperor Constantine was much closer to the original. One of the few people in Córdoba capable of translating it was Hasdai.

The manuscript was in Greek, and Hasdai worked closely with a Greek monk to make sense of its more arcane passages and translate them into Latin. Hasdai then used both the Latin and the Greek texts to create a complete version in Arabic.

Muslim Spain never did cement an alliance with Christian Byzantium, but relations remained cordial, and intermittent trade, facilitated by Jewish merchants, continued. So did the transmission of knowledge and learning. Spain remained a crucial conduit for Western Europe, and in pursuit of translations and manuscripts, creed took a backseat to expertise. No Muslim ruler cared whether the people translating works by the likes of Dioscorides were Jewish, Christian, or Muslim. The only relevant consideration was skill. All who possessed the linguistic tools and intellectual capacity to render these texts into Latin and Arabic were welcome to participate, and they were rewarded for speediness and success. Hasdai may have been charming and politically adept, but what made him stand out was his knowledge of multiple languages.

Throughout this period, the Jewish community of Córdoba was left to itself. Courts were not composed of layers of bureaucracy, at least not by modern standards, and rather than micromanage the affairs of Jews or other religious minorities, Muslim rulers preferred not to get involved with marriage, inheritance, or the social relations of their subjects. While there were laws governing the interaction between Muslims and other People of the Book, there were hardly any for relations between Jews and other Jews, or Christians and other Christians. Jews and Christians were subject to the poll tax, but it was left to each community to collect it. They could not build churches or synagogues outside of their quarter, but within the quarter, they lived in their own world governed by their own laws and traditions.

However, it was necessary for at least a few members of the community to interact regularly with the court. These intermediaries lived in both worlds, and they had to to navigate both. Men like Hasdai formed a bridge between the cultures, and by all accounts, the most adroit of them garnered universal respect.

Hasdai's position at the court led to at least one odd and unexpected encounter. When Hasdai met with the Byzantine delegates, he was told of a Turkish tribe on the borders of the Byzantine Empire that had, to the surprise and evident fascination of everyone who heard the story, converted to Judaism. The Khazar Turks lived north of the Caspian Sea, and in time would migrate and become the dominant tribe of the Crimean Peninsula. For reasons that are shrouded in the mists of time, one of their rulers decided that he and his people would become Jews. The Jews of Spain were in the habit of making contact with Jewish communities throughout the world, to explore opportunities for trade and to reinforce the solidarity of the Jews in exile from the Holy Land. So it was natural for Hasdai to write a letter to Joseph, the king of the Khazars, when he learned of the conversion.

"I, Hasdai, son of Isaac, son of Ezra, belonging to the exiled Jews of Jerusalem in Spain, a servant of my lord the King, bow to the earth before him and prostrate myself towards the abode of your Majesty from a distant land. I rejoice in your tranquillity and magnificence and stretch forth my hands to God in heaven that He may prolong your reign in Israel." Hasdai expressed the hope that regular relations could be established between them, and he asked Joseph to describe how it was that the Khazars had adopted Judaism and if they had any insight into when, if ever, the long exile of the Jews from Jerusalem might come to an end.

It was several years before Hasdai received a response from Joseph explaining the complicated history that had led to the conversion of his people. Apparently, sometime in the middle of the eighth century, the Khazars were visited by envoys from both the Byzantines and the Arabs, each of whom hoped to convert them and make them allies. The king at the time was a cautious man, not easily convinced, and he sent for a Jewish scholar to test the strength of their arguments.

According to Joseph in his letter to Hasdai,

The King searched, inquired, and investigated carefully and brought the sages together that they might argue about their respective religions. Each of them refuted, however, the arguments of his opponent so that they could not agree. When the King saw this he said to them: Go home, but return to me on the third day. On the third day he called all the sages together and said to them, "Speak and argue with one another and make clear to me which is the best religion."

They began to dispute with one another without arriving at any results until the King said to the Christian priest, "What do you think? Of the religion of the Jews and the Muslims, which is to be preferred?" The priest answered: "The religion of the Israelites is better than that of the Muslims." The King then asked the qadi [a

Muslim judge and scholar]: "What do you say? Is the religion of the Israelites, or that of the Christians, preferable?" The qadi answered: "The religion of the Israelites is preferable." Upon this the King said: "If this is so, you both have admitted with your own mouths that the religion of the Israelites is better. Wherefore, trusting in the mercies of God and the power of the Almighty, I choose the religion of Israel, that is, the religion of Abraham. If that God in whom I trust, and in the shadow of whose wings I find refuge, will aid me, He can give me without labor the money, the gold, and the silver which you have promised me. As for you all, go now in peace to your land."[5]

This world—of Jewish doctors, Muslim princes, and Khazar kings—is very different from the remembered history of Islam and the interaction between the faiths. Think of it: a Turkish kingdom on the banks of the Volga River in modern-day Russia adopts Judaism after its king listens to representatives from each faith debating the merits of their system. Later, a Jewish official serving at the court of the Muslim ruler of Córdoba writes a letter in Hebrew to the Jewish ruler of the Turkish tribe after learning of their existence from Christian emissaries, sent by the Byzantine emperor, who were hoping to establish an alliance with the Muslims of Spain against the Abbasid Empire in Iraq.

None of this would have struck any of the people involved as strange. While religion was central to their identity, faith did not create absolute barriers to interaction. Even in the realm of marriage, the walls were porous. Muslims, Christians, and Jews weren't supposed to intermarry, but in places like Spain where the populations lived side by side, they inevitably did, and people found ways to deal with it. Usually, the woman adopted the religion of her husband, but if the woman was Muslim, then the husband would usually convert. These marriages weren't common, but they weren't unheard of either.

The historian William McNeill once wrote that vibrant societies are often the product of unexpected and jarring interactions with strangers. His point was that unless people are forced to confront alien groups, different habits, and unfamiliar customs, they become rigid, brittle, and complacent. Spain was a place where such meetings were unavoidable. Muslims, Christians, and Jews lived side by side, and they in turn were connected to international communities of other Muslims, Christians, and Jews, whom they visited and traded with and who visited and traded with them. There was also war, which though deadly and violent was also a form of jarring interaction, and it forced rulers to be alert and creative in order to defeat their enemies and remain in power.

The competition between the faiths was one reason for the rapid spread of monotheism beyond the Mediterranean. The Khazar king, if the story is to be believed, would never have converted to Judaism had it not been for Christian and Muslim delegates trying to win his allegiance. The interaction between the faiths also fed intellectual creativity. The Muslims of Córdoba would not have gained the valuable medical wisdom of the ancients if there had not been Spanish Christians and Jews with linguistic skills that no Muslim possessed. And the Jews would not have thrived as merchants throughout the Mediterranean world without the Pax Islamica that extended to Jews the protections granted to the People of the Book.

Trade was the primary focus of most Jews living in the Muslim world, but in Spain, and especially in Córdoba before the eleventh century, they became prominent not just as merchants but as scholars, courtiers, generals, and poets. War and poetry marked opposite ends of the culture spectrum, one devoted to destruction, the other to creativity. Muslim Spain, and indeed much of the Muslim world, celebrated the poet and the warrior in equal measure. Few people were great poets or great warriors. Samuel ibn Nagrela, known as the Nagid, was that rare person who was both. That in itself was extraordinary; the fact that he was a Jew who commanded Muslim armies was even more so.

In the eleventh century, the power of the caliph in Córdoba began to wane, and the political unity of Andalusia disintegrated. The chaos and flux were both a boon and a bane to Jews and Christians. Where most things had revolved around the court in Córdoba, now multiple cities and rulers competed for power. Each of these required not just armies but also translators and administrators, and Jews possessed many of the skills needed to fill these positions. They were literate, multilingual, and loyal to their patrons.

Samuel was the son of a merchant. He learned both Arabic and Hebrew, and prepared for a quiet, prosperous life. Instead, he found his world plunged into turmoil as the caliphate collapsed. Political tumult took a toll on business, and when the situation became so dire in Córdoba that Samuel could no longer be assured of personal safety, he, along with thousands of Christians, Muslims, and other Jews, fled. He went to Málaga and eked out a living as a shopkeeper near the palace of the vizier of Granada. Word of his skill as a letter writer reached the court, or so later legend claimed, and he soon found himself employed as a counselor to the Berber ruler of Granada. After several timely deaths and various palace intrigues, he became the second-most-powerful person in the city and the general of its armies for more than twenty years, until he died in 1056.

With his rise to power, Samuel earned the title Nagid, which is a Hebrew term for "governor" or "worthy." As such, he was a central figure in the public life of Granada during a chaotic time. Protected by mountains and situated high above a fertile plain in southeastern Iberia, Granada, an isolated fortress demesne, would eventually be the last redoubt of Islam and the only surviving Muslim state after the peninsula was reconquered by Christian armies in the thirteenth century. During Samuel's life, however, Granada was simply one of many competing principalities, known as *taifa*s. Whether it would survive was very much in question, and had it not been for the Nagid's skill, it might not have.

Samuel led campaigns against other city-states, both Muslim and Christian. He oversaw public works and buildings, and tried to imbue the fortress of Granada with the glory of Cordoban architecture. Córdoba had been a city of mosques, fountains, courtyards, and palaces, and during Samuel's time; Granada acquired these as well. He also built a library that housed the greatest texts of Hebrew, Arabic, and Latin. These included Hebrew commentaries on the Torah, Latin works of medicine and philosophy, and Arabic works of poetry, astronomy, and material science. As one later hagiographer wrote, in Samuel's time, "the kingdom of science was raised from its lowliness, and the star of knowledge once more shone forth. God gave unto him a great mind which reached to the spheres and touched the heavens; so that he might love Knowledge and those that pursued her, and that he might glorify Religion and her followers."

Samuel did not just collect knowledge; he added to it. He was a grammarian who wrote extensively on Hebrew and its various dialects. He believed in the power of knowledge to transform a man and his society. As he wrote in one of his many poems,

Man's wisdom is at the tip of his pen,
His intelligence is in his writing.
His pen can raise a man to the rank
That the scepter accords to a king.

He was a scholar of the Torah and of Talmudic commentary. He wrote ballads in Arabic and Hebrew, including one celebrating a recent victory in which he dubbed himself "the David of his age." Self-aggrandizing, yes, but it was an apt comparison. Like David, Samuel was an unlikely hero who rose higher than many would have believed possible given his origins. He was not only a military leader but a protector and sponsor of Judaism and Jews. He sent money to Jerusalem to help the small Jewish community maintain its synagogues. And he worked to support trade as well as the familial networks that had been so assiduously created over the previous centuries and that were now threatened by the breakdown of the political order in Andalusia.

Yet, Samuel was like David in less flattering ways as well. "And David slew twenty-two thousand men of the Syrians," says 1 Chronicles, in the Old Testament. Just as David massacred adversaries and showed little mercy for those who opposed the kingdom of Israel, Samuel was an avid warrior. As he wrote triumphantly after one of his many successes on the field,

> The slain we left for the jackals, for the leopards and wild boars; their flesh we gave as a gift to the wolves of the field and the birds of heaven. And great was the banquet, all were satiated. Over thorns and thistles were their limbs dragged; the lionesses stilled their young with them.... Great and rich was the banquet prepared, and all were filled, drunk on blood without measure. The hyenas made their rounds, and the night was deafened with the cries of the ostriches.

A David for his age he may have been, but that meant not just power, fame, and culture. It meant reveling in the art of death and pursuing his enemies until they were utterly broken.[6]

The world inhabited by Samuel was nasty and brutish. One day of the week, a courtier might compose an ode to the beauty of a fountain, or to the serenity of courtyard lit by the moon. If he was Muslim, he might have chanted with Sufis the next evening and praised the unity of God. If he was Jewish, he might have prayed with the rabbis. He might even have felt himself stirred by the joy that came with glimpsing the love of the creator. And the next day, that same courtier might have marched out at the head of an army of several thousand men and butchered his adversaries.

Samuel was succeeded by his son Joseph, who tried to maintain the legacy of the father but could not. The Berber princes of Granada were never secure for long. Rivals from within and marauders from outside were a constant challenge, and court life was precarious. Joseph attracted enemies not just because he was a Jew, but because he had influence. He was targeted, just as the prince he served was targeted. Factions that were on the out used whatever weapons they could find, and the fact that Joseph was Jewish was adroitly exploited by his enemies. If he had not been Jewish, his rivals would have tried to defame him in other ways. They would have whispered to the prince that he had a secret agenda, or ill-gotten gains, or designs on one of the prince's wives. Instead, they seized on the fact that he was Jewish and used it to their advantage.

The most effective and vicious of his enemies was Abu Ishaq, who had fallen out of favor and got his revenge by bringing Joseph down. According to Abu Ishaq, the prince had made a mistake because he had

> chosen an infidel as his secretary, when he could, had he wished, have chosen a Believer. Through him the Jews have become great and proud and arrogant—they, who were among the most abject.... And how many a worthy Muslim humbly obeys the vilest ape among these miscreants. And this did not happen through their own efforts but through one of our own people who rose as their accomplice. Oh why did he not deal with them, following the example set by worthy and pious leaders? Put them back where they belong and reduce them to the lowest of the low, roaming among us, with their little bags, with contempt, degradation and scorn as their lot, scrabbling in the dunghills for colored rags to shroud their dead for burial.

As for Joseph, Abu Ishaq concluded,

> He laughs at us and at our religion and we return to our God. Hasten to slaughter him as an offering, sacrifice him, for he is a fat ram and

do not spare his people for they have amassed every precious thing. Break loose their grip and take their money.... They have violated our covenant with them so how can you be held guilty against violators. How can they have any pact when we are obscure and they are prominent?[7]

The result of this campaign was disastrous. Joseph's palace was raided by a mob. He was dragged out, beaten, and crucified. Hundreds of other Jews in positions of prominence in Granada were then subject to days of terror and death.

It is almost impossible to revisit the massacre of the Jews of Granada in 1066 without seeing it as evidence of the inherent animosity between Muslims and Jews. It sorely tests the idea that there is any substance to the Quranic injunction about fair and tolerant treatment of the People of the Book, and for later generations, it has been easy enough to draw a line from Muhammad and the destruction of the three Jewish tribes of Medina through Granada in 1066 to the conflict between Muslims and Jews in the twentieth century.

Doing this, however, distorts the past. It is a lens formed by the bitterness and hatred of our present. It is easy to scour the past and find examples of conflict—if that is what one wants to find. Granada happened in 1066; the massacre of the Banu Qurayza happened in 627. But many other things also happened, and those episodes of extreme violence perpetrated by Muslims against Jews were few and far between. Four hundred years separated Muhammad and the massacre of Granada, and it would be hundreds of years more before another such event. There was nothing common about this type of treatment, not when compared to the routine persecution of Jews in Europe during these centuries and not when contrasted with the centuries during which Jews flourished commercially and culturally, often working with Muslims and for Muslims, and in the case of Samuel the Nagid, even ruling Muslims.

THE SHIFTING SANDS

RELATIONS between the People of the Book in general, and between Muslims and Jews in particular, comprised a matrix. One quadrant was defined by violence and yes, hatred. But there were others, ranging from disdain to grudging respect to active cooperation for a common goal. Usually, that common goal involved the pursuit of knowledge and the task of translating the philosophy and wisdom of the ancient world. But there was also pedestrian cooperation between Christian and Muslim farmers in Andalusia, who often celebrated each other's holidays and prayed side by side. Everyone needed to have good harvests, and a Christian saying the prayers of a Muslim or a Muslim intoning the liturgy of the Christians would help guarantee that the rain would fall, the lands would be irrigated, and the grain would be reaped.

To identify moments of violence and call those more true and more representative warps the past beyond recognition. History becomes polemic. It would be just as egregious to portray the golden age of Córdoba as typical of how Muslims and the People of the Book interacted, but that distortion is less common, either in the contemporary West or in the Muslim world.

Isolating and highlighting moments of interfaith violence also distorts in other ways. Relations between *all* adversaries—regardless of religion—were ugly and violent. Muslims fighting other Muslims were no less brutal with one another than Muslims such as Abu Ishaq were toward the Jews of Granada. The warring states of Andalusia in the eleventh century were frequently ruled by Berbers who had built up centuries of resentment against the Arab elites. Their armies, in turn, were often staffed by a mix of Arabs, Berbers, and Christian mercenaries, and when they took a rival city, especially after a long siege or difficult fighting, they could be merciless and wanton. The Muslim Berber prince who sacked Córdoba at the beginning of the eleventh century allowed his troops to expiate the rage and shame of having been treated as uncivilized men of limited intelligence by an arrogant Arab aristocracy. They burnt the palace; they destroyed the library; and they massacred the city's inhabitants. Such treatment of conquered peoples did not happen frequently. It was more typical to terrorize, loot, and rape. But the behavior of the Berbers was not beyond the pale.

Muslims and Christians were rarely more charitable with each other. While massacre was atypical, it did happen. The shifting border between the Christian kingdoms of León and Aragon in the north and the Muslim city-states of Andalusia in the central and southern portions of the peninsula meant that at any given time after the tenth century, some Christian king was fighting some Muslim prince. The reason that massacre was the exception and not the norm had little to do with morality. Massacre as a policy was impractical and would have been the medieval equivalent of nuclear war. Soon enough, each side would have decimated the other. There would have been no one left to conduct trade or grow crops. Instead, Christians and Muslims in Spain worked out a system of organized slavery and equally organized ransom procedures. This was one way of making the loser pay, literally, while avoiding the depopulating effects of killing one another in large numbers.

At times, these conflicts were cast in religious terms, but that doesn't mean that they were fought because of religious differences. A Muslim prince would occasionally declare that his struggle against the Christians was akin to the early conquests of the companions of Muhammad, and that the cause was a holy war. For their part, Christians sometimes framed the reconquest of Spain and Portugal as a war spurred by the church and demanded by fealty to the cross. But because alliances often transcended religion, and because the political landscape shifted so frequently, it was more common for wars to be fought without clear religious ideology. Berbers from North Africa competed with Berbers who had lived in Spain for centuries, who in turn fought with Arabs, and in their efforts to unseat one another, they allied with Christian rulers who could provide money and soldiers. No one seems to have thought that such alliances violated an unwritten boundary between the faiths.

The kaleidoscope of coalitions could be dizzying. In the middle of the eleventh century, for instance, the Muslim ruler of Toledo signed a treaty with the Christian prince of Navarre for help against the Muslim city of Guadalajara. The price was steep, and included a large payment of gold. In turn, the Navarre Christians were given the right to harvest a portion of the crop of Guadalajara, if the city was captured. In response, the Muslim elites of Guadalajara concluded a treaty with the Christian king of León-Castile, and those soldiers then sacked Toledo. The Muslims of Toledo responded by sending emissaries of their own to the king of León, who demanded a large sum of gold from them in return for breaking his initial treaty and switching sides.[8]

During these battles, both Christians and Muslims prayed to God for aid. The irony that they were praying to the same God surely escaped them. However, the cosmopolitan Muslims of Andalusia, as opposed to their Berber allies in North Africa, were usually uncomfortable describing conflict with Christians as a holy war. That must have been a deliberate choice. In the other parts of the Muslim world, the Shi'ite conquerors of Egypt and Tunisia claimed that their wars against the Sunni Abbasids were a manifestation of God's will, and the Berber tribes of North Africa and Morocco united behind the banner of Islam. In contrast, the Muslims of Andalusia rarely used doctrinal differences to justify war against Christian enemies. Aggressive Christian princes wanted to remove Muslims from Spain and annihilate them; that was reason enough to fight.

In addition, for both Christians and Muslims passions could dissipate as quickly as they formed. At the end of the eleventh century, the Muslims of Toledo might have described their war against Christian León as a holy one, but then they might have been attacked from the south by another Muslim principality, looked to León for help, and quickly dropped the holy war concept. It has always taken some effort to get men to kill one another, and shouting holy war was one way to motivate soldiers; ordering them to bang their shields with their swords was another. The goal in either case was pre-battle frenzy. Holy war was more often a tactic rather than a strategy, and it would be a mistake to apply to the Muslims and Christians of eleventh-century Spain the ideological passions we associate with the early twenty-first century.

It wasn't long, however, before something happened that shifted the balance in Spain and led Christians to think in terms of holy war. The principalities of what would later become France and Germany had regular contact with the Christian kingdoms of northern Spain, and as the eleventh century progressed, they became more involved in the contest between the Christian north and the Muslim south of the peninsula. As Andalusia fragmented, the Christian states of Aragon and of León and Castile became more powerful, winning battle after battle and acquiring territory. They developed closer relations with princes in southern France, and in the process, fell under the influence of a monastic order centered in Cluny.

The Benedictine order of Cluny was founded early in the tenth century. At a time when the organization of the church could be charitably described as anarchic, the monks of Cluny were disciplined, focused, and intent on imposing order. The array of fiefdoms in France, northern Italy, and Christian Spain had always been chaotic, but with the breakdown of the Carolingian system, established by Charlemagne, the situation became much worse. It may be a cliché that nature abhors a vacuum, but it is also true. And in that wilderness of the late tenth and eleventh centuries, the Cluniacs filled the void.

Acting as a mini state, Cluny sent envoys to the kings of León and Castile and funded the establishment of satellite monasteries in northern Spain. As the wealth of the Cluniacs grew, so did their power. Bishops were appointed from their ranks, and these bishops looked to the order for guidance. The order, in turn, favored rulers who at least gave lip service to the church. That meant framing battles and campaigns against the Muslims as divine acts, sanctioned not just by the church but by God. Alfonso VI, king of León, was particularly adept at fusing his family's dynastic ambitions to expand into Muslim Iberia with the rhetoric of a holy warrior, and he established close relations with the Cluniacs.

The rise of Christian power in Spain corresponded with the decline of Muslim unity, but victors rarely credit their foes' weaknesses as a reason for success. Both the church and the state interpreted their hard-won victories as a sign of divine favor, and as a testament to their skill as warriors and rulers.

Had it been left to the inhabitants of the peninsula alone, the Christian reconquest probably would have been completed by the end of the eleventh century rather than dragging on until 1492. But the vigor and zeal of the combined kingdom of León-Castile provoked a counterreaction. Since the Muslim conquest, Berbers who had settled in Spain had maintained close contact with their brethren across the Strait of Gibraltar. At the same time that Cordoban power disintegrated, a dynasty emerged in the Atlas Mountains of present-day Morocco. Called the Almoravids, they established a base at the new city of Marrakesh, and fanned out north and west until they reached Ceuta on the Mediterranean. Then, sometime after 1085, they crossed into Spain and confronted not just the forces of León's Alfonso VI, but also Muslim rulers in cities such as Seville. Though the Almoravids suffered the occasional setback, challenged not just by the tenacity of Alfonso but by the quirky brilliance of the mercenary warrior known as El Cid, before the end of the century they had created a new dynasty stretching from Marrakesh to the middle of Spain.

The only problem, at least for those Muslims, Christians, and Jews that fell under their rule, was that the Almoravids abhorred the cosmo-

politan live-and-let-live attitudes that had characterized much of Cordoban history. They were puritans intent on restoring what they believed was the lost piety of early Islam. They roused their followers to
fight against injustice and for righteousness in the path of Islam, and they
viewed the decline and collapse of the Muslims of Spain as a sign of
divine displeasure. Muslims had strayed, and God had punished them by
giving the Christians the upper hand. It was the duty of the Almoravids,
and of all Muslims in Spain, to cleanse the community, rid it of impurities, and reverse the tide.[9]

The Almoravids succeeded in stemming the Christian advance and
then ruled what remained of Muslim al-Andalus with far less tolerance
for the People of the Book. Under the Almoravids, Christians and Jews
were subject to heavier taxation and more restrictions. Had the dynasty
lasted, the noose of cultural chauvinism might have tightened even
more. As it turned out, once ensconced in the palaces of their predecessors, the Almoravids began to feud with one another. The glue of holy
war could form only an initial bond, and once the object was attained, it
weakened.

As for the Christians, the success of the war against the Muslims of
Iberia did not escape the notice of the church in Rome. Western and
Central Europe may have been fragmented, but across the small world
of elites, news traveled. Monks traded manuscripts and ideas, and
princes and barons intermarried. At the very end of the eleventh century, the former prior of Cluny was elected pope, and he took the name
of Urban II. He had lived most of his life in the region now called Bur-
gundy, and he had played a central role in the rise of the Cluniacs to
such prominence. His selection as pope in 1088 was a triumph for the
order, and it raised the hope that he would be able to magnify the power
of the papacy throughout Christendom. Those hopes were not disap-
pointed. In 1095, in the town of Clermont, closer to Cluny than to Rome,
Pope Urban dramatically shifted the focus of Christian holy war away
from Spain. He called on all good Christians to turn their efforts to
retaking Jerusalem. And so they did.

CHAPTER FOUR

THE CRUSADES

IN PURELY MILITARY TERMS, the Crusades were negligible. At least seven times over the course of two centuries, armies from France, Germany, Italy, and England invaded the Near East. Initially, these armies were led mostly, though not entirely, by second-tier nobles and third sons who faced dead-end lives as retainers. Later, they were led by kings and princes who sought both temporal and spiritual glory in campaigns against the Muslims. At their height, the Crusader states of the Near East comprised a narrow band that barely included present-day Israel, Lebanon, and slivers of Jordan, Turkey, and Syria. While the crusading urge took centuries to dissipate, by the beginning of the fourteenth century the Crusades as a mass movement were over, and the Crusader states were eradicated. The movement began in a burst of religious fury, but in the end it probably did more harm to the Christian Byzantine Empire than it did to the Muslim states of the Near East.

In purely symbolic terms, however, the Crusades became the perfect metaphor for conflict between Islam and the West. Out of the sorry, often pathetic history of the Crusades, the myth of endless conflict was forged.

The Crusades were launched by Pope Urban to liberate the holy city of Jerusalem from the grip of Muslims, who were described as uncouth infidels defiling the holiest of holies and as "a race alien to God" who had desecrated ground sanctified by the blood of Christ.[1] It would take thick rose-colored lenses to transform the Crusades into a symbol of harmony. The blood-soaked streets of Jerusalem, taken after a long siege in 1099, and the armies of Christendom indulging in what even later Western propagandists admit was a wild orgy of death, make that impossible. But the killing fields of Jerusalem lasted days. Crusader states were enmeshed in the Near East for more than two hundred years. In between the intermittent battles, there were long periods of calm and poignant moments of amity.

Even with the Crusades, therefore, the memory that has survived is incomplete. It is a memory framed by prejudice, and whatever doesn't fit the history of conflict has been elided, forgotten, and buried. In the long years that separated the actual Crusades, Muslims lived uneventfully under Christian rule in the Near East. While there was far less of the cultural interaction that made Muslim Spain so dynamic, there was also little animosity. Indifference may not be the stuff of legend, but it more accurately describes the decades of live-and-let-live that separated the brief but exciting episodes of armies mustering, sieges laid, and battles fought.

While the Muslims of Egypt and the Near East were accustomed to clashes with Christian Byzantium, the arrival of the first Crusaders from Western Europe took them by surprise. The ferocity of the Crusaders stunned them, as did the simple intensity of their faith. By the end of the eleventh century, Muslims of the Near East had only the faintest connection to the early fervor of Muhammad and the Arab conquests. They were used to war, but not to war inspired by religious passion.

The exception, perhaps, was the animosity between Sunnis and Shi'ites, which seemed to worsen with each passing century. The sudden rise of the Shi'ite Fatimid empire in Egypt in the tenth century was seen by the Sunni majority of the Near East as a grave threat, and for good reason. The Fatimids forged an unlikely coalition of North African tribes, and then swept across the desert from Tunisia and into Egypt. Their leader proclaimed himself caliph, which meant that in the middle of the tenth century no fewer than three people simultaneously donned that mantle, one in Baghdad, one in Córdoba, and one in Cairo. Then Hakim, the Fatimid caliph of the early eleventh century, declared that he was also the messiah, and began to persecute those who did not bow to him. Instead of showing tolerance, he stripped the People of the Book of their rights. Like a Muslim Caligula or Nero, his behavior was erratic, confusing, and often cruel. He demanded that shops in Cairo stay open all night on the off chance that he decided to stop by, and he instituted a lottery where some were rewarded with gold, others with death.[2]

Hakim meted out draconian punishments to everyone—Sunni, Shi'a, Christian, black, brown, or fair-skinned—who might challenge his legitimacy. The persecution of Christians, however, had consequences that he neither foresaw nor lived to see. In 1009 his soldiers desecrated and then partly destroyed the Church of the Holy Sepulchre in Jerusalem to punish Christians for their refusal to embrace his new revelation. Word of that deed spread to the West, and though the pope and the royals of Europe could do little more than rail against the Fatimids, the memory did not fade. Instead, it festered over the next decades, until it sparked what became the First Crusade.

By then, however, Hakim was long dead. He had made far too many enemies, and he finally alienated one too many faction. His end was suitably bizarre. He rode out of Cairo on a donkey and disappeared. He had been in the habit of leaving the palace with only a small retinue of guards, and that was his undoing. But the absence of a body provided one group of followers with a sliver of hope. Various Shi'ite factions over the years had declared that their imam had not died but had instead removed himself from visible society to wait until the time was right for him to appear again. When Hakim vanished, a few steadfast followers refused to believe that he had been assassinated and claimed instead that he had gone into hiding to await the end of times. Hounded out of Egypt, these followers became known as the Druze, a secretive, close-knit community that survived in the mountains of Lebanon, Syria, and Palestine.

When the Sunnis were not fighting the Fatimid Shi'ites, they were fighting one another. The tenth and eleventh centuries saw the rise of Turkish power. The Turks had filtered into the Near East and Anatolia from Central Asia and had slowly converted to Islam after they were hired as mercenaries by both the Abbasid caliph and other Arab rulers. The emergence of the Turkish Seljuk dynasty in the eleventh century threatened all of the established powers in the region, especially the Byzantines and the Fatimid Shi'ites.

Because the Near East of the eleventh century was wracked by internecine conflicts between Muslim sects and Muslim states, it was ripe for a foreign invasion. Even so, no one expected a war with Christians from Europe, and few of the inhabitants of the Near East had any dealings with the West. Spain was far removed from the daily world of Damascus, Antioch, Jerusalem, or any of the other city-states of the

Near East. Though Jewish clans kept in touch with one another across the thousands of miles spanned by the Mediterranean, most Muslims were more provincial. Merchants traveled widely, and men of learning did as well, but even these had little contact with the backward states of Europe. As a result, the sudden appearance of thousands of European knights claiming a divine mandate to liberate Jerusalem was not something Muslims in the Near East had ever imagined.

It was unexpected for Western European Christians as well. They had never launched a campaign against so distant a goal. They had, however, fought "crusades" against non-Christians and heretics. While scholars have analyzed the various strands that led to the First Crusade, there are heated academic debates about how new the Crusades actually were. There had been campaigns against pagans in northern Europe and against Muslims in Spain and in Italy. Christian rulers routinely whipped up the passions of their soldiers by linking sacrifice in battle to Christ's sacrifice on the cross. But there was a difference between evoking Christ in pre-battle speeches and calling for a military holy pilgrimage thousands of miles away.[3]

Regardless of how novel the idea was, the result of Pope Urban's call was unprecedented. Never before had an army of Christians from the West been raised against the Muslims of the Near East.

THE CALL IS ANSWERED

THE GIST of Urban's speech at Clermont in late 1095 was simple: Christians had a sacred duty to liberate Jerusalem from Muslim rule. No official version of the speech has survived, and the various contemporary accounts differ considerably in detail and in tone. But they all suggest that Urban urged the bishops and princes of Christendom to assemble an army for the sole purpose of taking Jerusalem. In some accounts, Urban dwelt on the purported atrocities being committed by Muslims against pious Christians and pilgrims. In classic demagogic fashion, he listed the tortures that Christians were supposedly suffering, ranging from disembowelment and intestines twirled around filthy metal instruments to unfathomable acts committed within the Church of the Holy Sepulchre, including the forced circumcision of monks on the bloodstained altar. Other accounts of the speech stressed the redemptive power of liberating the city. Urban admonished the princes that they had been living lives of sin and had themselves committed atrocities in their petty wars with one another. For that, Urban declared, they would be held responsible on judgment day, unless they dedicated themselves to the noble cause of Jerusalem.

"Let therefore hatred depart from among you," Urban announced; "let your quarrels end, let wars cease, and let all dissensions and controversies slumber. Enter upon the road to the Holy Sepulchre; wrest that land from the wicked race, and subject it to yourselves." The Holy Land itself, Urban continued, was crying out for help.

> That land which as the Scripture says floweth with milk and honey, was given by God into the possession of the children of Israel. Jerusalem is the navel of the world; the land is fruitful above others, like another paradise of delights. This the Redeemer of the human race has made illustrious by His advent, has beautified by residence, has consecrated by suffering, has redeemed by death, has glorified by burial. This royal city, therefore, situated at the center of the world, is now held captive by His enemies, and is in subjection to those who do not know God, to the worship of the heathens. She seeks therefore and desires to be liberated, and does not cease to implore you to come to her aid.

And those who answered the call, Urban promised, would be rewarded. "All who die by the way, whether by land or by sea, or in battle against the pagans, shall have immediate remission of sins. This I grant them through the power of God with which I am invested." The task at hand was one that every believer had a duty to undertake, provided they had the means. The alternative, Urban declared, was unacceptable.

> O what a disgrace if such a despised and base race, which worships demons, should conquer a people which has the faith of omnipotent God and is made glorious with the name of Christ! With what reproaches will the Lord overwhelm us if you do not aid those who, with us, profess the Christian religion! Let those who have been accustomed unjustly to wage private warfare against the faithful now go against the infidels and end with victory this war which should have been begun long ago. Let those who for a long time, have been

robbers, now become knights. Let those who have been fighting against their brothers and relatives now fight in a proper way against the barbarians. Let those who have been serving as mercenaries for small pay now obtain the eternal reward.... Let those who go not put off the journey, but rent their lands and collect money for their expenses; and as soon as winter is over and spring comes, let them eagerly set out on the way with God as their guide.[4]

Those listening to Urban could have been forgiven for thinking that Jerusalem had only recently been captured by Muslim hordes. In fact, Jerusalem had been under the rule of one Muslim prince or another since the seventh century, and Christian pilgrims had rarely been denied access. Even the brief, albeit shocking, depredations of the mad caliph Hakim had taken place nearly a century before Urban stood in Clermont and made his history-altering speech. But the motivation for launching the Crusade had less to do with goings-on in Jerusalem than with the situation in Western and Central Europe.

As many have noted, the Crusades proved to be a brilliant solution for the anarchy and chaos of Europe. The princes of France in the eleventh century, aside from the successful Norman invasion of England in 1066, were engaged in constant battle with one another, and the situation wasn't much better to the east, in Germany. The church, aside from centers like Cluny, functioned at the whim of nobles. By calling for the liberation of Jerusalem, Urban hoped to focus the energies of the princes on something other than infighting and thereby increase the prestige and influence of the church. He enjoined the knights to wear the symbol of the cross in order to mark themselves as soldiers of Christ, and he instructed his bishops to spread the word. They did, and the response was immediate. The Normans were especially keen. So were the peasants of central Germany, led by an enigmatic figure known as Peter the Hermit, whose rough-shod, ill-clad army assembled around the Danube and followed it south and east

The road to Jerusalem went through Constantinople. While some of the Italian cities had ships, there was no fleet in Europe capable of transporting an army of fifty thousand and its retainers across the Mediterranean. The legions of the West had to go overland, and that meant a journey of thousands of miles to Constantinople and from there across Turkey and into Syria and Palestine.

The First Crusade was blessed with extraordinary, perhaps even divine, luck. The timing could not have been better. Much as the early Muslim conquests took place at a nearly perfect juncture just after the Byzantines and the Sasanians had exhausted each other after decades of war, the Crusaders arrived in Constantinople just as both the Byzantines and the Seljuk Turks were struggling to retain their empires. By the eleventh century, the Seljuks had replaced the Abbasids as the primary threat to the Byzantines. In 1071, at the battle of Manzikert, the Byzantine army was annihilated by the Turkish sultan, and the emperor was captured. As a result of this decisive and humiliating defeat, all of Asia Minor except for the ancient imperial city of Nicaea, a scant few hundred miles from Constantinople, fell under the control of the Seljuk federation.

After Manzikert, however, the Seljuks fragmented. They had never been a centralized federation, and each Seljuk prince commanded the loyalty of his own small army. With multiple marriages, the number of princes tended to balloon. Corralling them into a unified force was the exception, not the rule, and in perfect illustration of the law of entropy, the Seljuk state disintegrated into dozens of small units almost as soon as it had formed. These units then dissolved into even smaller units, until many of the cities that ringed Jerusalem, including Antioch and Damascus, were ruled by different and often antagonistic Seljuk factions, none of whom were willing or prepared to come to the aid of the others. Quite the contrary. As long as they themselves were not the object of a Crusader assault, they were perfectly content to let the Christians eliminate rival city-states on their way to Jerusalem.

Not only were the Seljuks disunited and the Byzantines hobbled, but the Fatimids of Egypt, who still nominally controlled Jerusalem and much of the territory of Palestine, were also a shadow of their former selves. Unable to mount an effective challenge to the splintered Seljuk emirs in Syria, the Fatimids welcomed the Crusaders as an effective deterrent. When the Fatimid caliph in Cairo learned that Christian armies from Europe were advancing toward Syria from Constantinople, he sent envoys offering them assistance. The enmity between the Sunni Seljuks and Shi'a Fatimids could hardly have been greater, but neither of them had strong feelings about the princes of Europe. The Crusaders were unfamiliar, and their motives were a mystery. The Fatimid caliph unfortunately overlooked the most trenchant detail, which was that the ultimate goal of the Crusaders was not Syria but Jerusalem, which was then ruled by the Fatimids themselves.[5]

In short, when the Crusaders set out for Jerusalem, not a single strong state stood in their way. Had the movement begun only a decade earlier, the Seljuk sultan who orchestrated the victory at Manzikert would still have been alive, and the Crusaders would not have stood a chance against him. At any other time in the eleventh century, they would have faced a powerful and hostile Byzantine emperor in Constantinople, as well as a cohesive Fatimid empire, had they somehow managed to make it to southern Syria.

Not only were the Crusades blessed with good timing, but they were also graced with adversaries who had scant knowledge of their tactics, ambitions, and ideology. In retrospect, the First Crusade was clearly a holy war waged by Christians against Muslims, but it is striking how unaware of that fact Muslims at the time were. The Seljuks and then the Fatimids viewed the initial forays by the knights of Europe as a nuisance and then as a military challenge, yet even after the fall of Jerusalem, there was no sense in the Muslim world that this was a religious war or a clash of civilizations.

In fact, it is stretching matters to even speak of a "Muslim world." There was no unity among Muslims even when faced with a Christian invasion of the Levant. As we will see, after the success of the First Crusade, some Muslims tried—and failed—to create a pan-Muslim alliance against the Christians. Even when, nearly a century later, Saladin united the disparate city-states and led them to retake Jerusalem, he succeeded primarily because of his abilities as a military commander, not because of people rallied to a pan-Islamic banner. In the years after the First Crusade, while there was no shortage of platitudes about Muslim solidarity in the face of a Christian challenge, few in a position of authority did more than give lip service to the idea of a unified Muslim community.

In short, religion mattered, except when it didn't, and it didn't matter, except when it did. The link between faith and action is blurry. The call of Urban spurring armies to march on Jerusalem in the name of God is often treated as proof that men will fight and die for their religion. The reaction of Muslims almost a hundred years later, when Jerusalem was retaken in 1187, is treated the same way. But what about the times when Muslims or Christians called on their brethren to rise up in the name of God and no one listened? What about the periods in between the fighting, after the fall of Jerusalem? Where was religion when Christian knights formed alliances with Sunni Muslims to fight Shi'a Muslims or when one Christian lord looked for help from a Muslim Kurd in order to subdue another Christian lord? If religion mattered more than anything, how do we explain those times when it mattered hardly at all?

Though the Crusades eventually became synonymous with conflict between Christianity and Islam, at the time the picture was decidedly more ambiguous. It's not that the war to take Jerusalem and the subsequent efforts of various Muslim rulers to retake it were not colored by religion. It's that religion was one of several reasons for fighting. Omitting these other factors reduces the Crusades to one dimension. Yes, faith was vital—at least for the Christian knights. From what we can tell at many centuries' remove, they were driven by piety, which Pope Urban tapped but did not create. They believed that the struggle to liberate Jerusalem would serve as a penance for their sins and lead to rewards in the hereafter. They were drawn by a potent promise of material and spiritual rewards, and they were moved by the image of the city where Christ played out his passion being occupied by people who had little regard for that blessed legacy. But even here, the fury of the Crusaders was easily channeled not just against Muslims, but also against Jews or other Christians who did not see the universe in quite the same way. Conflict between faiths was one of many conflicts, and not always the one that mattered most.

The intra-Muslim rivalries and antagonisms were mirrored by similar divisions among the Crusaders themselves and between the Catholic Crusaders, who at least nominally followed the edicts of the pope in Rome, and the Eastern Rite Byzantines, who had their own clerical establishment and refused to recognize the pope's supreme authority. Arriving at the borders of the Byzantine Empire, the Crusaders expected to be greeted warmly by the emperor Alexius Comnenus, and to be welcomed as allies in the war against the infidel. This was in spite of the fact that the Eastern and Western Churches had split in 1054 when the papal legate in Constantinople excommunicated the patriarch for heresy, in the Church of Hagia Sophia, which was the Eastern equivalent of Saint Peter's Basilica in Rome. The Byzantines did not appreciate the public insult to their church father, and had someone loudly insulted the pope in Saint Peter's, the reaction would have been much the same. Among the reasons for the schism, the Byzantine church refused to accept

Rome's addition to the Nicene Creed of the word *filioque*, which signified that the Holy Spirit flowed from both the Father and the Son, and not, as the Eastern Church believed, from God the Father alone. There was also the delicate and inflammatory matter of the use of unleavened versus leavened bread in the Eucharist. These issues were enough to cause a rupture.

In the decades before the First Crusade, both churches had attempted to heal the wound. As a result, by the end of the eleventh century, the princes of Europe viewed Byzantium as a natural friend in the war against the infidels, and they tended to overlook the chasm that had opened between the Catholic and Orthodox religious establishments.

The Byzantines were skeptical. Alexius, the heir to a rich and sophisticated tradition, understood that Jerusalem was not cause enough to align his interests with the Crusaders. He was a shrewd man, erudite and hard-nosed, who was also graced with a favorable biographer in his daughter. When he ascended to the throne, the empire was in disarray and in need of leadership. The Turks were only one of several threats, and Alexius had to repel Slavic and Serbian tribes invading from the northern Balkans as well as the vulturous Venetians and Normans. The tax system was in shambles; the army was undermanned and fragmented; and while the court and the palaces of Constantinople remained as magnificent as ever, there was a dispiriting sense that the end might be near.

Alexius reversed the tide. He rallied the army, appointed skilled governors, replenished the treasury, and looked to the West for mercenaries, especially Normans. He had fought Norman princes in Sicily and in the Balkans, so he knew that they excelled at combat and chafed at being ruled, but he was willing to take the risk of hiring them in return for the reward of using them. In a similar vein, he intended to use the Crusaders to loosen the grip of the Seljuks on Asia Minor, but he had to make sure that they did not keep what they conquered. In addition, their armies were not under his command, and when they needed food and supplies, they tended to loot. Alexius was faced with a challenge that a man of lesser abilities could not have met. He wanted to exploit the Crusaders for his purposes without allowing them to jeopardize his lands. As the price of his assistance, he demanded that the princes swear an oath that if they captured any territory that had previously been ruled by Constantinople, they would return it to him.

The cultural gulf between the Byzantines and the Crusaders could hardly have been wider. Byzantine splendor had faded, but it still shone brighter than anything in Europe. The proud Byzantines saw the Crusaders as ignorant peasants, albeit well armed and pious. While some chroniclers called the Byzantines "Greek" because of the language they spoke, the Byzantines called themselves "Romans," because they saw themselves, with justification, as the heirs of the empire that had been founded a millennium before by Augustus. While the Crusaders were also descendants of the Romans, they had long since lost touch with Roman learning and culture, so much so that they were dependent on the Muslims of Spain for the wisdom of antiquity. The Muslims referred to the Crusaders as the "Franks," because most of them, including the Normans, were from Frankish lands once ruled by Charlemagne. The Byzantines, however, referred to the Crusaders as "barbarians," which was what the ancient Greeks had called the uncultured, uncivilized tribesmen of Central Europe.

The Crusaders were a curiosity to the Byzantines, and the emperor's daughter Anna Comnena recorded her impressions of them with the critical, bemused eye of an anthropologist writing about a primitive tribe. She was particularly struck by the character and physique of the Norman prince Bohemond of Taranto. According to Anna, he "was so tall in body that he exceeded even the tallest men by almost fifty centimeters.... The flesh on his body was very white.... His hair was light brown and did not hang on his back as it did on other barbarians.... Some charm also manifested itself in this man, but it was obscured by the fear he inspired all around him." Anna's account, penned years after the fact, was undoubtedly colored by the fact that Bohemond went on to become ruler of Antioch and an uneasy, often antagonistic vassal of the emperor. Other Crusaders, such as Godfrey of Bouillon and Baldwin of Boulogne, later of Edessa and later still king of Jerusalem, also merited description, but Bohemond stood out as the archetype—the faithful, barely civilized knight heading to Holy Land as a warrior for God.[6]

And at the time, that is all they were. The term "Crusader" was not invented until the thirteenth century, although the absence of the word does not mean the absence of the concept. Scholarly debates notwithstanding, the men who set off for Jerusalem in 1096 thought of themselves as what one French historian called "armed pilgrims."[7] There was a long and established history of pilgrimage to Jerusalem, especially as penance for sins, and Pope Urban and his messengers had dangled the promise of spiritual reward for taking up arms to restore the Holy Land to Christian control. These armed pilgrims may have exhibited behavior that our contemporary morality would condemn as brutal and barbaric, but however greedy and rapacious they may have been, they lived in a world of deep and simple faith, one that not only coexisted with the sins of the flesh but was often fueled by them. The Crusaders knew that they had committed petty and not-so-petty sins, and that made the act of pilgrimage far more significant.

While the shifting sands of Near East politics were ultimately a gift to the Crusaders, the fate of Peter the Hermit and his followers, who had set off first, provided them with additional unexpected help. Peter's farce of an army had, by virtue of sheer size, managed to massacre the Jews of several towns along the Danube, but it was no match for the Seljuks. Alexius and his court were appalled at the filth and chaos of Peter's rabble, and the emperor made sure that the peasant "army" was quickly transported across the Bosphorus and away from the city. Once on the Asian side, they were cut to pieces by the local sultan, who naturally took them as representative of what the Franks could offer. When the far better disciplined and outfitted armies of the Normans and the other knights arrived soon after, the Seljuk emir mistakenly assumed that they were more of the same.

The local Seljuks may not have taken the Crusaders seriously, but Alexius did. Having persuaded most of them to swear allegiance, he had them escorted out of the city and across the Bosphorus into Asia. They took Nicaea (known as Iznik in Turkish) in May 1097 and then advanced south to the same pass that had welcomed Xerxes and Alexander in centuries past. The narrow Cilician pass between the mountains of southern Anatolia separated Asia Minor from Syria, and once through, the Crusaders laid siege to the ancient city of Antioch. Until its capture by the Seljuks in 1085, Antioch had been one of the most important Christian cities in the world, along with Jerusalem, Constantinople, and Rome.

After an arduous eight-month siege, Antioch fell to the Crusaders in June 1098. The task had been made easier by the squabbling that divided the Arab and Turkish factions trying to defend the city's formidable walls. Antioch was also home to a large Christian population that had lived there since the first century, and when the Crusaders arrived at the gates, the Turkish governor expelled them. "Antioch is yours," he told them, "but you will have to leave it to me until I see what happens between us and the Franks." He promised to look after their wives and children, but he did not allow them to return. These exiles received a cool reception from the Franks. Primarily Greek Orthodox and Armenian, they spoke different languages and worshiped with different rites, and the Franks treated them with suspicion and disdain. The feelings were mutual, and the proud Christians of Antioch, who traced their lineage to Saint Paul, felt less allegiance to the Crusaders than to the Arabs and Turks whom they had lived with, largely in peace, for the previous centuries. Though they served as useful intelligence agents for Bohemond and the other commanders, they did not trust the motives of the invaders.

Antioch finally succumbed after the Crusaders gained the aid of a Turkish general disenchanted with the local faction. Bohemond then allowed his soldiers, who had suffered through long months, to ravage the once-great city. And as in other cities on the road to Jerusalem, the Crusaders did not stop to ask whether the home they looted was owned by Christians, or whether the women they raped could recite the Nicene Creed or the opening verse of the Quran.[8]

After several days of indiscriminate pillaging, the princes reined in their army. The treatment meted out to Antioch seemed extreme at that time, but it was hardly out of the norm for Frankish and German warfare, nor did it compare to what was in store for Jerusalem. The duplicity of Bohemond shocked both the Muslims and the Byzantines but would not have raised eyebrows in Europe. He did not honor his commitment to Alexius to return Antioch to Byzantine control and instead set himself up as its king. That alienated not only the emperor but Bohemond's fellow knights as well. One of them, Baldwin, veered east with his army in a fit of jealousy and took the city of Edessa. The remaining forces, now significantly depleted, continued south.

The siege and capture of Antioch roused the Seljuk princes, as well as the Fatimid caliph in Cairo, to take serious notice. One twelfth-century Muslim chronicler later described the Christian victory at Antioch as the culmination of years of aggression against Islam that had begun with the fall of Toledo in Spain to the Christians in 1071, and then continued with the Norman invasion of Sicily, led by kinsmen of Baldwin of Edessa. The pattern, at least to one Muslim historian, was clear: Christians had been waging an international battle to turn back Muslim advances, and the assaults on Antioch, Edessa, and Syria were only the latest in a series.[9]

But even after Antioch, not all Arab and Turkish elites of the Near East took the Crusaders seriously. That would change forever when Jerusalem fell in 1099. Compared to the eight-month siege of Antioch, Jerusalem was taken easily, in less than two months. But while the Crusaders had camped under the walls of Antioch mostly during winter and spring, the contest for Jerusalem was waged during the scorching heat of summer. After more than three years of nearly continuous warfare in unfamiliar territory, the Crusaders were exhausted and anxious for the end of their mission. Perhaps that explains what happened when the walls were finally breached.

As it had been for centuries, Jerusalem was then inhabited by a mix of Jews, Christians, and Muslims. The Jewish quarter had existed since before the time of Christ, and the major Christian sects each had a sliver of the city and some responsibility for maintaining the holy stations along the Via Dolorosa. But the city's defenses were under the control of the Fatimid governor, and he viewed the local Christian and Jewish population as a potential fifth column. He made a Solomonic decision; the Christians he ordered out of the city, and the Jews he allowed to stay. Most Christians left, with the exception of the guardians of the Holy Sepulchre, which was still not fully reconstructed since Hakim's desecrations.

The siege was straightforward, and in mid-July 1099, the soldiers of Godfrey of Bouillon, by dint of formidable towers, heavy battering rams, and brute force, breached the walls. Some of the city's Christians aided the attackers, as the Fatimid governor had feared. They probably hoped that the victorious armies would reward them for their aid. Had they known what would actually happen, they would have fought to the last man to keep the Crusaders from occupying the city.

The Muslim accounts of the fall of Jerusalem described the usual outrages, but what sets Jerusalem apart in the annals of cold-blooded conquest is that the Christian chroniclers were equally shocked at what happened. The Crusaders had journeyed for an elusive goal, and once they had achieved it, their rage exploded. Whatever the reason, the city wasn't just sacked; it was desecrated and its inhabitants were massacred.

In spite of the paltry efforts of Godfrey and the other Christian general, Tancred, to exercise restraint, their soldiers swept through the city and killed every single soul they found. The massacre was not limited to Arab and Turkish Muslims. The Jews of the city took refuge in their synagogues only to be locked inside and burned alive. Eastern Orthodox monks tried to keep the shrine of the Holy Sepulchre from being looted by soldiers more interested in booty than in blessings, but they were cut down where they stood. There were stories of infants dashed against stones, of torture that lasted for days to amuse the troops, of beheadings, impalings, flayings, dismemberment, and corpses everywhere; and now and then, neat piles of heads surrounded, almost artistically, by pools of blood.[10]

LIVE AND LET LIVE

THE SACK of Jerusalem deeply disturbed the Muslim world. Muslims venerated the city, and the brutality of its conquest by the Christians was a wound that never quite healed. It's not that the treatment meted out to the unfortunate inhabitants was extraordinary by the standards of the day. But the fact that it happened in Jerusalem, a city so revered, was unsettling, and not only to Muslims. The proverbial morning after, even the Crusaders were shamed by what had transpired, judging from the Christian accounts of the city's capture. The massacre of Muslims who had taken refuge in Al-Aqsa Mosque may have been marginally acceptable, but the slaying of Eastern Rite Christians in the sanctuary of the Holy Sepulchre was not.

In time, the fall of Jerusalem became a rallying cry for the Muslims of the Near East, but in the immediate aftermath, the outrage was not met by action. Poets wrote laments about what had occurred, and some called for a campaign to repulse the Christian invasion. These had no effect. The Turkish emirs of Damascus and Aleppo were too weak, too antagonistic to the Fatimids, too suspicious of the rulers of Mosul and Iraq, and too competitive with each other to form an alliance capable of challenging the Franks. Calls for Muslim unity in the face of a foreign incursion were not persuasive enough to overcome the political, cultural, and theological divisions between the various factions that controlled the Near East. "The sultans did not agree among themselves," wrote the Arab historian Ibn al-Athir, "and it was for this reason that the Franks were able to seize control of the country."[11]

It is tempting to identify the Crusades as dramatic chapters in the war between Islam and the West, especially given the way Jerusalem fell in 1099. And that temptation is bolstered by some of what took place after the First Crusade. As the twelfth century progressed, it became common to view the Crusades as one prong of an international campaign conducted by Western Christians against Muslims. Both Christian and Muslim scholars of the Crusades, beginning centuries ago and resuming in the nineteenth century, lumped the various battles, waged by very different factions thousands of miles apart, under the banner of religious war. Polemicists at the time, again both Muslim and Christian, also had good reason to create this framework.

Yet the fact remains that *at the time*, holy war did not hold enough appeal to the rulers or to the people of the Near East to function as an effective rallying cry. The later tendency in both the West and the Muslim world to focus on the Crusades as war between religions makes it seem as if religion were the only factor, but in truth, it was only one factor, whose importance waxed and waned unpredictably. Put simply: if wars between religions had been of such overriding importance, then Christians throughout Europe would have rushed to fight side by side with their Byzantine brothers, and Muslims would have overcome their divisions and joined hands to fight a common adversary. That did not happen.

Instead, the First Crusade was led mostly by Frankish knights, and then the Franks—rather than fighting a perpetual war against Muslims—became part of the political fabric of the Near East. The victory in 1099 led to a dramatic increase in the number of pilgrims to Jerusalem, as well as a mini migration of settlers. Though exact numbers are impossible to come by, it seems that tens of thousands of people from Western and Central Europe immigrated to the new kingdoms of Jerusalem and Edessa. Some of these were petty nobility looking for a new start; others were artisans, soldiers, or peasants brought by their lords or drawn by a new frontier. Still others were merchants from Genoa, Pisa, Venice, or Amalfi who settled in the coastal ports such as Acre, Tyre, and Jaffa. The Italians, with their superior ships and vibrant commercial networks in the Mediterranean, took control of what they hoped would be lucrative trade routes stretching into Central Asia, India, and beyond.

Popular histories of the Crusades in both the West and the Muslim world focus exclusively on the conflict. Even the contemporary chroniclers, writing in the twelfth and thirteenth centuries, rarely devoted attention to daily life. There was little drama in that, and no heroism. The relentless focus on war has been a problem of history writing in general, and not confined to the subject of Muslims and Christians in the Near East. Until the second half of the twentieth century, few who wrote history—whether they were Muslim, Christian, Jew, or Hindu—wasted time on farming, trade, immigration, domestic life, and the humdrum aspects of getting through the day. History writing has thus exaggerated the frequency and centrality of war, revolution, mayhem, and changes in government. The consequence for the Crusades is that we remember the fighting, but not the peace. For two centuries, however, Western Europeans lived in the Near East, and while a year rarely passed without some skirmish against some adversary, there were long periods of quiet.

Recent historians have made concerted efforts to fill in the blanks of daily life in Europe at the time, but far less effort has gone into painting a complete picture of Near Eastern societies under the Franks. Since the middle of the twentieth century, and with very few original threads, scholars of medieval societies have expertly pieced together a tapestry of the so-called Dark Ages. Yet that skill has barely been employed to flesh out the contours of everyday life in the Crusader states.

As a result, for most of the past nine hundred years, histories of the Crusades—both in the West and in the Muslim world—have told a simple narrative of religious clash, begun by the papacy, fought by the knights of Europe, and then continued at the end of the twelfth century with equal fervor by the Muslims of the Near East and their savior, Saladin. That story has become part of the collective memory of both Westerners and Muslims. In the West, within a few years of the creation of the kingdom of Jerusalem, it was already being told in Europe, especially by those who used the First Crusade to create a more centralized church and more powerful states in Europe. Then the story made its way into ballads and epic poems, meant to inspire and entertain. Over the centuries, long after the last of the Franks had been evicted from the Near East, the memory seeped into popular culture through novels, plays, and eventually, in the twentieth century, movies.

In the English-speaking world, the nineteenth-century novels of Sir Walter Scott did more than anything to establish the popular image of the Crusades. Borrowing liberally from Edward Gibbon, Scott celebrated Saladin and Richard the Lionheart as icons of the contest between Islam and Christianity, and his books were later taken by Hollywood as the source material for films. In novels such as *The Talisman* and *Ivanhoe*, Scott portrayed Saladin as an aristocratic adversary, a Muslim warrior who respected the code of honor held so dear by Christian noblemen and knights. But Saladin was the exception to the rule that portrayed "Saracens" as heretical brutes.

Central to the popular story were the orders of religious knights: the Templars and the Hospitallers. The Templars, with their chain mail girded with white linen emblazoned with a red cross, became archetypes of the Christian warrior. Named after the Temple of Solomon in Jerusalem, where they lived, the Templars received the official sanction of the church early in the twelfth century. Not only was the temple the purported center of the first Israelite kingdom in the Holy Land, it was also where later Muslims had built Al-Aqsa Mosque. As a religious order blessed by the pope and sponsored by Bernard of Clairvaux, the Templars represented the fusion of the soldier and the priest, and their fame and wealth survived long after they departed the Holy Land. They and the Hospitallers eventually retreated to Mediterranean islands such as Malta and Rhodes, until the Ottomans supplanted them. As the order disappeared, however, the legend grew until the image of the Templars was permanently imprinted on Western consciousness. They became Crusader icons. They have graced forgettable Victorian novels, French romances, Hollywood films, and international best sellers, and have been cast as sinister characters pulling the levers of history, a dark, hidden force along with the Masons and the Illuminati.

But while the religious orders were prominent in Frankish society in the Near East, they were a small, albeit powerful, minority of all European settlers in the Orient and arguably less important than the Italian merchants who controlled trade but did not fight wars. Even generous estimates suggest that the Templars and Hospitallers never had more than a thousand armed knights at any one time. Yet a quick glance at a library catalog will yield thousands of entries on the crusading orders, which dwarfs the literature on trade. Merchants may have mattered more in the greater scheme of things, but what they did was less compelling to writers and polemicists, either at the time or centuries later. What would a romantic novelist do with a dull Genoese merchant in Acre? Much better to focus on knights, castles, war, and men in shiny chain mail. For Arab and Turkish court chroniclers, the Templars made a perfect foil, proof of the greed and rapaciousness of the Christians. A spice merchant from Pisa arranging shipments in Sidon was of far less interest.

In the workaday world of the Crusader kingdoms of the twelfth century, however, those merchants, artisans, and peasants outnumbered the Templars and Hospitallers, who were important as vassals of Rome but did little to shape everyday society in Syria, Lebanon, or Palestine. The orders were integral to the ambitions of the pope, but they were only one element of the balance of power in the Near East.[12] The actual history of daily life during the age of the Crusades is more mundane and lacks dynamic characters and dominant leaders. The names of the people who lived and died are obscure, if recorded at all. The princes and kings of the Frankish states in the Near East are kept alive by scholars, and most battles of consequence were recorded by either Muslims or Christians. The long lulls in between were not.

Part of the explanation is prosaic: lulls make for boring reading. Until the late twentieth century, no one wrote a novel about a hum-drum life, or filmed a movie with no plot. And it is not only that periods between the wars are less dynamic. They also make history more complicated and ambiguous, and thereby undermine the black-and-white story of conflict. Neither Western cultures nor Muslim cultures have wanted to focus on coexistence. Yet, for much of the twelfth-century in the Near East, daily life was shaped not by heroic warriors but by small Western Christian city-states ruled by a few nobles and bureaucrats who were surrounded by Muslim Arabs and Turks and by Eastern Christian peasants and elites who had never converted to Islam. Their history, largely forgotten, is neither glorious nor ignominious.

The conquest of Jerusalem was followed by the creation of the Frankish kingdom of Jerusalem and the crowning of its first king, Godfrey. He soon died and was succeeded by Baldwin of Edessa, who became King Baldwin I of Jerusalem and remained so until his death in 1118. Frankish armies pushed to the coast of Palestine, attacked Tripoli, and battled both the Fatimids and the Seljuks. As the new Christian states established themselves, they re-created Western Europe feudalism. The kingdom of Jerusalem nominally ruled many of the city-states in what is now Israel and the Palestinian West Bank; the lords of Antioch claimed sovereignty over large parts of present-day Lebanon; and the kingdom of Edessa carved out several thousand square miles inhabited mostly by Armenian Christians.

The Frankish princes ruled over a sparsely settled countryside dotted with towns. Many Muslims had fled just before and after 1099 as word of Christian barbarity spread. Jerusalem was nearly emptied of its inhabitants through the combined effects of flight and massacre, and even a decade later, the population of the city was only in the low thousands. Outside of Jerusalem, the areas controlled by the Crusaders were populated by a mix of Christians and Muslims. Most scholars agree that the Near East even at this point, nearly five hundred years after the first Arab conquests, was still home to a large Christian population, which in many regions was in the majority. That meant that Crusaders found themselves ruling states with substantial numbers of Christians. The conquerors, however, looked down on them because they spoke an incomprehensible language, had alien ways of celebrating mass, and held theological positions that had long ago been declared heretical in the West.

At first, the Franks treated the local Christians as conquered peoples. Though there was some loosening of social constraints, the locals remained second-class citizens. The Franks did not even lift the unpleasant poll tax that Muslims had imposed on the People of the Book. Instead, they maintained the tax, added Muslims to the lists, and continued to assess native Christians and Jews. In essence, most of the population, whether Christian or Muslim, found their lives little changed.

Eastern Christians neither rose up against the Crusaders nor fully embraced them. They served their new masters, just as they had served their old, but they at least shared a basic belief in the centrality of Christ to their lives. The Franks may not have respected the local Christians, but the local Christians found new opportunities for social advancement, primarily as intermediaries between the Muslims of the Near East and the new Crusader kingdoms.

In addition, Eastern Christians had an easier time getting hired as mercenaries by the Crusader states than they had by the Seljuks or the Fatimids. Unlike the Templars and the Hospitallers, who answered mostly to themselves and nominally to the pope, Eastern Christian mercenaries did the bidding of the prince or king who hired them. It was a good arrangement for both the Frankish rulers and the local population. The Maronite Christians of Mount Lebanon, who had been moving ever closer to Rome, benefited enormously from the establishment of trading posts along the coast, and they found lucrative employment as soldiers for the princes of Acre, Sidon, and Tripoli. They also served as translators and intermediaries for Italian merchants who wanted to access the Seljuk-controlled trade routes east of Damascus and Aleppo. The legacy of close relations between the Maronites and the Franks (French) lasted well into the twentieth century and culminated in the creation of the modern state of Lebanon.

Gradually, however, the Franks began to assimilate. They changed how they dressed, the language they spoke, and even who they married. The majority of intermarriages occurred between Franks and local Christians; marriages between Christians and Muslims were frowned upon by both sides. But men and women have a way of circumventing social controls. Knights who had come to fight and then stayed needed women. Sex was easy enough to obtain, for a price or from a slave, but marriage was a bit more challenging. The aristocrats could arrange marriages to cement alliances between crusading states, between ruling Frankish families in the Near East and Byzantine royals, or with nobility in Europe. But for the rest, the most promising avenue was the easiest one—women from the local population. Often these were Christian, but not always.

The increase in intermarriage drew the notice of the chronicler Fulcher of Chartres. Writing around the year 1127, he observed that the Crusader states had become as corrupt, petty, and divisive as their counterparts in Europe. "Occidentals have now been made Orientals. He who was a Roman or a Frank is now a Galilean or an inhabitant of Palestine.... We have now forgotten the places of our birth.... Some already possess here homes or servants which they have received through inheritance. Some have taken wives not merely of their own people but Syrians, or Armenians, or even Saracens who have received the grace of baptism."[13]

As part of the process of assimilation, Western Christians in the Near

East became more tolerant of religious diversity than they had been in Europe. While they disdained the rites of Eastern Christians and treated Muslims (and Jews) as lost souls, they neither proselytized nor went out of their way to make life untenable for these subjects. In part, that was out of necessity. They were vastly outnumbered by Christians of different sects and by Muslims whose aid and support they often needed. Once the goal of retaking Jerusalem had been accomplished, the Franks confronted the daunting task of creating viable states, without a master plan for governing. They were forced to improvise, and faced with the more sophisticated societies that they had conquered and now ruled, they borrowed liberally.

The Crusader states emulated not just the dress and mores of local Christians but also the policies of the Muslim rulers they had supplanted. The result was a grudging culture of toleration. As long as taxes were paid, most of the local populace was left alone, free to enforce their own social and religious mores. One Muslim chronicler, who was unstinting in his hostility to the Franks, nonetheless acknowledged that they did not interfere with the right of Muslims to worship God as they pleased and "did not change a single law or cult practice." The courts set up by the Franks, while privileging the testimony of Christians, provided protections to Muslims as human beings "like the Franks."

The new rulers of Jerusalem did convert Al-Aqsa Mosque into a church, with a monastery for the Templars. They also set aside space for Muslims to worship there. It was understood that when major centers were occupied by Christians or by Muslims, the main church or mosque would be symbolically switched over to reflect the religion of the rulers. As a result, there was no Muslim outcry when Al-Aqsa was transformed into a church. Given the image of the Crusades as a period of unmitigated holy war, the lack of outrage is difficult to reconcile. A similar event in Jerusalem today would plunge the region into chaos.

In the first half of the twelfth century, however, there was no ingrained culture of religious war in the Near East. It was as common for Franks to fight Franks or Byzantium as it was for Franks to fight Muslims. Most Muslim states expended more energy scheming and plotting against one another than they did against the Christian invaders. That seems to have dismayed few inhabitants of Damascus, Aleppo, Mosul, or Cairo. Although the occasional cry for war against the infidel was not unheard of, later polemicists—in the interest of giving muscle to the

clash-of-civilizations perspective—have excavated those and emphasized them out of all proportion to their frequency. Muslim calls for holy
war in the twelfth century were much like calls to end poverty in the
twentieth—no one could disagree with the noble ambitions, but few
were interested in actually doing anything.

In fact, Muslims who found themselves under Christian rule, rather
than resisting their new overlords, began to emulate them. Much as
Christians in Andalusia learned Arabic and tried to ingratiate themselves with the Muslim ruling class, Muslims of the Crusader states did
what they could to win the favor of the new lords. Some found that
Christian rulers were more equitable than the Muslims they had
replaced. In a refrain remarkably like that of the Córdoba martyrs of the
ninth century who despaired when they saw Christians embracing Muslim culture, the chronicler Ibn Jubayr moaned that Muslim peasants
preferred Christian landlords. "Their hearts have been seduced.... This
is one of the misfortunes afflicting the Muslims. The Muslim community bewails the injustice of a landlord of its own faith, and applauds the
conduct of its opponent and enemy, the Frankish landlord, and is accustomed to justice from him." And it wasn't just Muslims under Christian
rule who accepted coexistence. Local sultans signed treaties and established fruitful trade alliances with the Crusader states. According to the
chronicler Ibn al-Qalanisi, the Muslim governor of Ascalon sent emissaries to King Baldwin of Jerusalem to arrange a treaty because "he was
more desirous of trading than fighting, and inclined to peaceful and
friendly relation and securing the safety of travellers."[14]

It is a truism that most people, most of the time, follow the path of
least resistance. Faced with a new political order, people tend to adapt
rather than resist. That was true of Christians in Muslim-ruled Spain,
and it was true of Muslims in the Christian-ruled Crusader states of the
twelfth century. Until recently, most scholars assumed that the few
Franks and Italians who immigrated to the Near East lived only in the
coastal cities, in Jerusalem or Edessa, or in the fortified castles that lined
the north-south corridor from Krak des Chevaliers, between Beirut and
Damascus, to Kerak, south of present-day Amman in Jordan. In part,
these assumptions were based on the absence of records listing land own-
ership, but they were also fueled by a long-standing belief that the Crusaders would never have settled in the midst of a hostile and alien rural
population. But they did, and the local populace accommodated them.

While many Westerners did settle in cities, others carved out rural estates comparable to what might have been found in France or the Rhine Valley. These estates were tended by Christian and Muslim peasants whose particular creed mattered less to their masters than their ability to tend to crops, herds, and other agricultural business. For the better part of a century, Christian rule over those peasants generated no more, though perhaps no less, tension and animosity than what would have been found in feudal Western Europe at the time. Peasants resented their lords; barons disdained the peasantry. People gossiped, occasionally dreamt of a different world, and almost never did anything about it. The one thing everyone—high and low, Christian, Jew, or Muslim—abhorred was chaos. Injustice was hardly desirable, but it was preferable to revolution. In the world of the Crusader states, what mattered most was class and economic status, not religion.[15]

Though there are few surviving accounts of relations between Westerners and Muslims, one Muslim aristocrat did leave a vivid memoir of his life and times. Usama ibn Munqidh grew up in the city of Shayzar in northern Syria. He was, in the words of his translator and master scholar Philip Hitti, "a warrior, a hunter, a gentleman, a poet, and a man of letters. His life was the epitome of Arab civilization as it flourished during the early crusading period." As a young man, Usama received the typical education of a genteel urban aristocrat and learned classical poetry, grammar, calligraphy, and of course, the Quran. As an adult, he dabbled in rhetoric, philosophy, mysticism, and the arts of war, but to the end, he had a fatalistic view that God determined all moments of all lives and that all anyone could do is live out his allotted days. Toward the end of his life, after the entire region had been unified under the rule of Saladin the Kurd, Usama sat down and recorded his memories.

Usama delighted in the human condition and loved the absurdity of human existence. He recorded the story of a man named Ali Abd ibn abi al-Rayda who had made a name for himself as a soldier and a marauder raiding caravans. He served a local Muslim prince who was killed, and then was hired by a Frankish noble. With his knowledge of the region and his experience intercepting Muslim caravans, Ali helped his new Christian master become rich at the expense of local Muslim traders. Not only did that not please his former companions, it also deeply offended his wife. One night, she hid her brother in her home, and when her husband returned, they attacked and killed him. She claimed that she was "angered on behalf of the Muslims because of what this infidel perpetrated against them." But she also took all of her murdered husband's belongings and relocated to the city of Shayzar, where Usama lived. He reported that she was treated with great respect by the neighbors. In another story, Usama told of a Frankish maid taken captive during a battle who caught the eye of the local Muslim emir. She bore him a son, who became the prince when his father died. Rather than living in luxury as the esteemed mother, however, she left the castle and married a Frankish shoemaker.

Usama was fascinated with the Franks. Much like the Byzantines, he was alternately bemused and appalled by how crude they could be. "Mysterious are the works of the Creator, the author of all things," he wrote. "When one comes to recount cases regarding the Franks, he cannot but glorify Allah and sanctify him, for he sees them as animals possessing the virtues of courage and fighting but nothing else; just as animals have only virtues of courage and fighting." Usama was particularly amazed at Frankish medical practices, which were so rudimentary that they tended to kill the patient. He wrote of an Eastern Christian physician who healed a Frankish knight with an abscess on his leg and saved a woman suffering from a mysterious affliction. The physician applied a poultice to the leg that absorbed the infection, and he altered the woman's diet until she showed signs of renewed health. The Franks, however, did not trust the remedies and sent their own physician, who scoffed at the treatments. The Frankish physician, refusing to believe that the knight's leg was getting better, said to him, "Which wouldst thou prefer, living with one leg or dying with two?" Faced with this choice, the knight said he'd rather have one leg than no life. So the physician called for an ax and had a few strong men hold the knight down while another chopped off his leg. The blow wasn't accurate. It cut the patient's bone and artery, and he promptly bled to death. As for the woman, the Frankish physician took one look at her and declared that she was possessed by the devil. He had her head shaved, fed her nothing but garlic and mustard, watched as she became weaker, carved a crucifix in her skull, peeled off the skin, rubbed the exposed bone with salt, exorcised the demon, and killed the patient.

To be fair, Usama also described instances when Frankish medicine succeeded in healing patients with treatments unknown in Syria at the time, such as a concoction of ashes, vinegar, burnt lead, and clarified butter applied as a balm for a neck wound. But on the whole, he was both appalled and amused by the raw ignorance of the Franks.

Their sexual mores also astonished him. Usama was hardly the first or last person titillated by lurid tales. He recalled the time he was staying at an inn that served both Muslim and Christian travelers, and the innkeeper told him that a Christian man had come back to his room only to find another man sleeping with his wife. Naturally, he was a bit perturbed and woke the fellow up. "What are you doing here with my wife?" he asked the man. "Well, I was tired," the man replied. The wife was already in the bed, and it would, he told the irate husband, have been rude to wake her.

Usama also recounts a story told to him by the Muslim owner of a public bathhouse. One day, the owner went to the bath accompanied by a Frankish noble, and he was surprised at how immodest the Franks could be. He put a towel on before entering the bath, but found that the Franks didn't cover themselves. One of them came up to him and yanked off his towel, which promptly revealed another cultural difference. The owner, like most cultured gentlemen of the Near East, kept his hair trim—*everywhere!* The Frank looked and demanded that the Muslim trim him accordingly. The Frank liked the outcome so much that he called for his wife to be brought. He told her to lie on her back and then asked the owner to do the same for her and offered to pay for it!

The only editorial comment Usama made in telling the story was that the Franks seemed immune from both jealousy and modesty. The fact that the bathhouse owner had shaved the pubic hair of both a Frankish knight and his wife in public was apparently unremarkable to Usama. The only oddity from Usama's perspective was that the knight had asked. Presumably, the fact that the owner obliged was simply good manners.

Usama was also struck by the rough justice of the Franks. Muslim jurisprudence was well advanced by the twelfth century. Judges could call on centuries of legal precedent as well as volume upon volume of law books in order to apply the principles of the Quran to the case at hand. There was no equivalent among the Franks, who had forgotten most of the Roman legal system and long since abandoned the careful deliberations that had characterized Roman law at its best. In one episode relayed by Usama, a local Frankish blacksmith was accused of aiding several thieves, and he in turn challenged his accuser to a duel. Rather than trying the case in a court, the local lord agreed, and the blacksmith and the accuser then beat each other to a pulp. The blacksmith won, dragged the corpse away, and then hanged it in an act of ritual humiliation. Usama also described an "ordeal by water" trial. The accused was bound and then dropped in a cask of water. If he sank, he would be presumed innocent, but if he floated, he would be declared guilty. Given that human bodies do not tend to sink immediately, he bobbed a bit, and as a result he was found guilty and punished by having red-hot rods inserted in his eyes.[16]

Usama was a Muslim aristocrat who served the emir of Aleppo and Damascus and frequently fought against Frankish armies. But he also had warm relations with Christian knights. On several occasions, he went to Jerusalem to pray in Al-Aqsa Mosque and then shared a meal with the Templars who occupied the grounds. He referred to the Templars as "my friends," and seems to have spent considerable time in their company. He may have been alternately amused and repelled by the Franks, but his world was not so different. It too was punctuated by routine acts of violence, and by casual attitudes toward life, death, and slavery. In his memoirs, people live, people die, they kill and they get killed, and little of it shocks him.

Today's notions of religious conflict would have made no sense to Usama. Unlike Osama bin Laden, Usama ibn Munqidh did not see religious identity as all-encompassing. His faith was vital, and Allah's will was paramount. The Franks were infidels—and risked damnation—but so were the Shi'ites and the Fatimids. One month, he might be at war with them; the next, he might be the guest of the Templars at Al-Aqsa Mosque.

Though he was an unusually astute observer of human nature, Usama was also a man of his times. The way he related to his Christian and Frankish neighbors was typical for a person of his class and occupation. Traders and soldiers traveled frequently and freely throughout Syria and Palestine, in spite of dangerous roads and shifting political landscapes. Alliances were fleeting and made and broken promiscuously. When it was convenient, Franks signed peace treaties with the Seljuks or the Fatimids, and when it was advantageous they fought alongside Muslims against mutual enemies. Frankish nobles were as prone to wars with other Franks as they were to waging campaigns against Muslims. Just as

Spain had seen shifting coalitions depending on who was fighting whom, Frankish soldiers fought alongside Turks one year and against them the next. Sometimes religion was the fault line; often it was not.

Until the middle of the twelfth century, the Crusader states had the upper hand in the Near East. Then the tide shifted. Several talented Turkish emirs unified Syria and eventually Egypt. While their motive was to build powerful dynasties, they used the rhetoric of holy war, and when possible, they defined the politics of the Near East in terms of Muslims versus Franks. Whether or not they believed their rhetoric, in what was otherwise a divided region, it united Arabs and Turks, Syrians, Egyptians, and above all, Kurds and transformed them into a potent force capable of expelling the Crusaders from the Near East. The first to urge all Muslims to fight the Franks was a Turkish emir named Zengi, but the most famous was a Kurdish prince, born in the town of Tikrit along the Tigris, named Yusuf, son of Ayyub, later known by his surname, Honor of the Faith, Salah ad-Din.

❧❧❧ ❧❧

CHAPTER FIVE

SALADIN'S JIHAD?

THE SOLDIERS APPEARED on the outskirts of Jerusalem in late September, just before the autumn solstice in 1187. It had been nearly a century since the Franks had occupied the city, and no Muslim army had come close to retaking it. After the massacre of its former inhabitants in 1099, the kingdom of Jerusalem entered a long period of calm and prosperity. Pilgrims from Europe came and went freely, and the king enjoyed the tribute of towns and estates up and down the coast of Palestine.

Over the decades, however, the Franks failed to extend their initial victories. By the fall of 1187, though the rulers in Jerusalem were aware of the looming threat, they were still ill prepared when it finally arrived at their walls. The military backbone of the kingdom had been shattered just months before, when Saladin, the sultan of Egypt and lord of Damascus and Aleppo, decimated the armies of the Templars and the Franks at the battle of Hattin. The king of Jerusalem was captured and held hostage, and the administration of the city was left to the queen, Sibylla, and the patriarch. Word of Saladin's advance on Jerusalem, after an attack on Ascalon, preceded his arrival, but the queen could do little but watch as the city came under siege.

For his part, Saladin was overcome with the magnitude of what he was about to accomplish. He had, over the prior fifteen years, changed the political landscape of the Near East and created a new dynasty that united Egypt and Syria for the first time in centuries. During years of tactical battles against both Christians and Muslims, he had one goal in mind: the expulsion of the Franks and the creation of a new empire with himself as sultan in the service of God. Now, with his armies arrayed and prepared to capture Jerusalem, he remembered why he was there in the first place.

Just weeks before, outside of Ascalon, a delegation of Jerusalem merchants had approached him with an offer of peace. Their proposal was that Jerusalem proper would remain independent and intact, but Saladin would become master of its environs. Saladin, whose reputation for fairness was even then legend, took their suggestion seriously. He knew what had happened the last time the city had changed hands, when it had been emptied and its holy places turned into scenes of carnage, and he wanted no replay. "I believe," he told the delegation, "that Jerusalem is the House of God, as you also believe, and I will not willingly lay siege to the House of God or put it to assault." He said that in exchange for the surrender, he would permit the Christians to retain their possessions and some of the land. It was as good an offer as they could have hoped for, yet they refused.

At any other point during the previous century, that would have spelled the end of the city and its inhabitants. But Saladin was of a different mold. Determined to honor Jerusalem, he forced Balian, a nobleman charged with the hopeless task of defending the city, to come to terms. After the Muslims breached the walls, Balian, on the urging of the patriarch, went under the flag of truce to Saladin's tent. The only weapons he had left were words, and he warned Saladin that the knights of Jerusalem, and the Templars and the Hospitallers above all, were prepared to die as martyrs defending the city. They might lose in the end, he said, but they would make it costly. Saladin dismissed the warning as the bluff of a defeated man, and he reminded Balian what had happened when the Christians had taken the city decades before. Did Balian want to be responsible for an even greater slaughter? It was not an idle threat. Saladin had a reputation for tolerance, but he had also shown flashes of rage and ruthlessness. Like any successful ruler of that time and place, he was capable of violence. Faced with the reality of defeat, the Franks surrendered.

On Friday, October 2, 1187, Saladin's troops took control of Jerusalem. They were scrupulously fair toward the conquered. Discipline held, and the city changed hands quickly and bloodlessly. Saladin's men repossessed the Dome of the Rock and Al-Aqsa Mosque, and they did so on a day full of symbolism. By the Muslim calendar, it was the anniversary of Muhammad's night journey, when, in honor of Christ's passion, he had been transported on a magical horse-like creature, the Buraq, to the Dome of the Rock and from there to heaven.

Saladin was humbled by the enormity of what he had achieved. He interpreted the recapture of Jerusalem as a sign of God's pleasure, and he was determined to show his respect. Later court chroniclers tripped over themselves to describe what happened. After securing the city, Saladin focused on the purification of Al-Aqsa Mosque. Because it had been occupied by the Templars for so many years, that was no easy task. But with men working around the clock, it was soon restored. Then, according to the chronicler Imad ad-Din,

> The Quranic readers arrived, the official prayers were read, the ascetics and pious men congregated.... They joined in groups to pray and prostrate themselves, humbling themselves and beating their breasts, dignitaries and ascetics, judges and witnesses, zealots and combatants in the Holy War, standing and sitting, keeping vigil and committed to prayer by night.... The traditionists recited, the holy orators comforted men's souls, the scholars disputed, the lawyers discussed, the narrators narrated.

Though a fair number of the Christians of the city were held for ransom, they were treated honorably. Given Saladin's commitment to the basic tenets of Islam, that made sense. He took the Quranic injunctions about the People of the Book seriously, and that may have guided his choice of the preacher who gave the first sermon in the resanctified Al-Aqsa Mosque: the chief judge of Aleppo, known for his eloquence and learning, who delivered an impassioned lecture about the significance of Jerusalem to Muslims everywhere.

"O Men," he cried,

> rejoice at good tidings. God is well-pleased with what you have done, and this is the summit of man's desire; he has helped you bring back this strayed camel from misguided hands and to restore it to the fold of Islam, after the infidels had mishandled it for nearly a hundred years. Rejoice at the purifying of this House.... It was the dwelling

place of your father Abraham, the spot where the Prophet Muhammad, God bless him, ascended to Heaven, the *qibla* to which you
turned to pray in the early time of Islam, the abode of prophets, the
resort of the saints, the grave of the saints, the place where God's revelation came down, and where all mankind must gather on the Day
of Resurrection and the Day of Judgement.... It is the city to which
God sent his servant and apostle, the Word which entered into Mary
and Jesus.[1]

The retaking of Jerusalem was the culmination of a dream for Saladin. Early in his life, he had dedicated himself to the unification of Syria
and Egypt as a necessary prelude for a coordinated assault on the Crusader states and their jewel, the kingdom of Jerusalem. Donning the
mantle of holy war, he had achieved his life's ambition and evicted the
Christians from the Dome of the Rock. And yet, in that moment of glory,
his chosen preacher gave a triumphant sermon that linked Jerusalem to
the biblical tradition of Abraham and Jesus.

Jerusalem was holy to Islam precisely because it had been holy to the
Jews and to the Christians. It later became sacred to Muhammad and to
the Muslim community, but only because it was the city of apostles. In
short, Jerusalem was sanctified in Muslim eyes not in spite of but
because it had been the holiest of holies for the People of the Book. For
Saladin, Jerusalem was the glue binding the People of the Book to Islam.
His holy war had been fought against both Muslim and Christian states
that stood in the way of the unification of the entire community of
believers—Christian, Jew, and Muslim—under the banner of Islam and
the house of Saladin.

This is a far cry from how this period is commonly viewed. The simple black-and-white of us versus them, Muslims versus Christians,
doesn't come close to explaining why Saladin did what he did, and the
modern understanding of holy war doesn't help. Though Saladin is one
of the few historical Muslims who enjoys a favorable image in the West,
that does not mean he is understood. He may have been a noble soul in
comparison with his contemporaries, but he was also a man of his era.
He waged a jihad against the Christian invaders from Europe as part of a
grand strategy to build a dynasty and restore the Near East to the glory
of the seventh and eighth centuries.

HOLY WAR

SALADIN WAS NOT the first to use the language of holy war, but before him, it had been ineffective. Even with the failure of the Second Crusade in 1147 and the inability of the Christian princes to capture Damascus, Jerusalem remained untouched and unchallenged. The Turkish and Arab emirs of Syria and Egypt remained at least as committed to fighting one other as they did to fighting the Franks or the Byzantines. Sometime in the middle of the twelfth century, however, the landscape began to change. A succession of strong Turkish and Kurdish princes cobbled together a formidable state to rival Jerusalem. The first crack to appear in the Frankish façade was the fall of Edessa, and the next was the Christian debacle at the gates of Damascus during the Second Crusade. Stepping into this breach was the ruler of Aleppo, Nur al-Din.

The political balance in the Near East was defined by two rivalries: one between Aleppo and Damascus, the other between the kingdom of Jerusalem and the surrounding Muslim states. In Aleppo, Nur al-Din, known as "the Saint King," succeeded his father, Zengi, in 1146. His father cast a long a shadow, so feared that the rival emir of Damascus had entered into an alliance with the king of Jerusalem solely to contain him. It was a classic case of "the enemy of my enemy is my friend." It was also business as usual in the Near East at the time. One month, armies were arrayed on the side of faith, and Christians squared off against Muslims. Then, as one set of princes died, or were killed, old alliances melted away and new ones formed, based not on creed but on who wanted what. In the shifting political sands of the region, the Byzantines, transplanted Franks, intermittent Crusaders from Europe, the Fatimids of Egypt, Seljuk sultans, and Arab emirs jockeyed for preeminence. Strategically placed on central trade routes and standing between the Frankish states of the Mediterranean coast and the Turks inland, Damascus was the prime prize.

The ruler of Damascus, pinned between a cold alliance with the Franks to the west and the threat of Aleppo and Nur al-Din to the north and east, tried to have it both ways. While technically maintaining his pact with Jerusalem, he aggressively wooed Nur al-Din, who eventually agreed to a partnership. That upset the balance between Damascus and the kingdom of Jerusalem, and helped trigger the Second Crusade. Nur al-Din then seized the opportunity created by the departure of the failed Crusader armies after 1147 to extend his reach. Seven years later, he did what the armies of the Second Crusade could not and captured Damascus.

The annexation of Damascus not only transformed Nur al-Din into one of the most powerful players in the region; because of his unusual character, it also set in motion a shift in tone. Nur al-Din was less inclined to accommodate the Franks. Instead, he wanted to remove the transplanted Westerners. Unlike most Muslim warlords, who were feared for their ferocity or ridiculed for their timidity but rarely, if ever, praised for their character, Nur al-Din was lauded for humility and devoutness. And unlike so many before him, he was driven not just by ambition but by faith.

The image of the Muslim warrior riding into battle with the Quran in one hand may be familiar, but to Muslims of the Near East in the twelfth century, it would have been alien. Nur al-Din was remarkable not because he was an archetype but because he was so different. Ambition was commonplace, but piety was a rare quality in a prince. Muslim jurists, recognizing that rulers used the Quran mostly when it was convenient and did what they wanted when it was not, had come to the conclusion that it was better to suffer the cruelties of a mercurial, even unjust ruler than risk the chaos that might come with trying to overthrow him.

The result was a political philosophy of accommodation. Muslim theologians were hesitant to challenge the legitimacy of a ruler, whether or not that ruler honored the laws of Islam, which rulers rarely did. With the decline in the power and prestige of the Baghdad caliphate, Muslim scholars adopted a pragmatic approach to the warlords and draped it with religious justification. That was not overly difficult, given that Islam, at heart, involved submission to the ultimate authority, God. Faced with political fragmentation, the *ulama* emphasized the duty of Muslims to submit obediently to the ruler. If the ruler was unjust, he would ultimately answer to God, and in the interim, it was the responsibility of the individual Muslim to submit to the ruler's authority. The *ulama*, for their part, had a duty to ensure that religious law, the sharia, was preserved and honored, if not by the ruler, then at least by judges and scholars.

The ethos of accommodation and obedience was often challenged by individuals, but without a unified church, the *ulama* were less able to resist the will of any particular ruler than bishops, cardinals, and popes were in Europe at the time. Occasionally, some scholar would denounce a ruler for his actions, but usually from a distance. A judge living in Baghdad could safely inveigh against an emir in Syria, but he would risk his life if he said the same things in Damascus. It was the rare individual who took a stand against a perceived violation of religious law by a ruler, and it was the even rarer individual who did not then have to flee to escape that ruler's rage.

By contrast, Europe at the time was in the midst of a centuries-long struggle between church and state. The Crusades were a means to an end for the Catholic Church, which used the rallying call of war against unbelievers as a way to gain influence and power. Crusades were waged not just against Muslims in the Near East but also against pagan tribes in the Baltics, against heretics in Europe, and of course against Muslims in Spain. Most of these Crusades were spurred by a church and a papacy that were competing with political leaders for a dominant position in society.

But in the Muslim world, the political class was preeminent. In Baghdad, the Abbasid caliphate continued to exert a pull on the collective heartstrings of parts of the Muslim world, primarily because it was a reminder of an ideal of unity. The fact that such unity had rarely existed was less important than the fact that the ideal had always been central. No one could dispute that the Muslim world had been fractured for centuries, but the yearning for a unified community (*umma*) never faded. If anything, it grew stronger the more the reality of the Muslim world underscored its absence. As a result, while the invasion of the Crusaders did not initially lead to a counterreaction, the seeds were there. The inability of the Muslim states of the Near East to repel the Franks was a stark reminder of their divisions. After a tepid, shell-shocked response during the first part of the twelfth century, the political and military leaders of the Near East began to channel the unease and use it to craft a new balance of power capable of challenging the invaders.

It is impossible to understand the rise of Nur al-Din, and of his successor Salah ad-Din, without this context. Muslims were not only divided in the face of Western Christians, but they suffered from a debilitating legacy of doctrinal schisms that had afflicted the *umma* since the time of Ali and the formation of Shi'a. For the Sunnis, the Shi'ite Fatimid state in Egypt was just as disturbing as the Crusader states in Palestine.

Both represented the dire consequences of disunity. Both demonstrated what would happen to the *umma* if it fragmented.

When Nur al-Din died in 1174, he was praised throughout the Near East as a ruler of wisdom, maturity, and piety. But it was not immediately clear who would succeed him. The most likely candidate was his deputy, Saladin, the governor of Egypt who had spent more than a decade dealing with Frankish invasions and the intrigues of the rapidly decaying Fatimid state. Year by year, Saladin had acquired more influence, aided by the fortuitous death of assorted rivals. His battlefield victories were impressive, but his political instincts were also remarkably keen. After years of delicate maneuvering, he finally ended the life of the feeble Fatimid empire and ordered that the name of the Fatimid caliph be omitted from the Friday prayer and the name of the Sunni Abbasid caliph be included instead. Then, when he learned of the death of Nur al-Din, he moved with alacrity.

It was natural for Saladin to believe that he was the rightful heir to Nur al-Din. Like his former master, he professed a deep commitment to bringing the Near East under one Sunni overlord. At least that is the impression that has survived the centuries. Judging from the few contemporary histories that survive, it is hard to believe that Saladin was a man of flesh and blood. Either he was a master of propaganda or he was truly blessed with grace and nobility and motivated by a genuine passion to make the Muslim community whole. In truth, he may have been both.

It is ironic that Saladin is so celebrated in the West. In his day, he was the greatest defender of the concept of jihad in the Muslim world. In the words of one his biographers,

> Saladin was extremely diligent in waging this holy war, and it was constantly on his mind. One could swear by one's right hand without fear of contradiction that, from the time he first set out, intent on jihad, until he died, he did not spend a single gold or silver coin except on jihad and pious works. His heart and mind were so taken over by this burning zeal for jihad that he could speak of nothing else. Out of his desire to fight for God's cause, he left behind him his family, children, country, home.

In addition to being a dedicated holy warrior and man of God, he was "sociable, well mannered and entertaining.... The purity of his character was always evident: when in company he would allow no one to be spoken ill of in his presence, preferring to hear only their good traits; when he himself spoke, [he was] never disposed to insult anyone."[2]

If that were not enough, he was also—apparently—handsome, with kind, clear eyes and a finely trimmed beard. He was prone to acts of generosity and gentle in his interactions with women and children. It was said that he would share his food with supplicants and visitors, in honor of the old custom of the Arabs, rather than hide behind the elaborate rituals of later monarchs. He prayed regularly and publicly and delighted in listening to the verses of the Quran recited by expert readers. He was distrustful of philosophers and mystics who went beyond what the Quran and the tradition dictated. It was said after his death that one of his only regrets was that he had never been able to make the pilgrimage to Mecca. At the end of an expansive list of Saladin's remarkable traits, which stretched to many pages and thousands of words, one of his biographers explained that those were "simply a few examples of his soul's lofty and noble qualities. I have limited myself . . . in order not to extend this book unduly and bore the reader."

By the time Saladin encountered the armies of the Third Crusade, his image had been burnished to perfection. But in the years immediately after Nur al-Din's death, there were some who disagreed with the haloed portrait. Where most surviving accounts are unabashed hagiographies, not everything written about Saladin was so flattering. One satirist described drunken orgies, stupid scribes, humpbacked ministers, and cowardly generals who fought only when victory was certain. Like the court jester in Europe, satirists were allowed to poke fun at the powerful, to a point. The dark side of Saladin's piety may well have been a lack of humor about himself, and he was so offended by one description that he had the author banished. The poor soul was hurt and surprised, and wrote a bitter letter asking what he had done to deserve such treatment. "Why have you sent away a trustworthy man who has committed no crime and no theft? Banish the muezzins [who call the faithful to pray] from your lands if you are sending away all those who speak the truth."[3]

These sour notes, however, were drowned out by the chorus of praise, not just in his own time but in later generations. Western historians were particularly impressed. One of the premier twentieth-century scholars of Near Eastern history, H. A. R. Gibb, summarized Saladin's legacy in language that would have done a court historian proud. "For a brief but decisive moment, by sheer goodness and firmness of character, he raised Islam out of the rut of political demoralization." High praise from a sober English don, but nothing compared to the fulsome portrait left by Edward Gibbon in the eighteenth century. Gibbon, who rarely hesitated to use his pen to commit character assassinations, elevated Saladin high above the rank and file of humanity. He wrote that Saladin, having been fond of wine and women as a youth, saw the error of his ways and transformed himself.

> The garment of Saladin was of coarse woollen; water was his only drink; and while he emulated the temperance, he surpassed the chastity, of his Arabian prophet [Muhammad].... The justice of his divan was accessible to the meanest supplicant against himself and his ministers.... So boundless was his liberality that he distributed twelve thousand horses at the siege of Acre... and in a martial reign, the tributes were diminished, and the wealthy citizens enjoyed, without fear or danger, the fruits of their industry.

Yet Gibbon was not blind to Saladin's core. "In a fanatic age, himself a fanatic, the genuine virtues of Saladin commanded the esteem of the Christians; the emperor of Germany gloried in his friendship; the Greek [Byzantine] emperor solicited his alliance; and the conquest of Jerusalem diffused, and perhaps magnified, his fame both in the East and West."[4]

Gibbon, who embodied the swirl of contradictions that flowed through English society of the eighteenth century, which was still attached to the church yet testing the limits of that allegiance, recognized that Saladin was both a believer to the core and an empire builder. Which took priority in Saladin's soul is impossible to determine. But it is safe to assume that resurrecting an imperial Arab state and serving God were one and the same for him. His political ambitions were fully compatible with his religious passions, and his religious fervor gave him a strength and determination that most of his rivals lacked.

Some Western historians have argued that Saladin was primarily a dynast who manipulated religious imagery and language to justify his actions and craft his image. They note, correctly, that between 1174, when Nur al-Din died, and 1187, when Jerusalem was taken, Saladin spent nearly three years actively fighting other Muslim rulers, and little more than a year fighting Christians. Yet even when battling other Muslims, Saladin used the justification of holy war. Against the Shi'ite Fatimids, that was easy: wars between competing Muslims sects were every bit as vicious and ideological as wars between Christian sects could be. And judging from the Old Testament, battles between different Israelite tribes were hardly civilized affairs. But Saladin also relied on the language of holy war to validate his campaigns against other Sunni Muslim states.

Throughout his career, Saladin wrote letters to the Abbasid caliph in Baghdad, hoping to receive a blessing. Even in its absence, he claimed that he was acting as a loyal servant of the Commander of the Faithful and as the caliph's sword. As such, he would sweep away heretics and bring the errant Muslim city-states of the region once more into the fold of the community of believers. Those cities that resisted his entreaties he attacked because they were standing in the way of God's will. When the emir of Mosul refused to bow, Saladin claimed that the city was a key element in a master plan. With Mosul safely in Saladin's camp, the rest of the region would follow as surely as night follows day. Every other holdout would succumb, and then Jerusalem and finally Constantinople, "until the word of God is supreme and the Abbasid caliphate has wiped the world clean, turning the churches into mosques." Later, face-to-face with the leaders of Mosul, Saladin stated that he had only one reason for wanting the city, and it had nothing to do with his Kurdish roots. "We have come," he declared, "to unite the word of Islam and restore things by removing differences."[5]

For Saladin, the ends ultimately justified the means. Though he didn't seem to take any pleasure in war, he saw it as a necessary instrument. At each stage in his career, he was able to identify what was required to get to the next stage. After he had solidified his position in Egypt, he knew he still could not mount a credible challenge to the kingdom of Jerusalem. To do so would require the combined resources of the various states of the Near East. Unless they voluntarily submitted to him, he would force them to join him. If that meant war, then he would fight.

Yet Saladin's jihad was not the jihad of the twenty-first century. It was not a holy war of hate. It was a war of restoration, a struggle *for* orthodox Islam rather than *against* Christians or against Muslims who deviated from the Sunni path. There was a reason that Saladin spent more time fighting against other Muslims—including the fierce, fanatical, and at times suicidal cult of the Assassins, who were the al-Qaeda of their day—than he did against Christians. But that reason had nothing to do with doctrine. It was tactical. Only a unified Muslim Near East could defeat the Christian kingdom of Jerusalem.

If holy war is understood primarily as a struggle against non-Muslims and Muslims who have strayed, Saladin doesn't make much sense. But the problem here is not Saladin's jihad; it is how jihad has come to be defined by both Westerners and Muslims in the modern world.

As Islam evolved, so did the idea of jihad. Traditionally, there are two types of jihad in Islam: the greater jihad, which is an individual struggle for purity, and the lesser jihad, which is a campaign against those who dishonor or defeat the community of the faithful. The greater jihad is something all devout individuals must wage against their desires, especially those desires that contradict the central teachings of the Quran. The mystics of Islam often spoke of jihad as a dark night of the soul, where the striver is faced with his demons and must confront them in order to stay on the path toward God. The lesser jihad can take the form of a war against unbelievers, but it can also be any focused effort to restore Muslim society. War is one tool; political reform might be another; and economic policies could be as well.[6]

When Saladin spoke of jihad, he meant the remaking of Muslim society in the Near East, both because that was the right thing to do and because only then could Muslims once again rule Jerusalem. Not once was he accused of hypocritically using the language of jihad to advance selfish ambitions, in large measure because he first tended to his own spiritual house. In short, he seems to have embraced the greater jihad before he embarked on the lesser. And there lies the explanation why Saladin, the holy warrior par excellence, is nonetheless admired in the West and remains an icon in the Near East and in many parts of the Muslim world.

THE THIRD CRUSADE

BUT AS LAUDED as he was and still is, Saladin was also a flesh-and-blood warrior. The Saladin admired by most Westerners is so good and pure that he is almost a caricature. The real Saladin, however, was not always disposed to forgive his enemies or treat them with leniency. He had little tolerance for mystics who refused to fight and instead retreated from society to probe the inner meaning of the Quran, and he developed an obsessive hatred for at least one Christian adversary, named Reynald of Châtillon. This Saladin, the angry general, the stubborn commander who was neither curious about theology nor kind to those who were, has been safely tucked away in the past.

That said, it was not as though Reynald was undeserving of contempt. He had a checkered career, as an adventurer, knight, and political prisoner who married well in 1176 and thereby became lord of one of the most imposing fortresses in Jordan, the castle of Kerak. Its ruins still inspire awe, perched high above the Dead Sea in the biblical land of Moab. Before Reynald became a castellan, he was known for his brutalities, one of which entailed beating the patriarch of Antioch, then smothering the wounds on his face with honey and leaving him out in the middle of the summer in the Syrian desert to be tormented by flies and assorted carrion fowl until he agreed to pay an exorbitant ransom. Once in control of his own fortress, Reynald apparently took unseemly pleasure in casting enemies off its ramparts.

Saladin could not have cared less about what Reynald did to the patriarch of Antioch or other Christians who crossed him, but he took offense at Reynald's attacks on pilgrimage caravans headed to Mecca. Not only was the north-south route through Syria a central artery for pilgrims, it was—as it had been for centuries—a primary trade route. Disrupting the caravans, harming the pilgrims, and stealing their goods posed a serious challenge to Saladin. So did Reynald's successful raids along the Red Sea. Any ruler who had aspirations of being accepted as a viable sultan had to be able to protect access to the holiest place of Islam. If Saladin could not guarantee the safety of pilgrims making the annual hajj to Mecca and Medina, he could not claim the respect of the Muslim world. Reynald's attacks also jeopardized Saladin's revenue. Protecting the caravans meant not just respect, but the right to collect moderate payments for the service.

The raids staged by Reynald provoked a lethal response. Saladin declared war, raised an army of more than twelve thousand cavalry, and invaded the kingdom of Jerusalem. The Franks, recognizing the magnitude of the threat, patched over their differences. The count of Antioch, who had been flirting with Saladin and had even entered into a preliminary alliance with him, fell into line and made peace with the Templars and Hospitallers. The Crusader states assembled a formidable army, but that only made their subsequent defeat worse. Their military strategy was poorly conceived and proved to be no match for their adversary. They were gulled into meeting Saladin at a place of his choosing, on terrain that he desired, and at the hour he elected. The result in 1187 was a devastating battle at the Horns of Hattin, a labyrinth of barren hills just west of the Sea of Galilee.

On the morning of July 3, 1187, the Frankish armies woke to no dawn. Instead, the skies were filled with burning smoke. They had spent the previous day in the arid vale of Hattin, and though they knew that Saladin was near, they did not know precisely where. That morning, engulfed by the smoke generated by the brushwood and dry grass fires set by Saladin's forces, the disoriented Franks were surrounded and annihilated. The king of Jerusalem and the masters of both the Templars and the Hospitallers were captured. So was the hated Reynald and a precious, irreplaceable relic: a piece of the True Cross.

With the dead still on the battlefield, the captives were brought to Saladin's tent. According to one Frankish account of what happened, Saladin

ordered that a syrup diluted with water in a cup of gold be brought. He tasted it, then gave it to the king to drink, saying: "Drink deeply." The king drank, like a man who was extremely thirsty, then handed the cup on to Prince Reynald. Prince Reynald would not drink. Saladin was irritated and told him: "Drink, for you will never drink again!" The prince replied that if it pleased God, he would never drink or eat anything of his. Saladin asked him: "Prince Reynald, if you held me in your prison as I now hold you in mine, what, by your law, would you do to me?" "So help me God," he replied, "I would cut off your head." Saladin was greatly enraged at this most insolent reply, and said: "Pig! You are my prisoner, yet you answer me so arrogantly?" He took a sword in his hand and thrust it right through his body. The mamluks who were standing by rushed at him and cut off his head. Saladin took some of the blood and sprinkled it on his head in recognition that he had taken vengeance on him. Then he ordered that they carry the head to Damascus, and it was dragged along the ground to show the Saracens whom the prince had wronged what vengeance he had had.

Muslim accounts differ only in slight details. In one, Saladin denounced Reynald for attacking pilgrims on the way to the holy places of Islam. But all agree that Saladin himself executed Reynald, and then spared the life of the king of Jerusalem and the others.[7]

The victory at Hattin opened the way for the subsequent fall of Jerusalem, which in turn aroused another wave of European Crusader armies determined to reclaim the city. Neither the occupation of Jerusalem nor the vengeful killing of Reynald sullied Saladin's reputation. Instead, Reynald received the brunt of history's ire. Though some contemporary Christian polemicists denounced Saladin and described him as the devil incarnate, in time the picture born of wartime propaganda faded and a softer version emerged.

In the nineteenth century, Sir Walter Scott turned the execution of Reynald into a metaphor for Saladin's nobility. In *The Talisman,* Reynald is the grand master of the Templars and a duplicitous schemer loyal only to his own twisted greed. His death is presented not as an act of vengeance but as a heroic deed. The scene begins with Saladin entertaining Richard the Lionheart and his retinue in a battlefield tent replete with "carpets of the richest stuffs with cushions laid for the guests," along with whole roasted lambs, sweetmeats, "and other niceties of Eastern cookery." Then, as the guests are enjoying their iced sherbet, Saladin suddenly unsheathes his scimitar and slices off the head of the grand master of the Templars. Before his horrified guests can draw their swords, Saladin explains that the dead man has been plotting against Richard's life. In this telling, therefore, Scott recast the execution as the selfless act of a prince who treasured honor and chivalry.

Noble character notwithstanding, in taking Jerusalem, Saladin had seized the jewel of the Crusader crown. The kings of Europe, urged on by the pope, responded with the Third Crusade. Richard the Lionheart of England, Philip Augustus of France, and Frederick Barbarossa of Germany prepared for war. By now, the crusading idea had been woven into the fabric of Western and Central Europe. No longer a movement attractive primarily to younger sons, crusading became a central focus of both the church and the nobility. The armies of the Third Crusade were the elite of Germany, France, and England, and they might have succeeded but for the misfortune of Frederick Barbarossa drowning in a river after a convincing victory over the Seljuks of Anatolia. The rivalry between Richard and Philip hardly helped, and Richard's bullheadedness, while an advantage on the battlefield, did not make him an easy ally.

The Third Crusade is remembered, if remembered at all, for the epic struggle between Richard and Saladin. Militarily, the two were evenly matched, but Saladin, aging, with his acute skill as a general in decline, still outmaneuvered Richard. The only thing worse than defeat and stalemate on the battlefield is reputational defeat off it. Here Richard lost. Though each had court historians and partisans, Saladin emerged the undisputed champion in the propaganda war.

Except for a glowing aura in the story of Robin Hood, King Richard survives as a fearless and crude ruler driven by avarice, lust, and rage. Though we will never know what he was truly like, there is probably more than a grain of truth in the image that survives. The child of Henry II and the even-then-legendary Eleanor of Aquitaine, Richard developed an early and lasting reputation as a leader for whom subtlety and statecraft were alien concepts. This was not a question of wartime ethics, though here too, Richard managed to offend even the callous sensibilities of his day. It was a question of culture. England was barely removed from illiterate tribal confederations, and English society had only the slightest overlay of Christianity with a smattering of literacy confined to the monasteries. Saladin's Egypt and Syria, on the other hand, had experienced six centuries of Muslim rule and had benefited from the high culture of Damascus and Baghdad. That culture, which prized literature, art, science, medicine, astronomy, engineering, law, and agriculture, had been built on the foundations of Greece, Rome and Byzantium, and then blended with the courtly tradition of ancient Persia. The Crusaders did surpass the Muslims in certain areas—especially in the building of castles and, not coincidentally, the construction of siege engines to capture them. But in most respects, the contest between Richard and Saladin, much like the initial fighting between the Crusader armies and the Muslims of the Near East a century before, pitted brawn against brain.

Brawn sometimes had a distinct advantage. Richard, a physically imposing redhead who would sooner rush into the fray than command from the heights, stormed the Near East by sea, captured Cyprus as an advance post, and then took Acre after a tortuous siege. The commander of the Acre garrison surrendered before receiving Saladin's orders not to, and Richard found himself in control of a large number of captives. The rules governing prisoners of war were straightforward: a ransom would be set, high enough to be profitable for the victors and punitive for the losers but not so high that it couldn't be paid. Richard, however, was anxious to maintain momentum and wanted to advance inland. He could go nowhere until the fate of his prisoners was resolved. The negotiations bogged down, and Richard decided he didn't need the money or the hassle. He ordered his soldiers to kill the three thousand men, women, and children of Acre who had been so unfortunate as to be captured. Said one Christian apologist, the soldiers—looking to avenge the Christians who had died at Saladin's hands—happily carried out the task of beheading the captives.[8]

Massacre was juxtaposed with camaraderie. For many months, Richard's armies and Saladin's fought to a standstill. Camped near each other, the knights and commoners of each side fraternized during the long periods of inactivity. According to some accounts, the combatants would even stop fighting in the midst of a battle if they perceived that neither side had the upper hand. Arms would be laid down; there would be conversation and storytelling; one side would extend an invitation to dinner. At other times, contests were held to see who had more prowess in the arts of war, and then all would celebrate the winners.[9]

These scenes hardly square with the image of fierce warriors of God confronting one another with the fervor of true believers. Rather than generating rage and hatred, Saladin's faith often produced compassion. He respected the Christian willingness to fight and die for Jerusalem, and simultaneously deployed armies to kill as many of them as possible. And with the exception of Reynald, he could do all of this without hate. His faith, if we are to believe that it was as genuine as the chroniclers claim, was grounded in humility. His Islam was the Islam of submission, based on the recognition that all humans are fallible and all are sinners. God is the path, and only God is the judge. Saladin waged a jihad for the glory of God and for Islam, not a jihad against his enemies. They were obstacles, but they were not the object.

The Christians also defy easy characterization. They could speak of the evils of the infidels and glory in their slaughter. They could travel thousands of miles to restore the Holy Sepulchre to Christian control and to cleanse the Holy Land of the impurity of Muslim rule. Yet not only were they willing to fraternize with these infidels on slow days during a hot summer war, but by the fall of 1191, they were also willing to call the whole thing off and get married.

It wasn't the most obvious solution, but after less than two years, Richard's armies were stretched, and the Frankish advance was stalled. Saladin had absorbed the most intense blows without crumbling, and other than his bloody victory at Acre, Richard had done little more than secure the coast that had until recently been firmly under the control of the kingdom of Jerusalem. With Frederick Barbarossa dead, the Germans in disarray, and Philip Augustus having fallen ill and returned to France, it was left to Richard to challenge Saladin alone. But word reached him that back in England, his brother John was attempting to usurp his throne, and Richard needed to make an exit. He had no wish to win in Palestine only to lose his throne in England.

What Richard did made perfect sense to him, though it surprised his contemporaries. He wrote to Saladin, "I am to salute you, and tell you that the Muslims and Franks are bleeding to death, the country is utterly ruined and goods and lives have been sacrificed on both sides. The time has come to stop this. The points at issue are Jerusalem, the Cross, and the land." Richard declared that he could not leave without securing the right of Christians to worship freely in Jerusalem, nor could he depart without the True Cross that had been taken by Saladin at the battle of Hattin. Saladin responded quickly, "Jerusalem is ours as much as yours; indeed it is even more sacred to us than to you, for it is the place from which our Prophet accomplished his nocturnal journey and the place which our community will gather on the Day of Judgment. Do not imagine that we can renounce it.... The land was originally ours, whereas you have only just arrived and have taken it over only because of the weakness of the Muslims living there at the time." As for Richard's other demands, Saladin did not say yes and he did not say no.

The negotiations then took an interesting turn. It's not clear who proposed what, but the proposal was simple: Richard's sister Joanna of Sicily would marry Saladin's brother Sayf ad-Din, and the two would become joint monarchs ruling from Jerusalem. All prisoners held by both sides would be freed; the True Cross would be restored to the Holy Sepulchre; and Richard would sail home to England.

When Saladin heard the terms, he instructed his delegates to say no, apparently because he thought it was either a trap or a joke. His brother took the idea more seriously, and tentatively agreed. Unbeknownst to

Richard, one of his erstwhile allies was also negotiating terms with Saladin, and Saladin, therefore, knew he had the luxury to bargain from a position of strength. But Richard's offer of his sister's hand was genuine, and to him at least, made good strategic sense. Wars between princes in Europe often ended with intermarriage between rival families. Having campaigned vigorously against a worthy enemy, he decided it was time to stop and move on. Marriage seemed a natural, and necessary, component to secure a lasting peace.

Other Crusaders were less ecumenical. Richard found that not only was his sister opposed to the idea, but she had rallied others to her side. He was pressured to retract the offer. Instead, he wrote to Saladin to amend the initial proposal. "The Christian people disapprove of my giving my sister in marriage without consulting the Pope," Richard wrote. "If he authorizes the wedding, so much the better. If not, I will give you the hand of my niece, for whom I shall not need Papal consent."

Saladin, for his part, may have been reluctant to sign a truce, given that the struggle to which he had dedicated his life was still short of its ultimate aim of evicting the Franks from Palestine. But he saw the ravages that the wars were causing, and with Jerusalem secure in the Muslim fold, he agreed to end hostilities. He was reminded by one learned judge that even the Quran advised making peace when it was advantageous. "If they incline to peace, you too should incline to it." According to Imad ad-Din, Saladin had to be convinced by his commanders that peace was needed, even though he had committed his life to jihad. It was a convenient portrayal, whether it was strictly true or not, because it allowed him to preserve his reputation as a warrior but not one so blinded by fervor that he could not do what was best for his subjects.

The result of these negotiations was a truce leaving the Franks in control of Antioch, Tripoli, and much of the coast. Merchants—regardless of their creed or country of origin—were permitted to keep trading without being subject to onerous duties. And most important of all, Saladin promised that any Christian who wished to make the pilgrimage to the Holy Sepulchre in Jerusalem would be granted safe passage and unhindered access.[10] With that, the Third Crusade came to an end.

And so, what are we to make of a jihad waged by a devout Muslim against a Crusade prosecuted by Christians that included massacres and beheadings but nearly ended with a wedding between the families of the two leading adversaries? How are we to interpret Saladin, who was at once the holy warrior par excellence and the noble adversary of Western imagination for centuries thereafter? And most perplexing of all, how do we square contemporary ideas about war, religion, and Islam with the world of the twelfth century?

Today's image of the jihadist as an individual whose entire identity is subsumed to an ideology bears only passing resemblance to Saladin. Indeed, the very notion of an ideology that dominates all aspects of life has been alien to most cultures throughout history. In the twelfth century, the daily realities of farming, transportation, shelter, surviving disease, and fighting arduous, labor-intensive wars usually trumped ideas.

Religion and beliefs were one part of a kaleidoscope. At times, the words of the Quran and the hadith (traditions) drove men like Saladin to act as they did. At times, the words of the Bible and the pope spurred men like Richard to fight, or not to fight. But at other times, family issues, dynastic challenges, health problems, and political rivalries mattered more. Sometimes men fought with the words of a holy text ringing in their ears; and sometimes they met on the battlefield, slapped each other on the back, and played games.

Before the fall of Jerusalem in 1187, the Crusader states governed over and coexisted with a large local Christian population and with an even larger Muslim population. The result was hardly equivalent to Córdoba, but neither was it a period of conflict defined by faith. The war between Saladin and Richard had the markings of a religious conflict, but in the end, it was just a struggle between rulers that ended in a stalemate and nearly in a peace secured by marriage. The root of conflict in the modern world can be found in the Crusades, but only by forgetting much of what actually happened.

While the crusading movement continued to flourish for more than a century in Europe, Jerusalem was not threatened again by Western Christians. In 1204, the armies of the Fourth Crusade, transported by the Venetian fleet, took a detour and landed at Constantinople. The city was ransacked and terrorized by Western armies whose purported goal had been the liberation of the Holy Land. The fury with which the Fourth Crusaders, a combination of Frankish and German nobles, attacked the bastion of Eastern Christianity had been building for many years. Ever since Alexius Comnenus sent the First Crusade on its way, resentment of Byzantium had grown. The Venetians also coveted Byzantine wealth and influence over the commercial sea lanes of the Mediterranean.[11]

Saladin died soon after Richard's departure, and his sons set up a dynasty that dissipated in a remarkably short amount of time. His heirs were everything he was not: despotic, hedonistic, undisciplined. The subsequent Mongol invasion that destroyed the Abbasid caliphate in 1258 would have continued on to Cairo and perhaps across North Africa had it not been for the slave army of Mamelukes who had first supported and then overthrown the sybaritic sons and grandsons of Saladin in their palaces in Cairo. The Mameluke army stopped the Mongols at the battle of Ain Jalut near Nazareth in 1260, and the horsemen never again threatened the Near East.

The Egypt of the Mamelukes was a stable, prosperous state, linked by trade to the West and the East thanks to a thriving merchant class of Jews, Christians, and Muslims of all denominations. The Franks and Germans understood the importance of Egypt, and the later Crusades of the thirteenth century targeted Egypt in the belief that it was the strategic key to Jerusalem. These attempts failed. Egypt easily repelled the armies of Europe, and Cairo was untouched.

The relative safety of Cairo was a magnet, and among the many it attracted was a Spanish Jew from Córdoba who arrived with little more than his clothes and a few books after fleeing from the violence and chaos that was then engulfing Andalusia. Having seen his homeland overrun by Berber armies from Morocco and his city, Córdoba, once again consumed by flames, he made his way across the Mediterranean to Egypt. Had he remained in Córdoba, he may never have written what he did, or learned what he learned. But because he was welcomed at the court of Saladin, he thrived, burdened with a deep sadness but driven by an intellectual hunger. Saladin's most significant legacy for Islam is the capture of Jerusalem. Without intending to, he also shaped the evolution of modern Judaism, when his chamberlain in Cairo hired a Jewish refugee, Moses Maimonides, to be a court physician.

CHAPTER SIX

THE PHILOSOPHER'S DREAM

MOSES MAIMONIDES was not a shy man. He knew his own heart, and he minced few words. He was not modest, and he did not suffer fools. His goal was at once lofty and simple: he wanted to illuminate the darkness and banish doubt and ignorance in order to help the enlightened seeker. "I am the man," he stated, "who when concern pressed him and . . . he could find no other device by which to teach a demonstrated truth other than by giving satisfaction to a single virtuous man while displeasing ten thousand ignoramuses—I am he who prefers to address that single man by himself . . . I shall guide him in his perplexity until he becomes perfect and he finds rest."

Maimonides wrote these words in the preface to his magnum opus, *Guide for the Perplexed*. He was by then an old man who had seen more of the world than he had ever intended or ever wished. He had been born in 1135 in Córdoba, a city that may have been a shadow of its former greatness but remained a beacon of culture. He was the child of a judge and descended from scholars and rabbis, and from the time he could talk, he was initiated into the family business. But when he was barely a teenager, Andalusia fell under the control of yet another puritan dynasty from Morocco, the Almohads, who like their Almoravid predecessors emerged from Marrakesh and expanded in wave after wave until they inundated southern Spain.

The Almohads considered themselves reformers who would use the Quran as the foundation for law and justice, but like many puritans, they conveniently ignored passages of scripture that did not fit their worldview. Though the Quran insists on respect and tolerance for the People of the Book, the Almohads were openly hostile to the Christians and Jews who populated the cities of southern Iberia. They placed restrictions on them, many of which were purely symbolic but nonetheless humiliating. In some areas, Jews and Christians were punished for wearing certain types of clothing, and unlike the Muslim rulers whom they supplanted, the Almohads did not welcome Jews or Christians into their courts.

Finding life uncomfortable and pathways to advancement closed, the family of Moses Maimonides left Córdoba and moved to Fez, in the heart of Almohad Morocco. At first glance that looks like a dubious decision, but Almohad rule in the Moroccan heartland may have been less restrictive than it was in the newly conquered and still insecure cities of Andalusia. The Almohads were not blessed with friendly chroniclers, and they were denigrated as narrow-minded tribesmen with no ear for music and no eye for culture. Later Jewish sources depicted the Almohads as fanatics bent on exterminating Iberian Judaism. When they conquered Morocco, they dealt harshly with anyone who did not embrace their brand of religion, including other Muslims and Jews. But Jewish accounts may also have been colored by "a narrative of persecution,"[1] which inclined Jewish writers to portray diaspora Judaism as a series of tests and trials similar to the tribulations suffered by the Jews in the Old Testament after the destruction of Solomon's Temple.

Maimonides rejected the cataclysmic, melodramatic interpretation of the Jewish experience. After a period in Fez, he traveled across North Africa, often by ship, and settled briefly in Palestine. But Palestine, divided between warring Christian and Muslim princes, was inhospitable, and Maimonides and his family relocated to Cairo, where he would spend the rest of his life. His family's commercial enterprises blossomed in Egypt, and his brother proved to be an adept and flexible merchant who increased the family's fortunes. Maimonides, fluent in Arabic, Hebrew, and Latin, absorbed the learning and culture of the Mediterranean world and evolved into a philosopher whose advice was sought by Jews, Christians, and Muslims alike. He was a voluminous writer, a voracious reader, and a generous teacher, and he had only scorn for those who preferred to play the victim. The world was not kind, and it was foolish, he believed, to expect otherwise. Equally foolish, in his view, was to bow one's head and accept punishment and oppression. God had given man ingenuity and choice, and thus the tools to survive and thrive.

In fact, one reason that Maimonides and his family may have been able to relocate to Fez was that they converted to Islam. In the long history of relations between the faiths in Spain, false conversion was common. The Almohads were unusually harsh toward nonbelievers, and the advantages of converting were obvious. No one can see into the heart of another, and recognizing that simple truth, persecuted religious minorities developed a practice known in Arabic as *taqiyya*. Translated literally as "dissimulation" or even "diplomacy," *taqiyya* was in essence a prudent form of faking it. Early Shi'ites had done the same thing under hostile Sunni rule, and some Jews and Christians in Spain decided that, faced with hostile Muslim rulers, the pragmatic thing was to pretend to be Muslim and practice their own faith in private and in secret.

Maimonides had no patience for those who took a purist line and advocated martyrdom and death rather than survival. Defending martyrdom, he said, was "long winded foolish babbling and nonsense." In his view, temporary conversion was acceptable, though it was best if those who did so eventually moved somewhere that would allow them to practice their rites openly.

Though he was certain that no one can know God's will, the goal, for Maimonides, was to live a philosophical life, dedicated to understanding God's wisdom and helping others do the same. He had grown up in an environment that nurtured philosophy. The rabbinical tradition handed down to him by his father encouraged questioning and demanded intellectual rigor, and twelfth-century Andalusia teamed with singular minds who continued to fuse the legacy of the Greeks with the theology of Islam. Though it was a Muslim society, Jews and Christians were supporting characters who played vital roles in translating and interpreting the texts of the ancients. While Jewish scholars had distinguished themselves as astronomers and as commentators on the Old Testament, Maimonides evolved into much more than a brilliant Jewish philosopher and became one of the great synthesizers of Christian, Muslim, and Jewish wisdom.

For much of his life, he was acutely aware that he was an exile. Wandering defined him, and wandering taught him. "Every righteous and intelligent person will realize that the task I undertook was not simple.... In addition, I was agitated by the distress of our time, the exile which God decreed upon us, the fact that we are being driven from one end of the world to the other. Perhaps we have received reward for this, inasmuch as exile atones for sin." He feared that the fact that he was an exile might lower his status and lead others to take him less seriously. But rather than accept that fate, he turned the fear into fuel. He was an exile from his home; Jews had been exiled from their Holy Land; and mankind was in exile from God. Instead of passively accepting his fate, he used his exile, and it became his spark.

His output was extraordinary, even in an age of thinkers and philosophers who routinely wrote thousands of pages on all aspects of human existence. Maimonides composed lengthy treatises on the Torah, Talmud, and the Mishnah; he carried on correspondence with Jews and learned men throughout the Muslim world; he delved into mathematics, astronomy, and medicine; and he crowned his career with his magisterial synthesis of philosophy and theology, *Guide for the Perplexed.*

THE MYSTICS AND THE LAW

AS A DOCTOR at the court of Saladin, Maimonides won the trust of the ruling class. Like Hasdai ibn Shaprut, Maimonides' erudition and meticulous approach to diagnosing and treating the ills of the human body made him an invaluable servant to Muslim rulers. Medicine was not yet a distinct branch of knowledge. It was instead an amalgam of philosophy, science, mysticism, and theology. Anyone who wanted to be counted among the learned needed to have working familiarity with each of those, as well as fluency in Arabic and Latin, at the very least. A physician's study began with the ancients: Hippocrates, Galen, and Aristotle. It may seem odd that Maimonides, who began his formal study of medicine only late in his life, became a court physician with such a flimsy medical background. But in that day and age, he was qualified to be a doctor for one unimpeachable reason: he knew about as much as any man could know.

Though many of his treatises focused on Jewish law and scripture, he frequently wrote in Arabic. That was one of the languages he learned as a child, and it was the language of scholarship throughout the Muslim world and much of the Mediterranean. His fluency allowed him to absorb the works of the most prominent philosophers in the Arab-speaking world, and he built on what they had created.

Maimonides was not the first Jewish scholar to use the methods of Greek and Arab thinkers to unlock the keys to Jewish scriptures, but he was surely among the most masterful. He moved easily between the rabbinical tradition and the writing of Muslim scholars. The eleventh and twelfth centuries in Persia and the Near East saw a flourishing philosophical tradition that continued what had begun in Baghdad and Iraq centuries earlier. Over time, however, the arguments became more arcane, to the point where only those immersed in the corpus could understand the references and relate to the questions. Andalusian thinkers also contributed to the debates, especially Ibn Rushd, who was known in the West as Averroës and who like Maimonides had been born in Córdoba but unlike him carved out a niche as a court intellectual under the puritanical Almohads.

While this fraternity of Arabic-speaking philosophers differed greatly in their actual answers, they shared common questions: What was the role of human reason in explaining the world? To what degree could men rely on their intellect to unveil God's plan, and how much should they look to faith and belief instead? Could the intellect act as a conduit to the truth, or was it a distraction that would keep man from God? Maimonides lived at a crucial juncture when the balance shifted decisively in the direction of faith over reason, belief rather than philosophy, and heart over mind.

Philosophers such as Averroës and the Persian Ibn Sina (known in the West as Avicenna) were themselves suspicious of pure philosophy. They believed that reason had a place in explaining God's wisdom but only in conjunction with theology and faith. Much of what they wrote was esoteric. Thousands of pages were consumed by questions such as: How eternal is eternity? Was the universe created by God "in time" or before time itself was created? Does God have foreknowledge of all details of human history and action, or simply access to all details but no advance knowledge? Unless one had spent long years steeped in these issues, the references and the logic were difficult if not impossible to follow. But threading through the esoterica was a portentous debate about the proper relationship between reason, free will, and faith.

Standing in the way of the philosophers were the jurists. The philosophers emphasized the role of reason and looked to Aristotle and Plato for guidance on how to interpret the Quran. The jurists ranged from those who accepted only the most literal understanding of holy texts to those who embraced a limited amount of interpretation based on the early schools of law. The philosophers and the jurists disliked each other, and their disputes occasionally turned lethal. By the eleventh century, the traditions were deadlocked; neither side had managed to eliminate the other, much to their mutual frustration.

Just before Maimonides was born, Abu Hamid al-Ghazali of Baghdad attempted to resolve the apparent split between philosophy and theology. He embraced the methods of the philosophers in order to prove the supremacy of faith. Al-Ghazali was as essential to the evolution of Muslim theology as Thomas Aquinas was to the development of Catholicism. His brilliance was to synthesize science, philosophy, mysticism, and law. He had drunk deeply at the well of each. He became a scholar of Aristotle and sat at the feet of Sufi masters learning the mystical traditions. He then delved into the arcana of Muslim law, analyzed how the traditional schools interpreted the Quran, and absorbed dense and lengthy canons of jurisprudence.

After years of study, al-Ghazali composed a series of treatises that marked the apex and the end of a certain type of Muslim scholarship. In his quest to answer unresolved questions, al-Ghazali drew definitive conclusions, and among them was that both philosophy and mysticism were flawed. Only submission, the Quran, love of God, and respect for the law could lead a believer to live a proper life. While philosophy, science, reason, and mysticism each had something to offer, none was sufficient as a path to the truth. According to al-Ghazali, the philosopher risked turning the human intellect into a god, while the mystic often came close to worshiping his own soul rather than submitting to God's will. Al-Ghazali was urbane and sophisticated, but he was also, in the end, a conservative. Worried that Muslim societies had lost direction and purpose, he tried to find a new formula that would restore the pure, powerful faith of the Prophet and the companions.

Using the tools of the philosopher in order to discredit many of the claims of philosophy, and embracing the path of the mystic while rejecting many of the beliefs of mystics, al-Ghazali developed a complex system with a simple core: God is all-powerful, and Islam is the true path. He made mysticism respectable, but at a price. He insisted that all Muslims, mystic or not, were bound by the Quran. The path of the Sufis did not give them the right to live outside the law. The same principle applied to philosophy. Reason and intellect could never take priority over the Quran and the tradition of the Prophet.

In his own time, al-Ghazali was respected, but after his death, he was sanctified. The questions that he asked ceased to be asked, and Islamic philosophy began to ossify. It was said that after al-Ghazali, the door of interpretation (*ijtihad*) closed. For centuries after Muhammad, there had been active debates about the true meaning of the Quran and the hadith, about the proper tools of interpretation and the way one could approach God. But after al-Ghazali, debate was discouraged. Islamic law and theology became more rigid, and schools became repositories of received wisdom rather than generators of new ideas.

Men like Maimonides, who lived more than a generation removed from al-Ghazali, still probed, but whether as a direct result of al-Ghazali's influence or not, they began to recede from the world. They did not reject philosophy, but they narrowed their audience. They divided reality into outer truth and hidden truth. The outer truths could be learned by the masses, but the inner truths were for the select. These attitudes transcended religious differences. Maimonides was Jewish, but he had more in common with Muslim and Christian scholars than he did with most Jews. Regardless of creed, scholars and mystics shared a sensibility; they asked similar questions and employed similar methods to find answers.

Where Maimonides probed the gulf between man and God, others attempted to close the gap, and no one did so more poignantly than the Andalusian philosopher Ibn Arabi. In a world replete with brilliant minds and passionate seekers, Ibn Arabi was among the most brilliant and the most passionate. He confronted the ancient human dilemma of loneliness. Why, he wanted to know, was there such a distance between God and his creation? Was mankind forever doomed to the excruciating pain of separation from God? That plaintive question had been asked by Jewish scholars ever since they had begun to interpret the story of Adam and Eve's expulsion from Eden, and it had been a central concern of early Christian monks and mendicants. Ibn Arabi, however, drew on centuries of Jewish, Greek, Christian, and Muslim learning to arrive at a unique conclusion: man's separation from God was a product not of God but of man's limited ability to perceive the truth. A more aware mankind would realize that the gulf was an illusion, and that God and man were as close as two could be without being one.

Ibn Arabi wrote almost as extensively as Maimonides. Like the Jewish sage, he was born in Spain but then traveled for years before finally settling in the Near East, in Damascus. In his work, he touched on most major areas of human knowledge, but unlike so many others, he expressed a new idea. The distance between man and God was not real, he claimed. Duality was not real. Instead, creation is defined by unity, and by the unity of man and God above all. God created man as a mirror in which to view himself and his creation. Throughout history, there had been a "Perfect Man," who embodied that unity. All of the prophets and the great Sufi saints had been emanations of the Perfect Man, and the path of the mystic was to emulate them.

Ibn Arabi's style was metaphorical, elliptical, esoteric, and challenging. He fused the Greek concept of Logos, which was at the center of the New Testament gospel of John, with Muslim-Greek philosophy. He added to the mix Sufi wisdom, which sometimes used words as guides and sometimes used language to mislead the uninitiated. Embedded in his work was a bare, unadorned statement about every believer: "God is the mirror in which you see yourself, as you are His mirror in which he contemplates His names." In the primordial unity of being, man is God's way of seeing himself and God's way of knowing himself.

How ironic that twelfth-century Andalusia, ruled as it was by a dynasty with a numbingly narrow ideology, nurtured some of history's most profound thinkers about man and God. Even more ironic that a dynasty that tried to cleanse Islam produced thinkers who were the product not just of Muslim diversity but of multiple cultures. Ibn Arabi, Ibn Rushd, and Maimonides stood at the apex of more than fifteen hundred years of human civilization, some of which was Muslim, much of which was not. We will never know if they could have thought what they thought and written what they wrote had they been steeped only in their own traditions. We do know that they were immersed in Greek, Latin, and Arabic scholarship and that they drew on that accumulated wisdom not to write polemics but to explain the meaning of life. And we know that they deployed their intellect and channeled their passion not to attack but to illuminate. They walked the path of love and compassion, and served as guides to seekers trying to find their way to God.

And none more than Maimonides. With his days filled by his medical duties, he lived a busy life, and his descriptions of his routine as doctor to the royal family in Cairo do not convey the sense that he loved his day job. "My duties to the Sultan are very heavy," he wrote. "I am obliged to visit him every day, early in the morning; and when he or any of his children, or any of the inmates of his harem, are indisposed, I do not quit Cairo, but stay during the greater part of the day in the palace." Then, when he returned home late in the day, he usually found his house full of Jews, Christians, and Muslims seeking his counsel for ailments both physical and spiritual. At the close of the day, he was so spent that he barely had time for his writing and his studies.

Yet this was the same man, weary from his long hours, who was able to write *Guide for the Perplexed*. In it, he divided the world into those who can learn the inner truths and those who cannot. "It is not the purpose of this treatise to make its totality understandable to the vulgar or the beginner in speculation," he announced in the introduction, "nor to teach those who have not engaged in any study other than the study of the Law—I mean the legalistic study of the Law." It was a treatise for philosophers and for seekers. It was a guide for those who were advanced in learning yet still had unanswered questions. It was a map drawn by a master for those who had glimpsed behind the curtain separating the learned from the vulgar, who had started on the path but found themselves confused and uncertain.

Maimonides believed that there were truths that the masses could grasp and messages that any common man could hear and that there were truths accessible only to the learned, the wise, and the religious. In time, hidden truth became the foundation of the Jewish mystical tradition. The study of the kabbalah, which probed the inner meanings of the Torah and the Jewish holy texts, flourished in late medieval Spain and owed a considerable debt to the legacy of Maimonides. Though he would have been uncomfortable with the degree to which later kabbalists turned away from the world, he too believed in a hierarchy of truth and in the notion that only a select few are qualified to see God's plan in all of its glory.

Maimonides was a seeker who rejected the notion that all are created equal. The democratic side of Islamic and Jewish mysticism said that all believers could establish a personal, intimate relationship with God—provided they were willing to walk the long and arduous road. But as articulated by Maimonides and men like Ibn Arabi, there was also an elitism, which said that the world is inherently corrupt and that the true path is open only to those pure and wise enough to take it.

The consequence of these attitudes for Judaism was an increasing disengagement from society. The consequence for Islam was a growing unwillingness to engage new ideas. While the Jews of Spain may not have been able to prevent their marginalization by Muslim and Christian rulers, the Muslims of North Africa and the Near East suffered from the shift away from creative thought and away from grappling with the contentious questions that had been part and parcel of the Mediterranean world since the days of Plato and Aristotle. As the majority turned to orthodoxy and a minority turned toward a dynamic but secretive mysticism, Muslim culture in the Arab world slowly began to wither.

As for Maimonides, he died as he had lived: a pious man, who in spite of his erudition and willingness to learn what there was to learn, identified himself as simply a child of Abraham in long exile from his home. He believed that the Jews of Spain and the Near East had brought their fate upon themselves, because of the sins of their forefathers, and that their subjugation to the Arabs had been foretold by the scripture. He prayed throughout his life that God would allow the Jews one day to return and enter the Temple in Jerusalem once again, and until that day, he prayed that Jews would learn from their exile and, through love of God, be forgiven.

Had he been asked if his life demonstrated the possibility of coexistence between Islam and Judaism, Maimonides would almost certainly have said no. From his vantage, Jews under Muslim rule were constrained in what they could do and dependent on the sufferance of their rulers. Identified as he was with his tribe, he could hardly have felt otherwise. But even a wise individual is not always the best guide to his own life. As we have seen, Maimonides was not just a Jew. He was steeped in multiple cultures and a product of all of them. In much the same way, Ibn Arabi believed himself to be a Sufi seeker, but he too was the product of diverse cultural streams. The beauty, intensity, and sophistication of their visions were the result of that diversity. They represented the juxtaposition of religious traditions, whether they realized it or not. They were and are a testament to what is possible.

The intellectual and spiritual creativity of these men appeared to be in vivid contrast to the Almohad dynasty that ruled southern Spain. But on closer examination, even the Almohads were less rigid than history has made them. Their creed called for a return to the unadorned piety of Muhammad, yet they looked to logic and reason to defend their vision. "It is by necessity of reason that the existence of God, Praise to Him, is known," went one line of the Almohad *Doctrine of Divine Unity*. They took a hard line against the philosophical tendency to interpret the Quran in terms of analogies and had contempt for the notion that God had human characteristics. "Minds have a limit at which they stop and which they do not exceed," and when people attempt to explain the inexplicable, they tend to latch on to "anthropomorphism," which was, according to the Almohads, "absurd."[2]

In essence, the simple piety of the Almohads was not so simplistic. They drew on the same philosophical tradition that supported Maimonides and Ibn Arabi, even though they arrived at radically different conclusions. Both the Almohads and the Almoravids are rightly seen as early versions of what would later evolve into "Islamic fundamentalism." But their history shows that there was nothing unsophisticated about them. They were not ignorant country rubes. They knew the intellectual and spiritual terrain just as well as their adversaries, and they proffered a vision of Islam that relegated interpretation and human reason to small supporting roles and elevated the literal text of the Quran above everything. They saw the intellectual fancies of the elite as decadence, and they saw decadence as weak. But in spite of themselves, they shared more with those elites than they wished to acknowledge, and their success was not a function of military prowess alone. Only a few thousand Almohads and Almoravids settled in Andalusia, yet they managed to rule. They tapped a dormant chord of unease, a belief among the Muslims of Spain that the growing power of the Christians was a reflection of God's displeasure. It was the same alarm that Jewish prophets had sounded from time immemorial—that the strength of the enemy was God's punishment for communal sins.

Twelfth- and thirteenth-century Spain is one of the crucibles of history. The philosophical glories of Ibn Arabi confronted the puritan Almohad reaction, and the puritans won. The multicultural Islam of Andalusia confronted the renaissance of Christian power and lost. While the philosophical tradition never disappeared, it became less significant, and while the puritan tradition never fully triumphed, it became more dominant. Throughout the Muslim world, similar developments took place. There had always been considerable pockets of intolerance and animosity, whether toward the People of the Book or toward new ideas, but these had only occasionally had the upper hand. If the balance had been in favor of openness and inquiry before the twelfth century, it shifted the other way after. The inclusiveness of medieval Baghdad and Andalusia gave way to exclusivity. Flexibility was replaced by rigidity. And champions of orthodoxy, who had never had much success in the Muslim world, were increasingly able to silence dissent.

THE CYCLES OF HISTORY AND
THE CHRISTIAN RECONQUEST

TO A CONSIDERABLE DEGREE, these reactions went hand in hand with a change of political fortunes. In Iberia, the Christian kings of Castile, Aragon, and Portugal were becoming more powerful at the expense of Muslims. In the Near East, the Crusaders had shown just how easy it would be to conquer weak and divided Muslim city-states. Then, in the thirteenth century, wide swaths of Iran and Iraq were conquered by the Mongols. The Abbasid caliphate was swept away, and the last caliph was executed. In Turkey, the Seljuk Turks were decimated by another central Asian invader, Timur the Lame, more commonly known in the west as Tamerlane.

For the first five centuries of Muslim history, the story had been one of military, political, and cultural dominance. Suddenly, the tide was reversing, and Muslims suffered defeat upon defeat. Before, the only time Muslim states were overthrown was by other Muslims. Now, pagans, animists, and Christians seemed to be crushing one Muslim dynasty after another.

One response was to close ranks and try to recapture the formula that had brought Muslims their success. This was not nearly as self-conscious or systematic as the reaction to Western power that gave rise to the fundamentalist movements of the twentieth century. But the pattern is similar: Muslims responded to the challenges by looking back and turning inward, hoping against hope to reclaim the early glories of Islam's past.

This pattern did not go unnoticed by at least one astute contemporary observer. Writing in the fourteenth century, Ibn Khaldun was a North African version of Gibbon and Herodotus who attempted to describe the forces of history that had resulted in the world as he knew it. His theory of Muslim history was that success had always been the product of a tight-knit tribal culture. The first example was the Arab tribes of Mecca and Medina, led by Muhammad. They were bound by strong ties that created what Ibn Khaldun called *asabiyya,* which translates as "group cohesion" or "communal spirit." The cohesion of the Arab tribes was the product of ethnicity and ideology. The rigors of desert life hardened them, and the intense faith of early Islam bound them. As a result, they were able to erupt from the desert and obliterate what should have been two formidable adversaries—the Byzantines and the Persians. By the second and third generation, the piety and discipline that had generated such strength began to dissipate. The new conquerors moved to cities. The Umayyads became a dynasty and built palaces in Damascus. They took on the airs of royalty. No longer hardened by the desert, they became soft and corrupt. By the third generation, they were ripe for defeat, and were in turn supplanted by another group whose *asabiyya* was strong, the Abbasids. And then the cycle started again.

Ibn Khaldun believed that this pattern explained Muslim history. A tribe bound by ties of family and faith is forged on a desert anvil and then sweeps away an established empire. That tribe then creates a state, and decay sets in. Soon, cohesion gives way to selfishness, greed, and hierarchy, which leads to decadence and makes the group weak. Ibn Khaldun saw the emergence of the Almohads and Almoravids as the latest example of a pattern that had been occurring for centuries, and they did indeed fit his thesis. But later critics of Ibn Khaldun noted that they may have fit it too well. Reared in what is now Tunisia, Ibn Khaldun was acutely aware of the tension between desert tribes like the Berbers and the more settled cities along the Mediterranean coast. He knew how frequently tribes had emerged either from the mountains or the fringe of the Sahara to overthrow the established dynasties centered in cities such as Marrakesh and Tunis. But however well that described the history of North Africa, it was less true of the Near East and beyond. For Ibn Khaldun, however, the theory explained not just Muslim North Africa, but the entire history of Islam.[3]

The strength of his analysis far outweighed the weaknesses. He did what all great historians have done: he identified a pattern that shed light on why things happened as they did. The tribal element fused with a strong faith did give groups such as the Mecca-Medina Arabs, the Seljuk Turks, the Almohads, and others a unique strength. It also characterized a new force then emerging in the Muslim world, a Turkish tribe named after its putative founder, Osman, that became known as the Ottomans.

Much as Ibn Khaldun would have predicted, the zealous North African dynasties who conquered Andalusia began to run out of steam. Challenged in Morocco by Berber tribes and in Andalusia by the Christian kings of Aragon and Castile, they at first held their ground and then rapidly lost it. Córdoba fell to King Fernando III in 1236; Valencia (which had once seen Muslims and Christians serving together in its army) fell in 1238; and Seville surrendered after a siege that lasted from the end of 1247 until November 1248. By the middle of the thirteenth century, all that remained of the once-powerful Muslim kingdoms of Spain was the small enclave of Granada in the southeast, guarded by a ring of mountains on one side and the sea on the other. The kingdom of Granada would survive for two centuries, the last, lonely bastion of Andalusian Islam. In return for a hefty annual tribute to the Christians, Granada remained a Muslim state, but it was isolated. Its rulers turned their palace complex into a monument to past glories, and just before it fell at the end of the fifteenth century, the Alhambra was completed. It was a testament to what Muslim Spain had been—an architectural marvel combining the most sophisticated elements of Christian and Muslim art and engineering, its walls a mass of inlay, its courtyards hushed and cool even in the heat of summer, with only the soft melody of fountains breaking the stillness.

Where Ibn Khaldun dispassionately wrote of the natural rise and fall of dynasties, the capture of Seville and Córdoba in the thirteenth century was interpreted by the Christians of Spain as a validation of their faith. The crusading spirit animated the royalty of Castile, León, and Aragon, and the resounding defeat of the Muslim kingdoms ushered in a new era of Christian triumphalism on the Iberian Peninsula. The Muslims recognized that the shift was significant, and the capture of Seville, in particular, was seen as a catastrophe. Assessing the change in fortunes, one Muslim poet described the collapse as the inevitable decay of all human endeavors, and though he may have strived for detachment, his pain was all too evident. "Everything declines after reaching perfection," he wrote, "therefore let no man be beguiled by the sweetness of a pleasant life." All past empires had fallen, and the fate of Seville was no different, except that for him, it was.

> *Where is Cordoba, the home of the sciences?*
> *Where is Seville and the pleasures it contains, as well as its sweet river*
>   *overflowing and brimming full?*
> *They are capitals which were pillars of the land, yet when the pillars are*
>   *gone, it may no longer endure!*
> *[We] . . . weep in despair, like a passionate lover weeping at the departure*
>   *of the beloved, over dwellings emptied of Islam that were first vacated*
>   *and are now inhabited by unbelief;*
> *In which mosques have become churches wherein only the bells and*
>   *crosses may be found.*
> *O you who remain heedless though you have warning in Fate; if you are*
>   *asleep, Fate is always awake.*[4]

Outside of Spain, the conquest of Andalusia save for Granada did not shake the Muslim world in the same way that the fall of Jerusalem had. The Iberian Peninsula had always been at the outermost edge of the community of believers, and had been the scene of back-and-forth wars for almost half a millennium. But to the Muslims of Spain, the reversal of the thirteenth century was a calamity from which they never recovered. Unlike the fall of Jerusalem, the surrender of Seville and Córdoba did not spur other Muslim states to organize and launch a counterattack. The Christian triumph was not only decisive; it was permanent.

The Christian victories changed the nature of Muslim, Christian, and Jewish coexistence. For hundreds of years, the three had lived in Spain, but mostly under Muslim rule. The conditions of coexistence had been determined by Muslims, first by the Cordoban caliphate and then by different city-states. While Christians had ruled Muslims and Jews in the north of the peninsula, they had not made much of an effort to develop a governing philosophy. After the fall of Seville and Córdoba, that changed. Christians found themselves in the position of administering a large population of Muslims and a small but economically important community of Jews. In time, the demographics changed, but for most of the thirteenth and early fourteenth centuries, Christian over-

lords depended on a passive and productive Muslim population for revenue, farming, trade, soldiers, and stability.

At first, the governments of Castile and Aragon treated the conquered Muslims and Jews much as the Muslims had treated the People
of the Book. When the coastal port of Valencia fell to the soldiers of
Aragon in 1238, its Muslim inhabitants were forced to leave the city with
only those possessions they could carry. They had committed the unforgivable sin of resisting, and they paid a steep price—but not the steepest.
They were granted safe passage, which was one indication that the Christians were not secure enough or strong enough to depopulate and reset-
tle all of Andalusia.

More common were treaties with the local population guaranteeing
the same freedoms of movement and worship that the Muslims had
granted the People of the Book. For instance, the king of Aragon promised the Muslims in the vicinity of Valencia that they would be able "to
make use of waters just as was custom in the time of the Saracens. And
they may pasture their stock in all their districts as was customary in the
time of the pagans [Muslims].... Christians may not forbid preaching in
their mosques or prayer being made on Friday...but the Muslims are to
carry on according to their religion." Muslims could still determine
local laws, and their own judges could decide all issues of marriage,
estates, and contracts. In addition, Muslims were given the right of free
passage by land or by sea and were not to be forced to pay extra tariffs or
taxes.[5]

With the change of regimes, there was a considerable amount of land
redistribution and new settlement of Christian knights on formerly
Muslim estates. Most of that came at the expense of the defeated Muslim nobility and did not take the form of outright seizures from local
farmers or peasants. Instead, Christian lords replaced Muslim lords as
the recipients of taxes and tithes.

Initially, Christians were humbled by the victory they had achieved.
They recognized the Muslims of Andalusia as a worthy adversary, and
they shared with them the peculiar intimacy that comes with years of
war. Christian writers simultaneously condemned Islam and praised
Muslims. "If we wish to consider the nobility of the Muslims," wrote
one, "who can be unaware of the many kings, princes, and noblemen who
have arisen from among them?"[6] Crusading fervor had helped turn the

tide, but once the goal of reconquest had been achieved, Christian rulers appropriated the system that the Andalusian Muslims had created, and their culture as well.

The first Christian king to rule in peace over this new world was Alfonso X of Castile. Unlike his warrior father, Fernando, who had brought the great cities of Muslim Spain to their knees, Alfonso inherited a stable kingdom that had recently vanquished its enemies. War had defined Castile, but now an administrator was needed. On that score, Alfonso's record was mixed. He was not a meticulous soul, and he had little enthusiasm for administration. That may be one reason that so much of the existing order was maintained. To do anything different would have required energy and innovation. Alfonso possessed both, but no interest in applying them to either war or bureaucracy. To the joy of scholars and poets, Alfonso had one obsession. He loved literature, music, and history, and he dedicated his court and its considerable resources to their preservation. Over the course of a thirty-two-year reign, beginning in 1252 and ending in 1284, he did his best to rival the cultural output of Baghdad and Córdoba. And his best was very, very good.

An early sign of Alfonso's predilection was the tomb he erected for his father. Though he had fought by Fernando's side during the siege of Seville, Alfonso's design for his father's sepulcher was more literary than martial. It included inscriptions in Latin, Arabic, Castilian, and Hebrew in honor of the four cultural streams that had converged because of Fernando's efforts.[7]

Soon after Alfonso was crowned, he gathered the greatest minds of Spain to his court to work on a plan of breathtaking scope. He wanted to create a written monument to Spanish culture—its history, literature, poetry, astronomy, music, philosophy, law, mathematics, and of course, religion. His intent was to leave a compendium of human knowledge that could be read in Castilian and that would include the seminal texts of Muslims, Jews, and Christians. It was not only an ambitious undertaking; it was an expensive one as well, and not everyone shared his conviction that it was worth the price.

During the three decades of his reign, Alfonso was rarely popular, but he achieved his cultural goals. The teams he assembled produced a comprehensive history of Spain, illuminated manuscripts charting the stars, complicated musical scores, love poems, legal codes, and even a book dedicated to games, their rules, origins, and the best strategy for playing them. These achievements earned Alfonso the sobriquet *el Sabio*, the Learned. His lust for learning won him the lasting admiration of scholars and academics, and they have repaid him with a favorable historical verdict. He cherished the arts, and his dedication to culture was extraordinary even compared with the later patrons of Renaissance Italy. But it was not just personal passion that motivated him. He was certain that the success of the new kingdom that his father had cemented depended on its unique fusion of Muslim, Christian, and Jewish history. If no effort were made to preserve and record that legacy, it would inevitably be forgotten. Alfonso believed that this would be more than a cultural loss. He feared that unless these elements were purposely woven into the fabric of Castile and Spain, the kingdom would decay. Detached from its history, it would wither and fade.

Alfonso turned the city of Toledo into the hub of his kingdom. In addition to being his birthplace, the town was blessed with an old and established intellectual community, including a considerable number of Jews. Like many of his predecessors, Alfonso employed Jews as his court physicians, and they also served as translators for a number of the works compiled at his behest. Jewish doctors tended to know the major languages needed to complete the project, and they were able to render Hebrew and Arabic into either Latin or Castilian. Usually, they worked as leaders of translation teams. That in itself had been standard practice in Spain for centuries, but the scale of Alfonso's enterprise was much larger and required both more people and more organization.

Among the translations were a catalog of the known stars, Arabic books on the construction of clocks and on the proper manufacturing of measuring devices like the astrolabe, and a description of Muhammad's night journey to heaven. No one seems to have objected that the man appointed to render the Arabic version of this sacred Muslim story into Spanish happened to be a Jew named Abraham of Toledo. Nor was it seen as odd that Abraham oversaw several other translations, including one in Latin and one in Castilian. Muslims, Christians, and Jews in Spain were both separate from one another and entwined with one another. They shared a common heritage, and no one, the Castilian king least of all, would have denied that.

Alfonso was intent on translating both Jewish and Muslim religious texts in addition to scientific treatises. Though he was not the first Christian in Europe to create a Latin version of the Quran—Peter the Venerable, the twelfth-century abbot of Cluny, had already accomplished that—he was almost certainly the only one to insist on translations of the Talmud as well. His motives here were decidedly mixed. He wanted to preserve the heritage of the Iberian Peninsula, but he also wanted to establish the superiority of Christianity. According to his nephew, he "ordered the translation of the whole law of the Jews, and even their Talmud, and other knowledge which is called the *qabbalah* and which the Jews keep closely secret. And he did this so it might be manifest that it is a mere representation of that Law which we Christians have, and that they, like the Moors, are in grave error and in peril of losing their souls."[8]

This ecumenical translation project was a prime example of cooperation, but there was competition and hostility as well. An implicit recognition of common roots and the undeniable reality of a shared culture was offset by animosity that occasionally flared into outright aggression. Jews served as advisers to Christian and Muslim rulers, and as their physicians were entrusted with their lives and bodies, yet laws limited how intimate contact could be. Each community had strict prohibitions against intermarriage, as well as harsh penalties for sexual contact. It is a truism that no community ever passes laws designed to prevent something that isn't happening, and the intensity of these prohibitions is a sign of just how easy and how tempting it was to transgress. Even though each group lived in its own quarter, towns like Toledo or even cities like Seville had a small number of inhabitants by modern standards and people could not avoid interaction. The fact that so many people from each major group knew the languages of the others is itself an indication of how close relations actually were, even if sex was a line that was crossed only at great personal peril.

Alfonso's reign, unfortunately, did not herald a new era of cooperation in Spain. Instead, it marked the apex of Spanish Christian tolerance. Religious freedoms and coexistence gradually gave way to intolerance. Laws restricting the activities of both Muslims and Jews became more common, even though they were erratically enforced. Jews were permitted to worship, provided that they did so quietly and without "speaking ill of the faith of Our Lord Jesus Christ" and without attempting to preach to Christians or challenge their beliefs. That presented a problem for Jews when they were summoned to local courts to engage in theological debates designed to show the superiority of Christianity. These debates were a cultural pastime, much as they had been in Baghdad centuries before. The Jewish invitee, often a rabbi, had to tread the line between capitulating, which might anger the audience, and winning the argument, which might not only displease the audience but lead to legal jeopardy. Jews were rarely compelled to convert, because they were supposed to recognize their errors and come to God of their own free will. Until then, however, they were to be constrained in what they could do and how openly they could worship.

Muslims were treated in much the same way, but unlike the Jews, they were a majority of the population in the south, and remained so into the early fifteenth century. Converting the Moors became a preoccupation of the Spanish church, and as more land was redistributed and more Christians settled in what used to be Muslim Spain, Muslims began to convert or depart. Some Muslims, as well as Jews, hid their religion and after public conversion celebrated their old rites in secret. Scholars have long debated just how many Muslims and Jews went underground and practiced their religion in private even as they acted as Christians in public. But one result was widespread suspicion, even paranoia, in the Spanish church that Muslim and Jewish conversions were false. Beginning in the fourteenth century and gaining force in the fifteenth, this paranoia was enflamed by the office of the Spanish Inquisition.

The achievements of Alfonso notwithstanding, the contrast between Muslim and Christian Spain is startling. Muslim Spain saw long centuries of coexistence, interrupted by sporadic episodes of violence and brief periods of discrimination, much of which was not the result of tensions between Muslims, Christians, and Jews per se, but was simply an unremarkable aspect of medieval society. That Muslims sometimes punished or attacked the People of the Book is less significant than the fact that eruptions of violence between groups or between rival states were common and were as likely to occur within religious communities as they were between them. Christian violence toward other Christians and Muslim aggression against Muslims was ubiquitous. True, Jewish violence against Jews, except at an individual level, was rare, as was Jewish retaliation against Muslims or Christians—but that was because Spanish Jews never controlled the state and were always a small proportion of the population.

Christian Spain, however, did not cherish tolerance and coexistence. Instead, there was a culture of discrimination against Muslims and Jews, with only intermittent periods of harmony and cooperation. Under the

rule of Castile, Muslims were marginalized, disdained, and then targeted as aliens and enemies. Within a few generations after the fall of
Córdoba and Seville in the thirteenth century, the tolerance that marked
Alfonso's realm and that had been a central element of Muslim Andalusia evaporated and was replaced by a zealous intolerance that demanded
conversion and was often not satisfied even with that.

The hostility of Christian Spain to the Muslims and Jews grew even
as the power of Castile increased. It cannot be explained as reaction born
of insecurity. It wasn't as though Castile and Christian Spain was attacked
by a foreign power or was disintegrating within. Quite the opposite. The
contrast with Islam is stark. Muslim society, from the outset, had been
forced to think about the balance between Muslims and the People of
the Book. Christian Spain followed a different path, as did Western
Europe. Crusades against Muslims had gone hand in hand with the con-
solidation of Christian power. The success of Spanish Christianity, at
least in the political sense, cannot be separated from war with Muslims.

The stronger Christian Spain became, the more intolerant it grew.
Muslim Granada had been allowed to remain independent and then
proved difficult to eliminate. Its conquest became a national fixation, and
the monarchs of Castile and Aragon launched a crusade to capture it
once and for all. By the time Granada finally fell in 1492, antagonism
toward Muslims and Jews had reached a new peak. Secure in the reconquest, the king and queen of Castile and Aragon, Ferdinand and Isabella,
ordered the Moors and the Jews of Spain to convert or depart. While it
took many decades to fulfill the edict, Spain became almost entirely
Christian. Only the art and architecture that graced its cities remained
as reminders of what once was.

What we are left with, then, is two very different histories. One is of a
Muslim Spain that with notable exceptions rested on a foundation of
coexistence and cooperation between the three faiths. The other is a
Christian Spain that with few exceptions thrived because of a crusading
ideology that rejected Muslims and Jews. The Spanish monarchs of the
fifteenth century were convinced that both were a threat, and the campaign against them was given added urgency by what was happening on
the other side of the Mediterranean.

In 1453, with a suddenness that shook Christian Europe, the last
Christian empire in the Near East, the once great city of Constantinople, fell. Just as the Christian monarchs of Spain were achieving their

goal of cleansing the peninsula of Jews and Christians, a new Muslim empire emerged that had the will and the power to threaten the very existence of Christian Europe. Had that not occurred, the subsequent relationship between Muslims, Christians, and Jews might have taken a different path. Instead, it reinforced a belief, already prevalent in the Christian West, that Muslims were the enemy.

CHAPTER SEVEN

The Lord of Two Lands

WHEN THE END finally came, it was a calamity. It was also meaningless. After more than a thousand years, the city of Constantine, the seat of the greatest empire Christendom had ever known, was occupied by a Muslim army. But by the time that Sultan Mehmed II, ever after known as the Conqueror, marched into the Church of Hagia Sophia, in the heart of Constantinople, Byzantium had long since ceased to be an empire in anything but name.

Mehmed came to power burdened with a substantial Oedipal complex. His father, Murad, had significantly enlarged the scope of Ottoman rule, and when Murad died in 1451, Mehmed succeeded him—for a second time. After victories over the Hungarians and the Serbs, Murad had abdicated in 1444, only to be recalled by the court when the teenage Mehmed, obstinate and disdainful of his father's advisers, proved unable to govern effectively and unwilling to work with the vizier appointed by Murad to guide the young prince. Though there are no records recording what Mehmed felt at being installed and then abruptly shunted aside by his commanding father, it's unlikely that he took it in stride. In portraits, his face defined by the long, sharp nose and the classic beard of an Ottoman prince, it is difficult to discern his character. But his later behavior suggests that he never forgave or forgot what his father had done, and Constantinople paid the steep and fatal price.

His father had won almost every confrontation with almost every adversary that the Ottomans faced, but one prize eluded him. Constantinople had been taken exactly once, in 1204, but not by Muslims. The Venetians had done what no other power had accomplished—not the

Slavs, not the Huns, not the first wave of Arab armies to emerge in the seventh and eighth centuries, and not the Seljuk Turks in the eleventh. For fifty years after the brutal sack of Constantinople in 1204, the Latins ruled the imperial city, and the Byzantine emperor sat in exile. In the middle of the thirteenth century, the imperial family returned, but hardly in triumph. For the next two hundred years, Byzantium was more a name and a legend than a real power capable of determining what went on in the eastern Mediterranean or the Balkans. Controlling only a few thousand square miles of land, the latter-day rulers of a once-mighty empire watched helplessly as the Ottomans sealed them in their city.

Though Byzantium had shrunk and its emperor was reduced to a man in robes barely able to raise five thousand men to defend the city's ramparts, it remained a potent symbol as the last relic of Rome. For that reason alone, it was a target worthy of young Mehmed's ambitions. And even with a handful of defenders, the walls of the city and its strategic placement between the waters of the Golden Horn and the Bosphorus represented a formidable challenge to any adversary that wanted to take it. Siege technology was not advanced enough to breach the ramparts. From the heights along the water's edge, a few defenders could destroy ships that attempted a landing. Some of Mehmed's predecessors had tried to take the city and had failed, even with numbers on their side. Constantinople was weak, but it could still defend itself.

Mehmed was impetuous, arrogant, and seething with resentment, but even at the age of twenty-one, he knew better than to attack the city unprepared. He marshaled a large army, built a fleet, and commissioned the construction of an immense cannon before he began the attack on Constantinople in the spring of 1453.

The Byzantines did the best they could. Some Genoese and Venetian ships and mercenaries came to their aid, though most of Europe refused Emperor Constantine's request for help. Some Western Christians suggested that if the emperor were willing to bow to the pope, more active support might be forthcoming, but that was not a price he was willing to pay. While the Roman Church had established itself as the supreme doctrinal authority in the West, the Eastern Orthodox Church had never acknowledged that the pope was anything more than the bishop of Rome, worthy of respect but not obeisance. Given the choice between capitulating to the pope and surrendering to the Ottomans, Constantinople preferred the infidel. "Better the turban of the Muslim in the midst of Constantinople," the saying went, "than the miter of the Latin." The emperor Constantine was left with his guile, intimate knowledge of the walls that had been built by the emperor Theodosius a millennium before, and prayer. Those were not enough.

Though Constantine shared the name of the city's founder, he did not share the same luck. The Ottoman generals did what had been considered impossible and breached the iron gate that protected the Golden Horn from enemy ships. Mehmed had numbers on his side, and he exploited the thinness of the defenses and weaknesses in the fortifications. Tens of thousands of his soldiers poured into the city and overwhelmed it. Constantine ripped off his imperial insignia, charged into the onslaught, and died. He declared that he would not be remembered as the emperor who fled the greatest city in the world in the hour of its greatest need.

RELIGIOUS FREEDOM AND "THE CONQUEROR"

THE OTTOMAN ARMY entered the city on May 29, 1453. Because the Byzantines had refused to surrender, Mehmed gave his troops license to loot and pillage; they would have rebelled if he had not. But the city was already depopulated and all but a handful of churches and palaces were deserted. Some later Western accounts describe a horrific sacking, but there is little evidence of that. No matter how psychologically devastating, the physical damage was relatively mild, both to property and to people.

Mehmed made directly for Hagia Sophia. For a millennium, the church had stood as a monument to the empire, the center of Eastern Christianity. At the end of May 1453, an alien language was heard under its domes, and a conquering people replaced the old rites with theirs. The church echoed with the sound of the *shahada*, and with the Muslim call to prayer. Thereafter, Hagia Sophia would be a mosque, with the names of the first four caliphs surrounding its main dome. When Mehmed first entered, so legend has it, a soldier was attempting to pry loose the tiles in the floor. The sultan struck him with the flat of his sword, and said, "For you the treasures and the prisoners are enough. The buildings of the city fall to me."

The sultan soon halted the pillaging. The city was to be the capital of his empire, and he did not want to be burdened with unnecessary renovations. The place was in sorry enough shape as it was and in need of repair. In the ensuing months, the Ottomans refashioned the city, both physically and culturally. Some Byzantine nobles had escaped; others were taken captive; some were ransomed; and a few were executed. But Mehmed could not afford to have the entire city emptied of its Greek inhabitants. In order to keep it functioning, he did what he could to assure the population that their rights would be respected. He even tried to entice those who had left to return and offered to pay them restitution if their property had been damaged or destroyed.

As an added incentive, Mehmed promised that he would not interfere with religion. The Byzantine emperor had stood at the head of the Orthodox Church, and with him gone, the patriarch was the logical replacement. But at the time of the city's fall, the reigning patriarch was abroad, and in his place, Mehmed turned to Gennadius—one of the most respected monks in the city, who was known to be fiercely independent and equally fierce in his opposition to Rome—and announced that he would be the leader of the church.

It was later said that Mehmed ordered his officials to scour Constantinople for someone worthy of the appointment. In the words of one contemporary Greek chronicler, "Gennadius was a very wise and remarkable man.... When the Sultan saw him, and had in a short time had proofs of his wisdom and prudence and virtue and also of his power as a speaker and his religious character, he was greatly impressed, and held him in great honor and respect, and gave him the right to come to him at any time, and honored him with liberty and conversation." In January 1454, the sultan installed the new patriarch and granted him authority over the daily lives of the city's Christian populace, "no less than that enjoyed previously under the emperors."

The extent of the patriarch's power was spelled out in a charter drawn up by the sultan's vizier. Gennadius was more than the spiritual guide of the Greek Orthodox who had fallen under Ottoman rule. He was in many ways their king, with power to tax and judge and the authority to appoint local representatives throughout the empire. Much like the Byzantine emperor, he had more influence than the heads of other Christian churches in the East. While he ultimately answered to the sultan and to the Ottoman state, on issues ranging from birth to marriage to death, including estates, taxes, and intracommunal trade, he had wide latitude. The Ottomans may have ruled, but Mehmed II had no interest in micromanaging the daily lives of Christian subjects. That would have required more bureaucracy and more effort. Better to find a partner and delegate the dirty work of administration to him.[1]

It did not seem remarkable to anyone at the time that Mehmed could be simultaneously so merciless with the nobles and the ruling class and so merciful toward most of the people and their religious leaders. But it runs contrary to the modern notion that there is no separation between church and state in Islam. That lack of separation is said to be in contrast to the wall dividing secular and religious power in the West. Yet until at least the nineteenth century, those walls did not exist in the Western world, and the entire framework has never made much sense when applied to the Muslim world.

For instance, the Byzantine Empire, which the Ottomans ended, never had separate spheres for religion and politics. The emperor was simultaneously the head of the state and the head of the church—and that formula was replicated in other parts of the Christian world, including Reformation England, where the king demanded the obedience of the archbishop of Canterbury. Throughout Byzantine history, the emperor enforced doctrine, led military campaigns, and convened tribunals to punish those who dissented from the imperial orthodoxy. As we saw, the refusal of Egyptian Coptic Christians to bow to the authority of both emperor and the patriarch in Constantinople in the sixth and seventh centuries was one reason for the ease of the Arab conquest of Egypt soon after Muhammad's death.

In contrast, while there were occasions when Muslim rulers attempted to dictate doctrine, those times were the exception, and not the rule. In one sense, the Ottoman sultan had unlimited power over his subjects. He had power over life and death. But in other ways, he was as constrained by, and in theory just as subject to, religious law as any other Muslim. Like earlier rulers, he deferred to the scholars and judges who comprised the *ulama*. Even when the Ottoman sultan added the title of caliph in later centuries, he did not exercise total doctrinal authority. True, he could issue laws of his own whether or not those agreed with sharia (religious) law. But he still needed, and cultivated, the support of the *ulama*. The only sense in which it can be said that there is no separation between church and state in Islam is that there is no church. The possible exception is Iran. After the sixteenth century, Iran's Shi'a mullahs gradually coalesced into an institution that in its hierarchy and coherence resembled the Catholic Church, but without the ability to coerce errant believers. Almost everywhere else, Islam had no central, governing religious body. Throughout the history of Muslim societies, from the emergence of a clerical establishment in Baghdad during the Abbasid caliphate through the evolution of Sufism and other forms of individual piety, the political and doctrinal spheres were distinct and governed by different people.

The de facto separation helps explain why Mehmed could be so indifferent to the religion of his subjects. Like most imperial rulers, the Ottomans drew a distinction between the state and the people. Neither Mehmed nor any of the Ottomans evinced an interest in converting the Greek Christian population of Constantinople. To the contrary. The Ottomans provided incentives to encourage the Greeks to work with the new regime to revive the city and restore it to greatness. For their part, the Christians of Constantinople, their religious rights intact, seem to have accepted the new rulers. Greek Christian architects drew up plans to reinforce and reconstruct the decaying walls and fortifications that had in the end failed to protect the city. They designed mosques and helped Mehmed transform Hagia Sophia into a Muslim house of worship. They also built a vast new covered market, which would become the famed Grand Bazaar of Istanbul, and manned many of its stalls and shops.

Had Mehmed stopped with the capture of Constantinople, he would have earned his sobriquet "the Conqueror." But he was still very young, and his ambitions were not sated. He took on his father's old adversaries in Hungary and Serbia, and he solidified Ottoman control over much of the Balkans and the southern coast of the Black Sea. More often than not, cities surrendered, opening their gates to the sultan rather than suffer death and destruction. The Ottomans honored the flag of truce. When they promised to protect the rights of the local populace, they did.

Inevitably, after decades of leading his armies, Mehmed grew tired and ill. He did not age gracefully, and his accomplishments had not made him happy. He drank too much and became ever-more distrustful of those around him. At the risk of unfairly psychoanalyzing him from a distance of many centuries, it might be said that he did everything he could to banish the memory of his father, and he failed. Had he consulted a Sufi master, he might have learned that he could go to the ends of the earth, win every battle, and become rich beyond imagination, but unless he bared his soul to God, he would remain restless and unfulfilled. And so he was, until he died in 1481, fat, gout-ridden, surrounded by Jewish and Persian physicians helpless to heal him, an old man at the age of forty-nine.

Though the Europeans were dismayed at the loss of the city they had done so little to help and so much to undermine, whatever affinity they felt was an illusion. In truth, the Christians of Western Europe were more alien and more hostile to Orthodox Byzantium than the Ottomans. The Ottomans and the Byzantines had been fighting for more than a hundred years, and they had also lived side by side while each attended to other enemies. Mehmed's father had married a Byzantine-Serbian princess, which was neither the first and nor the last time that a Muslim Ottoman married a Christian woman for reasons of state. The two empires had been bound not only by marital ties, but by financial ones. For many years, before Mehmed, the Ottoman sultan paid an annual fee to the Byzantine emperor, because the Ottomans preferred a toothless Byzantium to a rival power in Constantinople guarding the vital cross-roads. Later, in the nineteenth century, the powers of Europe were to make the same calculations about the Ottomans, and the empire would survive not because it was strong but because it was weak.

EUROPE AND THE OTTOMANS

THE OTTOMAN EMPIRE lasted nearly five hundred years, longer than all but a handful of dynasties the world has known. Byzantium, and Rome before that, each survived more than a thousand years, but only the Ottomans could claim that the same family ruled in succession from the beginning until the end. Though there may have been some convenient rewriting of the family tree, there was an unbroken chain stretching from Osman in the fourteenth century through the last sultan, Mehmed VI, in the first decade of the twentieth. By way of comparison, European dynasties have rarely lasted more than a few hundred years and have usually ruled an area no larger than an Ottoman province. For the better part of five centuries, however, the Ottoman Empire encompassed the entire eastern Mediterranean. From the early sixteenth century until the early twentieth, it also ruled North Africa and Egypt; the Caucasus between the Black and Caspian Seas; the Crimean Peninsula and the surrounding regions; all of the Near East from present-day Israel to the borders of Iran; and the Balkans, including Greece, Serbia, Croatia, Bulgaria, Romania, and parts of modern Hungary.

In the collective memory of the West, the Ottomans loom large. More than the first wave of Arab conquests, more than the Muslims of Spain or Saladin and his armies, the Ottomans were woven into the consciousness of modern Europe. At the very time that the centralized monarchies of Western and Central Europe were emerging, they faced an adversary whose size, organization, wealth, and power dwarfed anything they could muster. The lords of Spain, France, England, the German lands, and the Holy Roman Empire may have thought of themselves as titans, but against the Ottomans, they barely rated as pygmies. Acting in concert, the fleets of the Italians, the knights of Spain and France, and the foot soldiers of Hungary, Poland, Austria, and Prussia were able to stave off total defeat, but until the eighteenth century, the shadow of what they called "the perfidious Turk" clouded even the brightest of their days.

Gradually, the Ottomans lost their comparative advantage, and in the late eighteenth century, the monarchs of Europe and Russia reversed the tide. Even then, the empire shrank but did not collapse. Unlike many other regions of the globe, the core of the Ottoman Empire was never occupied or ruled by the Europeans. The empire contracted, but the central lands of Turkey and large parts of the Middle East, including Iraq and Arabia, remained under Ottoman rule until the end of World War I.

Close in proximity, the Ottomans and the Europeans were separated by a wide cultural gulf. Religion, however, was perhaps the least important dividing line. The Ottomans were ruled by a Turkish family, whose origins were, as many scholars have noted, shrouded in obscurity. There is as little known about Osman, the dynasty's founder, as there is about Romulus and Remus, the mythic progenitors of Rome. There are almost no written records about the Ottomans for the first century of their existence, and their primary adversaries—Serbs, Hungarians, Byzantines, and the Turkish emirs in Anatolia, did not leave many accounts of the defeats that they suffered at Ottoman hands.

In time, Europe became familiar with the Ottoman state, but well until the nineteenth century, its inner workings remained opaque. The sultan and his harem became legendary, but few Westerners understood how the Ottomans governed, fought, or lived. Western ambassadors in Istanbul wrote accounts of the imperial capital, but they had limited contact with the elite and were shown only those aspects of courtly life they were allowed to see. Not until the nineteenth century, when the Ottomans were forced to open up more of their society to foreign scrutiny, was the veil pulled aside, and even then, only partway.

One result of ignorance was imagination. In fanciful, often salacious accounts, Westerners conjured a picture of a sultan serviced by a harem of willing women guarded by eunuchs from sub-Saharan Africa and defended by a slave army of men taken as captives while still young boys and trained to a hard life as warriors who would just as soon die at the sultan's command as breathe. In his throne room, surrounded by viziers plotting the next campaign against the West, the Ottoman sultan sat, shrouded in mystery. Like the Eastern potentates that he emulated, he seldom allowed visitors to gaze upon him, which only enhanced the aura of mystery. Westerners filled the gaps in their knowledge with fears and transformed the sultan into a holy warrior bent on extinguishing Christian power in order to fulfill what Muhammad had started and to avenge the Muslim world for the loss of Spain.

This mixture of half-truths and legends fed Western anxiety. Feared, loathed, and grudgingly admired, the sultan ruled a formidable empire on the borders of Europe. Though the Turks were only one of many different groups in the empire, the word "Turk" became a proxy for all things Ottoman, and not a positive one. For the English, as for most Europeans, "Turk" meant barbarism and savagery.[2]

In the absence of evidence to the contrary, caricature was taken as fact. Even after the Ottoman Empire was exposed as a state like any other, with its own strengths and more than its share of weaknesses, the image never fully faded. In fact, it outlasted the empire itself. The memory of Turkish warriors fighting in the name of a Muslim God against the armies of Christendom survived the fall of the Ottomans and lodged itself in Western culture. When Turkey applied for membership in the European Union at the start of the twenty-first century, French, German, and Dutch voices murmured uncomfortably that Turkey was still too alien, too other, and perhaps too Muslim. Laced through these concerns were hints that having fought the Ottomans for centuries and finally triumphed, Europe was not about to allow the Turks to enjoy the fruits of that hard-won victory.

The reputation of the Ottomans also suffered from the nationalist movements that swept the Balkans and the Near East in the nineteenth and twentieth centuries. First the Greeks in the 1820s and then the Hungarians, Serbs, Bulgarians, Romanians, and, finally, the Arabs of the Near East defined themselves as nations that had been conquered, brutalized, and silenced by Ottoman autocrats. For the Greeks and other Balkan peoples, there was an added religious element: the Muslim Ottomans, they claimed, had oppressed Christian peoples. Even the Arabs, who caught the infectious bug of nationalism just before World War I, distanced themselves from the Ottomans, though their main bone of contention was more ethnic than religious.

Here as elsewhere, conflict has received the most attention, and in the West the religious undertones have been emphasized. Without question, the early Ottoman rulers considered themselves Muslim warriors. They called themselves *ghazis*, which in Arabic meant "holy raiders," in order to link themselves to the companions of Muhammad and to the Arab dynasties that had ruled after his death. In their relations with the Christian West, the Ottomans were anything but peaceful. Once they had defeated Christian Byzantium and taken control of the Balkans, they turned to the last fortresses of the Frankish Crusaders on the islands of Rhodes, Crete, and Malta, and to the cities along the Danube, including Buda, Pest, and above all, Vienna.

But what is usually overlooked and forgotten is that the title of *ghazi* was only one of a long line of titles, which included not only Lord of Two Lands, but also Lord of Two Seas; Sultan of the Arabs, Persians, and Romans; Distributor of Crowns to the Rulers of the Surface of the Earth; Sovereign of the White Sea, Black Sea, Rumelia, Anatolia; Overlord of Rum and Karama, of Dulkadir and Diyarbakir, Azerbaijan, Syria, Aleppo, Egypt, Noble Jerusalem, Venerated Mecca and Sacred Medina, Jidda, Yemen, and Many Other Lands; and Thunderbolt of War, the World Conqueror. The Ottomans were proud of their victories, proud to style themselves as the heirs not just to the early caliphs but to Caesar and Rome and to the Persian monarchs of antiquity, proud to rule both Europe and Asia, both Jerusalem and the holy cities of Arabia, and proud that the monarchs of Europe feared and reviled them. The fact that the Ottomans were also Muslims who had won victories rivaled only by the caliphs of the seventh and eighth centuries was one laurel, but hardly the only one.

What is also forgotten is that for most of those five hundred years, the Ottomans were indifferent to the religion of their subjects. The empire was ruled by a small number of governors and judges and a formidable army barracked in the capitals of each major province. Except for the sultan and his family, membership in the ruling class was not based on race or religion. It was based on a system of organized enslavement of young boys. Taken from their villages, they were sent to schools in Istanbul, and in the imperial capital of Adrianople, and trained as soldiers or as bureaucrats. The soldiers were known as Janissaries, and many of them began life as Christian peasants, who then converted to Islam. Theirs was not, however, an orthodox Islam, but one suffused with the mysticism of a Sufi order known as the Bektashis that seems to have preserved many Christian rites.

Every year, Janissary corps would sweep through the villages of the Balkans and the Caucasus and collect a quota of children. Few aspects of Ottoman rule have generated as much controversy and ill will. By the nineteenth century, the practice had largely come to an end, but the memory was enough to rouse the Balkan peoples against their overlords. The Janissaries were slaves in the sense that their rights and their wealth, property, and status were at the whim of the sultan. But in many other respects, they were a privileged elite. Unlike the Africans enslaved in the Americas, the Janissaries were the ruling class of an empire and enjoyed the concomitant benefits. Though later generations of Westerners decried the forced recruitment, the opportunity to have sons rise high in the ranks of the empire was not seen as a grave injustice by many families. Besides, in the fifteenth, sixteenth, and seventeenth centuries, no peasants—whether Christian or Muslim—had expectations of Jeffersonian democracy. The Ottoman ruling class was harsh and unsentimental, but they differed from the rulers of Europe only in efficiency. When the kings of France or Spain needed to raise an army, their troops also entered villages and violently drafted eligible young men without asking permission. The recruitment of the Janissary corps in the Balkans and Greece was, in that sense, no different.[3]

While the Ottoman ruling class was Muslim, the empire was not, and Islam did not act as a glue holding together the disparate parts of the state. A majority of the population of the European lands controlled by the Ottomans was Christian and remained that way until the end. Even in regions such as Egypt and Iraq where Muslims were in the majority, the Sunni Islam of the Ottoman ruling class was somewhat different than the Islam of many Arabs. On the whole, while the sultan proclaimed himself caliph and protector of the holy cities of Mecca and Medina, he seems to have cared not one whit about the religion of his subjects. No efforts were made to convert Christians and Jews, nor did the Ottomans try to enforce one version of Muslim law. Being a Muslim was no guarantee of better treatment by local governors, and being Christian or Jewish was not necessarily a burden to overcome.

While the Ottomans fought against the Christian states of Europe, they fought against the Shi'ite shahs of Iran with just as much intensity. In neither case was the propagation of Islam a primary motivation. The Ottomans were a dynasty bent on expanding and perpetuating their own rule. As with the Romans, the Mongols, the Han, and other empires, power was primary, and all else was secondary. Religion was at best an instrument of control. If the mantle of religion could be used to justify expansion, all the better. If religious toleration helped pacify subject peoples and maintain stability, so be it.

JEWS UNDER OTTOMAN RULE

THE OTTOMAN FORMULA that stressed obedience to the sultan and indifference to the religion of subject peoples was developed before the fall of Constantinople, but it only became vital to the empire's success after. By leaving the religion of his subjects alone, the sultan was able to use them to enhance the power of the state. For instance, in his effort to restore the glory of Constantinople, Mehmed ordered thousands of people throughout the empire to relocate. Some of these were Turks and Muslims, but many more were not. Greek Orthodox from Anatolian cities with needed skills were told to move, and though they were given assistance and guaranteed an income and jobs, they were not given a choice. Nor were the soldiers of the sultan's armies, of course. And nor were thousands of Jews, many of whom lived in the Balkans. Their ability to act as intermediaries between the Muslim eastern Mediterranean and the Christian West meant that they could, and soon did, play a pivotal role in the commercial and economic success of the Ottoman state.

Under the Byzantines, Jews had been tolerated but hardly embraced. In Christian Constantinople, an affluent Jewish community performed the same function as economic intermediaries that they did in numerous other cities in the Mediterranean world. They were represented at the emperor's court by a chief rabbi who was both a leader and an advocate. In the Byzantine system, his authority was narrow. Under the Ottomans, however, the Jews gained more autonomy and in time became active supporters of the sultan's rule. After the conquest, Mehmed allowed the chief rabbi who had served the Byzantines to retain his position. This rabbi was not, as some have suggested, the head of all Jews in the Ottoman Empire, though in time the position would become the chief rabbi of Jewish lore. Initially, he was responsible only for the Jewish community of Constantinople, which was fairly small in 1453, but which soon swelled by thousands because of Mehmed's resettlement policies.

Faced with an underpopulated capital and insufficient numbers of people capable of carrying out complicated tasks, Mehmed ordered thousands of Jews to move to Constantinople. They were singled out not because of their beliefs, but because they were a close-knit group that possessed skills that the Ottoman state dearly needed. The forced relocation of Jews from various parts of the Balkans and Anatolia could not have been pleasant for those made to move their homes, and there have been heated debates among scholars about how to characterize Mehmed's edicts. Some have likened the removals to the pogroms and persecutions of the late nineteenth and twentieth centuries. Others, including the fifteenth-century Jewish poet Elijah Capsali, had little to say about the relocations and saw the Ottomans as a significant improvement over both the Western Christian regimes in Europe and the Eastern Christian rulers of Byzantium. Capsali, in fact, took the fall of Constantinople as a divine punishment against those who had abused the Jews and a sign of God's favor for those who showed tolerance.

In short, there was nothing about Mehmed's policies that discriminated against the Jews as Jews, or against any Christian denomination as Christian per se. The Ottoman bureaucracy treated all subjects as instruments of the state and servants of the sultan, to be used and disposed of as he saw fit. In that sense, all citizens of the empire were discriminated against by the sultan and the ruling elite, and had few rights separate from what the sultan permitted. In no part of the world in the fifteenth century was the situation dramatically different. While the Jews who were forced to relocate to the new capital may have suffered, only through a very particular contemporary prism can it be said that they suffered because of their religion.

And by the end of the fifteenth century, the Jews of Constantinople were thriving, and Jewish communities in other parts of the empire were living secure, prosperous lives. Skepticism and fear during the first years of Mehmed's reign gave way to acceptance and then outright enthusiasm. While Jews and Christians had to pay a head tax, these were offset by the tax benefits they received for setting up business first in Istanbul and then in other major cities. Jews dominated what primitive forms of banking there were, as well as trade in jewels, pearls, and satin. The Jewish community of Egypt remained intact, and when Egypt was finally conquered by the Ottomans early in the sixteenth century, they reaped economic benefits. And one foreign community of Jews found a home in the empire and were met with a warm embrace that contrasted sharply with what they had left behind.

In 1492, after the defeat of the Muslim kingdom of Granada, the triumphant monarchs of Spain fulfilled a long-standing ambition of the Spanish Catholic Church and ordered the expulsion of the Jews. With little time to prepare and in danger for their lives, thousands packed what they could and left the country. The cities of Western Europe shunned them, and North Africa was divided into petty principalities with little economic vitality. But the Ottomans announced that the exiled Jews of Spain were welcome and would receive aid and support, including transportation from Spain to the heart of the empire on the other side of the Mediterranean. Jews were allowed to move to Istanbul, but the sultan proclaimed that he would be particularly pleased if they settled in one of the oldest cities in the Balkans, Thessaloniki, also known as Salonica.

Not all who made the trip survived. Said one taciturn contemporary account, "A part of the exiled Spaniards went overseas to Turkey. Some of them were thrown into the sea and drowned, but those who arrived there the king of Turkey received kindly, as they were artisans." These transplanted Jews willingly shared their wisdom and learning with their new overlords, including knowledge about the arts of war. Jewish engineers and artisans helped the Ottomans manufacture advanced artillery and complicated siege engines, which the sultan put to good use against the Europeans in the sixteenth and seventeenth centuries. The outcasts of Spain thus became an asset for the Ottomans.[4]

Some of the exiles moved to Istanbul, but the bulk settled in Salonica. By the middle of the sixteenth century, the city had a substantial Jewish population and had established itself as a metropolis that could stand proudly in the shadow of Istanbul. The Jews of Salonica were self-governing, answerable to the Ottoman governor and ultimately to the sultan but not to the chief rabbi in Istanbul. That began to change in later centuries, as the sultan ceded more authority to religious leaders in the imperial capital, which meant enhanced powers not only for the chief rabbi, but for the patriarchs of the Greek and Armenian churches as well. Initially, however, the Jews of Spain who settled in Salonica competed not with the Jews of Istanbul but with the older population of Greek Jews who had lived in the city for fifteen hundred years and had hosted Saint Paul on his travels through the Roman world spreading the gospel. These rivalries faded, though never completely, and with each passing century, the Jews of Salonica became richer, more powerful, and more central to the commercial life of the empire.

The illustrious history of the Jews of the Ottoman Empire stands in sharp relief to the treatment of their brethren in Christian Europe until the mid-eighteenth century and of course during the Holocaust of the twentieth. The kingdoms of Europe cared greatly about the religion of their subjects and fought destructive wars in order to coerce belief and stifle heresy. The Ottomans were ruthless as conquerors but once they had achieved military victory, they preferred a lean and tranquil administrative system.

This tolerance may explain why few Christians and Jews converted to Islam during the Ottoman centuries, especially compared with the earlier rates of conversion in Andalusia or in the Near East, Egypt, and Persia after the coming of Islam in the seventh century. The presence of increasingly powerful Christian states in Europe, who represented the possibility, however unlikely, of a different order and a different regime may also have dissuaded Christians from converting. Other factors notwithstanding, the benign neglect of the Ottoman state allowed Jews, Greek Orthodox, Armenians, Catholics, Copts, and others to live in peace and security and to practice their beliefs unmolested. There are many reasons why the Ottomans were so successful and so resilient, but perhaps the most important was that they gave people just enough autonomy to keep them content, loyal, and uninterested in change.

SULEYMAN AND THE APEX OF EMPIRE

MANY OF TODAY'S inhabitants of the Balkans would dismiss the characterization of the Ottoman Empire as tolerant and relatively benign. Bulgarians, Serbians, and Greeks bear no affection for the Ottomans or for the Turks, and they recall an empire notable for its brutality and its ill treatment of them. The issue here is not whether the Ottomans were cruel; like most imperial powers, they could be. It is not whether individual governors took advantage of their power to steal, rape, and otherwise abuse their subjects. In their treatment of the peasants of the Balkans, however, the Ottomans were neither more nor less cruel than feudal lords in Europe were toward their peons. Some Ottoman governors were tyrants, others were not, and the ones who were tend to get the attention. There are many chronicles written by peoples that the Ottomans ruled that depict their masters in a very unkind light. Some of these highlight religion as the dividing line, but that does not mean that it was. The dividing line for the Ottomans was power, who had it and who did not.

The Ottomans did what was expedient. In today's terms, they were realists, not idealists. Sultans from Mehmed on may have described themselves as holy warriors when they took the field against enemies, but when it came to governing, they were pragmatists to the core. The unspoken formula was beautiful and elegant: the empire was ruled by a sultan with nearly unlimited powers, answerable only to God and in theory to the *ulama*, who almost always validated what he wanted to do. That included marrying Christians, employing Jews, and forging alliances with Catholic states—none of which were held to be incompatible with orthodox Islam as then understood.

The Ottoman bureaucracy, in turn, did not discriminate on the basis of religion or race. From the Janissary corps to the civil service to the palace eunuchs, the government was run by a motley collection of races. While becoming a Janissary did entail converting, there was often more form than substance to the Islam of the foot soldiers who fought the sultan's battles so ably.

Tartars, Serbs, Greeks, Arabs, Berbers, Copts, Armenians, Jews, Sunnis, Shi'ites, Druze, Nubians, Slavs, Bulgars, Hungarians, Georgians, and of course Turks combined to form a crazy quilt of languages, traditions, and rites. The Ottoman court in Istanbul and various provincial administrators also made use of Venetians, Genoese, Florentines, and Romans, as well as merchants and translators from France, Austria, Spain, and England. Not until the ruling class seized on the notion of "Turkishness" in the late nineteenth century was there anything particularly Turkish about the Ottoman state.

The sultans also viewed marriage through the lens of politics rather than race, religion, or love. Wives and the concubines of the harem came from a wide range of ethnic groups and multiple faiths. The goal was to bind the disparate groups of the empire to the sultan, and so he could hardly sleep with only Muslim women or only Turks. That in turn meant that most sultans—as the children of such unions—were of mixed ethnicity. The empire not only had a multicultural administration; it had a multicultural sultan.

The reality of the harem itself is at odds with the myth. The seductive mysteries of the harem became an obsession of Westerners who fantasized about lascivious nights, willing women, lots of silk, a surfeit of pillows, and black eunuchs with gold earrings and scimitar-laden cummerbunds. There was that, perhaps, though as the Western women who penetrated the harem later reported, there was much less sex and much more tea drinking and sewing. While one purpose of the harem may have been to gratify the sultan's desires, the primary aim was to make sure that there was at least one male heir and that the pool of possible mothers reflected the diversity of the empire. It was, in that sense, a version of sexual democracy unburdened by concerns of race, class, or religion.

The willingness to ignore religion in order to focus on realpolitik defined the reign of the empire's greatest sultan—Suleyman. Though he was known as "the Magnificent" in the West, his primary sobriquet in the Ottoman world was different, and telling. To his subjects, he was "the Lawgiver." During his reign of more than forty years, the empire reached its apex. His conquests brought the Ottomans to the gates of Vienna in the West and deep into Persia in the East. All of North Africa came under his nominal control, and the last of the Crusader principalities, the demesne of the Hospitallers on the island of Rhodes, which had resisted all challengers for more than two hundred years, fell after a long and gritty battle in 1526.

But while Suleyman led his armies to victory on the periphery, the core of the empire was peaceful, prosperous, and stable. After centuries of struggle, the Ottomans were able to consolidate their rule. Suleyman's forty-six years in power were dramatic, but less because of external pressures than because of familial squabbles that turned deadly, as they often did among Ottoman princes. In most other respects, it was a placid and stable time. Suleyman formalized and codified the administrative practices that he had inherited from his father and grandfather, and for nearly three hundred years thereafter, his laws governed the state. During his reign, revenue flowed into the coffers in Istanbul; the Janissaries recruited their own version of the best and the brightest; provincial governors were dispatched from the capital to rule comfortably in the sultan's name; and only the Safavid shahs of Iran to the east and the Habsburgs of Austria to the west prevented the Ottomans from extending their reach from China to the English Channel.

Every apex is also the beginning of decline. Suleyman's armies achieved such rapid victories against the Hungarians in 1529 that they unexpectedly were able to advance up the Danube to Vienna. The army had not prepared for a long siege of the city, and was not equipped for winter. After weeks of stalemate, Suleyman, ensconced in a tent more opulent than many of the palaces of Europe, decided that it was more prudent to withdraw than submit his Janissaries to a winter campaign. The march on Vienna had been so easy that he imagined he could return again the following spring. Instead, it was a lost opportunity, and Ottoman forces would not seriously threaten the city again until 1683, when they would fail once more.

During these years, European diplomats and merchants had more contact with the Ottomans. Suleyman was an imposing, enigmatic figure, but he did grant audiences, and a number of diplomats wrote their impressions. Much of what they said reinforced the sense that the Ottomans, with Suleyman at their head, were utterly alien and brutally effective.

Regular diplomacy and occasional interaction did begin to peel away the mystique. In 1520, a Venetian envoy described a young Suleyman as "tall and slender, with a thin and bony face. The sultan appears friendly and in good humor. Rumor has it that he...enjoys reading, is knowledgeable and shows good judgment."[5] He had the same aquiline nose as his great-grandfather Mehmed, and an even narrower face adorned with the sparse Ottoman beard favored by his family. That look did not change over the decades, though he grew paler and more sallow with the passing years. Toward the end of his life, the sultan received a perspicacious emissary named Ghiselin de Busbecq while "seated on a rather low sofa, not more than a foot from the ground and spread with many coverlets and cushions embroidered with exquisite work.... His expression...was anything but smiling, and had a sternness which though sad was full of majesty." Suffering from gangrene, heavily made up, and deathly pale, Suleyman exuded a potent and painful combination of grandeur and tragedy.

He had every reason to be sad. His victories notwithstanding, his personal life was a shambles. He had broken the cardinal rule of the Ottoman ruling class and married one of his concubines. Sultans were not supposed to love the mothers of their children, but Suleyman did. She, in turn, used her position to champion her sons and turn her husband against the children of his other mistresses. The result was death all around. Suleyman ordered the execution of two of his sons, and another's life ended under questionable circumstances. When his wife died, his two remaining sons by her turned on each other, and on him. He had yet another executed, along with several grandchildren, leaving only Selim, who would succeed him.

These dramas were duly recorded by the European envoys in the city. Much as the Roman emperors had combined an exquisite ability to rule the known world with dark and depraved family dramas, Suleyman and his heirs led lives rent by passions, intrigue, sex, and murder. While some of these stories fed the European imagination about the lascivious Turk, more to our point is that religion never entered the equation.

To wit: Suleyman commissioned the construction of a major mosque in Istanbul, the Suleymaniye. It was the most important Muslim monument of its day, but over half of the workers and artisans who built it were Christian. In addition, the sultan may have believed himself to be a devout servant of God, but as was true of the clergy in Rome at the time, such devotion didn't preclude sin. The Medici and Borgia popes commissioned works of art, kept mistresses, and tried to ensure the well-being of their many illegitimate children. The Ottoman sultans conducted themselves in a similar manner.

The absence of a rigid, doctrinal Islam was in stark contrast to the role of religion in the West. As the Ottomans drew closer to Europe, they held up the mirror to Western Christians who were descending into a long period of intolerance. Disgusted with the corruption of the Catholic Church, the German monk Martin Luther set in motion a chain of events that produced both the Reformation and decades of war in Europe. Luther viewed the Ottoman Empire under Suleyman as an exemplar of religious toleration. Though he did decry the Ottomans as "servants of the devil," for Luther that was a mild critique compared to what he said about the pope and about Jews. Luther hoped that a reformed and purified church could one day emulate the Ottoman model.

Several decades later, the French philosopher Jean Bodin, committed though he was to his Catholic faith, wrote favorably of the Ottomans, "The great emperor of the Turks doth with as great devotion as any prince in the world honor and observe the religion by him received from his ancestors and yet detests he not the strange religions of others; but to the contrary permits every man to live according to his conscience... and suffers four diverse religions: that of the Jews, that of the Christians, that of the Greeks, and that of the Mohametans." Having lived through the wars of religion that were sundering Europe in general and France in particular, Bodin had witnessed the costs of intolerance. Protestants and Catholics regarded each other with contempt, hurling invective and promising punishment in this life and damnation in the next. The Ottoman Empire presented an alternative that Bodin could not help but admire.

The Islam of the Ottomans did not create obstacles to allying with Christian states, and Suleyman became enmeshed in the politics of Europe, not just as an adversary but as a strategic partner. Europe was cross-hatched with divisions, especially between Protestants and Catholics and between two royal families, the Habsburgs and the Valois, whose feud was acrimonious and intense. The Habsburgs ruled Spain, and under Charles V they governed the central European lands of the Holy Roman Empire as well. The Valois controlled France and posed a challenge to Habsburg hegemony. Under Francis I, the animosity between the two families became personal. The two monarchs developed an abiding hatred for each other, which was based less on direct experience than on dynastic aims. But that did not make the hatred any less intense, and it led Francis I to court the enemies of the Habsburgs, no matter where they were or what God they worshiped.

The Habsburgs had more territory and more wealth (especially given the flow of silver from the new lands of South America), but they also confronted more enemies. Not only was Charles V faced with Francis, but he also had to contend with Protestant German princes, rebellious Dutch burghers, an increasingly unpredictable England, and of course, a restive and expansionist Ottoman Empire led by a sultan who could draw on seemingly inexhaustible resources to outfit his army. Having conquered the Hungarians, Suleyman came face-to-face with the Habsburgs. Watching from Paris, Francis decided in the early 1520s that the enemy of his enemy was a friend, and he reached out to Suleyman for an alliance. Suleyman, recognizing the strategic advantage, agreed.

For the remainder of Suleyman's life, the French and the Ottomans worked together to humble the Habsburgs. The pincer alliance was a constant irritant to Charles V and his heirs, but they never succumbed, in part because of skilled leadership and in part because Central Europe was never a prime objective for Suleyman. Persia presented a more immediate threat to the Ottomans, as did Venetian raiders interrupting trade in the Mediterranean. But as one historian has written, "The French alliance was the cornerstone of the Ottomans' European diplomacy." Suleyman knew that his partnership with France kept the Habsburgs on the defensive, and that freed him to pursue other ambitions. He also undermined Habsburg power by stirring the pot inside the Holy Roman Empire. He reached out to Protestant princes and offered his protection, claiming that the Protestants, because they had risen up against the idolatry of the Catholic Church, were in their way much like the first Muslims who had rejected the idolatry of the Meccans.[6]

These snapshots from Suleyman's life barely do justice to his reign of more than forty years, but they reveal an Ottoman state that was no more, and no less, defined by creed than the Habsburgs were defined by Christianity or the Romans by whatever pagan cult was in vogue. Islam was part of the governing creed, but it shared space with the imperatives of maintaining order, propagating the dynasty, and jockeying for position in foreign affairs. The sultans at times used Islam as a spur and justification for war, but they drew on the legacy of Muhammad and the warrior culture of the early Arab conquests only when it suited them. When they wished to do things that might be seen as problematic in light of Islamic law and jurisprudence, they did so without hesitation, knowing that even in the unlikely event that one of the *ulama* objected, others would support whatever the sultan did. Many of their actions should have raised such flags, if Islam had been the vital force keeping the empire together. There was no way to justify fratricide and rebellion using the Quran or the hadith, nor was the harem or the system of eunuchs easy to reconcile with Islamic law.

The Ottoman legacy also forces us to reconsider what we mean when we say "Islam." The alliances that Suleyman cemented with the Catholic French did not lead anyone to question his bona fides as a Muslim. The autonomy that Mehmed granted to the Jews, Greek Orthodox, and Armenians did not trigger challenges to his standing as a devout believer. Islam, like any great religion, is an umbrella that encompasses a wide range of virtues and a multitude of sins. Scholars and judges may have retained a right to criticize the sultan, but they almost never exercised it. Rulers were seen as a necessary element because they held back the chaos that would inevitably ensue if the state collapsed.

Suleyman's death did not immediately remove the Ottomans as a threat to Europe. A century later, in 1683, another sultan again menaced Vienna, and he came very close to taking the city. But even had he succeeded, it is unlikely that the Ottomans would have overrun Europe. The Russians had become a formidable foe, as had the French and the English. And while its rivals had evolved, within the empire, little had changed. The Ottomans were slowly losing their competitive edge. After 1683, Europe began to push back, and the balance tipped. For centuries, the Ottomans had stood as monument to equilibrium. Then the empire began to fray, and when it finally collapsed in the early years of the twentieth century, relations between Muslims, Christians, and Jews took a turn for the worse.

✦✦ ✦✦

CHAPTER EIGHT

The Tide Begins to Turn

For THE FIRST thousand years after the death of Muhammad and the initial Arab conquests, the world of Islam expanded. There were setbacks, of course, some major and some not. The Crusades were a brief interregnum of Christian rule in the Near Eastern heartland, and the fall of Spain represented a significant loss. The Mongol invasion that decimated Baghdad and came close to overrunning North Africa was a severe test, but one that was ultimately met. The coming of the Ottomans in the fifteenth century revitalized the Muslim world, and thousands of miles away, the Moghuls, another Muslim dynasty, expanded south from what is now Pakistan into northern India. At the same time, Muslim merchants, fanning out from these centers, carried Islam across the Sahara into Western Africa and across the Indian Ocean to Indonesia. By the end of the sixteenth century, the reach of Islam was greater than it ever had been, and the call to prayer could be heard five times a day from Morocco to Java.

But while millions across continents identified themselves as Muslim, they did not form a cohesive community. In the second half of the twentieth century, as travel became safer, faster, and accessible to the masses, unprecedented numbers of Muslims became hajjis and journeyed to Mecca. There, they were thrust into contact with Muslims from around the globe, and that experience connected them as few things did to a sense of an international Muslim community. But before the innovations of the industrial age, before the telegraph, radio, television, airplanes, and automobiles, few Muslims made the pilgrimage to Mecca, and few had contact with anyone outside their family and village. Some trading centers bustled with merchants from far-off places, and cosmopolitan cities like Alexandria in Egypt, Istanbul and Salonica in the eastern Mediterranean, and Zanzibar on the coast of East Africa were crazy quilts of languages, foreign dress, and multiple currencies. On the whole, however, while Islam spanned the globe, most Muslims had little in common.

That meant that, save for a shared knowledge of the opening verses of the Quran and a few Arabic words memorized for daily prayers, a camel merchant in Khartoum was almost as alien to a fisherman in Java or a mason in Konya as each was to a tailor in London or a count in Versailles. Even within the Ottoman Empire, there was no one Islam. There was a religious establishment in Istanbul, with the *sheikh ul-Islam* nominally at the head of the religious class. He was appointed by the sultan, and like the chief rabbi or the Orthodox patriarch, he had the authority to issue edicts on questions of religious law that were binding on the *ulama* and on judges (*mufti*) throughout the empire. As often as not, however, the *sheikh ul-Islam* was either silent or his decrees were quietly ignored and trumped by local mores. The result was that hundreds of variants of law and traditions characterized Islam in the Ottoman world.

Complicating matters even further was the amorphous nature of Sufism. While Sufism first emerged as a mystical tradition, it also evolved into folk religion. Some Sufi lodges retained their mystical focus, and nurtured monasticism and meditation. Others, however, combined Muslim practices with whatever pre-Muslim traditions had existed before Islam took root. North Africa was home to Sufi "saints" who practiced magic, charmed snakes, and read auguries, and whose shrines became pilgrimage sites after they died. In the heart of Anatolia in the city of Konya, dervishes spun themselves into ecstasy chanting the words of their great master Rumi. In Indonesia, the bare-bones Islam of Muslim merchants fused with local variants of Hinduism and animism to form a religion that bore some of the trappings of traditional Islam but would have been as strange to the camel nomads of Arabia as it was to the Calvinist burghers of Amsterdam. In its many forms, Sufism became a grab bag of Islam and pre-Islamic traditions.

It is both familiar and convenient to talk of a "Muslim world" stretching from Morocco to Indonesia, but that has led to a widespread tendency to assume that Muslims historically had one cultural identity. Yes, there was a notion of an *umma,* of a Muslim community united in faith, just as there were vague notions of a Christendom united under the banner of Christ. But like Christianity, Islam splintered into hundreds of rival sects, and whatever cohesion it might initially have promised evaporated. In both "Christendom" and the "house of Islam" (as Muslims have called their world), religion was one identity among many. And what that identity meant to the political, social, or cultural life of any particular village, town, state, or society is beyond generalization.

Of the three religions, Judaism was perhaps the most cohesive, though Jews from northern Europe bore little resemblance to Jews from Yemen. Few in numbers and scattered across the Ottoman and European worlds, Jews during thousands of diaspora years had come to identify themselves as a scattered people divided into hundreds of villages, towns, and cities. As merchants, artisans, and bankers, they had developed international networks that survived different regimes, multiple dynasties, war, plague, and revolution. While the more agrarian Jewish peasants of Russia and the northern steppe slowly lost contact with the more urban, educated Jews of Western Europe and the Mediterranean, most Jews in the Ottoman Empire perceived themselves as one community. For Christians and Muslims, the picture was more ambiguous.

THE MILLET SYSTEM AND THE RISE OF THE WEST

OVER TIME, the semiautonomous religious communities of the Ottoman Empire became known as *millet*s and each had a leader appointed by the sultan. Each *millet* was self-governing, and its leader was responsible for assisting the Ottoman state in collecting taxes. The Jews had a chief rabbi, and the major Christian groups had a patriarch or bishop. There were also groups within groups. The Christian sects included the Greek Orthodox and the Armenians. There were also Maronites in Lebanon, Copts in Egypt, and Assyrians (also known as Nestorians) in Iraq. Even the Jews were divided into several millet communities.

The *millet* system did not resolve all conflicts. When issues arose between different *millet*s or between a member of a *millet* and a Muslim, the matter was referred to an Ottoman court. Sometimes, Christians or Jews tried to have internal disputes decided in an Ottoman court when they believed that Islamic law would render a more favorable verdict. Christians occasionally attempted to have their divorces validated in a Muslim court because the provisions for divorce under the sharia were less onerous. Catholics in particular were antagonistic to the idea of divorce, while Muslims, in general, were more flexible. Both Christian men and women looked to Muslim courts for assistance, and there were cases when a husband or wife, desperate to escape a bad marriage, converted to Islam for the sole purpose of ridding themselves of a troublesome spouse. And different Christian groups, who had been fighting one another for more than a thousand years, often took their disputes to Muslim courts because mutual animosity prevented either from respecting the other's laws and traditions.

Limitations aside, the *millet* system enjoyed the active support of its members. Jews in the Ottoman world were well aware of how much better it was to live in Salonica, Istanbul, or Izmir (Smyrna) than almost anywhere in Europe. The Ottoman ruling class continued the tradition begun by earlier Arab dynasties of employing Jews as physicians, and for most of his reign, Suleyman himself was attended to by a Jewish doctor in Istanbul. Prominent Jews had the ear of court officials, and used the Ottoman system to discredit or undermine rivals. On occasion, Jews served as intermediaries to European powers, especially during periods when diplomatic relations between the Ottomans and the princes of Western Europe were strained or severed.

The diverse Christian communities, though rarely satisfied with their status, understood that the autonomy they enjoyed under the Ottoman system was an improvement over what had come before. That didn't stop them from competing for influence, and throughout the seventeenth, eighteenth, and nineteenth centuries, Christian *millets* waged quiet campaigns against one another in provincial courts and in palace chambers in Istanbul. But these internecine conflicts existed under the watchful eye of the Ottoman state, which kept ancient rivalries from spinning out of control and into outright violence. Hatred and resentment festered, but actual fighting was kept to a minimum.

That fact did not go unnoticed or unappreciated. In the eighteenth century, the Greek patriarch in Jerusalem, who was well acquainted with the struggles between different Christian groups, lauded the Ottomans for all that they had done to keep the peace.

God raised out of nothing this powerful empire of the Ottomans, in place of our Roman [Byzantine] Empire which had begun ... to deviate from the beliefs of the Orthodox faith.... The all-mighty Lord has placed over us this high kingdom, for there is no power but of God, so as to be to the people of the West a bridle, to us the people of the East a means of salvation. For this reason he puts into the heart of the Sultan of these Ottomans an inclination to keep free the religious beliefs of our Orthodox faith and ... to protect them, even to the point of occasionally chastising Christians who deviate from the faith.[1]

For centuries under the Byzantines, a sizable minority of Christians had nurtured grievances and built up resentments against the Greek Orthodox, who dominated political and religious life. While the Orthodox were able to retain a measure of influence under the Ottomans, their story was one of relative decline. Other Christian communities took the defeat of the Byzantines as an opportunity to make up lost ground. The Armenians initially thrived under the *millet* system, and were able to carve out a sphere of autonomy and prosperity. Armenian merchants captured a monopoly on the trade of valuable items such as silk, and in provincial Anatolian towns such as Diyarbakir they had nearly as much power as at any point in their storied history.

Later, in the nineteenth and early twentieth centuries, the Armenians suffered from the emergence of Turkish nationalism, and more than a million were killed as a result of Turkish policies during World War I. But the treatment of the Armenians at the hands of early-twentieth-century Turks is in sharp relief to their success earlier in the empire's history. Only in the late nineteenth century, in its attempts at reform, did the Ottoman Empire move away from the decentralized *millet* system and begin to emulate the European model of centralization and modernization. With that came a more explosive and destructive force, nationalism, which was hostile to religion, rested on a secular view of the world, and would prove far more lethal to groups like the Armenians than the Ottoman ruling class ever was.

Until then, in many corners of the empire, Christians lived peacefully and securely. The island of Cyprus and much of the Peloponnesian Peninsula of Greece, for instance, were predominantly Christian when they fell under the control of the Ottomans, and they remained that way until the empire disintegrated. Conversion was less typical than it had been under the Umayyads and Abbasids. The Ottoman authorities did not encourage it, and at times actively discouraged it. Being Muslim was not a requirement for playing a meaningful role in the life of the empire.

True, non-Muslims never occupied the innermost sanctums of power in Istanbul. Politics, however, have always been local, and the Ottoman Empire was no exception. Christians tended to focus on their local community and region. The Orthodox Christians of Crete wanted dominion over the island, and so long as the Ottoman authorities were willing to abet those ambitions, they were content. Though Crete saw a higher rate of conversion than other parts of the empire, that was more a function of Cretan peasants looking to join the Janissaries than any active attempt by the Ottomans to evangelize. On the contrary, Ottoman governors and elites worked with the heads of the *millets* to prevent non-Muslims from converting. Given that the primary goal of the Ottoman state was to keep the family of Osman in power and the sultan's treasury full, conversion served no purpose. To the contrary, it threatened the delicate status quo. Conversion was change, and if there was one thing the Ottomans did not welcome after the sixteenth century, it was change.[2]

Unfortunately, change was forced on them. Uncurious about their enemies, the Ottomans after Suleyman complacently rested in the knowledge that they were the most powerful state in the world. The navies of Venice and the Habsburgs triumphed at the battle of Lepanto in 1571, but the Ottomans shrugged off the defeat the way an elephant shrugs off a gnat. They rebuilt their fleet within a year, and the balance in the eastern Mediterranean shifted hardly at all. But their enemies learned a crucial lesson from the victory: the Ottomans, formidable and feared, were not invincible.

It is hard to imagine a world frozen for more than two hundred years, but from the middle of the sixteenth century until late in the eighteenth, the Ottoman state was rarely as innovative as its European rivals. Some laws were rewritten, administrative districts were redrawn, and titles were changed. Sultans lived and died; inconclusive battles were fought against the Persians to the east; somewhat more conclusive ones were waged against the Hungarians, Austrians, and Russians to the north and west. But through it all, the core of the empire was untouched and undisturbed. The recruitment of the Janissaries, once so dramatic and disruptive, became routinized. The Janissaries were supposed to be celibate and loyal only to the sultan, but over time, they devolved into an interest group bent on their own self-perpetuation. They turned to commerce and industry to augment their income. Their officers took wives, and with that came familial ambitions. As the children of Janissaries themselves became Janissaries, the need for fresh blood decreased. The Janissaries lost the edge born of a harsh system of recruitment and training; they became less effective and less feared. Soon, they were simply one group—albeit a heavily armed one—competing for influence and prestige in Istanbul. They were the subject of endless gossip, the butt of countless jokes, a dangerous, independent force still living in barracks near the imperial palace, immersed in networks of graft and marriage with the elites of the capital, and a bulwark against any who might even think about reforming a system that was becoming a shadow of its former self.

Meanwhile, the states of Europe began to fight one another less and turned instead to conquering the world. After the Thirty Years' War nearly destroyed Central Europe, the princes and premiers gathered in Westphalia in 1648 and agreed not to wage wars over religion. The strength of the "Westphalian system" has been lauded and overstated, but it did lead to fewer pitched battles in the heart of Europe for the next century and a half, until the twin earthquakes of the French Revolution and the rise of Napoleon. For much of the seventeenth and eighteenth centuries, Europeans focused less on the Ottomans than on expanding across the seas. The Mediterranean remained a vital link in world trade, but the Venetian stranglehold on commerce in what was otherwise an Ottoman lake spurred the Spanish, Portuguese, Dutch, and English voyages of exploration that led to the discovery of the New World and the extension of European influence throughout the globe.

The Venetians and the Ottomans continued to skirmish over Crete, Malta, and other strategic islands. At the same time, Venice was the European gateway for trade with the Ottoman world, conducted through intermediaries such as Jews, Greek Orthodox, and Armenians who resided in cities such as Salonica, Alexandria, Smyrna, Istanbul, and Beirut. The regular flow of foreign goods was an important source of revenue for the Ottomans, and the state welcomed European merchants even as the sultan retained designs on conquering Europe itself.

Until 1683, the Ottomans had good reason to believe that they might achieve what Suleyman had not. In that year, a new army was raised for the sole purpose of taking Vienna. The other cities of the Danube had succumbed to Ottoman rule, and Vienna was all that remained between the sultan and the fertile lands of Germany and Poland. The sultan's armies, led by the grand vizier Kara Mustafa, seemed on the verge of victory when an unexpected ally came to the rescue. The Polish king, Jan Sobieski, at the head of a substantial force, injected new life into the defenders, inflicted severe casualties on the Janissaries, and caused the Ottomans to withdraw in confusion. The defeat led Sultan Mehmed IV to order the gruesome execution of Kara Mustafa. It also permanently shifted the momentum from the Ottomans to the West. The war between the Ottomans and the Habsburgs technically ended in a stalemate, but in truth, it was a defeat for the sultan.

For the next century, the empire drifted. While the ruling class hardly noticed, others did. Slowly, quietly, almost imperceptibly, the non-Muslims of the empire became less content with the status quo. At times, that triggered a reaction. Local *ulama* would issue edicts designed to put the People of the Book in their place. These included restrictions on dress and attempts to make it more difficult for Jews or Christians to build churches or synagogues. But these were isolated incidents, short-lived and usually ineffective. Ottoman Jews found themselves less secure, but the reason had less to do with the Ottomans than it did with the influence of Europeans. As the states of Europe started to expand internationally, they looked to the Christians—and not the Jews—of the Ottoman lands as natural allies. Those Ottoman Christians welcomed the support, and they began to supplant Jewish merchants and businessmen.

But there was one other reason for the shifting fortunes of the Jews of the Ottoman Empire, which spoke to both the strength and the weakness of the Ottoman order. In 1665, a Jew from Smyrna proclaimed himself the messiah. It was not the first time such claims had been made, nor was it to be the last. But it was certainly one of the most divisive and disruptive, as much for its ending as for its beginning.

SABBATAI SEVI

SABBATAI SEVI was born to a prosperous merchant family. His father, Mordecai, had been a successful chicken merchant who was not content with the life of a poulterer. In Smyrna, on the Aegean coast of Anatolia, he switched careers and became an intermediary for European merchants. It was common for European businessmen to hire locals who could serve as translators and as representatives who would ensure that goods were delivered and paid for on time. Mordecai Sevi helped make at least one English merchant quite wealthy, and that merchant in turn enriched him. Unfortunately for Mordecai, his successful life and what might have been a decent legacy were obliterated by his son.

Sabbatai had not lived long when people began to notice that there was something strange about him. Few records of his life are unbiased; his chroniclers were either defenders or prosecutors. But friends and foes agreed that Sabbatai, from a young age, was not like others. Manic at times, sullen at others, he entered an altered state while praying, and at synagogue he was a powerful, disturbing presence. To his acolytes, he was a teenager who showed signs of divinity, including miraculous and inexplicable actions. It was said that he glowed when he prayed, that he was given to loud and disturbing outbursts, that his body emitted a faint yet unmistakable perfume that marked him as an anointed one. To his detractors, he bore all the marks of a madman, and that was why, barely into his twenties, he was asked to leave his home city and forced into an exile that would eventually take him to the Holy Land. His community could have tolerated his odd behavior. His obsessive interest in the kabbalah, uncomfortable though it was for the rabbinical establishment, could also have been accepted. But his very sudden and very public declaration that he was the messiah—that was going too far.

Expelled by the rabbis of Smyrna, he made his way across the Aegean to Salonica, which then had a Jewish majority. He was welcomed and honored as a scholar of the Lurianic kabbalah. The mystic rabbi Isaac Luria had lived and died in Safed, in Palestine, in the sixteenth century and had developed a secretive reading of the Torah that explicated the relationship between God and man. By design, the complexity of Luria's system defies easy explanation. It was a stew that combined the major religious and philosophical traditions of the Near East. Luria held that the Genesis stories of creation and the expulsion from the Garden of Eden were metaphors for the fragmentation of the divine. Centuries earlier, Ibn Arabi of Spain had spoken of the unity of God and man, a unity that was continually obscured by human inability to see the truth. Luria went a step further, and suggested that the divine had been splintered and that the point of human life was to help it reassemble. At some point, an intermediary would appear who would enable both God and man to become whole once again. Sabbatai Sevi claimed to be that someone.

Once it became clear to the rabbis of Salonica who Sabbatai Sevi thought he was, they expelled him. Sabbatai had enthralled many of those who came to listen to his interpretation of the Torah, and that disturbed the conservative rabbis, who saw him as both mentally unstable and a threat to their status. He did little to assuage their concerns, and in fact seems to have taken delight in flouting their authority. They responded predictably, and sent him on his way. This pattern was repeated in city after city as Sevi moved from Salonica to Athens to Cairo to Jerusalem and finally to Gaza, where in 1665 he proclaimed his mission—to lead an army of followers to Istanbul, announce the coming of a new age, and supplant the Ottoman sultan.

News of this new messiah spread quickly throughout the Jewish world. Sabbatai provided ample grist for the international gossip mill. He violated one of the cardinal rules of Judaism and spoke the name of God; he allowed women to recite the Torah in public; he declared that the laws of the Hebrew Scriptures were null until a new testament could be written; he appointed deputies as kings (and queens) of various parts of the Ottoman Empire and Europe; and he claimed that his disciples were the reincarnated souls of long-dead prophets.

From Poland, Germany, and Italy to the metropolises of the Ottoman Empire, Sabbatai Sevi gained adherents. Steeped in the mystical end-of-times prophecies of the kabbalah, Jewish communities throughout the Near East and Europe were receptive to the message that a new messiah had finally arrived, one who would overturn the old laws, announce a new covenant, and restore the kingdom of the Jews. Sevi interpreted the international euphoria as a favorable sign. He marched to Istanbul convinced that the waters would part, the sultan would bow, and a new age would begin. As for his followers, thousands left their homes and converged on Istanbul, certain of "the imminent establishment of the kingdom of Israel, the fall of the Crescent and of all the royal crowns in Christendom."[3]

The sultan and his vizier, who were occupied with a war against the Venetians over the island of Crete, viewed Sevi as a minor threat. In the greater scheme of the empire, he was insignificant, but even the insignificant can irritate. As long as he remained in the provinces, he could be ignored. He may have been important to his followers, but he was a nonentity to the Ottomans—until he marched on Istanbul proclaiming the end of the empire and the coming of a new kingdom. Then he aroused a response.

Soon after arriving in Istanbul, Sevi was arrested. He might have been left in jail indefinitely, but the influx of pilgrims who had come to greet the new messiah was not something that the sultan was prepared to tolerate. On the orders of the vizier, who astutely used the movement to solidify his status as the sultan's most humble servant, Sevi was taken to the summer palace a hundred miles from Istanbul in Edirne (Adrianople), and offered a choice: he could suffer execution for inciting rebellion, or he could renounce his faith and convert. To the horror and astonishment of his followers, he decided to convert. According to most accounts, he did so willingly, even cheerfully, and required little coaxing before he denounced the religion of the Torah, recited the Muslim profession of faith—"There is no God but God, and Muhammad is his Prophet"—in Arabic, in front of the sultan, and took a new name, Aziz Mehmet Effendi.

The story, however, does not end there. Sevi was released from prison, and most of his followers drifted away, shocked that their messiah had committed an act of apostasy and embraced Islam rather than dying for his faith. A few, however, did not quite see it that way. Rather than interpreting what had happened as a repudiation, they claimed that Sevi's actions were part of a master plan revealed in the kabbalah. His supposed conversion was a test of his followers. Jewish communities became sharply divided between those who remained faithful to Sevi's vision and those who renounced him for having renounced them.

As for Sabbatai himself, he remained in Istanbul and Edirne, supported by a smaller group of acolytes. Some of them converted; some did not. Surrounded by an unlikely community composed of Jews, Muslims, and Jews who had converted to Islam, Sevi was once again at the center of his world, looked to for leadership and guidance. Soon after his release from prison, he proclaimed that he and his Muslim disciples were not really Muslims but were indeed fulfilling a mysterious kabbalistic prophecy. In 1672, the Ottoman authorities reacted to the provocation and exiled Sabbatai and his group to a remote part of the Albanian coast on the Adriatic, where he died in 1676.

For the sultan and his court, Sabbatai Sevi's movement was a sideshow that for a brief moment looked as if it might lead to an uprising of the empire's Jewish population. Revolts by disaffected groups were not uncommon but neither were they frequent. They happened, and they required attention. When the issue could not be resolved by suasion and money, it was handled with swift and brutal efficiency by the Janissaries. Sabbatai Sevi spared his followers certain death by his act of conversion, though whether that was part of his motivation we will never know. His memory survived in Jewish communities, and his life gave rise to legends and kabbalistic prophecies about the end of days. For the Ottomans, however, the movement barely registered.

That is itself a testament to the supreme capacity of the Ottomans to maintain order. Faced with an uprising led by a man who loudly announced his intention to overthrow the sultan, the government reacted calmly, deliberately, and effectively. The fact that the man was a Jew who claimed to be the messiah, as well as the fact that he proclaimed that his revelation would supersede not just the Old Testament but also any subsequent messages in the New Testament and the Quran, did not in and of itself agitate the Ottoman authorities. They were secure enough to tolerate outrageous claims. When Sevi crossed the line from rabble-rouser to rebel and marched on the imperial capital, only then was he arrested, imprisoned, and sentenced to death. His crime had less to do with creed than with law and order.

Sevi's movement tells us a good deal about the nature of the Ottoman state and about the status of non-Muslims within it. One of the most striking things was how quickly Sevi's message spread throughout the empire and into Europe. Within months of announcing his mission and marching on Istanbul, word had reached every Jewish community in Europe and the Near East. The seventeenth century was hardly notable for the ease of travel and communication, yet knowledge of Sabbatai Sevi penetrated the farthest corners of Poland, Russia, Greece, and the Near East with remarkable speed. That shows how connected the Jewish community was, even though it was spread out among different states. Jews were international conduits not just of commerce but of information as well. Sevi's story also highlights that one way the Ottomans were able to remain in control of their vast territory was through well-developed and equally well-maintained networks of both communication and transportation.

The movement also demonstrates just how indifferent to religion the Ottomans could be. As long as Sevi didn't challenge the state, his actions were permitted. He could travel freely and unencumbered from one part of the empire to another, say what he wished, and never be required to answer to any Ottoman authority outside of Istanbul. He was forced out of different places not by the Ottomans, but by conservative rabbis who were concerned about their own positions and his potential to unseat them. Sabbatai Sevi lived his entire life in the Ottoman Empire, but even as a rebel, his contact with the state was limited. Once he had converted, he was left alone, and only after repudiating his conversion and hinting that his movement would again challenge the sultan did the state once again take action against him.

STRENGTH BECOMES WEAKNESS

THE WAY that the Ottomans handled Sevi is emblematic of the way they managed an imperium of different races, religions, and peoples. They took Occam's Razor to heart, and believed that the simplest solution was usually the best. They understood that in matters of state, less was often more, and that to maintain the equilibrium, they would take action only when it was forced upon them.

That allowed communities as diverse as Jews, Armenians, Greek Orthodox, Moroccans, Egyptians, Bulgars, Serbs, and Turks to thrive. The tolerance that permitted communities to go about their lives and pursue their own particular ambitions was a strength. The fact that Istanbul contained Janissaries, Ottoman princes, Armenian and Greek merchants and craftsmen, and Jewish doctors, to name a few, contributed to its greatness. Some of the world's most vital urban centers have been the product of different groups living next to one another, if not actually with one another. Rome in its imperial grandeur teemed with peoples from every corner of Europe and the Mediterranean, and New York in the nineteenth century flourished with a population that consisted mostly of immigrants.

Ottoman diversity amazed the elites of Europe. In the early 1700s, Lady Mary Wortley Montagu, the colorful, erudite wife of the British ambassador to the Ottoman court, wrote an astute account of Ottoman life. In addition to deflating some of the cherished English myths of the lascivious harem, Lady Montagu described an Istanbul defined by variety. "My grooms," she wrote, "are Arabs, my footmen, French, English and German, my nurse an Armenian, my housemaids Russian, half a dozen other servants Greeks; my steward an Italian; my Janissaries Turks, [and] I live in the perpetual hearing of this medley of sounds." There was nothing unusual about the Montagu household retinue. It was a microcosm of a cosmopolitan society. Little did Lady Montagu realize that the empire was slowly decaying.

When the empire finally crumbled in the late nineteenth and early twentieth centuries, one of the first casualties was tolerance. Armenians suffered near annihilation, and Christians in the Balkans were brutalized. But these events should not stand as an indictment of earlier centuries, or be used as a proxy for five centuries of Ottoman history. Tolerance and coexistence were real, even if they dissipated at the end.

If tolerance was an Ottoman strength, lack of curiosity about the wider world was a weakness. The states of Europe, locked in deadly competition with one another, could not afford to be insular. As they jockeyed for advantage, they spread throughout the known and the unknown world. That meant not just voyaging to the Americas and beyond, but also paying more attention to the Ottomans.

Lucrative trade was reason enough to attract the revenue-hungry European states. Given that the Ottomans were less interested in coming to them (at least not until the eighteenth century), they came to the Ottomans. The empire accommodated them with the same level of indifference that it accorded to protected minorities, but Ottoman officials did make it clear that European merchants and official representatives were to limit their activities to trade. That was fine with the Europeans, who proceeded to open consulates and offices in the major ports and trading centers. The only condition they demanded was the right to be tried in their own courts. The Ottomans, accustomed to allowing the *millet*s to govern themselves, agreed. They also permitted select nations to pay lower tariffs on the goods they imported and exported, which was a boon to trade but ultimately a bane to the Ottoman treasury. Known as "capitulations," the self-governance that foreigners in the empire enjoyed became a wedge that helped the states of Europe undermine the Ottomans. Though the system initially spurred economic activity to the mutual benefit of European merchants and the Ottoman state, as European power grew and Ottoman influence waned, the Ottomans came to regret the concessions they had made.

By the middle of the eighteenth century, it was clear to the major European powers that the Ottomans were becoming weaker. The Janissaries were no longer a premier fighting force, and instead were corrupt, undisciplined, and unable to compete with the more technologically advanced armies of the West. While the Ottomans suffered significant defeats on their borders north of the Balkans and in the Caucasus, these were not yet severe enough to shake the complacency. Said one wise European envoy,

> The Ottomans will probably persist in their errors for some time, and submit to be repeatedly defeated for years, before they will be reconciled to such a change; so reluctant are all nations, whether it proceeds from self-love, laziness, or folly, to relinquish old customs: even good institutions make their progress but slowly among us.... The Turks are now an instance of the same; for it is neither in courage, numbers nor riches, but in discipline and order that they are defective.[4]

The end of the eighteenth century brought more military setbacks. The Russians, flush from the reforms of Peter the Great decades earlier, expanded their reach. As the tsar's armies advanced south, the Ottomans were swept aside. The Russian victories signaled to the other states of Europe that the Ottomans were now an easy mark, and had it not been for the French Revolution and the subsequent wars that racked the continent, the empire might have faced even greater pressures. Instead it was given a respite, and successive sultans used the opportunity to make the first tentative steps toward change.

For too long, the Ottoman ruling class, not to mention most of the empire's inhabitants, mistook internal stability for strength. At the end of the eighteenth century, the court still treated foreigners with disdain, and still demanded obeisance from European envoys. Ottoman emissaries to foreign states expected the sort of deference that the Romans had demanded from the Gauls and were shocked and appalled when that was not forthcoming. Many Europeans saw through the veil of vanity and observed an arrogant, decrepit state. In the words of one English envoy:

> It is undeniable that the power of the Turks was once formidable to their neighbors not by their numbers only, but by their military and civil institutions, far surpassing those of their opponents. And they all trembled at the name of the Turks, who with a confidence procured by their constant successes, held the Christians in no less contempt as warriors than they did on account of their religion. Proud and vainglorious, conquest was to them a passion, a gratification, and even a means of salvation, a sure way of immediately attaining a delicious paradise. Hence their zeal for the extension of their empire; hence their profound respect for the military profession, and their glory even in being obedient and submissive to discipline.
>
> Besides that the Turks refuse all reform, they are seditious and mutinous; their armies are encumbered with immense baggage, and their camp has all the conveniences of a town, with shops etc. for such was their ancient custom when they wandered with their hordes. When their sudden fury is abated, which is at the least obstinate resistance, they are seized with a panic, and have no rallying as formerly. The cavalry is as much afraid of their own infantry as of the enemy; for in a defeat they fire at them to get their horses to escape more quickly. In short, it is a mob assembled rather than an army levied. None of those numerous details of a well-organized body, necessary to give quickness, strength, and regularity to its actions, to avoid confusion, to repair damages, to apply to every part to some use; no systematic attack, defense, or retreat; no accident foreseen, nor provided for....
>
> The artillery they have, and which is chiefly brass, comprehends many fine pieces of cannon; but notwithstanding the reiterated instruction of so many French engineers, they are ignorant of its management. Their musket-barrels are much esteemed but they are too heavy; nor do they possess any quality superior to common iron barrels which have been much hammered, and are very soft Swedish iron. The art of tempering their sabers is now lost, and all the blades of great value are ancient. The naval force of the Turks is by no means considerable. Their grand fleet consisted of not more than

seventeen or eighteen sail of the line in the last war, and those not in very good condition; at present their number is lessened.[5]

By the early nineteenth century, even the sultan, who would have been the last to be informed that he was not wearing any clothes, noticed that the comparative position of the empire was becoming untenable. It was one thing to observe that fact, but it was quite another to know what to do about it. Not surprisingly, successive sultans and their advisers tackled that portion of the problem that seemed amenable to a solution: the military. If the deficiencies of the empire were most apparent in battles with the powers of Europe, then it made sense to remake the military. If European guns and ships were overwhelming Ottoman forces, then it was obvious that the sultan needed new guns, new ships, and soldiers capable of using them. But no matter how much the Ottomans tried to revamp the army, they kept losing battles. Having suffered a series of humiliating defeats, the Ottoman elite in Istanbul finally recognized that the changes required were more extensive than buying new guns.

The pivotal figure was Mahmud II, who came to power in 1808 after Sultan Selim III had been overthrown in a plot concocted by enraged Janissaries who feared (rightly) that Selim meant to build a new army and make them obsolete. Having survived a tumultuous two years during which the Janissaries attempted to rule the empire through a puppet sultan, Mahmud vowed that he would respect the status quo, but he lied, and lied brilliantly. He had no intention of allowing the Janissaries to retain a monopoly on military affairs. The Balkans were beginning to exhibit disturbing signs of unrest. The Arabian Peninsula had recently seen the emergence of the religious puritan Muhammad ibn Abd al-Wahhab, who in alliance with the Saudi tribe called for a return to the simple faith of Muhammad and was willing to eradicate anyone who did not agree. And Egypt and Palestine had fallen under the control of an Albanian mercenary appointed by Istanbul, who managed to fend off the Europeans while signaling to Istanbul that he would no longer heed the sultan's orders.

Until the nineteenth century, most of the millions who lived under the Ottoman state would have been unaware of these large trends. The wars of Europe, the military innovations of the French, Germans, and English, and the changing patterns of world trade were so distant as to be nonexistent. Before the sudden, unanticipated French invasion of Egypt in 1798, daily life in Cairo in the eighteenth century wasn't markedly different from daily life in the sixteenth or seventeenth centuries. The same could be said of Morocco and Syria and central Anatolia. The *millet* system continued much as it had, becoming more refined and more tightly organized as part of the modest reforms of Ottoman administrative system in the late seventeenth century, but not in ways that would have made a Christian in the Peloponnesus or a Jew in Smyrna perceive any radical shift in status.

What did change, inexorably, was the place of the Ottomans in the world, and that had much to do with events beyond their control. The reason for the sudden and dramatic rise of the West at the expense of the rest remains one of the great unsolved riddles of the modern world. There is no lack of theories, but there is no one settled answer. The countries of Europe had fought one another to a standstill for so long that they had been forced to innovate, and to find new sources of revenue and better technology. European nations were forged in a cauldron of war and hatred, and emerged on the world stage uniquely capable of fighting. They combined the ruthlessness of all great powers past and present with the means to enforce their will. The Ottoman Empire was only one of the many obstacles that stood between them and the world, and it withstood the onslaught better than most.

For the first time in the history of Muslim societies, however, the trajectory shifted from offense to defense. As we have seen, there had been earlier setbacks, during the Crusades, in Spain, and for the brief but devastating Mongol interregnum. But then the Ottomans had appeared and restored the narrative to its proper form, with Sunni Muslims ruling and the People of the Book ruled or on the defensive. Early in the nineteenth century, it became clear to both the Ottoman elite and to the Europeans that the empire could no longer resist the expansion of the West. The thousand-year history of Muslim dominance had come to an end.

Muslim societies spent more than a millennium accustomed to power. They have spent the past two hundred years dealing with the loss of it. They met the challenges of dominance; they are still struggling with the challenges of defeat.

CHAPTER NINE

Brave New Worlds

T HE SHIFT FROM dominance to decline occurred gradually. There was no one pivotal military loss that marked the end, but the reversal was shocking all the same. From the early decades of the seventh century until the nineteenth century, states ruled by Muslims had validated the promise of the Quran and the early Arab conquests. They had vanquished or outlasted all rivals; they had carefully constructed social orders based on the preeminence of Islam relative to other religions; and for the most part, they had enjoyed the rewards of success. The ascendency of the West in the nineteenth century, therefore, was as revolutionary and disruptive as the rise of Islam had been twelve centuries before.

To reiterate, until the nineteenth century, relations between Muslims, Christians, and Jews had unfolded in the context of Muslim dominance. Even in those periods and places where that wasn't the case, such as the twelfth-century Crusader states and Spain after the thirteenth century, the patterns that had been established under Muslim rule conditioned how the three different faiths interacted. Religion, as we have seen, was only one of many factors shaping these societies, but it did define boundaries and it did set limits. At no point was it a simple matter for a Christian to marry a Muslim, or a Jew to marry either, and that in itself guaranteed a degree of separateness. But over the centuries, under Muslim rule, Christians and Jews had been able to lead their lives and contribute in meaningful ways to the shape and success of their societies.

Beginning in the nineteenth century, the states of Europe came to dominate the Muslim world. This included the Ottoman Empire, as well as Persia, India, and Indonesia, each of which had substantial Muslim populations—and in the case of India, a Muslim emperor. The expansion of Europe was, as political scientists might say, "overdetermined." There was no one reason; there were many, ranging from economic to political to religious and ideological. But insofar as most inhabitants of these European nations were Christian, it is fair to call them "Christian states." Just as Islam was a central part of the identity of the Muslim world, Christianity was woven into European manners, mores, and attitudes. Granted, European nations had an ambivalent relationship to Christianity, at times bringing the gospel to the unconverted masses around the globe, at other time abjuring religion in the name of secular progress. But while it has been common to overstate the place of religion in both the Muslim world and in Europe, it would be a mistake to go too far in the other direction. Especially at times of head-to-head competition between states whose rulers were Muslim and states whose leaders were Christian, religion could be central. Just as Muslims had both implicitly and explicitly taken their worldly success as a sign of divine favor, Christian states in the nineteenth century attributed their strength not only to country but to God as well.

With few exceptions, the nineteenth century has gained a bad historical reputation. American historians may glory in the history of the United States during these years, and historians of science can point to discovery after discovery. On the whole, however, the century has been seen as the placid middle child between the revolutions of the eighteenth century and the transformations of the twentieth. Generations of writers and scholars in the second half of the twentieth century heaped scorn on the nineteenth century as a period of harsh industrialization marked by a rapacious West sweeping across the globe in a fit of nationalist, capitalist imperialism that despoiled the riches of countless societies and left them hobbled. That remains the prevailing thesis, and it is fair to say that the nineteenth century has a dowdy image in comparison to the Enlightenment, the Renaissance, or (thankfully) the horrific drama of the first half of the twentieth century.

The rise of the West and its effects on the rest of the world also have their known history and their forgotten. A vocal minority defensively celebrate the civilizing mission of the West in spreading liberalism and democracy throughout the world, and they trumpet the Industrial Revolution as a vital step in the march of modern progress. But more preva-

lent today is history that treats the West as a malign force and empha-
sizes the destructive effects of imperialism on the non-Western world.
This perspective holds that Muslim societies suffered acutely from the
rise of Europe, and that the roots of the present problems confronting
states from Morocco to Afghanistan were planted in the 1800s.[1] This
vision of the nineteenth century and of relations between the West and
the rest paints a dark picture of Western power and its effects on the
globe.

To be fair, these debates are more active in academia than in popular
culture, especially in the United States. In England, there is an audience
for popular books about the Victorians and what they wrought, but few
nonacademics in the United States pay attention to what happened in
the mid-nineteenth century outside America. While textbooks in England try to give a sense of the pros and cons of empire, the tendency in
the past decades on both sides of the Atlantic has been to decry the negative effects of empire. As for the Middle East and other parts of the
world, the nineteenth century is seen as a sorry, sad period of setbacks
and decline punctuated by Western imperialism. It is said that the
humiliation of Muslim societies at the hands of Western states, and of
the Arabs, Persians, and Turks in particular, produced a legacy of hatred
and animosity that eventually led to the fundamentalism, violence, and
terrorism of the late twentieth and early twenty-first centuries. The
nineteenth century, therefore, carries a heavy burden—even without
including the forces of nationalism that originated in the later part of the
1800s and have been held responsible for the wars that not only eviscer-
ated Europe but wreaked havoc on much of the world between 1914 and
1945.

The problem, once again, is not that this history is wrong, but that
it is incomplete. Side by side with military defeats and Western expansion was a spectrum of coexistence and cooperation. While nationalism
eventually proved to be a destructive force in the wars of the twentieth
century, in its early forms it was closely linked to liberal, progressive
ideals. While the imperial experiment ultimately left a sour aftertaste, it
had redeeming features. Fueled by the Enlightenment and by the forces
unleashed by the French Revolution, Europeans spread across the globe
and exported a hodgepodge of ideals that included an unshakable belief
in human progress. And while there was ever and always a racial component to European attitudes toward everyone else, there was also a will-

ingness to view all human beings as capable and able to attain the highest levels of civilization.

In the Muslim world, nineteenth-century European expansion triggered both resistance and accommodation. Unable to defeat the states of Europe on the battlefield, Muslim rulers from Istanbul to Cairo to Persia and India did what they could to adapt. It was more than a simple tale of European aggression. The notion of progress was appealing and infectious. It held out the possibility that with reform, any state and any society could join the ranks of the elite, and that the gap between Europe and the rest would be a temporary phenomenon.

The belief in progress was dealt a severe blow by the wars of the twentieth century, but on the whole, it remains deeply entrenched in both the United States and Western Europe. Even Communism was a utopian system based on the notion that a better world was within reach if only society could be reorganized. The American creed that everything is possible embraces progress as an essential component to life, liberty, and the pursuit of happiness. It is difficult, therefore, to remember that the notion of progress is a recent phenomenon, a product mostly of the past few hundred years. Medieval Europe at best promised a better world in the hereafter. The idea that the future could and would be better than the present was alien. Few embraced change for its own sake, and most resisted it. In the nineteenth century, as Europeans distanced themselves from both organized religion and the divine rule of kings, the belief in progress filled the void.

There was something naive yet seductively universal about the cult of progress. It was critical of the old systems that had purportedly kept mankind from realizing its full potential. That meant disdain for established religion and for political systems that had governed people from time immemorial. The guiding spirit of the cult of progress was the French Revolution, which enshrined the notion that any state could reform and thereby unleash the full potential of its citizens. Imbued with the spirit of innovation, people could transform the material world using technology and remake society using the tools of philosophy and science.

The belief in progress shaped how Muslim societies and Western Christian states interacted. Just as the American Revolution cannot be understood without looking at the ideas of liberty and freedom that fueled it, the interaction between Muslims, Christians, and Jews in the nineteenth century was framed not just by Western expansion but by a potent set of ideas about the untapped potential of human beings and the promise of a future better than anyone had ever known.

Here, as throughout this complicated story of relations between Muslims, Christians, and Jews, it is not a question of either-or. There are ample episodes of rapacious greed, racism, and abuse meted out by the imperial powers of the West on the rest. There are numerous times when they found surrogates to do their bidding. None of that negates the other history, of coexistence and cooperation.

So while it is true that Western states used raw power to dominate the world, it is also true that they found willing and avid partners who were devoted to the progress of their societies. Unfortunately, most of those who joined hands with Western states to work for progress, many of whom were heroes at the time, became scapegoats in the twentieth century, denigrated as fools and collaborators in their own subjugation by the West. Some were fools, no doubt, but not all, or even most. A closer look reveals that they often understood the ways of the world better than those who caricatured and lampooned them a century later. They recognized the weakness of their societies, confronted their limitations, and partnered with Western states in order to reform. They were willing to undertake the hard work of change. They were Muslims who decided to cooperate with Christian states, who did not look first to religion for answers, and often not even for guidance. And at times they were met not by Europeans who wanted to subjugate them but by Westerners who looked to them as allies in a common, human cause.

THE SICK MAN OF EUROPE

THROUGHOUT the nineteenth century, the fate of the Ottoman Empire was inextricably entwined with European politics. From Napoleon's invasion of Egypt in 1798 through World War I, the states of Europe fought over who would claim which Ottoman lands. As the century wore on, the empire shrank, and province after province either was absorbed into Europe's orbit or became an independent state in its own right.

After the Congress of Vienna in 1815, which ended the long period of war that had wracked the continent since the French Revolution, the countries of Europe competed with one another, not by fighting directly but by carving up the globe. The balance of power in Europe was maintained at the expense of anything but a stable balance of power globally. The Ottoman Empire, sitting directly on the frontiers of Europe, was both more vulnerable to European encroachment and more able to ward off annihilation.

By midcentury, the Ottomans became a crucial player in European politics. The empire was treated as a hobbled but important component of the diplomatic system that kept peace on the continent. Too weak to defend themselves on the battlefield, the Ottomans survived because no European state wanted another European state to occupy Istanbul and thereby gain control of the sea lanes connecting the Black Sea to the Mediterranean. The empire was kept on life support, but the sultan understood that in order to keep Europe at bay, his diplomats would have to become master manipulators—and they did. Astute at survival but never strong enough to compete militarily, the empire became known as the "Sick Man of Europe."

For much of the nineteenth century, European ministers jockeyed for influence in Istanbul, and the armies of Europe nibbled at the empire's edges. Every foreign ministry had a department dedicated to the "eastern question," and more than once during the century, the system established at the Congress of Vienna threatened to disintegrate in the face of a crisis involving the Ottomans.[2] This was usually the result of a European state attacking an Ottoman province or demanding unreasonable concessions from the sultan and his vizier. But some of the challenges came from within the empire, and one of them nearly ended its life.

In 1798, Napoleon Bonaparte invaded Egypt. His career in Paris was at a standstill, and his plans for a cross-channel assault on England were not going well. Convinced that if he stayed in Paris he would become lost in the political labyrinth, and even more convinced that it was his destiny to reshape the world, he decided to undermine England by striking at its empire. By taking Egypt, which was then under Ottoman control, Napoleon hoped to disrupt England's plans in India and beyond. The choice of Egypt was strategically questionable, and Napoleon remained in the desert land for only two years, until Admiral Nelson destroyed the French fleet off Alexandria. But while Napoleon's invasion was a sideshow to the larger continental conflict between France and everyone else, it set in motion a chain of events that fundamentally altered not just the Ottoman Empire but the future history of Muslim societies and their interaction with the West.

Since its conquest by Suleyman at the beginning of the sixteenth century, Egypt had been left alone by Istanbul. The old Mameluke elite still dominated the country, and though the Ottoman governor was in theory the most powerful official, the appointees sent by Istanbul depended on the Mamelukes to make sure taxes were collected and order was maintained. Egypt was also home to a large and prosperous Coptic Christian population, and Cairo and Alexandria sheltered an affluent and established Jewish community. Napoleon shattered that calm. The Mamelukes, who had not fought a battle of consequence for centuries, were comically overmatched. The French, even in the dead of summer, even after a scorching, debilitating march across the desert from Alexandria to Cairo, destroyed the Mameluke army in an afternoon.

The ease of the victory did not surprise Napoleon. He knew how weak his adversary was, and he had planned for the occupation of the country by bringing administrators and civil servants on the expedition. He also gathered a group of scholars, known as the *savants*, who were tasked with the study of Egyptian life and history. These mathematicians, engineers, geographers, linguists, and historians were given the responsibility of classifying and cataloging Egyptian culture. They had the eye of clinicians and they were acolytes of the religion of progress, which had triumphed when the French king was humbled, deposed, and finally executed. The French Revolution represented the demise of a social order based on God and king, and the intellectuals who accompanied Napoleon, as well as Napoleon himself, looked to a new world where reason and science would trump faith. Trained at the Polytechnic School in Paris, the *savants* treated Egypt as a canvas primed for a new tableau.

The French Revolution, whose radical leaders renamed 1793 as "Year 1," embodied the spirit of an era when men (and they were mostly men) believed that society could be purged of past impurities. Organized religion was perceived as one of those impurities. The revolutionaries treated religion, and Catholicism in particular, as a primitive force, hostile to inquiry and reason, and inimical to science and progress. The *savants* were scarcely more forgiving of Islam, but Napoleon at least was sensitive to the vital role of religious authorities in maintaining the status quo in Egypt. With less than fifty thousand troops, he intended to govern a large, mostly desert country, and he needed the tacit cooperation of the *ulama* to achieve that. In both Alexandria and Cairo, he issued proclamations declaring that he had no fight with Islam, only with the Mamelukes. Earlier, in Italy, Napoleon had ordered his troops not to interfere with religious leaders, including rabbis. He reiterated those commands in Egypt: "Deal with them as you dealt with Jews and with Italians," he commanded. "Respect their *muftis* and their *imans*, as you respected rabbis and bishops. Show the same tolerance towards the ceremonies prescribed by the Koran that you showed towards convents and synagogues."

Not since the fall of Granada in 1492 had a Christian power occupied a major Muslim metropolis. Though Napoleon and many of the revolutionary soldiers did not think of themselves as Christian armies, the inhabitants of Cairo did. They were shocked at what they took to be the barbarity of the French. Napoleon had scarcely begun to establish himself in the city when a revolt broke out. As he had demonstrated in suppressing rebellions in Italy, Napoleon was ruthless when challenged. His artillery shelled densely populated areas, and his soldiers occupied the precincts of Al-Azhar Mosque. The behavior of the French, both during these weeks and after, fueled the anger of at least one notable Azhar sheikh, al-Jabarti. In his meticulous multivolume history of the French occupation, al-Jabarti was scathing in his denunciations of the French and was appalled at how filthy, rude, and uncultured they were. He expressed the outrage of many of Cairo's leading citizens about the disrespectful way French troops behaved in Al-Azhar, alleging that "they treated the books and Koranic volumes as trash, throwing them on the ground, stamping on them with their feet and shoes.... They soiled the mosque, blowing their snot in it, pissing and defecating in it. They guzzled wine and smashed their bottles in the central court."[3]

What al-Jabarti interpreted as disrespect for Islam, however, was something rather different for the French army. At that time, flush with the spirit of the French Revolution and imbued with the fervor of their charismatic but somewhat amoral general, the French were at best indifferent and at worst acutely hostile to religion in general. They had no particular animus toward Islam as Islam. In fact, they almost certainly had more rage toward Catholicism, which they saw as an impediment to the evolution of humanity. They scorned Islam, not because of its particular attributes but simply because it was a religion.

The French expedition survived barely two years, long enough to give Egypt a taste of the West but not long enough to reshape Egyptian society. After Nelson destroyed his fleet, Napoleon escaped to France. With the Mamelukes scattered but still dangerous, Egypt was left in a vacuum, which both the Ottomans and local factions attempted to fill. Though the country was hardly a priority for the sultan, who was then engaged in a power struggle in Istanbul with the Janissaries, it was important. The grand vizier looked for a governor who would be loyal to the sultan, and in 1805 he chose a rising young star. The new governor saved Egypt, but he almost destroyed the empire.

MUHAMMAD ALI

BORN IN ALBANIA, Muhammad Ali served the Ottoman armies as a loyal mercenary. Given the state of the empire at the turn of the century, that was not such an oxymoron. The Janissaries had ceased to be an effective fighting force outside of Istanbul, and the sultan and his cabinet relied on a motley assortment of paid soldiers and officers to keep the peace within the empire's borders. Muhammad Ali was an unusually capable soldier of fortune who went to Egypt in 1801 precisely because he perceived an opportunity in the turmoil. By the time officials in Istanbul appointed him governor in 1805, it was largely a formality. In his four years in the country, he had consolidated his hold through an adroit combination of guile and force.

Muhammad Ali Pasha ruled Egypt for more than forty years, and under his stewardship, the country went from a quiet province of the Ottoman Empire to a pivotal actor in world affairs. Alexandria blossomed as a commercial center, home to merchants and bankers from every major country in Europe, and Egypt emerged as a vital link between Europe and India, which had become the fulcrum of the British Empire. The pasha himself became a legendary figure, known throughout the world as the man who modernized his country and nearly brought down the sultan.

As gifted as he was, Muhammad Ali made one major miscalculation.

Earlier than most in the Ottoman world, he recognized the superiority of Western armies. Unlike the officials in Istanbul, he had seen close up what the French army could do and watched as Napoleon had easily overrun Egypt. He also witnessed the unparalleled skill of the British navy, and the discipline of both the infantry and sailors in battle. He recognized that armies and navies like these were the product of more than good training. They were the result of a radically different society, with an education system designed to foster both independence and loyalty, and state bureaucracies capable of extracting considerably more revenue than the Ottomans.

After becoming governor, Muhammad Ali plotted for nearly six years to end the threat of the Mamelukes. Finally, in 1811, he invited them to a banquet in the Citadel in Cairo, sealed the doors, and had his soldiers massacre them as they ate. All but one of the Mamelukes were killed, and the pasha emerged as the sole power in Egypt, answerable only to the sultan.

He then embarked on a campaign to modernize the country. He sent promising young men to school in Europe. Some were dispatched to Italy; Italian merchants were well represented in Egypt, and closer relations would be a financial boon. Others went to Paris, which inaugurated more than a century of Egyptian Francophilia. There, they encountered Turkish civil servants who had been sent by the sultan, Mahmud II, with a similar goal. Among the young Egyptians in Paris in the 1820s was an Al-Azhar scholar named Rifa'a al-Tahtawi. Though he had been studying at the most established Muslim university in the world, a bastion of tradition, Tahtawi embraced the new and the foreign. The pasha himself had commissioned translations (into Turkish, not Arabic, which the pasha never learned to read) of Voltaire, Montesquieu, and Machiavelli, and he wanted the students he sent to Europe to exhibit the same curiosity. Even more, he expected them to learn engineering and science. But he did not approve of them fraternizing with the local population. Like the Russians who sent students to the West during the Cold War, Muhammad Ali had an intuitive sense of the dangers of "going native." The students were to take what they could from Europe and apply it to the betterment of Egypt.

Tahtawi quietly disregarded the pasha's orders. He went out and about in Paris, made friends, attended dinner parties, and took in the social scene. But there was never any danger of him being seduced by what he saw. In fact, the experience left him, as it left many subsequent generations of students from the Middle East, unsettled. To his eyes, the French were too liberal, too decadent, and too disorderly in their social lives. While he agreed that they had much to teach Egypt and the Ottomans about running a state and fielding an army, he returned to Egypt more loyal to the autocracy of Muhammad Ali than he had been before he had left.

Over the next decades, Tahtawi articulated a vision of a modern Egypt that was one part autocracy, one part Islam, and two parts Industrial Revolution. The result was a society that combined the unchallenged authority of a ruler like Muhammad Ali with cutting-edge techniques of farming, efficient organization of the state bureaucracy, and advanced technologies for communication and transportation. As for the place of religion, Tahtawi did not agree with the French example. The French believed that "national welfare and human progress [could] take the place of religion and that the intelligence of learned men is greater than that of the prophets," and they had banished Christianity from the public sphere and affairs of state. That was unacceptable to Tahtawi, who insisted that Egypt could modernize without antagonism toward Islam, a religion that he believed was firmly compatible with science, technology, and progress.[4]

As Albert Hourani noted in his studies of this period, Tahtawi "lived and worked in a happy interlude of history, when the religious tension between Islam and Christianity was being relaxed and had not yet been replaced by the new political tension of east and west." That meant that forward-looking Egyptians could pick and choose those aspects of the West that fit their model of an emerging Egypt and reject the rest. Unburdened by a sense of civilizational clash, they looked on France and on Europe as challengers and competitors who had distinct strengths. They understood that it was important to learn from those strengths, and they dedicated their lives to modernizing Egypt using the European model as a guide. Muhammad Ali and much of the Egyptian ruling class took an à la carte approach, selecting those aspects that they liked while rejecting those they did not. Educational reform they approved of; democracy and secularism held little appeal. The same process was unfolding in Istanbul under the sultan, though the entrenched interests there made reform far more difficult. And that was why Muhammad Ali nearly replaced the sultan, not once but twice, in 1833 and again in 1839.

It wasn't that the pasha intended to challenge the sultan, at least not at first. In fact, he had repeatedly come to the sultan's aid, notably in Greece when the powers of Europe intervened to support the independence movement, and on the Arabian Peninsula when the followers of Ibn Abd-al-Wahhab captured Mecca and Medina and massacred pilgrims making the hajj. But by the late 1820s, having nearly suppressed the Greek revolt before the English fleet sank Egypt's navy in Navarino Bay, Muhammad Ali came to the conclusion that the real danger to his future and that of Egypt and the Near East wasn't Europe. It was the ineffectual Ottoman sultan, who ruled in Istanbul while the empire disintegrated around him.

Convinced that the Europeans would destroy the empire if he did not prevent them, Muhammad Ali sent his son to invade Syria and Turkey. Between 1830 and 1833, Egyptian armies inflicted defeat after defeat on Ottoman garrisons and detachments. By the middle of 1833, the pasha's forces had advanced to within 150 miles of Istanbul, and his recently rebuilt fleet was moored near the Bosphorus. Panicked, the sultan asked the Russians for help. The tsar had long nurtured a desire to establish Russian dominance in Istanbul, and he decided to save the sultan and thereby become the protector of the empire. In order to keep Russian influence in check, the English and the French then closed ranks and issued communiqués informing Muhammad Ali that they would not permit him to occupy the capital. Faced with the combined might of the European powers, Muhammad Ali negotiated terms. His armies departed, but he was now lord not just of Egypt but of Syria, Arabia, and the Sudan as well. Having suffered no setbacks on the field, he remained a formidable threat.

The sultan, Mahmud II, knew that, and it was intolerable. He had spent most of his decades in power one step behind Muhammad Ali, and the humiliation of 1833 made him determined to established his authority over the Egyptian upstart. However, he needed European support to succeed. By the end of the decade, Ottoman diplomats had successfully convinced the English that Muhammad Ali had to be humbled. The pasha himself had made no moves against the sultan, and had sought only to make his family hereditary rulers of Egypt and Syria. But in the summer of 1839, assured of English backing, Mahmud sent his new army to challenge Muhammad Ali in Syria, and the result was a disastrous defeat for the sultan. Soon after, the Ottoman fleet, whose commanders had been seduced by the promise of titles and gold, deserted to the Egyptian side. Mahmud, suffering from tuberculosis, died before he learned of these disasters. In great pain and weary after thirty years in power, he drank himself into a fatal stupor just before messengers arrived in the capital bearing the grim news.

Once again, however, the states of Europe defended the sultanate against the Egyptian vassal. This time, Muhammad Ali did not blink. He refused to withdraw. But in his age and pride, he had forgotten just how strong the English were, and his fleet was destroyed in the harbors of Acre and Beirut. The pasha was forced to withdraw his army from Turkey and Syria, and while he was allowed the face-saving gesture of a decree establishing his sons and heirs as rulers of Egypt, the damage had been done. Egypt never again threatened the integrity of the Ottoman Empire. Unfortunately, the Ottomans had to confront the fact that their continued existence now depended on the European countries that had rescued them.

THE OTTOMANS REFORM

THE CHALLENGE posed by Muhammad Ali and the humiliation of needing to turn to Europe for survival precipitated the next wave of Ottoman reforms. While the Ottomans never ceased to identify them-selves as a Muslim dynasty that was part of a long and noble tradition stretching back to the first four caliphs, religion was all but invisible as a factor during these decades of reform. The Ottomans wore their Islam lightly, especially when it came to governing. Their lack of dogmatism made them flexible and resilient, and even though the state had stag-nated, that underlying strength remained. With Europe a critical threat to their power, the Ottomans tried to adapt, and their version of Islam did not stand in the way of change. As a result, the reforms of the nineteenth century owed more to Europe than to the Quran, and the Ottoman state became barely distinguishable from that of its European rivals.

Mahmud had wanted to modernize the army but tried to keep the traditional structure of the empire unchanged. Though the Ottoman elites dabbled with the ideas unleashed by the French Revolution, they had no appetite for liberal reform. But with the death of Mahmud and the near death of the Ottoman state, a new generation came to power.

Many of these young men had spent a few years in Paris along with the Egyptian students sent by Muhammad Ali. They had studied the success not just of European armies but of European bureaucracies. With the passing of Mahmud, they engineered a stunning new wave of reform.

The *Hatt-i Serif of Gulhane* (Noble Edict of the Rose Chamber) was issued on November 4, 1839. It was read out loud by the dynamic foreign minister, Mustafa Reshid Pasha, in front of the assembled nobles of the court, including the sultan and the grand vizier, in a formal garden beneath the Topkapi Palace. No one who listened that day failed to appreciate its significance. Along with the 1856 *Hatt-i Humayun,* these edicts were to the Ottoman state what the Declaration of Independence and the Constitution were to the American republic. These decrees set the empire on a path of reform that simultaneously centralized the state and granted specific and unalienable rights to its citizens.

The Rose Chamber decree began with the simple, uncontroversial statement that all law in the empire flowed from the Quran and the sharia, and that those two pillars were the foundation of the state. "But in the last 150 years," it continued, "former power and welfare turned into weakness and poverty. It is absolutely impossible for a country not ruled by shariah rules to survive.... [As a result], we decided to issue some new laws to govern our sublime state and our country through the mercy of God and guidance of our Prophet." Having established the reasons for the decree, Mustafa Reshid then described the new laws. First, the life and property of all citizens of the empire, whether they were Muslims, Christians, or Jews, were to be treated with the utmost respect and no punishment was to be meted out without due process in courts of law. The old system of tax farming, often abused by capricious officials, was abolished and replaced with a new tax code; and military conscription was ended.

The subsequent edict of 1856 built on these foundations The sultan, basking in his semi-victory over the Russians during the Crimean War, declared that all subjects of the empire, Muslim and non-Muslim, were equal, and that henceforth the *millet*s would be integrated into the bureaucracy. In essence, each religious community would retain its self-government for certain matters and also become part of a centralized system based in Istanbul. In addition, every inhabitant of the empire, regardless of religion or ethnicity, was considered a citizen, and all citizens had rights and obligations. Some of these would be protected and enforced by the *millet*, while others would be guaranteed by the government in Istanbul.

Collectively, these reforms were known as *Tanzimat*, the reordering of Ottoman society. For most of its history, the empire had been, as one English writer cleverly put it, "less like a country than a block of flats inhabited by a number of families that met only on the stairs." The families were the various religious and ethnic communities, and the flats were the *millet*s. As a result of the decrees of 1839 and 1856, however, some of the walls separating the families came down, and the sultan became a more active presence. Having lived semiautonomously for centuries, the citizens of the empire were now told they were members of a single political community with the sultan at the top and Istanbul at the center. While this change temporarily strengthened the Ottoman state, it also led to its demise.[5]

The *Tanzimat* was nothing if not contradictory. The reforms were initiated by a ruler who had rarely been answerable to anyone but God and by ministers who borrowed from the secular French Revolution to enshrine notions of individual rights and civil law. While increasing the power of the *millet*s, the reforms were designed to strengthen the central bureaucracy and allow the government in Istanbul to collect more revenue so that it could outfit a larger, more modern army and navy. And while the movement declared its respect for ethnic and religious diversity, it unleashed the same forces of nationalism that ultimately pushed both the empire and the states of Europe away from inclusiveness and toward arrogant intolerance.

The official language of the Rose Chamber decree invoked God, the sharia, and the Quran, yet the actual reforms steered the state away from its traditional pillars. In fact, the entire history of these decades highlights just how minimal a role religion played in the evolution of the Ottoman Empire and the Near East in the nineteenth and early twentieth centuries. The ruling elites of the empire were culturally Muslim, yet there was nothing about their Islam that precluded turning to the Russian tsar, who was the head of the Russian Orthodox Church, for help against an Albanian Muslim ruler of the mostly Muslim but partly Coptic province of Egypt. Nothing in their Islam precluded alliances with the thoroughly Protestant England or with the adamantly secular

French state. And their Islam fluidly accommodated the melting-pot nationalism in vogue in Europe.

On the borders of the Ottoman Empire, the Austro-Hungarian Empire, ruled by a Catholic monarch, was a mix of Catholics, Orthodox, Protestants, Jews, and Muslims. The Catholicism of the ruling class was the top layer of a multiconfessional society, and while the emperor demanded the loyalty of his subjects, he did not insist that they worship as he did. That was the model that the sultan emulated.

It was an easy shift. Centuries of Ottoman jurisprudence and practice supported the live-and-let-live approach that the decrees of 1839 and 1856 enshrined. The ancient Quranic prescription that the People of the Book should be allowed to practice their religion and should not be subject to coercion was in harmony with liberal notions of freedom and equality. And the *dhimmi* framework that had been established in the early centuries of Islam, which required Christians and Jews to pay the state a tax in return for living peacefully under Muslim rule, fit neatly with the nineteenth-century efforts by the Ottomans to rationalize and modernize the tax collection system.

In essence, the reforms of the *Tanzimat* era were less of a departure than they seemed; they made explicit what had been implicit. The decrees announced that all religions would be tolerated and that the *millets* would form the basis of administrative units, but this was more a change in form than substance. The goal of the reformers was to replace the traditional hidebound Ottoman bureaucracy with a modern state apparatus capable of raising revenue and defending the borders in the face of aggressive European competitors. But in doing so, the reformers built on a framework that had divided the empire into ethnic and religious communities for centuries.

The contradictions should have been apparent. Rather than forcing the inhabitants of the empire to see themselves as "Ottomans," the reforms instead led each group to become more conscious of its religious and ethnic distinctiveness. Greeks, Armenians, Arabs, Turks, and Jews became more attuned to their own identities, and in short order began to resent the attempts of the government in Istanbul to forge them into one Ottoman nation.

And yet, here as elsewhere, the picture is complicated. In the end, the Ottoman state did not successfully transform itself, but large numbers of

people within the empire found the notion of progress, equality, tolerance, and citizenship appealing. In cities such as Smyrna and Istanbul,
the second half of the nineteenth century was a heady, exciting time.
Greek, Jewish, and Armenian merchants were at the forefront of substantial social and political changes. Not only did they serve as economic
and social middlemen connecting Europe and the empire, but they also
saw a possible future when the last vestiges of discrimination against
them would dissolve. In Egypt, Alexandria (which was staunchly independent but still part of the Ottoman ecosystem) grew into a cosmopolitan city that prized its diversity and prospered in a way it had not since
the days of Cleopatra. In the Balkans, the city of Salonica continued to
be a trading hub, and in the eastern Mediterranean the sleepy ports of
Acre, Beirut, and Tripoli, which in the twelfth and thirteenth centuries
had bridged Europe and the Near East, once again became centers of
trade and culture.

Throughout the Muslim world, there was a concerted effort to move
closer to Europe. The sultans who succeeded Mahmud II worked tirelessly to establish themselves as respectable monarchs who would be
welcome in the halls of Europe. The family of Muhammad Ali devoted
themselves to transforming Egypt into a nation worthy of European
respect. "Egypt," said Khedive Ismail, Muhammad Ali's grandson and
ruler during the building of the Suez Canal, "must become part of
Europe." In order to show just how European he was and could be,
Ismail built rail lines, palaces, military barracks, and roads. Not only did
he underwrite the construction of the Suez Canal, but he also spent lavish sums of money to turn Cairo into the Paris of the Near East, complete with an opera house, a museum, wide tree-lined boulevards, and
hulking overdecorated edifices to house the new bureaucracy he created.
Unfortunately, in order to pay for these endeavors, he went heavily into
debt to European banks, and soon found that his reach had exceeded his
grasp.

In Istanbul, the sultans and their ministers did the same. A new imperial residence, the 250-room Dolmabahce Palace, was built along the
water in the modern section of the city, at an extraordinary cost for what
amounted to a knockoff of Versailles. Crystal chandeliers lit overly large
formal dining halls and ballrooms, and almost every piece of furniture
was imported from Europe. The Ottoman ruling class exchanged its traditional robes for the latest fashions from Paris and Vienna, and traded

divans and pillows for stiff-backed couches and armoires. They drank wine from German crystal goblets, dined with imported cutlery and imported ceramic plates, and dabbed their mouths with imported linens. They held balls where string quartets played the latest waltzes by Schumann, where the ladies danced in gowns that the empress Eugénie of France might have worn, and the men wore frock coats that would have suited any masquerade in Prague or Berlin.

In order to show the world that they were not the warriors of old, Sultan Abdul Aziz and Khedive Ismail of Egypt both went to Paris for the Exposition of 1867. To their delight and surprise, they were feted as celebrities. Prior to their arrival, they had underwritten the construction of sumptuous pavilions for the exposition in order to demonstrate the progress their societies had made, and to show that they belonged among the leading nations of the world. Though Ismail was still theoretically the sultan's vassal, the two were in competition, and they eyed each other warily. They were not the only Muslim rulers to jockey for favor in Europe. Several years later, the shah of Iran, annoyed that the sultan had been so well received in Paris, set out on an official tour of his own, by way of Russia. He was also feted, but he insisted that his wives return early after he discovered that the Europeans allowed the sexes to mingle in public.

Had a poll been conducted surveying Muslim attitudes toward the West in the second half of the nineteenth century, with samples drawn from Morocco, Algeria (which was then mostly under French control), Egypt, Syria, Turkey, Persia, and northern India, the response would have been overwhelmingly positive. By and large, European nations were admired for the rigor and efficiency of their armies and for the way they organized their societies in support of the state. While a strong undercurrent of rivalry and distrust remained, many believed that the future would see less war, more commerce, and more peaceful coexistence.

As always, there were exceptions: the Balkan provinces were anything but placid. The Serbs and the Bulgarians were seized with nationalist ambitions, supported by selective historical memory and overlaid with religious and ethnic grievances. The governing Turks viewed the Balkans with suspicion and disdain, and relations deteriorated as the century progressed, thanks in no small measure to the meddling of the Austro-Hungarians, the Russians, and the English. The Balkans eventually became the most contentious and unstable point of contact between

Muslims and Christians, which led to multiple small wars and eventually set off the conflagration of World War I.

Hindsight allows us to see what worked and what didn't in the nineteenth century, but at the time, the Ottomans seemed to be succeeding in wrenching a moribund bureaucracy out of its stupor and making the empire competitive. The army was retrained and acquitted itself respectably alongside the French and the English in the Crimean War against the Russians. The administration of the empire was rationalized, and the new taxation regime made it possible for the treasury to collect a steady stream of income. Roads, railways, and irrigation systems boosted economic and agrarian activity. Istanbul joined London, Paris, Saint Petersburg, Berlin, and Vienna as a leading European capital, and whenever the sultan toured Europe, he was greeted not just as a visiting dignitary but as a charismatic visionary responsible for bringing the empire into the concert of nations.

In private, European leaders were less respectful and scorned the empire for its weakness, but little was said about its religious makeup. Christianity and Judaism were in retreat from public life on the continent. There were exceptions, of course, Catholic Ireland being just one, but in general, religion in nineteenth-century Europe was less important than nationalism. The French and English looked down on the Ottomans as a backward race mired in ossified customs and traditions, and they certainly identified Islam as a factor contributing to the decadence of the empire. But they felt the same about the Indians and the Chinese and their religions and customs. In short, Western powers regarded all non-Western peoples as less civilized, and they tended to view traditional organized religion, including Christianity, as a source of weakness. Even with the missionary impulses of English and Scottish imperialists, religion as a spur to global expansion was never as potent as economic interests, political rivalries, and nationalist imperatives.

European expansion combined a passion for progress with pure power politics. The utopian impulse to create a better world, where human reason and ingenuity would invent technologies to make hunger, war, and disease obsolete, walked hand in hand with the ancient human desire to conquer and control. Until early in the twentieth century, the gloss on the nineteenth century was that it was a period of human progress, defined by the spread of liberalism emanating from Europe and by the scientific advances of the age. Later it became fashionable to excoriate the Victorians and the French of the many republics as hypocrites barely more civilized than the people they conquered. But reality is never quite so binary, and the nineteenth century was no exception.

For most of the century, however, religion was rarely a primary cause of either conflict or concord between Muslims, Christians, and Jews. The Ottoman Empire, along with other Muslim communities in Persia, India, and Indonesia, emulated the European powers, and that meant that Islam receded from public and political life. Though historians and polemicists have looked back at the nineteenth century and found the seeds of modern religious conflicts, at the time, few people thought of religious identity as an important factor propelling their societies. European expansion, science, technology, and ideas such as nationalism would have come to mind more readily, while religion would, more often than not, have been seen as a quaint anachronism.

Of course, religion as a source of tension had not been completely eliminated, but it was the supposedly secular Europeans who aggravated matters. While the French and the English, and in their own way the Russians, all moved away from the religious fervor of the Middle Ages and the Reformation, they still felt an affinity for their coreligionists. As a result, they developed bonds with those communities within the Ottoman Empire that shared their faith. French merchants needed partners in Lebanon and Syria, and found them in Catholics and Maronite Arabs. Russian diplomats and traders looked for bankers and translators and found them in Slavic communities in the Balkans that were still part of the Ottoman state.

The links between these groups and the European powers then became an excuse for intervention in the internal affairs of the Ottoman state. The old system of capitulations mutated into a series of laws that allowed Europeans to act with near impunity within the empire, untouchable by the Ottoman authorities, and European diplomats and merchants extended their protection to those who had helped them. That created tension between the Christians and Jews who worked for and with the Europeans and the Muslims who did not. What began as convenient relationships grounded in religious affinity became an irritant and then a wedge that jeopardized not only the Ottoman effort at reform but the internal stability and integrity of the entire state.

THE DARKEST HOUR AND THEN A NEW DAWN

DAMASCUS IN 1860 was a mélange of Christian sects, Muslims, Druze, and Jews, along with a powerful group of European merchants and envoys. The city had become a conduit for Mediterranean trade with the inland regions of central Anatolia and Iraq. As Lebanon was drawn into the orbit of France and its ambitious emperor, Napoleon III, the Maronite Christians grew not only wealthier but more independent. They formed tight networks with Catholics in Damascus, who also benefited from the increased economic activity.

These developments did not go unnoticed, especially by those who did not have the same advantages. In 1856, the *Hatt-i Humayun* granted the Christians in the Ottoman Empire full legal equality with Muslims. While theoretically this made Christian subjects eligible for military service, it was relatively easy for them to pay a fee instead of actually serving in the army. Furthermore, in Syria and in Lebanon especially, Christians enjoyed the protection of European consuls. Each of the major European powers in effect sponsored one of the Christian denominations. In addition to the French interest in the Catholics and the Maronites, the Russians became patrons of the Greek Orthodox, and the English extended their hand to Protestant communities as well as to the non-Christian Druze.

It was one thing not to have to serve in the army; even most Muslims did not begrudge that. But under the capitulations, Europeans and their clients were exempt from taxation and were outside the Ottoman legal system. Local businessmen took advantage of the capitulations by becoming affiliated with a consulate and thereby making their ventures essentially tax-free. That struck established Muslim merchants as cheating, because it gave the Christians a distinct advantage. The new relationships with the Western powers also disrupted the delicate equilibrium that had existed in the region for centuries. The average Muslim had no recourse to consular protection; he had no easy way of avoiding taxes; and it was only with great difficulty that he could avoid conscription. And as in any situation where the status quo changes dramatically and rapidly, there was resentment, and there was a backlash.

It began in 1858 in Lebanon. The Druze had been losing ground to the Maronites, and they struck back. The local civil war led to refugees, most of them Christians, fleeing over the mountains to what they thought was the safety of Damascus and Aleppo. But the influx proved to be a fatal spark for the simmering animosities of the Muslims of Damascus. Bitter after years of watching their relative status slip and that of the Christians, with their European protectors, increase, they retaliated. On July 9, 1860, Muslims massacred five thousand Christians in Damascus. There were also riots in Aleppo and nearby towns, and there might have been further violence but for the efforts of both Muslims and Christians to contain it. Hearing the news, Napoleon III of France threatened to send an army to restore order.

For their part, the Ottoman authorities responded forcefully. They understood the stakes. The Francophone foreign minister, Fu'ad Pasha, was dispatched to settle matters in both Syria and Lebanon. Druze and Muslim leaders who had incited the murderous mobs were sentenced to exile or execution. The government and the administrative districts of Lebanon were reorganized along denominational lines in order to give the Maronite Christian community more buffers. These measures placated the Europeans, and also reassured the Christians of Syria and Lebanon. Justice had been done, and life returned to normal.[6]

Much like the violence in Andalusia that culminated in the massacre of Cordoban Jews in 1066, the civil war between Muslims, Christians, and Druze from 1858 to 1860 has been taken as another exhibit in the case against Islam. But to indict Islam for this violence is the equivalent of condemning Anglicanism for the occasional depredations of the British army in its many wars of conquest in the nineteenth century, or to excoriate Catholicism because of French massacres of Algerians during the same period, or to charge American Protestantism for the slaughter of Native Americans at Wounded Knee in 1890. Religious identity and affiliation in all of these cases did contribute to "group cohesion," as Ibn Khaldun might have said. And religion was one way that groups differentiated themselves and distinguished "us" from "them." But in none of these cases, including what happened in Damascus, was religion the cause of the violence.

The year 1860 in Damascus was an anomaly that had more to do with the encroaching West than with relations between Christians and Muslims. We know that it was an anomaly because Muslims and Christians had lived side by side in Damascus for centuries without violence. Even during the time of the Crusades, when Muslims of Syria looked on native Christians and Jews as a possible fifth column who would open the gates (literally) to Western Christian armies, there were no comparable acts of retribution. What changed in 1860 was that the centuries-old balance between Muslims and Christians in Syria and Lebanon was disrupted by the presence of the West. After the Anglo-French intervention against Muhammad Ali, there was increased European involvement in the internal affairs of the Near East, which meant both more trade and a shift in the status quo. The eruption of violence in 1860 was one consequence.

Remarkably, within months after the riots, not only was order restored, but so too was something resembling the old harmony. Christians once again went about their lives as a flourishing minority in the midst of a Muslim majority. The *Tanzimat* reforms emanating from Istanbul promised equal rights and special privileges for religious communities in the empire, and the Christian sects of Syria and Lebanon were among the beneficiaries. Aided by Europe, Christians in the Near East enjoyed more rights and freedoms than they had before the deadly riots.

A casual observer in the years after 1860 would have been struck by the relative harmony that prevailed, and by the energy and hum of commercial and intellectual activity. But there were problems beneath the surface. The Ottoman reform movement established clear and nearly equal rights for religious minorities. That was supposed to make all citizens of the empire legally the same, but by building on the *millet* system, the *Tanzimat* created inadvertent problems. Loyalty to the *millet* community was almost always stronger than loyalty to the sultan or to the empire, and the concept of "Ottoman" citizenship was still unfamiliar. Though the *Tanzimat* reforms were designed to preserve, strengthen, and modernize the empire, they had the unintended consequence of sharpening religious and ethnic differences.[7]

As the nineteenth century neared its end, ethnic nationalism became more evident. The Turks began to imagine a new, smaller empire defined by its Turkishness. There was a parallel development among the Arabs of the Near East, who contemplated a future separate from the Ottoman Empire. They started to think of themselves as Arabs first, Muslims or Christian second, and distinct and different from the Turks who ruled them. They turned to the distant memory of the early Arab dynasties, and to their days of past glory. Interestingly, Arab Christians were forceful proponents of the ideas and programs that evolved into

Arab nationalism, and they unequivocally asserted that Arab nationalism could not be detached from Islam.

In the second half of the nineteenth century, these ideas were in their infancy, and were part of a mix that included Ottoman nationalism, European notions of a global community of peoples and nations freed by technology from the cycles of the past, and a belief in religious coexistence that would lead to a dwindling of old traditions in the face of that strange force known as modernity. Many Arabs and Turks viewed the mosque as a quaint institution, prone to superstition and backwardness. Some educated Syrians or Egyptians, like their counterparts in England or Germany, believed that religion was retreating from the public sphere and would eventually be relegated to the home and family. The *ulama* were seen as ignorant, though earnest, individuals who could not grasp the demands of the modern world but could make it more difficult for the Arabs to become part of it. Others, however, were not so quick to dismiss religion and tried to blend it with reform. They recognized that their societies needed to evolve and modernize but believed that it was possible both to "Westernize" the "Muslim" world and to keep Islam central.

As in any period when the old order is breaking down, there was no lack of ideas. These decades were tumultuous and chaotic, swirling with conflicting visions. The Ottoman Empire in the nineteenth century was in profound flux. The only constant was that the old was evaporating. Uncertain but hopeful, Arabs, Turks, Christians, Muslims, and Jews looked to a future of working with the West to construct a new order.

CHAPTER TEN

THE AGE OF REFORM

I N THE LAST DECADES of the nineteenth century and the early years
of the twentieth, European pressure intensified on all parts of the
Muslim world, and more territory was conquered. Morocco, the rest of
Algeria, and Tunisia fell under the direct rule of France. In 1882, Egypt
was invaded and then governed by England. France became the de facto
protector of Lebanon, and England extended its influence over both Persia and parts of the Balkans. Russia became more aggressive in its support for Bulgarian independence and came into conflict with the British
in remote parts of Central Asia. Successive generations of British politicians jockeyed with the Russians for influence in Afghanistan and Persia
because of Russian desires to expand south and England's desire to provide an ever larger buffer for its prize possession, India. While Russia was
England's primary rival in Asia and the Balkans, France was its main rival
in Africa. As the French moved south into the Sahara and toward West
Africa, the British tried to create an unbroken line of control stretching
from Egypt to South Africa. That led to friction with the French, which
at several points in the late 1800s nearly escalated into war.

The societies of the Muslim world reacted to these developments
with more reforms and more soul searching. What began as a trickle of
changes in the early nineteenth century became a roaring current in the
final decades. While Algeria was as different from Persia and India as
England was from Argentina, the way these societies reacted to Western
expansion was similar. In almost every part of the Muslim world, there
were some who enthusiastically embraced the mores and manners of the

West, and others who resisted at all costs. There were some who ventured abroad, studied the fundamentals of Western science and philosophy, and returned home to lead a new wave of reform; and there were others who retreated more deeply into the comfortable lassitude of the past, clinging to dreams that the West would retreat as surely as the Crusaders had left Palestine centuries before.

Almost everywhere, however, reform movements became the driving force. Some looked to remake the Muslim world along Western lines, with constitutions that mimicked those of France and, to a lesser extent, the United States. In Istanbul in 1876 and Tehran in 1905, constitutionalists inaugurated a new era of government that limited the power of the sultan, shah, or khedive and granted judges and legislatures a measure of autonomy and independence. The constitutionalist movements were careful to incorporate the ancient Quranic protection of the rights of the People of the Book, and they were models of multicultural toleration for religious and ethnic minorities.

Even as many leading voices argued for reform, attitudes toward the West remained ambivalent. It wasn't as if millions in the Muslim world suddenly decided that it was time to change. Change was forced on them—not all at once, but with each passing decade, it became impossible for societies ruled by Muslim leaders to deny that the balance had shifted decidedly against them and in favor of the West. The challenge at the beginning of the century and at the end was similar—how to compete with the West and remain independent—but the stakes seemed higher as the century wore on. The heirs of Muhammad Ali in Egypt and the second generation of reformers in the Ottoman Empire asked the same question, but with the added knowledge that France, England, and Great Britain were more likely to invade and rule directly than they had been before.

As the nineteenth century ended, the idea of progress became more deeply embedded. Reformers have to believe that the future can be better, and that the right choices made by the right people will create a stable, prosperous, and successful society. The late nineteenth and early twentieth centuries were the golden age of Muslim reform movements, and the outcome of these movements in turn shaped how Muslims, Christians, and Jews would interact in the twentieth century and into the twenty-first.

AN EGYPTIAN AFFAIR

THE DIPLOMATS of the Ottoman Empire continued to hone their skills of playing one European power against another. Internally, Ottoman identity fought what was ultimately a losing battle against Turkish identity, but for a time, that made for a vibrant intellectual life in Istanbul. Poets, playwrights, philosophers, and writers debated the virtues of "Ottomanness" and "Turkishness" with the same vitality that French intellectuals argued socialism, democracy, and class in the Third Republic. But the brief success of the constitutional movement was ended by a coup from above. Sultan Abdul Hamid II abrogated the newly passed document and used the reforms of the previous decades to create a harsh autocratic government interested primarily in collecting revenue to fund armies and railroads.

The Ottomans were able to keep the Europeans at bay, but the Egyptians were not. The building of the Suez Canal ensured that Egypt would be drawn more closely into the orbit of Europe. At first, that had been one of the selling points that convinced Khedive Said and then Ismail to join with the French entrepreneur Ferdinand de Lesseps to fund the construction of the massive hundred-mile-long trench connecting the Mediterranean to the Red Sea. With the completion of the canal in 1869, however, Ismail found himself heavily in debt to French and English bankers, who continued to extend his line of credit in the 1870s as he scrambled to remake his country. Soon, he was personally insolvent, as was the Egyptian treasury.

Forced by his creditors to hand control of Egypt's finances to a consortium of European banks, Ismail was then deposed, and his ramshackle treasury and tottering government were left to his young, untested son. English and French officials installed themselves as advisers in the major ministries. This takeover of the government did not go unnoticed, and a resistance movement formed. It was led by a native Egyptian army officer, and its aims were straightforward: to restore sanity to Egypt's finances, to make the government of Egypt less Turkish and more Egyptian, and to decrease the influence of England. It was, in short, the first major eruption of Egyptian nationalism.

Muhammad Ali and his heirs may have wanted to transform Egypt into a power to be respected, but they were an Albanian family surrounded by a Turkish elite governing an Arab-speaking populace. When the country's finances cracked under the weight of Ismail's ambitions, some Egyptians began to consider an alternate Arab Egypt that would be independent of both Europe and of the Ottoman elite. The sultan in Istanbul disapproved, but he was consumed with unrest in the Balkans. The British, however, with the newly opened Suez Canal linking Europe to Asia, were not prepared to let a popular Egyptian army officer take control of the government. When riots broke out in Alexandria in the summer of 1882, the British fleet bombarded the port, and a British army quelled the uprising with its customary, not to mention lethal, efficiency.

British control of Egypt lasted, in one form or another, until the end of World War II. Though Egypt was declared independent by Great Britain in 1922, British troops remained in control of the Suez Canal zone, and British influence over Egypt's foreign policy was close to total. In time, Egypt developed a robust nationalist movement that worked to end British rule, but in the immediate aftermath of the 1882 occupation, most Egyptian nationalists resigned themselves to the changed reality and looked for ways to reform the country. The soul searching produced at least one reformer who not only fused Islam with Western modernity but offered a template for dozens of other movements throughout the Muslim world in the twentieth century.

Muhammad Abduh was born in 1849 in a village in the Nile Delta. Life in that lush, fecund land was beginning to change, but it was still a world determined by the waxing and waning of the Nile floods, by peasants planting crops, by festivals full of music and noise and Sufi masters walking on coals and charming snakes, and by the village mosque with its imam preaching sermons that could have been heard a thousand years before. As a bright, precocious child, Abduh was sent to study at Al-Azhar, which was the oldest university in the Muslim world and still among the most prestigious. It was not, however, known for being forward-looking. Unlike most of his contemporaries, Abduh took his formal education, which would have included immersion in the Quran, the sharia, the hadith, and jurisprudence, and applied it to the pressing question of his day: what to do about the West?

The events of 1882 sharpened his answers, but even before, he had been intent on synthesizing the traditions of Islam with the philosophical and scientific innovations introduced by the West. While he excelled as a student and then as a teacher of the traditional curriculum of Al-

Azhar, he had been drawn into the orbit of progressive thinkers who congregated in Cairo in the 1870s. One of the leading lights of that circle was an itinerant teacher named Jamal al-Din al-Afghani. An Iranian who claimed to have been born in Afghanistan, he was in fact a Shi'ite who pretended to be a Sunni in order to broaden his appeal. Afghani spent most of his adult life in a peripatetic whirl. He was a decade older than Abduh, and by the time they met in the 1870s, he had become a minor celebrity, known for his lectures and his writings on science, Islam, and the West. He was charismatic and eccentric, and maintained an aura of mystery. He was part Pied Piper, part academic philosopher, and part agitator who gravitated toward the innermost circles of power and influence in both Europe and the Muslim world. At various points in his career, he was a confidant of the Ottoman sultan, a fixture at the court of the Qajar shah in Persia, a gadfly to the salon intellectuals of Paris, and a dinner guest of the Churchills in London. Like Socrates, he was known as much for the fame of his pupils as he was for his own teachings, and Abduh was his Plato.

Afghani had one creed: Muslim societies had fallen behind the West because they had strayed from the core strength of Islam. Unlike all other world religions, Afghani claimed, Islam celebrated science and reason. That was what had allowed the Abbasids and other dynasties to flourish, and it was why Muslim societies had been successful in the past. Over the centuries, Muslims had lost sight of that. They had closed the door to innovation and become antagonistic to change, with the result that the West had raced ahead. The so-called traditionalists who opposed Western science were, Afghani believed, forsaking the Islamic tradition. True Muslims should embrace the science, technology, and social advancements of the Western states and build on them. Then the community would be whole and strong once again, and a new golden age would begin.

These ideas were not only radical in the Muslim world; they were a direct challenge to the prevailing winds in Europe. In France especially, increasing numbers of the bourgeoisie were indifferent and often hostile to religion, and to organized religions such as Catholicism most of all. The intellectuals of the day, epitomized by the brilliant, arrogant scholar Ernest Renan, believed that all religions were antithetical to innovation, and that religion stood in the way of human progress.

In 1883, a series of electric debates took place between Renan and Afghani. The two men engaged in a multiround duel over the question

of whether Islam was compatible with science. In many ways, their dialogue was a latter-day re-creation of the tense rhetorical battles that
Christians, Jews, and Muslims had fought in front of courtiers in Córdoba and Baghdad centuries earlier. But there was one crucial difference: Renan did not defend Christianity; he denounced it, and he
denounced Islam. Renan was an avatar for the modern age, an ardent
acolyte of reason, a devotee of logic, and an enemy of what he thought
was cant and superstition in the guise of religion and faith. A onetime
seminary student, he was fluent in Hebrew, versed in the Quran and had
devoted years to the study of the Orient. He admired the Persians, but
had little respect for what Arabs had wrought over the centuries, and
that added to his antipathy for the deleterious effects of organized religion. In his view, the philosophical achievements of the Muslim world
during the Middle Ages were in spite of, not because of, Islam. The Persians had done better than the Arabs, he believed, because they were less
in thrall to orthodox Islam. Renan held that no religion nurtured the scientific spirit. No religion could afford to, because science was based on
the limitless capacity of human reason and intellect while religion
rested on the infinite power of God the creator.

Afghani had a different perspective. While he acknowledged that in
all religions there was tension between science and faith, he saw Islam as
unique in its embrace of reason and its warmth toward science. Drawing
on a corpus of works from eighth-century Baghdad through the flowering of medieval Andalusia, Afghani's argument was buttressed by evidence. He stressed that the great philosophers of Islam—Ibn Sina, Ibn
Rushd, Ibn Arabi—were often mystics as well. They used reason, and
they were also men of faith, who submitted to the mystery and power of
God even as they employed logic to probe the meaning of his creation. If
Muslims were to meet the challenge of the West, Afghani declared, they
would have to reclaim their lost inheritance.

Afghani had many disciples, but none more skilled than Muhammad
Abduh. While Afghani roamed restlessly throughout the Muslim world,
Abduh dedicated himself to the cause of Egypt. Afghani, wise in so
many ways, allowed himself to be used as an ornament by rulers such as
the Ottoman sultan, who pointed to his presence at their courts as proof
of how forward-looking they were yet had little intention of putting his
more radically democratic ideas into practice. Afghani believed that the
most important ingredient for change was education, and that only by

taking the curriculum out of the hands of the hidebound *ulama* and putting progressives like him in charge could a new generation be trained to
grapple with the West and implement real reform. Abduh took up that
mantle in Egypt. By the end of his life he had some success in turning
those ideas into a reality, but not without considerable anguish at the
failure of the nationalist movement in the early 1880s, and not before
being exiled by the British for five years.

When Abduh returned to Egypt, he reestablished himself at Al-
Azhar, and then emerged as one of the most serious, and influential,
reformers during the long years of British rule. Like Afghani, Abduh
took as his starting point Quran 13:11, which states, "Verily God does
not change what is in a people, until they change what is in themselves."
Generations of exegesis had taken the verse to mean that mankind has
free will. With free will comes reason, and reason is integral to progress.
Abduh, who had witnessed the absence of progress firsthand when he
was taught a curriculum at Al-Azhar that had been frozen for centuries,
believed that ignorance was a greater threat to Egypt and the Arab and
Muslim world than the West was. "If we continue to follow the method
of blind acceptance," he wrote, "no one will be left who holds this religion. But if we return to that reason to which God directs us in this verse
and other verses like it, there is hope that we can revive our religion."
And that religion, Abduh continued in other writings, "may be counted
a true friend of science, a stimulus into the secrets of the universe, and
an appeal to respected established truths, and we may rely upon it in
cultivating our spirits and reforming our actions."

Like his teacher Afghani, Abduh did not limit his aspirations to one
country. Afghani has been called, rightly or not, one of the creators of
pan-Islam, a movement that has been tainted as an early-twentieth-
century version of Islamic fundamentalism. But where Afghani tried to
spark a reformation everywhere, Abduh diligently pursued reform in
Egypt as an incubator for the rest of the Muslim world. His faith in reason, as it were, led him to excoriate the structure of the Egyptian state
that had evolved under both the Ottomans and Muhammad Ali and his
heirs. Law had been based on the whim of the ruler, supported by a
placid religious and judicial establishment. If Egypt was to change,
Abduh believed, it would need not only a better education system, but a
legal system that was more powerful than any one man.

Abduh's dedication and erudition impressed the British administration, and late in his life, in 1899, he was made grand mufti of Egypt, in charge of all religious law and jurisprudence. In that position, he revised the curriculum for training civil servants and imams alike. He attempted to reorient Egypt away from blind adherence to tradition and toward a reborn society that fused reason, science, and the Quran. Though he did not fulfill his own high ambitions, he did create a new way, one that demanded internal reform based on laws that honored the Islamic tradition but were in harmony with the modern world. That in turn was to be the foundation of a modern Egypt led by men trained to think, to question, and to learn, who not only accepted but fostered innovation, and who nurtured the spirit of scientific inquiry that had always been part of the glory and strength of Islam.

Though Abduh saw Egypt as an important test case, his ultimate goal was the renaissance of all Muslim societies. Unlike Afghani, he was less focused on active resistance to the West than he was on awakening the dormant spirit of Islam. In his reading of history, the past success of Islam was the product not just of fearless inquiry but of toleration for religious minorities. Abduh's vision embraced Christians and Jews as equal partners who had been vital to Muslim success in the past, and would be essential to success in the future. In short, his Islam not only was compatible with the modern ethos articulated by the West; it also predated it.

Science, military prowess, respect for law, and liberalism were among the cornerstones of Western culture in the nineteenth century, which along with more than a dollop of greed and rapaciousness led to the dominance of Europe relative to the rest of the world. But Europe's great weakness, Abduh believed, was that it had created a false tension between religion and modernity. According to Abduh's reading of the past, Muslim societies had once surpassed the West because that tension did not exist in the centuries after Muhammad. Unlike post-Enlightenment Europeans, the *Salaf* (the elders of the early community of Muslim believers) had prospered because they combined reason with faith. That meant that modern Egyptians, as the vanguard of Muslim states, had the potential not only to hold its own, but to set an example by adding religion to the mix instead of banishing it from the public sphere.

That, at least, was Abduh's dream. But he knew that until Egypt and other Muslim states did the hard work of wrenching themselves out of their stupor, they would follow the West and not lead the world. And as long as Muslim societies remained mired in ossified traditions, they would invite scorn and condescension. Abduh felt the sting of British disdain, but he understood that it was a natural and appropriate reaction to Egyptian backwardness. He reserved his most stringent criticisms not for the conquerors but for the failings in his own society that made it unable to resist Western encroachment.

Centuries earlier, with the passing of al-Ghazali and others, the Muslims of the Near East and North Africa had gradually retreated from interpreting the Quran and the traditions of the Prophet. Abduh represented a break from that unfortunate legacy. He claimed the right to interpret Islam and adapt it to the circumstances of his time, and he did so believing that this was the birthright of every Muslim and every human being. The fact that interpretation had been discouraged was the failing of Muslims and Muslim societies, but not indicative of the true Islam of Muhammad, his companions, and those who immediately followed them. Understanding that human beings were weak and prone to error, Abduh treated his countrymen with compassion rather than contempt, and regarded the Christians and Jews in his midst as people worthy of the respect that he believed the Quran demanded. In spite of the ossified culture of Egypt and of much of the Arab world, he rarely doubted that progress was possible, and that a new era of peace and prosperity was within reach so long as the Arab world in general and Egypt in particular recognized that they had lost their way and began the process of rebirth.

Abduh set the tone for a generation of activists and intellectuals who helped define Arab nationalism in the first part of the twentieth century. Slowly, however, his legacy was distorted by followers who were less convinced that the modern trappings of science and European liberalism were compatible with Islam and Arab independence. Other Muslim countries, Turkey and Iran among them, grappled with similar issues and experienced similar fissures between those who envisioned a future of peaceful rivalry with the West and those who resisted the changes that the rise of Europe had forced on the world. Some became bitter and angry that reforms did not yield immediate benefits, and as the West continued to dominate the economic, political, and military destiny of much of the Muslim world in the first decades of the twentieth century, that bitterness generated darker versions of Abduh's teachings. Abduh believed that the *Salaf* had been ecumenical and tolerant, but others saw them instead as a tight-knit community of believers whose strength lay in the rejection of the message given to the People of the Book and in their willingness to silence any who challenged the words of the Quran and the hadith. In fact, within Muslim communities, people known in the West as "fundamentalist" are often referred to as *salafiyya*, because they look to the founders of Islam for answers about how to confront the challenges of the present.[1]

Abduh would have been dismayed by the twentieth-century evolution of the *salafiyya*. He vigorously opposed what the British government had done in Egypt and elsewhere, but he warmly embraced the English and French friends he made in Cairo and in the capitals of Europe. One of his closest companions was Wilfrid Scawen Blunt, an Englishman who devoted his life to fighting against imperialism and to defending Islam to a skeptical English public. Blunt was a full-fledged member of the British ruling class, yet he was outside the mainstream. Having married the granddaughter of Lord Byron, he was drawn to the mysteries of the desert and the esoteric, and he shared with his wife an insatiable yearning for something other than what England had to offer. Seeking adventure, they shunned London society and spent nearly a decade riding their horses through the most desolate tracts of the African Sahara and the Arabian Najd, where they were guests of Ibn Rashid, whose family was then locked in a struggle with the Saudis and their Wahhabi followers. The Blunts also lived with the bedouin of the Euphrates in central Iraq, and they wrote a book about their experiences that was avidly read by the English public.

Among the bedouin, Wilfrid Blunt found what he had been looking for. Disillusioned by imperial Britain, he romanticized the moral code of the bedouin, their purity of faith, and their lack of hypocrisy. The bedouin were a society of merit, who through Blunt's rose-tinted vision offered "the purest example of democracy to be found in the world— perhaps the only one in which the watchwords of liberty, equality, and fraternity are more than a name." Their Islam had not been sullied by the ostentatious displays that marked the High Anglicanism of Blunt's England. While most of his contemporaries compared the Arabs to Europe and found them culturally deficient, Blunt concluded that it was the Europeans who were deficient. The Arabs may have temporarily fallen behind the West, but for that Blunt blamed the Ottomans. He believed that once the empire finally collapsed, the Arabs could restore their caliphate and rise again as a beacon of freedom and creativity that would put the West to shame.

In 1880, Blunt visited Egypt and met Abduh. Through Abduh, he was drawn into the nationalist movement that ultimately culminated in the British occupation, an event that Blunt did everything he could to prevent and that devastated him when it finally took place. The scorn that most of his countrymen felt toward Arabs and Islam was a disgrace, Blunt wrote on the eve of the invasion. Islam, he said, "must be treated as no vain superstition but a true religion, true inasmuch as it is a form of the worship of the one true God in whom Europe, in spite of her modern reason, still believes. As such it is entitled to whatever credit we may give true religions of prolonged vitality and while admitting the eternal truth of Christianity for ourselves, we may believe that in the Arabian mind...Islam too will prove eternal." He tried to persuade the British prime minister William Gladstone that Egypt should be allowed to manage its own destiny and that it was contrary to Gladstone's liberal creed and against the true tenets of the Christian faith to sanction an occupation of a country undertaken solely to appease European creditors. But Gladstone, anxious about any potential threat to the sea lanes from Suez to India, did not agree.[2]

The searing events that culminated in the British invasion cemented a bond between Abduh and Blunt that would span decades. Blunt continued to pound at successive British governments for the follies of imperialism, while Abduh worked within the system established by the British protectorate in Egypt and campaigned tirelessly for educational and legal reform. Both were critics of their respective societies, and in many ways, they were mirror images: Blunt the Englishman who rejected the bombastic self-assurance of imperialism and railed against the hypocrisy of a liberal society ruling an illiberal empire; Abduh the esteemed shaikh who rejected the moribund tradition handed down to him and demanded that his society remember what it had forgotten.

MERCHANTS, MISSIONARIES, AND MISFITS

DURING THE LAST decades of the nineteenth century, Blunt watched with dismay as the British Empire grew in scope and in arrogance. The old policy of intervention only when absolutely essential gave to way to intervention everywhere. The reason for the shift was the competition between the states of Europe. An emerging Germany after 1870 had altered the balance cultivated by the Congress of Vienna, and the major powers—England, France, Russia, Germany, Holland, and Italy— rushed to plant their flags on the remaining unclaimed parts of the globe, from sub-Saharan Africa to Southeast Asia and the Near East.

The Ottoman Empire continued to play one European state off the next, manipulating the hopes and fears of each of the contenders, but by the early part of the twentieth century, the Balkan provinces had declared their independence, North Africa was directly controlled by either France or England, Arabia was largely autonomous, the Caucasus was under the sway of Russia, and French influence in Syria and Lebanon made even collecting taxes difficult at best. In Africa, France and England nearly came to blows in the Saharan hinterland, while in southern Africa, the Germans tried to gain a symbolic foothold to demonstrate to the world that they too were a global empire. Even the United States, which had traditionally confined its expansionist ambitions to the Western Hemisphere, acquired its own colony in the Philippines at the expense of Spain in 1898.

Blunt was part of a vocal minority who believed that imperialism was not just wreaking havoc on the globe but destroying England and its cherished liberalism. In his eyes, the mores of imperialism were incompatible with the ethics of liberalism, and any country that used brute force to control the destiny of others would soon be incapable of nurturing the values of democracy and liberty in its own citizens. His ideal of mutual respect between cultures clashed with the views of many of his countrymen that Britain was superior not just militarily and economically but morally as well. Because he moved in elite circles, his words were listened to, but rarely heeded. He was the conscience of his class, a reminder to an increasingly self-satisfied imperial elite that power can corrupt.

Blunt was also a member of a select club of Europeans who were drawn to the Arab world and to Islam. The pull of the desert was lost on most of his contemporaries, but not all. The known history of the nineteenth century paints a stark picture of European conquest and disdain for the conquered, but the forgotten history includes a panoply of other reactions and interactions. It may have been the case that few Europeans traveled far from home, that even fewer traveled beyond the continent to the other shores of the Mediterranean, and that those who did by and large looked down on foreign cultures. But some fell in love, others felt complete, and still others were swept away with awe and respect for the alien societies they encountered. Blunt was one of them; Sir Richard Burton was another.

Burton's relationship to the Arabs was fraught, but so was his relationship with everyone else. He not only managed to pass as a Muslim in Mecca but provided the romantics back home with a tingling erotic translation of the *Arabian Nights*. Blunt and Burton's fraternity included not only eccentrics but also members of the elite such as the young Benjamin Disraeli. Descended from a Jewish family and struggling to find his place in English society, Disraeli looked on the Near East and Palestine as a realm of wonder, danger, and promise. Before entering politics, he penned several novels where East met West, and he might have merited a footnote as an author had he not risen to the heights as Queen Victoria's prime minister. In addition to Disraeli and Burton, the cohort included intrepid travelers such as Gifford Palgrave, Charles Doughty, Lucy Duff-Gordon, and anonymous seekers and misfits who were never comfortable in the parlors of London or Paris but were at home in the souks and oases of the Arab world.

Similar souls could be found in France, though their focus was not just the Near East but also the North African coast stretching from Morocco to Tunisia. Germans and Italians came late to the imperial party, but German universities excelled at producing scholars who could read and translate the classics of Arabic and Persian literature. They studied what Muslim societies had produced during their heyday and parsed the Quran as well as the rich philosophical and cultural heritage that had defined medieval Baghdad and Spain and that, as Abduh so acutely recognized, had begun to fade from memory in the contemporary Muslim world. Often, these "Orientalists," as they were called, took a condescending attitude toward their subject. The nineteenth-century imbalance between Muslim societies and the West was taken as proof of a fatal flaw in Islam. By carefully analyzing the central texts of Islam, the Orientalists hoped to solve the puzzle of why the Muslim world had fallen so far behind the West.[3]

The question was perfectly reasonable. It was the same question that reformers in Istanbul, Cairo, and Tehran asked. And for the most part, the answers suggested by both Westerners and reformers in the Muslim world were the same: Muslim states, at their height, had encouraged interpretation as well as adaptation of the Quran and hadith to the circumstances of the present. When those societies turned away from inquiry and shunned science in favor of unquestioned acceptance of the authority of the past, they lost touch with the spark that had made them so successful. The result was stagnation. Some Orientalists, like Renan, indicted Islam as a whole, but others drew a distinction between vibrant, classical Islam and what came later. These scholars focused on the conundrum of what went wrong in the Muslim world. While their immediate influence was on a relatively small group of like-minded students, their views were adopted by statesmen and diplomats, who had a more direct impact on the interaction between Western states and the Muslim world. In fact, one of the indirect consequences of Orientalism was the Arab Revolt in 1916, whose celebrated protagonist was T. E. Lawrence, made famous by the American journalist Lowell Thomas as "Lawrence of Arabia."

The "Orientalist" legacy was more than one of patronizing attitudes and flawed policies. Some scholars went native, and like Blunt became ardent critics of the West and avid defenders of the virtues of Islam and of Muslims. One of the strangest and most colorful of these was the improbably named William Marmaduke Pickthall. He was born in Suffolk, England, in 1875, and attended the famed Harrow school, which he hated. The only consolation of his wretched experience there was the beginning of a lifelong friendship with another student who suffered through its Darwinian rigors, Winston Churchill. Pickthall lost himself in languages but couldn't find an adequate Arabic teacher, so as soon as he reached eighteen and the end of Harrow, he set off for Port Said on the northern end of the Suez Canal. As it had been for Blunt, it was love at first sight.

Pickthall found a tutor and began reading the *Arabian Nights* in the original. He was enthralled. Recounting how he felt when he read the stories of Harun al-Rashid, he wrote that the old Arabic revealed to him "the daily life of Damascus, Jerusalem, Aleppo, Cairo, and the other cities as I found it in the nineteenth century. What struck me, even in its decay and poverty, was the joyousness of that life compared with anything that I had seen in Europe. The people seemed quite independent of our cares of life, our anxious clutching after wealth, our fear of death." As he traveled through the Near East, he confronted a society that seemed to him a perfect mix of community and individualism, and that practiced a truer form of democracy than what passed for it in Europe. Where most of his contemporaries saw decadence and decay, he saw personal liberties, freedom from the ominous hand of the state, and genuine piety. After a near-conversion experience in Damascus, he returned to England just as the century was ending, wrote a novel, and became a literary celebrity with his tales of the Orient.

Events in the Ottoman Empire drew Pickthall back. He was appalled when he heard his countrymen railing against the "infidel Turks" during successive wars that were fought between the Ottomans and the newly independent Balkan states before World War I. He was equally disillusioned by the Gallipoli campaign waged by his old schoolmate Churchill against the Ottomans during the war. In 1917, he renounced Christianity and very publicly converted to Islam. He went to India to support Mahatma Gandhi, and then began work on a translation of the Quran, which he published in 1930, a few years before his death. By then, he had become well known in India and throughout the Muslim world as a convert who spoke out against the injustices of European rule and who defended Islam against its many Western critics. Pickthall applauded the honesty and moral purity that he observed in Muslim communities, and was angered by the hypocrisy of the British. The West, he believed, claimed a moral high ground based on the principles of liberty, but then flagrantly violated those principles in the way it governed its empires and treated their people. For Pickthall, it wasn't Islam that needed reform; it was the West.[4]

Disenchanted souls like Blunt and Pickthall were not the only ones drawn to the Muslim world. There were also merchants who saw the Near East as a land of opportunity to make a fortune. Many of them were undoubtedly adjuncts to imperialism, interested in exerting control and extracting what they could. Businessmen, however, tended to be indifferent to ethnicity and religion and sought only to cement contracts. Europeans often relied on Christians in the Near East to act as intermediaries, but in other parts of the Muslim world—Algeria and Persia for instance, or northern Nigeria—they partnered with Muslims. Religion almost never intruded on these commercial interactions, and local Muslim merchants did not hesitate to work with European Christian businessmen. If an English aristocrat wanted to buy horses in Egypt, he could find a dozen Egyptian horse traders; if a French concern wanted carpets from Isfahan, Tabriz, or Van, it had only to demonstrate its willingness to buy in order to find many who wanted to sell.

As Europe became more involved in the Arab and Ottoman world, those regions became more tightly tied to the continental economy. In Lebanon and Syria, the increased influence of France in the second half of the nineteenth century was an economic boon. Textile and silk merchants and manufacturers enjoyed a burst of demand for their products. Beirut became an international center for the cultivation of silk pods and the production of fine silk thread, and the riots of 1860 only hastened the economic integration of the Levant with Europe. The British occupation of Egypt in 1882 also led to a long period of economic development. The rewards were unevenly distributed, but the country nonetheless saw the influx of considerable foreign capital. A similar process occurred in the still-independent Ottoman Empire, which late in the century under the autocratic and crafty Sultan Abdul Hamid II courted a rising Germany as a counterweight to France, England, and Russia. German banks worked closely with Ottoman officials to build the Baghdad Railway connecting the provinces of Iraq to central Turkey and Istanbul.[5]

It wasn't just Western merchants who ventured forth. In Beirut and in Cairo, American missionaries opened schools that shaped educational life for decades. The school that became the American University in Beirut was founded as the Syrian Protestant College in the 1870s by a group of Presbyterians and Congregationalists under the aegis of the aptly named Daniel Bliss. His missionary impulse was augmented by his zeal to educate. "We do not aim," Bliss said at the end of his career in 1904, "to make Maronites, or Greeks, or Catholics, or Protestants, or Jews, or Muslims, but we do aim to make perfect men, ideal men, God-like men, after the model of Jesus against whose moral character no man ever has said or can say aught." His creed was a liberal Christianity that championed religious freedom, and while he was adamant about the necessity of belief in a higher power, he was indifferent about what form the worship of that higher power took. "We wish every student to be religious," he proclaimed, but he did not force his students to be religious in any particular way.

The spirit of religious tolerance governed not only the curriculum but the choice of the school's name. When members of the board of trustees proposed that the name be changed to Beirut Christian University, Bliss's successors vetoed the suggestion, on the grounds that using the term "Christian" in the title "seemed to provide unnecessary emphasis on religious differences which might prove unfortunate." While the school never lost touch with its missionary roots, it always attracted a mix of Jews, Muslims, and Christians to study on the campus. There was occasional friction between them, but the only major complaint of the Jewish and Muslim students was that university officials were less than accommodating about respecting dietary restrictions in the choice of food served at the cafeteria. Even as sectarian tensions increased in the early twentieth century, the American University remained a haven. It set an example for toleration and coexistence that resisted successive waves of conflict in Lebanon but could not withstand the 1975 civil war that engulfed the entire country.[6]

Beirut was one melting pot, but perhaps the most extraordinary crossroads was Alexandria. This ancient capital of Egypt, founded by Alexander the Great and ruled by the Greek Ptolemies until their last descendant, Cleopatra, cuddled up with an asp and died, had dwindled to a cultural and economic backwater by the early nineteenth century. Then it began to stir under Muhammad Ali. As he looked to the West to reinvigorate his country, Alexandria connected Egypt to the ports of Europe. Foreigners flooded the districts just off the quays, and the city became a bustling hodgepodge of languages and cultures, home to a diverse assortment of Muslims, Christians, and Jews united by their common interest in lucre. Under the ambitious Khedive Ismail, Alexandria became even more central to the financial and economic life of the eastern Mediterranean, though its bombardment by the English navy in 1882 destroyed some of the gracious mansions lining the shore. The economy soon recovered, and Alexandria attracted bankers, merchants, artisans, archeologists, and wanderers who were drawn by the chaotic rhythms of a city planted partly in Europe, partly in Egypt, and fully in neither.

For a brief few decades, Alexandria was home to a permissive culture that winked and nodded at the offbeat sexual proclivities of many of its expatriate denizens. At the old century's end and the new century's beginning, it attracted a literary crowd that included most famously the Greek Constantine Cavafy, the American Lawrence Durrell, and the very British E. M. Forster. Like other cosmopolitan port cities, it was both part of and separate from its hinterland. Arabic was spoken, but so were Greek, French, Armenian, English, Italian, and Turkish. The call to prayer could be heard from the mosques along the shore and inland, but so could the ringing of bells from the churches, and the blowing the ram's horn on the Jewish holiday of Rosh Hashanah from one or more of the city's synagogues.

The locals were no more homogeneous than the expatriates and themselves formed a crazy quilt of ethnicity and religion. The Muslims were mostly Sunni, but the Christians represented almost every denomination. There were Greek Orthodox, Syrian Orthodox, Copts, Armenians, Latin Uniates, Greek Catholics, Maronites, Armenian Catholics, Presbyterians, Anglicans, and even a few members of the Church of Scotland. These Christian sects were usually friendly or indifferent to Muslims and Jews but could be quite antagonistic toward one another. The Copts said—correctly—that they had been there the longest and so deserved some sort of respect and primacy, but few of the other sects cared about tenure. Meanwhile, there was also a wealthy Jewish community that could trace its roots back to the Hellenistic period and claimed, with some justification, to be one of the oldest continuous Jewish settlements in the world. And though the Jews, Christians, and Muslims of Alexandria were aware of their sects and subsects, they all worked to extract what they could from a world dominated by Europeans. They were intrepid and entrepreneurial, and looked to a future where people and nations would be judged on what they did and how much they earned rather than on what they believed or the god they worshiped.[7]

NATIONAL HOPES AND DREAMS

As the nineteenth century came to a close, Europeans had exported not only technology but ideas, and the belief in progress had taken root almost everywhere. At times, it was an awkward graft, especially in Eastern societies that had a less linear sense of time and history. But in many parts of the Muslim world, it was an attractive formula. As Abduh understood, one of the strengths of classical Muslim states was their ability to evolve. The notion of "progress," if not the word itself, was embedded in their culture. And so when most of the Muslim world fell under the direct or indirect sway of Europe in the nineteenth century, there was no shortage of people who believed that change was possible.

When the reformers looked ahead, they envisioned a day when their countries would be able to stand with Europe when they wished, and against Europe if they had to. In the interim, they recognized that the playing field wasn't level, and they sought European financial, intellectual, and military advice and assistance. But even as they learned from the West, they knew that there might be conflict before there could be genuine coexistence. Until Europe ceased to rule, there could be no meeting of independent equals. Preferably, conflict would be minimal or nonexistent. In the face of pressure, protests, and resistance movements, the British and French would do what was prudent and withdraw. After that, there would still be competition, of course, but it would not need to take the form of war. Instead, the Ottoman elite, the rulers of Egypt who worked with the English occupation, and others looked to a time when the Muslim world and the West would trade and exchange ideas as equals. The first step was internal reform; the next would be to reclaim full independence.

The dream of progress, therefore, did not mean a passive acceptance of European rule. Quite the opposite. Progress for the reformers meant the end of European hegemony and the restoration of full independence. The humiliations of imperial rule were real. Lord Cromer, who almost single-handedly controlled what went on in Egypt from 1882 until early in the twentieth century, was undisguised in his contempt for the country. He treated its inhabitants as wayward children in need of instruction. "What Egypt required most of all," he said in 1883, "was order and good government. Perhaps...liberty would follow afterwards. No one but a dreamy theorist could imagine that the natural order of things could be reversed and that liberty could first be accorded to the poor ignorant representatives of the Egyptian people, and that the latter would then be able to evolve order out of chaos."[8]

Even those who agonized about the problems in their societies were repelled by these patronizing attitudes. Educated, cultivated Egyptians chafed at being treated like errant children. Who were the British, they mused, to lecture us about religious tolerance and liberty when Copts, Muslims, and Jews had lived side by side for fourteen hundred years "in the greatest unity and harmony"? Who were they to tell Egypt about civilization when the inhabitants of the Nile Valley had created a society thousands of years before the English had even learned to write? Admiration for what Europe could offer sat side by side with indignation about what Europeans often did offer.

These were the dominant themes, but, of course, some followed their own muses and approached these encounters from a different perspective. There were the voices crying in the wilderness like Blunt and Pickthall who believed that the hypocrisy of the West was a more damning weakness than any of the problems in the Muslim world. There were merchants on both sides who had no interest in these larger ideas. And there were missionaries who worked not to convert Muslims but to improve relations between faiths and cultures and who spent decades trying to build bridges.

In the final decades of the nineteenth century, however, nationalism complicated matters even further. In his book *Imagined Communities,* Benedict Anderson defines nationalism as a collective act of imagination. A nation "is imagined because the members of even the smallest nation will never know most of their fellow members, meet them or even hear of them, yet in the minds of each lives the image of their communion." The concept of nation is a product of European history. With the development of mass printing in the sixteenth century, individuals slowly began to imagine nations that were distinct from the religious community and the ruling dynasty.[9] As nationalism gathered momentum in the nineteenth century, organized religion in Europe declined. As God and the church faded, or were banished, from public life in Europe, the cult of the nation took their place.

Nationalism became a pivotal force in Europe and throughout the world. Bulgarian and Serbian nationalism led to independence from the Ottoman Empire in the final decades of the nineteenth century, and in turn helped launch a wave of Turkish nationalism that resulted in a cycle of violence in the Balkans. Inside the Ottoman Empire, Turkish nationalism became increasingly prominent at the end of the reign of Sultan Abdul Hamid II. As the Ottoman reforms failed to make the empire an equal competitor, and as North Africa, Egypt, and Lebanon became provinces of the West, a new generation of Turks distinguished Turkishness from Ottomanness. Disillusioned by Abdul Hamid, a group calling themselves the "Young Turks," many of whom were in exile in Paris, dedicated themselves to the cause of the Turkish nation. In their

reading, Ottoman greatness was Turkish greatness, and the Arab provinces were simply areas that had been ruled and acquired by Turkish
rulers. This revision of the Ottoman past, though it erased the rich legacy of multiethnic and multireligious cooperation, took root in Istanbul
and in Turkey itself. The Turkish nationalists did what all nationalists
do: they defined an "us" based on language, ethnicity, a shared past, and
a common religion. And they defined a "them" who spoke different languages, had a different past, and were not only distinct but lesser and
even inferior.

Nationalism accelerated the breakup of the Ottoman Empire. The
old *millet*s began to think of themselves as independent nations, as did
many of the provinces. Armenians demanded Armenian autonomy;
Egyptians fought for Egyptian independence; and the Arabs of Syria
agitated for an Arab nation. These ideas did not develop simultaneously.
Egyptian nationalism emerged before the Arab nationalism of the early
twentieth century. Nonetheless, the concept of nationalism took root
almost everywhere, from Morocco and Algeria in the west to Iran in the
east.

The process was not linear, and for many years, nationalism was a
phenomenon confined to the elite. A fellah working the fields in Upper
Egypt would not have spoken of an Egyptian nation any more than a
Turkish farmer in central Anatolia would have thought of himself as a
citizen of a place called Turkey. To confuse matters further, there were
competing nationalisms. There were Ottoman nationalists, who argued
that the empire, with its shared history, actually constituted a nation-
state. They had limited success convincing others of that, but their
campaign was no more or less futile than that of elites in the Austro-
Hungarian Empire trying to do the same. There was also a group of
Islamic nationalists who combined the modern European idea of a
nation-state with the Islamic ideal of the *umma* to argue that there was a
transnational Muslim community that had been fragmented for centuries but that should be reconstituted under the leadership of a new
caliph.

Later on, nationalism would reveal its darker side, of ethnic purity
and state control of what citizens said and thought. At first, however,
nationalism was allied to the ideals of progress and linked to the sense
that Muslim societies were changing for the better. An independent, sovereign nation was hailed as the fulfillment of Muslim hopes and dreams,

and independent states would be the reward for the arduous work of reform. The beginning of the twentieth century was heralded in Europe as the dawn of a better age of mankind, and that sentiment permeated the Muslim world. Just as the prevailing attitude in Europe was that war and disease would disappear in the twentieth century, it was widely believed in the Muslim world that the twentieth century would see an end to imperialism and the revival of Muslim societies. That would require effort and would not come about without a struggle, but there was optimism that everything would eventually work out.

The dream of a renaissance after reform was secular. Educated, elite Muslims did not see a prominent role for religion in public life. Nonetheless, their dreams were grounded in a past that had demonstrated the power of a covenant and the promise that if the word of God was heeded, earthly rewards would follow. The promise of the new century was similar, except that the terms were different. Instead of listening to the word of God, Muslims had to embrace the tenets of the modern world—science, innovation, education—in order to reap earthly rewards. The first decades of the century seemed to offer proof that with reform would come a rebirth. For a while, the vision of the reformers was vindicated—but only for a while.

CHAPTER ELEVEN

HOPE AND DESPAIR

A T THE BEGINNING of the twentieth century, religion as a central force in the fate of nations was almost nonexistent. It was commonly believed, at least by the educated and the elite, that religion would soon fade away, to survive perhaps as a quaint tradition kept alive out of sentimentality and habit but no more part of the modern world than magic and witchcraft. Insofar as Muslims embraced the attitudes and manners of the West, they shared similar sentiments.

As we now know, the death of religion was prematurely announced, and the story of the twentieth century is one of retreat followed by a regrouping and an advance, not so much in Europe, but in many parts of the world. Just as the rise of nationalism went hand in hand with the decline in organized religion, the failures of nationalism contributed to a new religious revival.

Failure is, of course, always defined in relation to expectations. Had the expectations been more modest, the story of the twentieth century would have been different. But nationalism and modernity embodied utopian dreams of a world without physical or spiritual want. They held out the promise that nations would be able to satisfy both the material needs of their citizens and the intangible ones as well. The nation would provide not just security but meaning and purpose. That was a tall order, and even if it was not bound to fail, it did.

A millennium of success, punctuated by challenges such as the Crusades and the Mongol invasions, had conditioned much of the Muslim world to believe that those who embraced Islam would in return be given power relative to those who rejected it. The tolerance that Muslim communities exhibited toward the People of the Book went hand in hand with that power, and it stood in sharp contrast to the intolerance that Christian societies displayed toward Jews and Muslims during the same centuries. Given that Christian societies were rarely secure in their power until a few hundred years ago, it's hard not to conclude that security is a precondition for tolerance. There are exceptions, including the early Muslims in Medina in relation to their non-Muslim neighbors. Theirs was tolerance born of expediency and weakness. But in general, tolerance is often a by-product of strength and an expression of confidence.

Throughout the nineteenth and early twentieth centuries, Muslim societies were anything but secure in the face of Western encroachments and expansion. Yet with the exception of Damascus in 1860, that didn't lead to intolerance. In fact, the reform movements trumpeted coexistence and protected religious diversity. Not only the *Tanzimat* reforms of the Ottoman Empire but the various constitutions written throughout the Muslim world all enshrined religious toleration as a cornerstone of the modern state.

This nineteenth- and early-twentieth-century spirit of tolerance is another overlooked chapter of history. In the West, the prevailing image of Muslim societies is that, at best, they discriminated against non-Muslims and at worst they treated other religions with outright hatred.[1] The forgetting of the past is just as acute within Muslim countries. In the late twentieth and early twenty-first centuries, the principle of tolerance for Christians and Jews has been denounced by extremists, and Muslim defenders of coexistence have had a difficult time being heard. That is in contrast to centuries of Islamic history, when respect had been so woven into the moral framework that no one thought to challenge it.

But however much the ideologies of intolerance have come to dominate the public realm, that does not mean that most people are intolerant. Societies have public faces that do not necessarily reflect what the people who inhabit them think and feel. Even in the contentious modern age, the quiet norm in the Muslim world has been a tacit acceptance of religious minorities and a continued willingness to work with the West when that is perceived as beneficial. That reality, less dramatic than angry sermons meant to stoke passions, has been almost completely obscured by fundamentalists who see the reforms of the nineteenth and twentieth century as a long march away from Islam and away from everything that had once made Muslims powerful.

There was nothing inevitable about public abandonment of tolerance and coexistence. Even as the West invaded and occupied parts of the Muslim world, the initial response was to find ways to accommodate and cooperate. There was no widespread call for jihad against the West in the early twentieth century. There were calls for a restored caliphate and for reforms that would generate an Arab or Muslim renaissance, but not for war against the West. And as long as the promise of independence and revival stayed alive, most Muslim societies distinguished between illegitimate Western domination, which was to be resisted, and continued coexistence between Muslims, Christians and Jews, which was to be preserved.

THE ARAB REVOLT AND
THE BALFOUR DECLARATION

Two events profoundly shaped how Muslims, Christians, and Jews interacted in the twentieth century. One was the Arab Revolt against the Ottomans, which was supported and encouraged by the British. The other was the creation of a Jewish state in Palestine, also supported and encouraged (at least initially) by the British. Both had their origins in World War I.[2]

In many ways, World War I was the direct result of the erosion of the Ottoman Empire and the outbreak of more virulent strains of nationalism. In the decades leading up to the assassination of the Archduke Franz Ferdinand in Sarajevo on June 28, 1914, the Balkans were a cauldron of nationalist zeal. The balance between the new Balkan states was continually disrupted by the powers of Europe, which treated them as pawns to be used and sacrificed. The Ottoman Empire was roiled by a struggle between Turkish nationalists who wanted to retrench and redefine the empire as a Turkish state and Ottoman nationalists who wanted to regroup and recapture lost territories. In the Balkans, the Russians aggressively asserted their claim to be the protector of Slavic states such as Bulgaria and Serbia, and thereby came into direct conflict with the Habsburg-ruled Austro-Hungarian Empire, which was itself wrestling to maintain its control in the face of nationalist movements. When Franz Ferdinand, the heir to the Austrian throne, was killed by a Serbian nationalist, a chain reaction led to war between the major European states. Soon after, the Ottoman Empire joined the fray on the side of Germany against the French, Russians, and English.

In the Near East, the war became a contest between England and the Ottomans. The British Empire depended on the Suez Canal to link Britain to its colonies in India and Asia. With the outbreak of hostilities, the British treated Egypt as a strategic center that could serve as a launching point for attacks on the Ottomans. They also viewed Egypt as potentially vulnerable, and redoubled their military presence in the canal zone. The other source of British concern was the three Ottoman provinces of Mosul, Baghdad, and Basra (which would eventually form the modern state of Iraq).

Within the Ottoman Empire, the war provided the government with a rationale for suppressing dissent. Given that most dissent came from ethnic and religious minorities who wanted independence, the result was predictable. Turkish governors dispatched by the cabal then ruling in the sultan's name showed no mercy in the Armenian provinces in eastern Anatolia and in the Arab provinces of Syria and Lebanon. The Ottoman Turks were so concerned about Armenian nationalism that they engineered the forced removal of millions of Armenians, many of whom died or were killed in the process. In the Near East, anyone who had spoken for Arab nationalism or for an independent Arab state faced imprisonment or execution. The empire, which had for centuries epitomized tolerance, became a police state.

In Cairo, a group of British officials set up an Arab Bureau in order to coordinate efforts to support Arabs who wanted to work with the Allies against the Ottomans. One of the junior officers assigned to the bureau was T. E. Lawrence, a young but preternaturally old and already eccentric student of classical Islamic castle architecture who had fallen for the desert. He idolized the bedouins as warriors pure of heart, humble in their faith, and still connected to the natural world. But though he celebrated their culture, his attitudes toward the Arabs he actually encountered were paternalistic and condescending. He saw them as lost souls, who had forgotten what had made them great centuries ago. Condescension aside, his interpretation was not much different than that of Muhammad Abduh or the Arab reformers, but unlike them, he was an

Englishman who didn't believe that the Arabs were capable of claiming their own destiny. Instead, he was convinced that they could move forward to a better future only if the more civilized and advanced England assisted them.

The Arab Revolt of 1916 had several triggers. One was the British struggle against the Ottomans. By sponsoring a revolt of the Arab provinces, the British High Command hoped to distract the Ottoman military and force the empire to direct precious resources to fight in what was otherwise the strategic backwater of Syria and the Arabian Peninsula. Another spark was the dream of national awakening that had been fostered in equal measure by sympathetic Europeans like Wilfrid Blunt and by hardheaded reformers like Afghani, Abduh, and their successors. Though Lawrence was at the outset only a staff officer responsible for implementing policy rather than making it, he fused the contradictory aspirations of the British Empire. As his influence grew, he then embodied the inevitable disillusionment that ensued once those visions ran up against great-power politics. Sent by the Arab Bureau to support Sharif Husayn of Mecca, Lawrence set in motion events that would remake the Near East.

"All men dream," he wrote in later years,

> but not equally. Those who dream by night in the dusty recesses of their minds wake in the day to find that it was vanity: but the dreamers of the day are dangerous men, for they may act their dream with open eyes, to make it possible. This I did. I meant to make a new nation, to restore lost influence, to give twenty millions of Semites the foundations on which to build an inspired dream palace of the national thoughts, and made them play a generous part in events: but when we won, it was charged against me that the British petrol royalties in Mesopotamia were become dubious, and French Colonial policy ruined the Levant.[3]

Lawrence, with his florid prose and profound sense of destiny, became a key player in the Arab Revolt as the liaison between the Arabs and the British. He was also a capable military commander, who favored the hit-and-run tactics that had been perfected over the course of centuries by bedouin raiders. In the eyes of the West, he was the public face of the Arab Revolt. Lionized as Lawrence of Arabia, he was pictured in bedouin garb and credited with organizing the tribal Arabs, mounted on camels and on horseback, against the stolid and better armed Turkish occupiers.

Yet the Arabs that Lawrence worked with were hardly passive pawns. They had their own plans and their own vision. They treated him as a partner, and in the end they used him just as he used them. By the time he wrote his memoirs, he had become an international celebrity, and the dreams of the Arab Revolt had collided with the postwar realities of the Paris peace conference and the refusal of the European powers to honor their wartime pledges. But in 1916 Lawrence still believed, with a naive, compelling fervor, that he was fighting for the restoration of Arab glory.

The movement was led, at least initially, by Sharif Husayn ibn Ali, who was the head of the Hashemite clan that traced its lineage back to the Prophet Muhammad. Though his family had governed the holy cities of Mecca and Medina for generations, he answered to the Ottomans and paid tribute to the sultan, and he had begun to chafe under the control of Istanbul. He was also facing a challenge from Ibn Saud, who controlled the central part of the Arabian Peninsula and could call on the formidable support of the puritanical Wahhabis. Even before the war, Husayn entered into a dialogue with the British authorities in Cairo, and the letters between him and the British high commissioner, Sir Henry McMahon, set forth the conditions under which he would agree to declare independence.

Husayn wanted more than to rule Arabia. He intended to create an Arab state stretching from Syria to Yemen that would potentially include parts of Iraq as well. Though he needed British military and economic aid in order to mount a credible campaign against the Ottomans, he was a proud, stubborn man with several ambitious sons, and he correctly perceived that he was in a position to make demands. As a result, the British guaranteed that his family would have the right to rule the lands "lying to the west of the districts of Damascus, Homs, Hama, and Aleppo." The terms would come back to haunt not just the British and Husayn, but the Hashemite clan, the Arab world, and the future state of Israel. The text of the letters excluded Lebanon but did not address who would control Palestine. Jerusalem and its environs were symbolically important both to the Ottomans and the British, and it isn't surprising that their status was left out of discussions between Husayn and McMahon. Yet the omission proved costly to the future of coexistence between the Arab world and the West.

With the parameters established, Husayn announced the Arab Revolt in June 1916. Soon after, he proclaimed himself king of the Arabs. Lawrence later claimed that he designed the military and political strategy adopted by Husayn and his sons, and while he almost certainly overstated his role, he did act as a trusted adviser. Husayn's sons Abdullah, later the first king of Jordan, and Faysal, soon to be the first king of Iraq, both relied on Lawrence's counsel, Faysal most of all. They knew he wanted the same thing for them that they wanted for themselves: an independent Arab nation allied with Great Britain. They saw themselves as walking in the footsteps of the first Arab conquerors, destined to inherit the legacy of Muhammad and the caliphs, their great-grandfathers many times removed. And in their most optimistic moments, preparing for an ambush on a Turkish outpost or readying an assault on the port city of Aqaba, they saw their dreams coming true and believed that the English, represented by Lawrence, were on their side, working for a common goal.

What Lawrence didn't know, or chose not to acknowledge, was that the British had no intention of honoring their promises to Husayn and his family. All may be fair in love and war, but that does not mean that there are no hurt feelings. Husayn, Faysal, and Abdullah led a revolt against the Ottomans at great personal peril, and they expected the British to keep their word. But the British were trying to win a war, and they were willing to make empty promises to gain allies. As important as the Arab Revolt was, it was a minor affair in the greater scheme of things, and less important than the Anglo-French alliance.

The French had their own designs on Lebanon and Syria, having worked tirelessly for much of the nineteenth century to secure their influence in those regions. Just as McMahon was promising Syria and more to Husayn, a British diplomat named Mark Sykes concluded a secret compact with a French diplomat named Charles François Georges-Picot. The Sykes-Picot agreement established a template for the postwar division of the Arab provinces of the Ottoman Empire: France would get Syria, Lebanon, and parts of oil-rich northern Iraq; Britain would get Palestine and southern and central Iraq.

To complicate matters further still, the British government made another wartime promise. This one had little to do with the war and did nothing to advance the campaign against the Ottomans. It was, instead, the culmination of years of effort by a nationalist group that had blossomed in the late nineteenth century. Like so many others, this group traced its origins to a distant point in the past and claimed the right of self-determination. But unlike so many others—unlike the Serbs or the Turks or the Arabs—this movement looked to a land that its people had not occupied in any great numbers in nearly two thousand years. That was what made Zionism different, and what made the declaration of the British foreign secretary in 1917 all that more unusual.

The idea that Jews were an ethnic group that had the right to self-determination and their own state was no more or less unusual than any other nationalist movement of the time. But the homeland claimed by the Jews was Palestine, and the ones claiming it were European Jews. Graced with well-connected and extremely disciplined leaders, the Zionists found a sympathetic audience in the inner circles of the British government. Just as there is a long and complicated history between Muslims and the People of the Book, there is also another history, of relations between Jews and Christians. Rarely had Jews fared well in Christian states. They had been barely tolerated, but with a lingering threat of violence that compared poorly to the climate of benign neglect in the Muslim world. In the nineteenth century, as most Western European states distanced themselves from organized religion, the position of Jews improved, especially in countries such as England, France, and Germany. But leading families like the Rothschilds were aware that the security of the present was not something to rely on. Only if the Jews had their own country could their survival be assured.

In England, support for Zionism stemmed from the same source as support for Arab independence. Most of the men who governed the British Empire had gone to schools whose curriculum was heavily influenced by both the Bible and the classics of Rome and Greece. The result was a deep affinity for the Holy Land, which in turn led to an ambivalent and troubled relationship to Judaism. There was shame and guilt over the ill treatment that Jews had suffered throughout most of the medieval and early modern period—and there was also anti-Semitism, which led members of the British ruling class to prefer the idea of Jews living somewhere else. Leaders of the Zionist movement toiled for years to gain the support of the British government (and the American government of Woodrow Wilson as well) for a homeland in Palestine, but as long as the Ottoman Empire was still intact, there was little the British were willing or able to do. With the war, however, the aspirations of the Zionists received an unexpected boost, and in 1917, the British foreign secretary, Sir Arthur Balfour, issued a stunning declaration.

"His Majesty's Government," Balfour wrote in a letter to the Lord Rothschild,

> view with favor the establishment in Palestine of a national home-land for the Jewish people, and will use their best endeavors to facil-itate the achievement of this object, it being clearly understood that nothing shall be done which may prejudice the civil and religious rights of existing non-Jewish communities in Palestine, or the rights and political status enjoyed by Jews in any other country.

The British government later claimed that it had informed Husayn before issuing the statement, as well as at least one of his sons, Faysal. Husayn, according to British accounts, had no objections, as he did not see Palestine as essential to the national aspirations of the Arabs. He also did not believe that the declaration precluded an Arab state governing the territory, as long as the rights of local Jews and any Jewish immi-grants from Europe were protected. In Britain, a number of prominent Jewish leaders, including a member of the cabinet, Sir Edwin Montagu, were less warm to the idea of the British endorsing Zionism. They were concerned that doing so would undermine the hard-won status of the Jews in England and in other countries in Europe. Hence the final words of the declaration, and hence, as well, why Balfour spoke only of a "national homeland" rather than a state, which left open a variety of possibilities short of actually nationhood.[4]

This triad of documents—the Husayn-McMahon correspondence, the Sykes-Picot agreement, and the Balfour Declaration—determined the shape of the modern Middle East. Even more, the hopes and expec-tations raised by these promises were the source of many of the conflicts both within the Arab world and between the Arab world and the West for the remainder of the twentieth century. After the Russian Revolution in 1917, the Bolsheviks, in order to embarrass and undermine the Allied war effort, made public a variety of secret documents, one of which was the Sykes-Picot agreement. Its revelation had the desired effect. British duplicity was exposed. The British had told Husayn that Syria would be his and then secretly assured the French that it would be theirs. Had Britain known how much bitterness these conflicting promises would generate, it may have thought twice, but in the heat of war, lies seemed a small price to pay for victory.

Few were more disillusioned by what happened in the aftermath of the war than Lawrence himself. He had been used and misled by his government no less than Husayn and his sons. After the war, he went to Paris, as did Faysal, to plead the case for Arab independence. Woodrow Wilson had opened the floodgates of nationalism when he announced before the peace conference that the postwar world would honor the self-determination of all peoples. Faysal was one of many supplicants who asked the victorious powers to grant his people a state, and he was one of many whose requests were politely, but firmly and perhaps cynically, rejected.

Faysal appeared at the conference not just as the representative of his father, but as the ruler of Damascus. In the final days of the war, the forces of the Arab Revolt occupied the city and Faysal was proclaimed king. Lawrence both reveled in the success and dreaded what he knew, or at least feared, would come after. The French coveted Syria, and they had no intention of ceding it to Faysal or the Arabs. In a similar fashion, the British wanted Iraq. In fact, with the exception of the unclear status of oil-rich Mosul, the map of the Near East had been drawn long before Faysal or Lawrence arrived in Paris.

But with American president Woodrow Wilson having unleashed the genie of self-determination, the powers of Europe could not simply brush aside Faysal's claims and those of others who were in a similar position. The result was a compromise between imperialism, nationalism, and Wilson's idealism: the Mandate System. Under its terms, various European nations were given control of specified territory under the condition that they established a timeline for eventual independence. Syria and Lebanon were declared French mandates; Iraq, Transjordan, and Palestine were awarded to the British. Faysal returned to Damascus, only to be forcibly removed by the French. The British, who needed someone to govern the new state of Iraq, decided to install the now-stateless Faysal as its new king in 1921. His brother Abdullah became the first ruler of the new state of Transjordan, and their father, Husayn, was left in control of the western part of Arabia.[5]

The subsequent fate of the Hashemites was mixed. Sharif Husayn, having been a hero to the Allied war effort, alienated the British because of his refusal to kowtow after the war. He soon found himself without sufficient aid and unable to resist the onslaught of Ibn Saud, who evicted Husayn from Arabia in 1924. Faysal remained king when Iraq became independent in 1932, and ruled until his death the following year. His heirs controlled the country, under the watchful eye of the British, until his grandson Faysal II was overthrown and assassinated in a coup in 1958. Only Abdullah's family survived much past midcentury as rulers of Jordan, though Abdullah himself was gunned down for the unforgivable sin of allowing an independent state of Israel to come into existence in 1948 and planning to make a separate peace with the Israelis. His legacy was continued by his grandson Hussein, who in turn was succeeded by his son Abdullah II, the current ruler of Jordan.

Outside of Jordan, it is rare today for those who remember these events to portray Husayn, Faysal, and their family as anything but puppets in an imperial game.[6] The regimes that replaced them in both Saudi Arabia and Iraq reviled their legacy and labeled them collaborators. They were viewed, at best, as benighted fools who had legitimate goals but who failed utterly in implementing them, and, at worst, as corrupt and venal manipulators who sold out the Arabs to the West. As for the British, the French, and the West in general, they were indicted for cloaking their greed for oil and for land in the noble language of the League of Nations and self-determination.

Without question, Western motives were ambiguous. Many genuinely respected the Arabs, admired the bedouin, and supported the right to self-determination. The contradictory promises that the British made were largely the product of incompatible goals. Men like Balfour and Prime Minister Lloyd George were both idealistic romantics and hardheaded practitioners of realpolitik. They genuinely supported a homeland for the Jews and a new Arab nation, and also wanted to make sure that the balance of power in the postwar Near East did not favor the French. They did not believe that either the Arabs or the Jews were ready for self-government without a period of tutelage, and they were willing and eager to be the tutors.

On the other side, men like Faysal and Husayn made their compromises knowingly. They were prepared to do what was necessary to achieve their ultimate goal. For Faysal, that meant accepting the loss of Syria in order to get Iraq. His aim was an independent Arab nation, and he was pragmatic enough to change tactics as the situation demanded. After the war, the British in Iraq were desperate for a credible ruler who could unite a country on the verge of revolt. In 1920, Iraq had been racked by a bloody insurgency, and though the British army and air force quelled the uprising, there was still no viable Arab ruler. Faysal was offered the throne of Iraq, provided he was willing to work under the terms of the British Mandate until the League of Nations determined that Iraq was ready for full independence. Winston Churchill, then colonial secretary, wired the British high commissioner in Iraq about British expectations: "You should explain to Faysal that...we must expect to be consulted so long as we are meeting heavy financial charges in Mesopotamia [Iraq]. He must show that he is capable of maintaining peace and order unaided...then he can become sovereign.... This will certainly take some time."[7] Faysal, who was almost as much a stranger to Iraq as the British were, agreed, and in 1921 he arrived in Basra. He soon won a rigged election that the British made sure he could not lose, and was acclaimed king by 96 percent of the population. Eleven years later, Iraq gained full independence.

Here as well, what is most remarkable in light of subsequent history is the almost complete absence of religion from the debates. In Iraq, the same divisions that define the country in the early twenty-first century defined the political landscape under Britain and Faysal. The Shi'ites were predominant in the south, the Sunnis in the central regions, and the Kurds in the north. But while the British played on regional and religious rivalries as part of their tactics of divide-and-rule, no one demanded a Muslim state or called for a government controlled by the *ulama*. Religious differences were secondary to tribal, ethnic, and regional divisions, and Iraqi elites argued not over the role of religion in public life but over the merits of the British, the virtues or faults of Faysal, and the shape of the nascent "Arab nation" emerging from the shadow of the Ottomans in the Near East.

Although the Hashemites became synonymous with collaboration with the West, they were architects of their own destiny and made strategic choices that involved collaboration with the British in order to achieve independence. As Faysal said in 1921, "The British and I are in the same boat and must sink or swim. Having, so to speak, chosen me, the British must treat me as one of themselves and I must be trusted." Stripped of the baleful context of later interpretations, the relationship between Britain and Faysal in Iraq was a marriage of convenience, but a marriage it was. It was an example of cooperation and coexistence, and it created a new state.

Similar relationships existed between the British and Abdullah in Jordan, between the French and nascent political parties in Syria and Lebanon, and between the British and nationalist leaders in Egypt. Throughout the Near East, and in Turkey under the charismatic leadership of Kemal Atatürk, elites made common cause with Western powers, who in turn looked to them as partners who would facilitate their access to oil. It was not a union of equals, as the West retained military and economic dominance. But neither was it a black-and-white case of an oppressive, rapacious West and passive Muslim states with puppet leaders. The West was ascendent, and presented a still unsolvable puzzle to Muslim societies, but within that framework there was a wide scope of cooperation, coexistence, and common ground.

Nationalism was the most fertile common ground. It was understood that Muslim societies would achieve full independence from the West only when they became modern nations. Politicians and intellectuals throughout the Muslim world ingested the history and ideas that had led to the emergence of the Western nation-state, and they then applied those to their own societies. That process had begun in the late nineteenth century, but truly blossomed after World War I, especially in the Arab world. While Arab nationalism aimed to remove the onerous presence of the Western powers, Arab states in the first half of the twentieth century was still dependent on and subservient to the West. The relationship was laced with tension, competition, and animosity, but there was also respect, shared goals, and similar world views.

EGYPT, SYRIA, AND ARAB NATIONALISM

AFTER WORLD WAR I, France remained in direct control of North Africa from Morocco to Tunisia, but in the Near East, the situation was more varied. Egypt was declared independent in 1922 after a popular uprising against the British, although Britain retained wide latitude to intervene in Egypt's internal affairs and had almost complete control over its foreign policy and its major source of revenue, the Suez Canal. Though Transjordan, Palestine, and Iraq had been awarded to the British, and Iraq became independent in 1932, Palestine remained under British rule until after World War II, and in Transjordan Abdullah depended on London's military support in order to rule an arid territory inhabited by a few hundred thousand bedouin. The French retained Syria and Lebanon and refused to allow either to emerge from mandate status. Saudi Arabia thrived as an independent country under the autocratic Ibn Saud, in part because he was so amenable to Western oil companies investing in the infrastructure necessary to transform the desert kingdom into a petro powerhouse. Non-Arab Iran and Turkey avoided direct European control, and were ruled by modernizing strongmen. Atatürk in Turkey and Reza Shah Pahlavi in Iran instituted a European-style education system, which meant removing the curriculum from the hands of the clerics and the *ulama.* They also stepped up the pace of economic and agricultural reform. They enacted laws to enforce a more modern dress code, especially for women, and the veil—a potent symbol of the old order—was outlawed.

Both Syria and Egypt were centers of Arab nationalism. In Syria, one movement was led by a Christian named Michel Aflaq, who was a founder of the Ba'ath Party. Aflaq had attended French schools, lived in Paris, and studied at the Sorbonne. Though initially more socialist, he later flirted with extreme forms of nationalism modeled on the fascism of Mussolini and Hitler. Aflaq lived a long life, and he witnessed first the victory and then the perversion of his legacy when the 1958 Ba'athist coup in Iraq eventually led to the dictatorship of Saddam Hussein. Though Aflaq wanted to create a modern state, he believed that Islam was a vital component of Arab unity. The irony of a Christian intellectual creating the framework for a nationalist movement that embraced Islam was lost on most at the time (and since), but Arab Christians in Lebanon, Syria, and Palestine were at the forefront of the development of Arab nationalism. Aflaq called Islam "the most precious element of Arabism," and he enjoined all Arabs, whether Christian or Muslim, to revere Muhammad as a hero.

The West was perceived as an obstacle and an adversary, yet in emulating European nationalism, socialism, and even fascism, Arabs were in some respect cooperating with the West. That may not be a legacy to remember fondly. Ba'athism was only one of many Arab nationalisms, of course, and in Syria alone, there were mainstream nationalist parties that rejected the philosophy of Aflaq. But while many of the principles of Ba'athism were distasteful and many of its subsequent leaders were corrupt, it was nonetheless a movement born of integration between Muslims and Christians, between the Middle East and the West. Aflaq wasn't shy about crediting French and German intellectuals for his inspiration, and the Ba'ath Party that he helped create borrowed heavily from both communism and the national socialism that burgeoned in Europe between the wars. Aflaq also defended the rights of the poor and the universal right to free speech, and he called for secular government in the Arab world. He had, at least, a moral compass, compromised though it may have been. Though he lived to see the Ba'ath Party come to power in both Syria and Iraq, and was appointed to a ceremonial ministerial post in Iraq, Aflaq was never comfortable with the politicians who led the party, including Saddam Hussein. In the 1960s and 1970s, Hussein used Aflaq and the Ba'athist label when he thought it convenient and ignored them when they were not.[8]

Aflaq and Ba'athism were one form of synchronicity with the West. The constitutional nationalist movement in Egypt was another. After World War I, Egypt was still directly governed by the British, but unlike Iraq, it was not part of the Mandate System. Egyptian opposition to the British coalesced around the Wafd Party and its grand old man, Sa'd Zaghlul. Zaghlul succeeded Muhammad Abduh as the leading reformer in Egypt at the turn of the twentieth century, and he was the driving force behind Egyptian independence. After his arrest by the British for organizing protests in 1919, he was deported to Malta. That triggered an uprising, which shook British resolve and led to Egyptian independence in 1922. Zaghlul, promising to decrease the influence of Britain over Egyptian affairs, became prime minister in 1924. While he did not succeed in diminishing the presence of the British in the Suez Canal zone, Egypt was admitted as a full member of the League of Nations in 1937.

The Wafd Party remained the dominant force in Egyptian politics for more than three decades. The party was infused with the dignity, probity, and pride of Zaghlul, but it was led by several equally formidable men in the 1930s and 1940s, who were faced with the same challenge of a Britain that was unwilling to yield its control of the canal or Egypt's foreign policy to a domestic, elected government. Some Egyptian nationalists then turned to Germany as a natural ally in the struggle against the British. It was a classic example of "the enemy of my enemy is my friend." The Germans challenged British hegemony in Egypt, especially during the early years of World War II, when the North Africa campaigns of the "Desert Fox," General Erwin Rommel, threatened to evict Britain from Egypt and the Suez Canal. The Wafd Party, however, resisted an explicit break with the British, and a Wafd prime minister was in fact forced on King Farouk in 1942 when British tanks broke down the gates of Abdin palace and ordered the king to change his government. But while supportive of the British war effort, the Wafd continued to work for full independence. One product of its struggle was the creation of the League of Arab States in 1945, which remained a prominent vehicle for pan-Arab nationalism into the twenty-first century.[9]

The Syrian Ba'ath and the Egyptian Wafd represented two different forms of nationalism. One veered toward socialism, the other emulated English liberalism. The Ba'ath saw nationalism as a force that transcended the artificial borders that separated the Arab world into states. The dream, in fact, was that one day there would be a unified nation—or *umma*—stretching from North Africa to Iraq, encompassing the entire Arabic-speaking world.

Arab nationalism had an uneasy relationship with religion. While Islam was supposed to bind Arabs together, it was neither the only nor the dominant force. It shared space with language, history, and vague notions of race. Christians like Aflaq were often more comfortable with placing Islam at the center of Arab nationalism than Muslims were. Almost all of the leaders of the nationalist independence movements had gone to school in Europe or were educated in schools with a European curriculum. They had been inculcated with the virtues of secular society and the scientific method, and they had been taught to treat traditional religions as bastions of backwardness. Many of them had also studied Islam at a local mosque, and their experiences with neighborhood preachers often reinforced their skepticism. Christians like Aflaq, however, could adopt a more utilitarian attitude. Unburdened by personal ambivalence about Islam, they articulated a vision of an Arab nation that was at once Islamic and tolerant of the People of the Book.

The promise of Arab nationalism, like the promise of the nineteenth-century reform movement, was simple: if the Arabs could find a way to erase the false divisions that separated them, if they could throw off the yoke of European dominance, and if they could demonstrate that they were capable of governing their own affairs, then there would be an Arab renaissance to rival the court at Baghdad and the glories of Saladin. Turkish nationalism under Atatürk and Iranian nationalism under the shah held out similar promises, though the Turks looked to restore the glories of past Turkish dynasties, and the Iranians the power of Persian monarchs both before and after the advent of Islam.

What happened in the Middle East in the twentieth century helped determine the framework for how Muslims, Christians, and Jews interacted throughout the globe. Even though most of the Muslim world lay outside the Middle East—including hundreds of millions of Muslims in India and Indonesia who had little or no contact with Christians or Jews—the Middle East in the twentieth century was a crucible, as it had been when this story began in the seventh century, nearly fourteen hundred years ago, and as it continues to be today.

THE BIRTH OF ISRAEL AND ITS CONSEQUENCES

THIRTY YEARS stood between the Balfour Declaration and the birth of the independent state of Israel. For most of those three decades, it seemed unlikely that the outcome would be a Jewish state. Jews in Palestine were a minority living amid Arabs, some of whom were Muslim and some of whom were Christian. In the end, because of a series of decisions made by both Palestinian and Zionist leaders, as well as because of events in Europe and in the world well beyond the control of either, what materialized was a Jewish state vehemently opposed by almost every Arab nation. The creation of Israel in 1948 is one of those rare before-and-after moments, one that disrupted a tenuous balance that had existed between Muslims and Jews from time immemorial and that has yet to be restored.

It is almost impossible to write about the creation of Israel without offending someone. The history has become so politicized and so partisan that there is simply no agreement about the facts. Emotion trumps all else when the subject of Israel is raised, especially in the contemporary Middle East. Israel has become a third rail for rational, sober discourse. If the Holocaust stands as a never-ending rebuke to relations between Christians and Jews, then the intractable conflict between the

Palestinians and the Israelis has come to color not just discussions about Judaism in the Muslim world but discussions about Islam and the West in general.

The creation of Israel is a historical Rubicon. On one side is a dynamic past of coexistence and cooperation along with episodes of antagonism and cruelty. On the other is an increasingly simplistic picture of hostile relations between the parties. In short, the creation of Israel led to disturbing revisions of the past in light of the present. Muslims, Christians, and Jews are all guilty of revisionism. Most books about "Muslim intolerance" use the lens of the Arab-Israeli conflict to categorize the entire history of Islam. The vehement anti-Israeli attitudes of the Arab world since the middle of the twentieth century have been beamed backward a millennium and a half into the past, the presumption being that if many present-day Arabs who are also Muslim hate or oppose the Jewish state of Israel, then it must be because of some essential component of Islam. In a similar vein, Muslims tend to collapse Judaism and the state of Israel into one. Detesting the existence of Israel, they implicate Judaism, and thereby forget the coexistence with Jews that marked so much of their shared history.

Increasingly, Muslims and Jews, as well as Western Christians who span the spectrum from the most secular in Europe to the most fundamentalist in the United States, treat the Arab-Israeli conflict as the latest episode in a long war between the faiths. The assumption in the Western world is that Muslims have always opposed the existence of Judaism, and nurtured an animosity toward Christians and the West as well. In the Arab world, the existence of Israel has become a symbol of Arab weakness, proof that the reformers and the nationalists failed in their goal of resurrecting Arab greatness.

Complicating matters even further is the loose use of words and confusion about who is fighting whom and why. There is an Arab-Israeli conflict, which includes Arab Christians who have opposed or fought the state of Israel. Arab Christians in Lebanon, in Israel itself, and in Egypt have at times been the most adamant opponents of Israel, and Christians have been prominent in the leadership of the Palestine Liberation Organization. With each passing decade in the twentieth century, the Arab-Israeli conflict was exported throughout the Muslim world, first as a symbol of the injustice of the West, then as a symbol of

Muslim failure, and finally as a vindication of the Muslim fundamentalist argument about the clash between Islam and the People of the Book.

Muslims thousands of miles from the conflict, in corners of Nigeria, India, Afghanistan, Indonesia, and the Philippines, identified with the Palestinians and came to view the conflict with Israel as the prime example of how far the Muslim world had fallen behind the West. The Palestinians became doppelgängers for all Muslims, and their fate was taken as a painful reminder of the wrong turn that the Arabs had taken. Muslims who had never met a Jew, and who may never have met a Christian, began to view both from the perspective of being an oppressed minority. It didn't matter whether they were living in a predominantly Muslim society. What mattered was an emerging transnational Muslim identity.

The creation of Israel alone cannot and does not explain the climate of animosity and distrust that has disfigured relations between Muslims, Christians, and Jews since the middle of the twentieth century. The legacy of European intervention and colonialism is at least as important, and the inability of numerous Muslim states to achieve the dreams of both the nineteenth-century reformers and the twentieth-century nationalists is perhaps the crucial element. Had Muslim societies in general, and Arab societies most of all, been able to transform themselves, maintain their sense of identity, and become competitive with the West, then Israel may never have become a lightning rod.

Until 1948, the creation of a state of Israel with a Jewish majority was itself in doubt. The Balfour Declaration had promised a "national homeland," but that did not necessarily mean a state. The British Mandate for Palestine was supposed to provide not just for the settlement of Jews in Palestine, but for the self-governance of the half-million Palestinian Arabs who lived in the region. In 1922, the British tried to allay Arab concerns and issued a disingenuous statement that His Majesty's Government had not "at any time contemplated, as appears to be feared by the Arab Delegation, the disappearance or subordination of the Arab population, language or culture in Palestine."[10] But unrestricted Jewish emigration from Europe sparked a violent Arab backlash, which led the British government to restrict the influx of Jews in 1939. British restrictions coincided with the rise of virulent anti-Semitism in Europe, especially in Nazi Germany. That caused more European Jews to emigrate, but they found the British government in Palestine hostile to Jewish settlement. By the end of the 1930s, the British had managed to alienate both the Arab and Jewish populations of Palestine, and were seen as an adversary by both.

The hope that a combined Arab-Jewish polity could be created under the benign and watchful tutelage of the British took time to die completely, but the Arab revolt in 1936, this time against both the Jewish community and the British authorities, shattered whatever illusions anyone may have had that such a state was feasible. Hajj Amin al-Husayni, the mufti of Jerusalem and one of the most prominent Palestinian leaders, disdained compromise with the Jewish immigrants and turned against the British for refusing to support Palestinian dominance. After the outbreak of war between England and Germany, Hajj Amin tilted toward Germany and the Nazis in order to gain leverage against Britain. He spent the war years in Berlin, where he was warmly received by Hitler and the Nazi leadership.

At the same time, the Jewish Agency, which was the Zionist organization responsible for governing Palestine's Jews, also increased its pressure on the British. Several splinter groups (most notably the Irgun Zvai Leumi, led in part by future Israeli prime minister Menachem Begin) used terrorist tactics—roadside bombs, assassinations, and targeting civilians—against the Palestinian Arabs and later against the British in order to force a change in British immigration policy, an end to the mandate, and the creation of a Jewish state.

In 1939, the British government issued a white paper that appeared to abandon the promises of the Balfour Delcaration. They were in no mood to placate the Zionists. Instead, needing stability in Palestine, they did their best to satisfy the Palestinians. The white paper promised an end to Jewish immigration within five years and an eventual Palestinian Arab state rather than a Jewish one. It also struck down the idea of a partition that would result in a two-state solution. The Jewish leadership was horrified, but war in Europe changed the landscape once again. Violence in Palestine escalated, and the British cracked down on Jewish resistance groups. The Jewish Agency, recognizing that the war and the Holocaust had raised the stakes, started to mend fences with the British, and the Palestinian leadership became even more disillusioned. The end of the war, with Britain victorious but exhausted and financially spent, signaled the end of the mandate, and the British government looked for a way out.

The end of the war also saw the fateful beginning of American involvement in the politics of the Middle East. U.S. oil companies had been active since the 1920s, and had assiduously courted the rulers of Saudi Arabia. But the scope of that involvement was minor compared to the years after World War II. As the British receded, the Americans stepped in to fill the void. In the case of Palestine, American interests were nebulous. Though Zionist leaders lobbied the Truman administration to support the establishment of a Jewish state, at the United Nations, they had to compete with Arab leaders who lobbied just as strongly against one. The postwar path from the mandate to the creation of Israel was chaotic and uncertain. The British asked the United Nations to take charge of the situation, and Palestine became one of the first issues that the U.N. attempted to solve.

In November 1947, after substantial back-and-forth, the U.N. General Assembly accepted a partition plan that would have transformed Palestine into an unwieldy checkerboard of Jewish and Palestinian areas. The problem, and a glaring one, was that the eleven Muslim members of the United Nations (including non-Arab states such as Turkey, Afghanistan, and Pakistan) voted against the plan. Denouncing it as "absurd, impracticable, and unjust," they vowed to prevent its implementation by any means necessary. True to their word, when Israel declared its independence on May 15, 1948, the armies of five Arab states (Egypt, Lebanon, Jordan, Iraq, and Syria) mobilized for war. The Israel Defense Forces raised thousands more men than the combined Arab armies and Palestinian militias, and proved to be far superior to their disorganized adversaries. By the fall, not only was the partition plan null and void, but 750,000 Palestinians had been turned into refugees, and Israel controlled large portions of territory that had at least nominally been promised to the Palestinians.[11]

Defeat was not followed by reconciliation. After long and painful months of U.N.-mediated negotiations, Israel signed armistice pacts with each of the Arab states individually. Not only was there no universal peace agreement, there was no peace agreement, period. Armed hostilities ceased, but Israel remained in a state of war with its neighbors. Internationally, the United Nations and its constituents were divided. The United States had, at the last minute, recognized Israel, but only after heated debate within the Truman administration. Most of official Washington was opposed to recognition, largely out of concern that the gesture would weaken the United States in its global campaign against the Soviet Union and undermine its ability to function diplomatically and economically in the Arab world. The Europeans were somewhat more favorable, largely because of guilt over the horrors of the Holocaust. On the whole, however, the new Israeli state found itself intact but isolated and ostracized. Its ability to buy weapons or seal economic agreements was hampered, and it was surrounded by hostile states whose lack of coordination made them ineffectual but whose daily animosity made them unpleasant and dangerous neighbors.

In the Arab world, the establishment of Israel became known as the *naqbah,* the catastrophe. All of the members of the Arab League, including those of North Africa and the Arabian Peninsula, vowed never to recognize Israel and refused to negotiate until there was a return of the refugees and a Palestinian state, with Jerusalem as its capital. The creation of a Jewish state was widely perceived in the Arab world as the ultimate indignity, a glaring example of the strength of the West and the feebleness of the Arabs. After more than a century of reform efforts, the Arab states—or their leadership at their very least—were becoming frustrated. The liberal, constitutional reforms of the nineteenth century and the nationalism of the twentieth century had led to a degree of independence from Europe, but by all measures, the Arab world still could not compete with the West. Algeria, Tunisia, and Morocco remained colonies of France, although the latter two were on the road to independence. Jordan, Iraq, and Egypt could not make foreign policy decisions without the approval of the British Foreign Office. Saudi Arabia was independent, but ringed by British protectorates in Kuwait and the emirates on the Persian Gulf coast and dependent on European and American oil companies for income.

The sense of humiliation grew, as Israel proved impossible to dislodge. In the late 1940s and 1950s, however, the Arab-Israeli conflict was confined to the Middle East. Many, but not all, Muslim countries outside the Middle East voted in sympathy with the Arab states if and when the subject of Israel came up at the United Nations, but Israel was not yet a central concern for their people or their governments. A century of pan-Islamic movements had succeeded only in creating a general sense of shared interests. The result was empathy with the political aims of the Arabs but not virulent opposition to Israel or to Jews. Outside the Middle East, the creation of Israel was taken as one more instance of selfish Western imperialism, but hardly the worst episode. On the other hand, for the central Arab states, and of course for the displaced Palestinians, it was seen as a tragedy that ended, once and for all, the dreams of reform and progress. For them, and soon for many parts of the Muslim world, 1948 was not a beginning but an end. From the ashes of the failed promise, a new set of ideas emerged—virulent, dark, and despairing—that ran counter to centuries of history.

The most immediate and destructive consequence was that hundreds of thousands of Jews were forced to leave their homes and emigrate to Israel. Iraq had one of the oldest Jewish communities in the world, with families that could trace their lineage to the time of the Babylonians, centuries before the birth of Christ. By the 1940s, there were nearly 150,000 Iraqi Jews, many of whom were prominent as financiers, businessmen, and doctors. Iraqi Jews had also played a behind-the-scenes role in bolstering the Hashemite monarchy, especially with loans. Yet after 1948, they came under extraordinary pressure from the Iraqi government, which passed laws limiting their property rights and restricting their freedom of movement, and which ultimately coerced them to leave with only a fraction of their property. By the early 1950s, barely four thousand Jews remained in Iraq; the bulk had left for Israel, with the rest scattered to England, the United States, and other parts of the world.

It was not just Iraq. Of the approximately 1.7 million Jews in Arab lands, hundreds of thousands emigrated to Israel, and hundreds of thousands more left for Europe, Latin America, or the United States. The emigration to Israel included a massive airlift of nearly fifty thousand Yemeni Jews, and the involuntary departure of tens of thousands of Jews from Egypt, Syria, Morocco, and Iran. For nearly two thousand years, Jewish communities had been rooted in these countries, and for most of that time, they had lived peacefully under the rule of Muslim governments. They enjoyed a level of autonomy greater than what they had known under the Babylonians, the Romans, or the Christian states of Europe. Muslim tolerance of Jews was often laced with contempt, but that did not prevent coexistence and occasional cooperation. Here too, it is important to remember that at very few moments in human history have ruling majorities treated minorities with respect, and they have rarely allowed them access to power, privilege, and prosperity. Within those parameters, Jews under Muslim rule lived about as well as any minority under any majority at any point in history.

That made the forced emigration in the late 1940s all the more star-tling. After 1492, Jews expelled from Spain were welcomed into the Ottoman Empire. Four hundred and fifty years later, that welcome came to an end. In light of nearly a millennium and a half of coexistence, what happened after 1948, and indeed what has happened between Muslims, Christians, and Jews since then, is an exception to the historical pattern of coexistence. It is tempting to ascribe these events to a deep dislike of Jews that began in Medina, when Muhammad turned on the Jewish tribes. But in order to draw that unbroken line, centuries of other history, of Hasdai ibn Shaprut, of Maimonides, and of their countless descen-dants, must be forgotten and ignored.

The events of the nineteenth and early twentieth centuries, and the inability of the Arab and Muslim world to compete with the West, led to an increasing level of bitterness and insecurity. Before the nineteenth century, Muslim states were rarely threatened by the People of the Book. Christians and Jews lived as protected minorities, and Christian states were more often than not on the defensive in the face of Muslim dynasties beginning with the Umayyads and continuing with the Otto-man Empire. The Crusades were an exception, but the Crusader states were quickly contained and, in the greater scheme, quickly defeated. Only in the nineteenth century were Muslim societies put on the defen-sive, and it took the establishment of Israel—and Jewish military victo-ries over the Arabs—to unleash the waves of intolerance that led to the exodus of the ancient Jewish communities of the Near East.

The Arab-Israeli conflict has focused attention on conflict between Muslims and Jews, and between Muslims and the West. But here too, the narrative that has become so familiar is incomplete. The relentless focus on conflict and its continuance in the present has left little room for other stories. The result is a numbing, never-ending litany of war, hatred, animosity, and death. The history of coexistence has been lost in that fog.

CHAPTER TWELVE

In an Otherwise Turbulent World

OVER THE PAST DECADE, and particularly after September 11, 2001, more people have become familiar with the story of how Arab and Muslim disillusionment provided the impetus for the evolution of a virulent strain of fundamentalism. Since September 11, there is a common understanding of why some fundamentalists embraced terrorism. "Common understanding" doesn't mean wide and deep awareness, of course, but many in Europe, the United States, and the rest of the world now have a basic sense that the creation of Israel and the inability of Arabs and Palestinians to prevent that produced widespread disenchantment with modernization and Westernization. The subsequent rise of extreme forms of fundamentalism epitomized by al-Qaeda has been dissected, studied, and debated. And after the U.S. invasion of Iraq in 2003, and bombings in Bali, Madrid, and London, the citizens of many nations have been forced to grapple with the rise of radical groups in Iraq, Europe, and Asia.

The picture is still unclear, but its outlines are straightforward. At some point in the middle of the twentieth century, a critical mass of despair was reached in the Muslim world. Both the reforms of the nineteenth century and the nationalism of the twentieth were judged as failures. At first, the reaction against Arab nationalism was muted. The Egyptian Muslim Brotherhood was an early proponent of a return to a purer Islam, and though its vision of the golden age of the caliphs was more fiction than fact, the Brotherhood did tend to the poor and to the newly urbanized and gave them a sense of place and belonging in a cold impersonal world. The Brotherhood was vigorously suppressed and its leader was killed in 1949. Egyptian fundamentalism then went underground, and the torch was passed to Sayyid Qutb, who turned his attention to the corruption of Arab regimes and the pernicious influence of the Western world. In his eyes, the bankruptcy of reform was the inevitable result of the turning away from Islam and toward the false gods of progress and modernization. In 1966 Qutb was executed, and became a sanctified martyr to generations of fundamentalists.

While the foundations for radical fundamentalism were laid in the Arab world, there were related movements in India, Pakistan, and Indonesia. Each shared a basic conviction that contemporary Muslim states were ruled by godless governments and that society had been corrupted and weakened by the influence of the West. They wove a vision of the past that glorified the first four caliphs and the early Muslim community, but their reading of history was highly selective. The ecumenical spirit of the Abbasid court, the medieval philosophical tradition that celebrated interpretation and reason, the mystical traditions that emphasized God's love, and the relaxed attitudes toward People of the Book were absent from their version of the past. Instead, they imagined a time when Islam was the alpha and the omega, when everyone from the caliph to the slave imbibed the piety of the Quran and the tradition of the Prophet, and then in return, God graced his believers with power, fortune, and security.

Muslim fundamentalist movements shared certain characteristics, but they were also deeply divided. Much like American Protestantism, Muslim fundamentalism of the twentieth century was decentralized and constantly changing shape. Groups would form, and then splinter. There was little agreement about tactics, and more to the point, no consensus about goals. Was the adversary the corrupt governments of Muslim states? Was it Israel? Was the goal the creation of new Muslim societies through revolution, through reform, through education, or through violence and chaos? Which enemy should be targeted—the so-called near enemy, such as secular Arab nationalists, Nasserists, local governments, and neighboring states? Or should it be the far enemy, such as the West in general or the United States as the most powerful Western country? Was the most pressing issue the plight of the Palestinians? Or was it the mass of disenfranchised Muslims who were forced to suffer under decadent monarchs like King Muhammad in Morocco, King Idris in Libya, the shah in Iran, the Hashemites in Jordan and Iraq (until 1958), and under atheistic nationalists like Nasser in Egypt and the heirs to Atatürk in Turkey? Decade by decade, the appeal of fundamentalism grew, but so did the divisions. In the 1970s, the most violent took to calling themselves jihadis, because they believed that armed jihad against unbelievers—apostates and secular governments, Jews and Christians, "Zionists and Crusaders"—was incumbent on all good Muslims and that the means, no matter how violent, justified the end of reestablishing a moral society.[1]

Even the jihadis were not united, however. They came from different regions with different historical experiences. There were Afghan jihadis whose worldview was informed by the 1979 Soviet invasion and the subsequent U.S. aid for the mujahideen (the "freedom fighters"), and who turned Afghanistan into a Soviet Vietnam War. There were disaffected Saudis who were disgusted by the rampant materialism of the Saudi royal family and their unholy alliance with Western oil companies. There were Algerians who rejected the socialist Algerian revolutionaries who had fought a bitter independence war against France. There were Pakistanis who followed the teachings of an early-twentieth-century preacher named Maulana Maududi (who influenced Sayyid Qutb) and who wanted to establish the sharia as the sole legal code for Pakistan and for Muslims living in India. And there were Palestinian Islamic radicals who organized Hamas in order to contest both the state of Israel and the leadership of Yasser Arafat and the PLO. To add to the confusion, there were also Shi'ite jihadis, who looked to Iran and Ayatollah Khomeini rather than to Sayyid Qutb for inspiration and who created parties like Hezbollah ("The Party of God") in Lebanon.

In short, while fundamentalism has been a significant force in the modern Muslim world, the notion that there is a single fundamentalist movement whose leader is Osama bin Laden is utterly incorrect. Even more troubling is the tendency of both jihadis and Western observers to read history through a fundamentalist lens. The result is a vision of the Islamic past where there is no separation between church and state, where reason is subservient to orthodox acceptance of revealed truths, and where there is no mention of the wild creativity of Córdoba and Baghdad, the eccentric individualism of Ibn Arabi and the philosophers, the piety of the Sufis or the modernist, Islamic synthesis of Abduh. This narrow version of the past is widely accepted by Muslims and non-Muslims alike, but that does not mean it is accurate.

The other unfortunate result of the contemporary obsession with radicals and jihadis is that history is read backward in order to find the roots of the present. Of course, no matter how much we might try to look at the past neutrally, some "presentism" always creeps in. But in seeking to explain the origin of the current struggles over Israel or the clash between Muslim extremists and the West, people have magnified the role of fundamentalism and the prevalence of historical conflict and minimized those aspects of the past that don't fit the mold of the present.[2]

In addition to misreading history, too many of us also misread the present and the recent past. Certainly, the creation of Israel ushered in a new and troubling period of relations between Muslims, Christians, and Jews, and contemporary Islamic fundamentalism and its most violent offshoots did emerge from disgust with nationalism and Western-style modernization. But fundamentalism, violence, and the Arab-Israeli conflict are hardly the whole story of the modern world. Conflict is only part of the picture. Even the creation of Israel has a hidden history. If the main plot was war, the subplots were accommodation, coexistence, and cooperation.

JORDAN AND ISRAEL

UNTIL THE END of the mandate period, and throughout the 1920s and 1930s, the daily interactions between Palestinians and Jewish settlers were often cordial and sometimes quite friendly. In fact, relations between Jewish settlers and Christian and Muslim Palestinians were warmer and more intimate than relations between the Crusader states and the local populace had been centuries before. There were joint business endeavors and shared agricultural projects. One early Jewish settler thought that the tension between Jews and Arabs could be decreased by marriage between the bedouin and the settlers. Chaim Weizmann, one of the leaders of the Zionist movement, met often with Arab leaders and tried to convince them to support an Arab-Jewish polity based on common interests rather than divided by different creeds. The socialist philosophy of the early Zionists tended to be hostile to organized religion. Judaism for them was an identity that owed more to ethnicity and history than religion. The Jewish immigrants were by and large agrarian laborers, who worked on farms bought from the Arabs, and tilled the soil alongside Arab farmers. Some Zionists, therefore, took the logical step of imagining a state designed to serve the needs of laborers, Arab and Jew alike. Of course, these attempts at concord gave way to successive waves of violence, caused by dispossessed Palestinians who hoped to halt Jewish immigration and then by Zionists determined to establish a national home. Moderation always has a difficult time in the face of extremism, and is usually trumped by it. Palestine was no different.

Relations between the Jewish Agency and the neighboring states were marked by animosity, especially on the part of the Arabs, but here as well there were periods of calm and concord. The Christian Maronite leadership of Lebanon welcomed a Jewish state as a possible counterbalance to a Middle East dominated by Muslims. More than a few Maronite leaders in the 1930s and 1940s made overtures to the Zionists and discussed the possibility of future alliances should a Jewish state come into being. At the time, the Maronites were struggling for the termination of the French Mandate, much as the Zionists were fighting to end British rule. In light of their parallel goals, the Maronite patriarch even signed a treaty with the Jewish community of Palestine, promising support and economic aid, as well as diplomatic backing for unlimited Jewish immigration. In return, the Jewish signatories promised to abet the establishment of an independent Maronite-controlled Lebanon.[3]

The most extensive collaboration between the Jews of Palestine and their neighbors occurred with Jordan and King Abdullah. Transjordan had been formed at the Cairo Conference of 1921 when British diplomats, including most notably an imperious Winston Churchill, literally drew lines on a map to determine the states of the modern Middle East. There was almost nothing organic about the boundaries of Jordan, except for part of its western border, which ran along the Sea of Galilee and the Jordan Valley, from which the state gets its name. Having received his crown as a consolation prize after losing Arabia, Abdullah worked diligently to make Jordan into a viable state.

The separation of Jordan from Palestine and Syria had little grounding in history, and the region was inhabited largely by bedouin tribes who respected Abdullah's Hashemite lineage but questioned his legitimacy as their ruler. His army was a British creation and was answerable to Sir John Glubb. While Glubb never shed his English identity, he became a loyal partisan of Abdullah. It was a particular sort of loyalty, tinged as it was with a patronizing attitude toward the Arabs and their capacity for self-government, but like T. E. Lawrence, Glubb felt at home in the desert among the bedouin. He and his wife adopted bedouin and Palestinian children, and he saw no contradiction in serving both Abdullah and the British government. By 1948, Glubb could look back at his years in the desert with pride, and he led an army that was by far the most professional in the region.

Faced with the establishment of a Jewish state, Abdullah took a less adversarial stance than the other Arab leaders. Though he publicly sided with the Arab League in the months before Israel declared independence in May 1948, he secretly negotiated with the Israelis to arrange an equitable division of Palestine that would leave Jordan in control of what became the West Bank. There was even hope that he would not have to use his army. A young Golda Meir, who would later become Israel's first and only female prime minister, disguised herself as an Arab woman and sneaked into Amman four days before Israel declared independence to try to conclude an agreement with Abdullah. But the king was unwilling to risk ostracism by the other Arab states. He told Meir that he "firmly believed that Divine Providence had restored you, a Semite people who were banished to Europe and have benefited by its progress, to the Semite East, which needs your knowledge and initiative.... But the situation is grave.... I am sorry. I deplore the coming bloodshed and destruction. Let us hope we shall meet again."

There was some cynicism at work here. Abdullah recognized that Israel was not going to be pushed into the sea, and that sooner or later, the Arabs would have to come to terms with its presence. Confident in his army and in Glubb as a general, Abdullah believed that he could put pressure on the Israeli defense forces in the West Bank, and even threaten west Jerusalem. Abdullah described his strategy to a friend: "I will not begin the attack on the Jews and will only attack them if they first attack my forces. I will not allow massacres in Palestine. Only after order and quiet have been established will it be possible to reach an understanding with the Jews." Throughout the summer of 1948, the Jordanian army hovered but, perhaps realizing it would lose if it confronted the Israelis too aggressively, never attempted to advance into the territory that had been assigned to Israel under the 1947 U.N. Partition Plan. The Jordanians kept civilian casualties to a minimum, and Israel regarded Abdullah as a respected adversary. It was an odd sort of war, and an odd relationship, which led one Israeli diplomat at the time to refer to Israel and Jordan as "the best of enemies."

As a result, the government of Prime Minister David Ben-Gurion embraced Abdullah's willingness to talk. In the fall of 1948 and into 1949, there were multiple clandestine meetings between Israelis and Abdullah and his court. One of the negotiators was Moshe Dayan, who would later become Israel's most famous general and whose rakish, one-eyed visage came to epitomize both the energy and the determination of the Israeli military. At the time, he was a junior member of a delegation led by Moshe Sharett, Ben-Gurion's foreign minister and later prime minister himself. The meetings were cordial but often awkward. At dinner one evening, Sharett managed to offend Abdullah by correcting him about whether China had been a member of the League of Nations. As Dayan wryly remarked in his memoirs, "A king never errs, and Abdullah stood by the statement." Other visits were laden with ceremony and formality, which tried the patience of the rough-and-tumble Dayan. "We would dine with the king prior to getting down to business and for an hour or so before the meal there would be political gossip of what was happening in the capitals of the world, an occasional game of chess, and poetry readings. In chess, it was obligatory not only to lose to the king but also to show surprise at his unexpected moves. And when he read his poems, in epigrammatic Arabic, one had to express wonder by sighing from the depths of one's soul."

As close as the Jordanians and the Israelis came to a formal peace treaty, in the end Abdullah would not break ranks with the rest of the Arab states. He could not afford to become isolated. The result was an entente with Israel but not an explicit peace. Though the king tried his best to keep the negotiations secret, too many high-level players were involved, and it was widely known that discussions had taken place.

Abdullah paid a high price. In 1951, while visiting Al-Aqsa Mosque in Jerusalem, he was gunned down by a Palestinian Arab. His young grandson Hussein was walking just behind him and watched in horror. He soon succeeded Abdullah, and as King Hussein, continued the delicate balancing act that his grandfather had begun.

For nearly fifty years, King Hussein—who could use his mellifluous baritone to recite classical Arabic to his subjects and then speak in a beautiful English accent for an address at the United Nations—maintained respectful relations with the Israelis, even as his goals and theirs were often diametrically opposed. He was a voice of moderation in the Arab world, at times accused, like his grandfather Abdullah, of being a pawn of the Western powers, and of the United States especially. He had to contend with a restive Palestinian population, and he lost the West Bank to Israel during the 1967 war. Yet Israel only reluctantly went to war with Jordan in 1967, and at no point did either Hussein or Prime Minister Golda Meir cease to describe each other as friends. To his dying day, through the most perilous times, during the extremism of the Palestinian Liberation Organization in the 1960s and 1970s and the Palestinian uprising known as the *intifadah* in the 1980s, he remained true to his vision of a Middle East governed by peace. In 1994, that vision was at least partly vindicated, and Jordan and Israel signed a peace treaty that led to formal diplomatic relations and agreements on everything from boundaries to water rights. Even as the accords between Israel and the Palestinian leadership disintegrated, the interaction between Israel and Jordan—ruled after 1999 by Hussein's son Abdullah II—was marked by an unusual level of mutual respect.[4]

The relationship between Israel and Jordan doesn't fit the familiar template of the Arab-Israeli conflict. While it is certainly possible to write a history of Israeli-Jordanian interaction as a series of wars separated by periods of cold peace, that requires ignoring far too much of the past, and the present. In his later years, King Hussein frequently remarked on the peculiar intimacy of Israel and its Arab neighbors. The bulk of Jordan's people live on the highlands above the Jordan River Valley, scant miles from the most inhabited areas of Israel, and they can literally gaze out over Israel and the West Bank when they watch the setting sun. In turn, many in Israel can look at the Jordanians every morning, stare at them from the beach resorts of the Dead Sea and from the Red Sea city of Eilat, which is separated from the Jordanian city of Aqaba by nothing more than a heavily fortified fence. Hussein took the ancient notion of the People of the Book very seriously. The kinship of race, history, and a shared God infused his sense of the region, as it still does for his son Abdullah.[5]

Even at its worst moments, the Jordanian-Israeli relationship has rarely been colored by *religious* animosity. The Hashemites take great pride in their lineage as descendants of Muhammad, but they have never supported the agenda of the fundamentalists. They have a conservative, hierarchical approach to government, which is more in the mold of classical Muslim states. Islam is central to their personal identity much as Christianity is central to British monarchs and politicians, and to American presidents. But Islam is not a political force per se, and the Jordanians have resisted calls to turn their country into a polity where the *ulama* have ultimate authority.

As for Israel and Judaism, some of the post-1967 Israeli settlers were motivated by zealous notions of a biblical re-creation of greater Israel. But the Israeli state has remained, in spite of the rise of Jewish fundamentalism, more secular than not. Some of the Palestinians who became Jordanian citizens turned toward Islamic fundamentalism in their opposition to Israeli policies on the West Bank. But the leaders of both countries have never used religion as an excuse to fight one another. To the contrary. The Jordanian royal family's sense of kinship with Israel derives from a basic belief that Jews and Arabs and Jews and Muslims are woven from the same cloth and are children of the same creator.

But because of the fraught nature of the larger Arab-Israeli conflict, the positive aspects of the Jordanian-Israeli entente have been downplayed by Israelis and Jordanians alike. Instead, war and extremism have dominated the Arab-Israeli agenda, and the nuance and moderation that have marked relations between Jordan and Israel have been pushed aside and neglected as a model for the present and the future.

LEBANON

LEBANON IS ANOTHER ambiguous story that can serve almost any vision of relations between Muslims, Christians, and Jews. Though its history is indelibly colored by the disastrous civil war that rent the country from 1975 until the mid-1990s (not to mention the more recent Israeli-Hezbollah war in the summer of 2006), for more than a century Lebanon seemed to be a shining example of Muslim-Christian coexistence. The Maronites occupied a central place in the political and economic life of the region, and they had been crucial in the independence struggle against France. They were not the only Christian sect, but they outnumbered the Greek Orthodox, the Greek Catholics, and the Armenian Orthodox. The Muslims were themselves sectarian, with a large group of Sunnis, a growing population of Shi'a, and a concentrated Druze community. Beirut was a cosmopolitan city, with a powerful Maronite contingent but with other groups well represented. It was also a commercial hub that looked more toward Europe than to the Arab world.

Outside of Beirut, each major group dominated a particular region, with the Maronites in the mountainous center, the Shi'ites mostly in the south, and the Sunnis along the coast and in the urban areas. Each of these communities was in turn led by a few powerful clans who could trace their lineage back centuries. The clan lords had fought one another in the past, but under the auspices of the Ottomans and the French, they had come to a modus vivendi. That balance was occasionally disrupted, as in 1858–60 and in 1958, usually after one group or another sought to change the status quo. These civil wars, lethal while they lasted, were always inconclusive, and were resolved by only slight changes to a system that gave each group sufficient autonomy and security.

The modern cornerstone of that system was an accord known as the "National Pact." In 1943, recognizing that no one group was powerful enough to dominate the whole country, the leading Maronite family and one of the influential Sunni clans made a deal. They agreed that the president of Lebanon would be Maronite, the prime minister would be Sunni, and the head of the chamber of deputies would be a Shi'ite. It was, according to one of its architects, "the fusion of two tendencies into one ideology: complete and final independence without resorting to the protection of the West or to a unity or federation with the East."

In the 1950s, the rise of Egypt's Gamal Abd al-Nasser and the pan-Arab ideology of Nasserism put pressure on conservative regimes throughout the Arab world. Nasser had led a military coup that overthrew the Egyptian king, and that put the other Arab monarchies on notice. The Hashemites reacted by looking to the United States for support. Jordan and Iraq also made common cause with the aloof Saudis, who gravitated toward their onetime Hashemite adversaries in the face of the anti-royalist threat of Nasserism. Lebanon and Syria became pawns in this struggle, and when Syria tilted toward Egypt, the Maronites of Lebanon appealed to the United States. The balance between the sects in Lebanon was stable but susceptible to external disruptions. After the king of Iraq was overthrown and killed in 1958, and after King Hussein in Jordan narrowly avoided a coup, the Maronite president of Lebanon asked the United States to send troops to prevent incursions of Nasserist forces from Syria. Concerned that another pro-Western regime was in jeopardy, President Eisenhower agreed. Within weeks, in the summer of 1958, more than ten thousand U.S. marines landed on the beaches of Beirut, where they found surprised sunbathers who were not aware that the country was in danger.

After this brief interruption, balance was restored, and Lebanon prospered in the 1960s. Beirut enjoyed halcyon days as a global entrepôt, filled with wealthy bankers and traders, and blessed with an enviable night life that welcomed the jet set no less than the French Riviera. The American University in Beirut attracted students from around the world and established itself as a premier research college. As Nasserism crested and then diminished, Lebanon looked forward to a period of calm, but that was not to be. The influx of Palestinian refugees after both the 1948 and 1967 Arab-Israeli wars was one factor; changing demographics were another. The Shi'ites were becoming a larger portion of the population, yet their share of influence was still limited by the National Pact, which had been drawn up when they were a distant third in numbers. The civil war that erupted in 1975 was in fact multiple wars between ever-shifting factions who made and broke alliances at a dizzying pace. By the 1980s, Israel, Syria, and Iran intervened, and the influence of each remained pronounced even after the fighting ceased in the 1990s. Israeli presence in the south, Syrian control of the interior and the Bekaa Valley, and Iran's support for Hezbollah hobbled the country and precluded any lasting stability.

Before 1975, the peace in Lebanon had been maintained through a combination of clan politics and a free-market economy in Beirut. The traditional leaders had managed the affairs of their own community, much as the *millet*s under the Ottoman Empire had, and the national government served as a town square for the notables to air disputes. But the country never developed a cohesive national identity, or a strong military, and when groups of Palestinian refugees began to use parts of Lebanon to stage operations against Israel and against various parties in Lebanon that they disliked, the equilibrium disintegrated into the civil war that lasted in one form or another for more than two decades.

Which of these stories best captures Lebanon? The decades of peace and harmony between Christians and Muslims, or the civil war that saw not only Christians fighting Muslims, but Sunnis fighting Shi'ites, pro-Syrian groups fighting Palestinians, and the Druze fighting just about everyone and Maronites most of all. Which is the "real" Lebanon—a failed experiment of what was known as "confessional democracy," which honored the rights of each religious community, or a successful example of coexistence and toleration destroyed not by problems from within but by troubles in the surrounding region? And which of these stories will be seen in the future as the "real Lebanon"? A history of the United States in 1862 might have displayed skepticism about the American experiment and how it had finally foundered on the shoals of slavery. In the 1960s, Lebanon was celebrated as a beacon of toleration and openness. After 1975, it was the subject of eulogies for shattered dreams and lost generations. But as the civil war recedes into the distance, the memory of a stable past comes back into focus. Even with the Israeli bombardment of Hezbollah in the summer of 2006, whether Lebanon will once again be taken as a model for how different religious communities can coexist will depend not on what has happened in the past but on what happens now and in the future.[6]

ANOTHER STORY

WE ARE ALL, to varying degrees, captives of our culture. With few exceptions, the current image of relations between Muslims, Christians, and Jews is negative, and the belief that conflict has been ever present is deeply entrenched. Yet if the stories told in these pages say anything, it is that there is another perspective. Throughout history, there has been active cooperation. There has been tolerance, and there has been indifference. The only way to describe the arc of fourteen hundred years as primarily a history of conflict is to forget and ignore not only the stories told here, but countless others that have been lost to history because no one thought that they merited recording.

This is not just a problem of how we see the past. When future generations look back at the second half of the twentieth century and the early decades of the twenty-first, they will have at their disposal an unparalleled amount of information. Yet unless they try to find other stories, they too will be left with the impression that these years—our present— were defined by a war between civilizations and by ever-increasing hostility between Muslims, Christians, and Jews. They will say that our time was marked by escalating violence, acts of terrorism, suicide bombings, and by fear that some group would obtain and use a weapon of mass destruction in the name of God. These future generations will be forgiven if they too look to the distant past and retell the familiar tales of hatred between the faiths that began with Muhammad and the Jews and continued episodically over the centuries.

Today, Muslims, Christians, and Jews are equal offenders in their relentless focus on conflict. Each tends to paint the past as a series of indignities suffered at the hands of the other two. Westerners, whether or not they adhere to an organized religion, are disposed to view Muslim societies as backward and intent on war and violence. And most inhabitants of the Muslim world tend to believe that the West bears ill will toward Islam and Muslims and wants not peace or coexistence but economic and cultural domination.

Indeed, in the past few decades, polemics about the coming war between Islam and the West have proliferated, as have what one clever critic dubbed "travel narratives from Hell." These are primarily penned by Western writers addressing a Western audience who explore the Muslim world and come back with reports of gloom and doom. We are told of new madrassas (schools) from Nigeria to Pakistan to Indonesia being funded by Saudi extremists preaching hate. We are told of generations that celebrate violence against Israel, against corrupt governments, against Europe and the United States. We are told of Muslim rage on every street, and of angry young men and women who watch helplessly as the modern world passes them by, their faces pressed to the glass gazing on possibilities that they can never obtain, while their own worlds decay and their traditions succumb to Coca-Cola and McDonald's.[7] There are, of course, books and articles that reject this framework and posit a different reading of Islam and of the past, that suggest the compatibility of Islam and democracy and Islam and the West, but it is fair to say that these have not gained the same level of influence as their more shrill counterparts.[8]

The history of conflict is not untrue. It is incomplete. By the same token, the reality of religious extremism in the modern world cannot and should not be downplayed. There are radicals who will dedicate their lives to inflicting pain and death on those who do not agree with their vision. And there is a still-simmering Arab-Israeli conflict that remains a source of pain and anger for all involved. Nonetheless, there are other stories that garner less attention but are no less part of the tapestry.

Take the Arabian American Oil Company, known as Aramco. It began as an arrangement between Standard Oil of California (which in time became Chevron), Texaco, and King Ibn Saud. The Saudi monarch had been wooed by both Europeans and Americans, but he ultimately felt most comfortable with the Americans, either because they charmed him or because they weren't the British. Aramco, with the involvement of Standard Oil of New Jersey (later called Exxon) and of New York (later called Mobil), remained the dominant Western oil company in Saudi Arabia for decades. In the 1970s, the Saudis began to purchase it, and within a few years, Saudi Aramco controlled not only half of Texaco and more than a thousand gas stations in the United States and Europe, but as much as one-quarter of all the proven oil reserves in the world.

The issue of oil and the Middle East has been peripheral to most of the history in this book. Oil did not become central for Saudi Arabia and Iraq until the 1920s, and only during World War II did the region take on global significance as a source of petroleum. By the end of the twentieth century, however, it was widely understood, both in popular culture in Europe and the United States and "on the Arab street," that American involvement in the Middle East has been motivated by three things: Israel, Christianity, and oil.

And yet, Aramco is an Arab oil company. Specifically, it is a Saudi company with close ties to the global petroleum industry. The Saudi state rests on two foundations: an alliance between the royal family and the puritanical Wahhabis, and a symbiotic relationship with the major economies of the world as the dominant producer of oil. The Saudi oil barons own land, businesses, and investments throughout Europe, Japan, and the United States. Many of them have been educated in American schools, and live a double life as tribal potentates and Western billionaires. Today, Aramco executives and workers inhabit the peculiar twilight zone of Dhahran, as they have for decades, with fathers often passing their positions to their sons, and in their walled and heavily guarded compounds, they live a life that is not quite Western and very definitely not Saudi.

Whether one views this relationship as symbiotic or parasitic, a testament to free-market capitalism or a sign of Western imperialism; whether there is a genuine partnership between the Saudi oilmen and

American executives and engineers or a cynical compact, the existence of Aramco is a product of cooperation between an austere Muslim state and an unabashedly Christian country, the United States.[9]

Then there is the saga of Turkey's struggle to gain full membership in the European Union. After World War I, Atatürk remade his country as a secular state, and it has stayed on that path. Throughout the Cold War, Turkey was an ally of the United States and a member of NATO. In the 1980s and 1990s, Turkey's government and its business class made a concerted effort to join the European Union, and after considerable debate, the EU decided to commence the official talks that could lead to Turkey's membership after 2010.

In both Turkey and Europe, there is unease and ambivalence. After decades of staunch secularism, Turkey in 2003 elected a prime minster, Recep Erdogan, who supported a more prominent role for Islam. That alarmed not only the Turkish military and the loyal inheritors of the Atatürk's legacy, but also the Europeans. The European Union says nothing per se about the religion of its members, but one of its official criteria is the vague category of "Europeanness." Suffice it to say that Islam has never been embraced as an aspect of European identity. To the contrary, Europe thinks of itself as having been forged in opposition to Islam, and to organized religion.

Erdogan, however, has consistently resisted attempts of Turkish Islamists to force traditional religion into the public sphere. He has refused, for example, to reconsider the ban on head scarves for women in public classrooms. Atatürk used reforms of traditional dress, including bans on head scarves for women and the fez cap for men, as a symbol that Turkey would be part of, and not distinct from, the modern world. That world was, he realized, governed by Western values and rules, and he wanted Turkey to become part of it. Erdogan belongs to a generation who, on the whole, accept that basic principle and yet also wish to integrate elements of traditional Turkish culture, including Islam. He personally is devout, yet that is no more antithetical to the "modern world" than the devoutness of American presidents.

The European Union, however, has been apprehensive about Turkey. Some Austrian opponents have explicitly raised the specter of the Ottomans at the gates of Vienna. Germans have also been suspicious. Millions of Turks live and work in Germany, but Germans, who outside of Bavaria have become increasingly less religious, express discomfort with the Muslim nature of the Turkish government—just as they have been uncomfortable with the evangelical Christian character of George W. Bush's administration. They have also questioned Turkey's economic development and its commitment to human rights, but the core arguments have all, in one way or another, circled around the issue of religion, identity, and politics.

The irony, of course, is that it is the avowedly secular Europeans who have been equivocal, whereas the Muslim party leading the governing coalition in Turkey expressed no reservations about relinquishing sovereignty to the European Union in return for closer economic ties. Turkey has also cultivated a cordial, though not exactly warm, relationship with Israel and maintained close relations with the United States, even through the highly charged atmosphere after September 11 and especially after the U.S. invasion of Iraq in the spring of 2003.[10]

Turkey's path challenges most generalizations about Islam and the West, but that is only because these generalizations are so incomplete. Few people imagine that it is possible for a state to be Muslim in cultural and religious identity and also be a full participant in the global economy. Even fewer believe that it can prize the rule of law, have a healthy interest in constructive ties with Europe and the United States, and simultaneously cherish Islam. That type of state does not fit the either-or template that says a society has to put religion into a confined box in order to be a full-fledged participant in the modern world, nor is it easily reconciled with the notion that the relationship between Muslims, Christians, and Jews is inherently unstable.

The status of Muslim immigrants in Europe often seems to support that notion. Riots in Parisian suburbs; the killing of the prominent, provocative Dutch filmmaker Theo van Gogh by a disaffected young Dutch Muslim; the increase of jihadi sympathy in the anonymous apartment blocks of English cities; and the bombings in Madrid in 2003 and London in 2005 have led to considerable anxiety in Europe about whether Islam and secular Christianity can coexist. Yet here as well, the daily lives of millions of immigrants who live and work in their adopted societies willingly and ardently is given scant attention. It is not just a problem of the "squeaky wheel" syndrome, where angry voices of protest get more notice. It is that other lives and other stories are actively ignored because they don't fit.

The result is that the cultural and economic cooperation that occurs so regularly and so effortlessly that it should be considered common-place is unmentioned or lost in the fray. In Jordan, King Abdullah II, heir to his father, Hussein, in so many ways, has tried to honor the tradition of intellectual openness, tribal solidarity, independence, and progress that marked the most vibrant days of the caliphs and the Ottomans. Jordan today is a hybrid of bedouin, Palestinian Christians and Muslims, a Muslim Brotherhood that participates (albeit grudgingly) in the politi-cal process, and a Western-educated and Western-leaning elite. That doesn't mean that all is well, simply that the country and its monarchs have tried to steer a course of moderation and international integration, working assiduously with governments and businesses abroad, from the United States to the European Union to Iraq, Iran, China, and Japan.

And then there is Morocco, which under both King Muhammad VI and his father, King Hassan, has tilted toward France. Cities like Mar-rakesh, Fez, and Tangier are cosmopolitan. Having once ruled Iberia, Moroccans never ceased to feel that they are as much a part of Europe as they are of North Africa and the Arab world. In the last decades of the twentieth century and into the twenty-first, Marrakesh for one has become increasingly entwined with Europe in general and France espe-cially. The French expatriate community has blossomed, and yet the city has maintained its eccentric Muslim culture. The call to prayer still blankets the old city at dawn and dusk, even as people drink alcohol in the Djemaa al-Fna, the airy open space that fills with crowds, food, and acrobats each night and that guards the entrance to the labyrinthine markets and to an old city whose tendrils extend from the twenty-first century back to the fifteenth.

And there are the 200 million Muslims of India, who live and prosper amid a billion Hindus, with flashes of conflict and long periods of indif-ference and communion. There are the young of Iran, an oil-rich coun-try that is ruled by a brittle mullocracy spending the dwindling political capital of the 1979 revolution but that now has a majority of population under the age of twenty-five who cannot remember the shah and who have little but scorn for the clerics. While the mullahs may yearn for nuclear weapons, the young dream vibrant dreams of the United States, and Hollywood, and of men and women being able to walk hand in hand without being confronted by thugs claiming the mantle of the Prophet. And there are the five million Muslims in the United States, a few of whom are African-American converts and many more who are immigrants and the children of immigrants from Pakistan, Bangladesh, and elsewhere, who go to neighborhood mosques and are appalled at the violence of distant men and women claiming to be the only true Muslims. And there are other stories, of people consumed not by religious fervor but by the daily, universal concerns of money, work, and family.

In a world where technology will make it easier for the angry few to do great harm, the perpetuation of a model of conflict is dangerous. Remembering that each of the three traditions carries the seeds of peace will not by itself heal the world. A more complete picture will not convert today's jihadis from war to love, and it will not alone force the Western world to reconsider Islam. But if these stories are integrated into our sense of the past and the present, it will be more difficult to treat religion as destiny. Religion is a force coursing through the past, but hardly the only force. Muslims, Christians, and Jews are entwined, but their history is as varied as the story of the human race. It points in no one direction, or in all directions. If conflict is what we want to see, there is conflict. But if peace is what we are looking for, then peace is there to be found.

᷂⋙⟶ ⟵⋘

Is Dubai the Future?

W E READ EVERY DAY news of death and violence in Iraq. The stories include Sunni Iraqis killing Shi'ite Iraqis, al-Qaeda assassinating rivals, Shi'ite factions in the southern part of the country skirmishing with one another, Iranian-funded groups fighting against Saudi-funded groups, and everyone fighting the Americans. Many people throughout the world no doubt long ago ceased to pay these reports much attention, but in Europe, the United States, and the Middle East, it is nearly impossible to avoid the news. The daily litany creates an indelible impression that Islam and violence keep close company.

Iraq has been only one element of that toxic brew. The continued struggle between Israel and the Palestinians is another, albeit familiar, ingredient. The presidency of Mahmoud Ahmadinejad in Iran has added a new dimension. The president has rarely lost an opportunity to inflame passions, which he seems to stoke with glee, calling one moment for the eradication of Israel and the next for a united Muslim front against the American-led West. Flush with an unexpected injection of petrodollars, thanks to China's increased demand for oil, Iran's government and its populist president have pursued a path of confrontation with the United States and with any who question Iran's right to a nuclear power program that might or might not go hand in hand with the capacity to produce a nuclear weapon.

And with the eruption of armed hostilities between Israel and the Iranian-backed Hezbollah in Lebanon in July 2006, it looked as if, once again, Muslims, Christians, and Jews were locked in a death dance, and that with the prospect of nuclear weapons in the hands of Iran and Israel, the conflict could one day have an Armageddon potential.

But five hundred miles south of Iran and Iraq, on the western shore of the Persian Gulf, lies the emirate of Dubai. Until 2006, few Americans—though a somewhat higher percentage of British and Europeans—knew where Dubai was, but that changed when Dubai Ports World, one of the largest companies of its kind, concluded a $6.8 billion agreement to purchase Britain's Peninsular and Oriental Steam Navigation Company, which operated a number of ports in the United States, including Newark, Miami, and New Orleans. The transfer of ownership seemed destined to be a quiet, uneventful event until Congress proceeded to bludgeon the Bush administration for gross negligence and dereliction of duty. The crime was allowing the sale of vital national security to an Arab state.

The criticism was not limited to Democratic opponents of the Bush administration. It was, in fact, a rare moment of bipartisan dudgeon, with heated rhetoric erupting throughout the country against the proposed deal. There were allegations that the government of Dubai was linked to terrorism, based on the fact that several of the participants in the 9/11 attacks had availed themselves of Dubai's banking system. While similar logic could have been used to denounce the government of Germany for abetting the 9/11 attacks, the fact that Dubai is a family-ruled Arab principality and that Dubai Ports World is controlled by the government was translated into proof that American national security would be endangered if the deal were allowed to go through. Said one outraged Republican congressional representative, "In regards to selling American ports to Dubai, not just *no*—but *hell no!*"

After a flurry of hearings and a wave of uproar, Dubai Ports World agreed to alter the arrangement so that the American ports would not be included. The emir of Dubai, in public, was tight-lipped, but in private he was apparently furious. More than almost any state in the Arab world, Dubai had embraced the logic of global capitalism, and yet it was still treated as a pariah by the American public and lumped together with al-Qaeda.

It was easy enough to read what happened as the latest chapter in the history of conflict. Yet here as well, all was not as it seemed. For while the ports deal was scuttled, other arms of the Dubai government were wrapping up the purchase of several luxury hotels and office buildings in Manhattan, including the Essex House on Central Park South and the W Hotel in Union Square. Two of the Park Avenue buildings bought by the Dubai company Istithmar were acquired from Boston Properties, which is controlled by Mortimer Zuckerman, who is not only a prominent New York developer but a publisher and an outspoken American Jewish financial backer of Israel. Another investment arm of Dubai purchased the second-largest private homebuilder in the United States, John Laing Homes, for $1.05 billion in the late spring of 2006, after the ports imbroglio. Around the same time, the international hotel and casino operator Kerzner International announced its intention to become a private company in a management buyout. Among other things, Kerzner owns the Atlantis complex in the Bahamas and is working on a Dubai project that will include a lavish resort on an artificial island, which may have the first casino in the Persian Gulf. The company's primary owners are the Kerzners, a South African Jewish family, and the royal family of Dubai.

Dubai was the beneficiary of the spectacular rise in the price of oil between 2004 and 2006, but unlike the other Gulf states, the country itself has few oil reserves. While it receives a share of the oil revenues of Abu Dhabi and the other states that comprise the United Arab Emirates, Dubai's wealth and power is a product of a purposeful decision by Sheikh Rashid al-Maktoum in the 1970s to align his strip of desert with the West. That policy was continued by his sons, who turned a weakness—the absence of oil—into a strength. Unable to rely on petrodollars, the royal family was forced instead to become entrepreneurial. The results have far exceeded Sheikh Rashid's ambitions.

With fewer than a hundred thousand citizens, Dubai in the early years of the twenty-first century became one of the largest construction zones in the world and home to more than 1 million people, almost all of whom were citizens of other countries drawn to Dubai by low taxes, loose credit, unintrusive banking, easy-to-obtain menial jobs, and countless opportunities to get rich. An odd amalgam of Las Vegas, Singapore, and Miami, Dubai is the only city in the conservative Gulf region to allow consumption of alcohol and to welcome Western and global tourists unconditionally. It is a free-trade and duty-free zone that built on its earlier foundation as a port and used the national airline to attract visitors to the dozens of malls that the city has to offer. Tourists from

Europe and Asia flock to Dubai for shopping holidays, as do Arabs from oil states. The Emirates Mall, opened in late 2005, includes a Ralph Lauren boutique, a Carrefour hypermarket, and a Harvey Nichols department store. It also has hundreds of boutiques, one of which offers custom-made burqas to cover upper-class women from Saudi Arabia; two shops over, La Perla displays nearly naked mannequins. A hundred yards farther on, there is Ski Dubai, a four-hundred-meter snow-packed ski slope fully enclosed and air-conditioned, with a Chili's restaurant providing a view of the surreal sight of people skiing in the middle of a desert where temperatures often exceed 110 degrees.

In spite of the furor over the ports deal in the United States, Dubai simply doesn't fit the images of a Middle East defined by conflict with the West, or images of Christians and Jews locked in a battle with Muslims. What are we to make of a Muslim ruling family doing business with a gambling and leisure company run by Jews? Or of a company owned by the royal family concluding real estate deals with an American Jewish real estate mogul who makes no secret of his ardent support for Israel? Or of a city-state that borders a puritanical Saudi Arabia and acts as an escape valve for the same Saudis who accept the stricture of Wahhabi dogma at home? Or of a burgeoning state that annually draws half a million British tourists, who are lured by the prospect of cheap shopping and beaches? What are we to make of Dubai, a city-state that epitomizes the excesses and successes of capitalism in a globalized age?

Contrary to predictions that the scuttling of the ports deal would imperil relations between the United States and Western-leaning regimes in the Middle East, within weeks it was business as usual. The virulent reactions of the United States did leave a bitter residue, but at the beginning of the twenty-first century—as in most of the prior fourteen hundred years—conflict and cooperation do not cancel each other out; they exist simultaneously.

Dubai is no longer ignored. It has too much glitz. It makes great copy for travel magazines and media outlets looking to observe the lifestyles of the rich and famous. It has a hotel shaped like a traditional fishing boat that rises a thousand feet above the water with rooms that start at $1,000 a night. It has sports tournaments and nightclubs that draw global sponsors and international celebrities, and it has resorts and condominiums that spring out of the dunes, along with a booming (and occasionally busting) stock market that piques the interest of international investors.

But Dubai as a counterpoint to the relentless drumbeat of civilizational war is unappreciated. It may be a shrine to greed and decadence, and it may be but a beneficiary of high oil prices and so will face hard times if those prices head south, but none of that makes it any less than a testament to the ability of Muslims, Christians, and Jews to find common cause.

And it is hardly the only one. In Egypt, a business dynasty led by the Coptic Christian Sawiris family has been trying to break out of the parochial backwater that has been the Egyptian economy. Perhaps in response to the petrodollars flooding the region and anxious to offset the rise in the fundamentalist movement, the Egyptian government of Hosni Mubarak finally realized that you can have political reform, you can have economic reform, but you cannot have neither. The loosening of state control over the economy—overseen by another Copt, the finance minister, Yousef Boutros-Ghali—proved to be a boon to the Sawiris clan, and especially to Naguib Sawiris, the fifty-year-old head of Orascom, the largest telecom company in the region. He seized the opportunity to create a new mobile phone network in American-occupied Iraq, and then negotiated a multibillion-dollar purchase of Wind, a subsidiary of one of the largest telecom operators in Italy.

Sawiris is strongly pro-American yet works assiduously to improve the lot of Gaza Palestinians by opening businesses in the impoverished region. He has been openly critical of Mubarak for the slowness of economic reform, and is unapologetically secular in his demeanor and outlook. He is, in short, a global capitalist who happens to be an Egyptian. He is a Coptic Christian who has created a company that employs tens of thousands of Muslims and offers its shares on international stock exchanges to Americans, Asians, Middle Easterners, and Europeans. And like any successful businessman, he is more likely to speak of the world becoming flat than he is to think in terms of any inherent antagonism between Muslims, Christians, and Jews.

And therein lies a final lesson and a real danger. Muslims, Christians, and Jews have been so enmeshed in a framework of conflict and so determined to view not only history but the present through that lens that they risk missing the next wave of history. Many parts of the world that are emerging in the twenty-first century have not been party to that history, and are neither interested in nor constrained by it, China most of all.

In no small measure, the rulers of Dubai and the Sawiris family have been able to turn their aspirations into reality because they are unencumbered by the history of conflict. They have shed the burdens of the past, and have instead taken advantage of the opportunities that cooperation and coexistence create and have always created. They are not trying to restore a golden age. They are not driven by a sense of grievance. They are simply working with the world around them. But whether or not they greet strangers with the word of peace, they are emissaries of it just the same. And so are the millions who go about their daily lives seeking only the betterment of themselves and their families, uninterested in dogma, theology, and hatred. That has been true for the entire history of Muslims, Christians, and Jews, even though that part of the story has been neglected, even though discord makes for better drama and more passion. It remains true today. Peace is woven into our collective past; it is there to be seen in our messy present; and it will be there in our shared future.

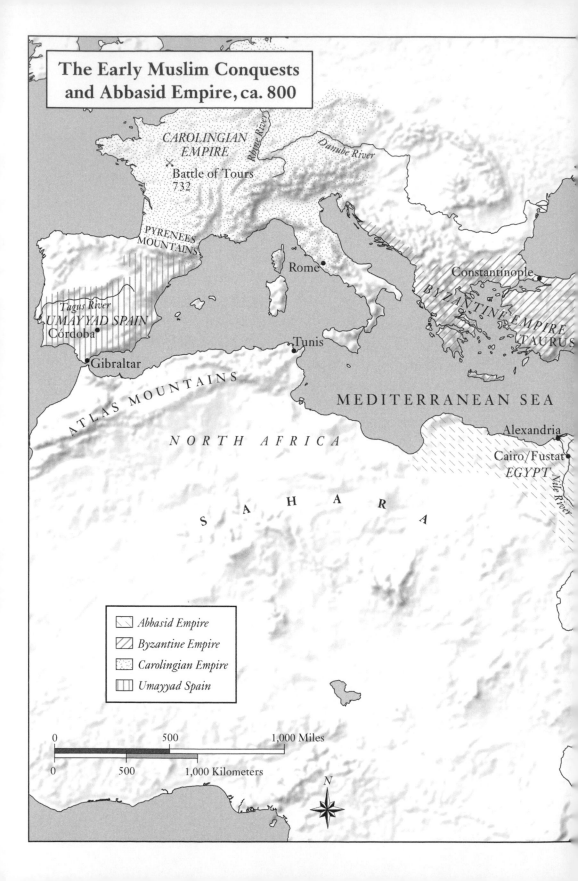

The Early Muslim Conquests and Abbasid Empire, ca. 800

CAROLINGIAN EMPIRE

Rhône River

Danube River

× Battle of Tours
732

PYRENEES
MOUNTAINS

Rome

Constantinople

BYZANTINE EMPIRE
TAURUS

Tagus River

UMAYYAD SPAIN
Córdoba

Gibraltar

Tunis

ATLAS MOUNTAINS

MEDITERRANEAN SEA

NORTH AFRICA

Alexandria

Cairo/Fustat
EGYPT

Nile River

S A H A R A

Abbasid Empire
Byzantine Empire
Carolingian Empire
Umayyad Spain

0   500   1,000 Miles

0   500   1,000 Kilometers

N

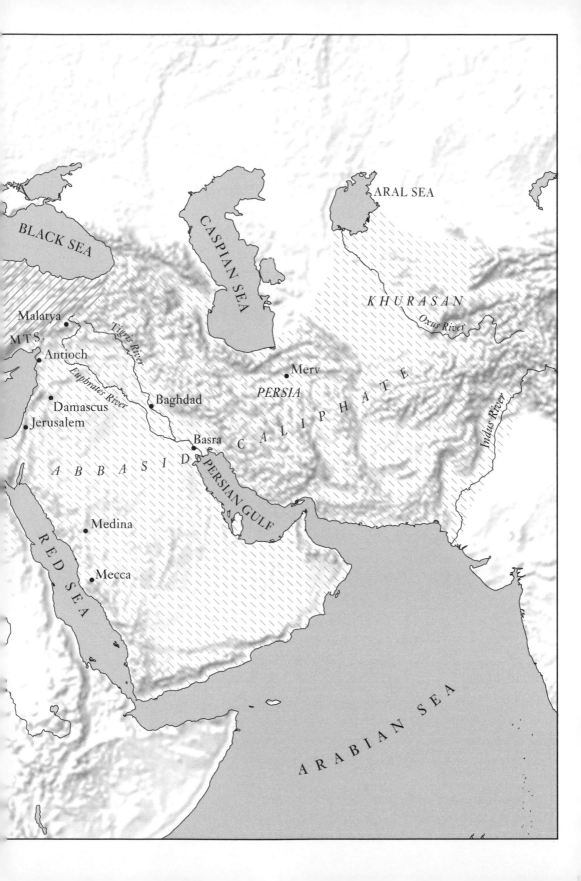

BLACK SEA

ARAL SEA

CASPIAN SEA

KHURASAN

Malatya

MTS.

Antioch

Tigris River

Euphrates River

Merv

Oxus River

PERSIA

CALIPHATE

Baghdad

Damascus

Jerusalem

Basra

Indus River

A B B A S I D

PERSIAN GULF

RED SEA

Medina

Mecca

ARABIAN SEA

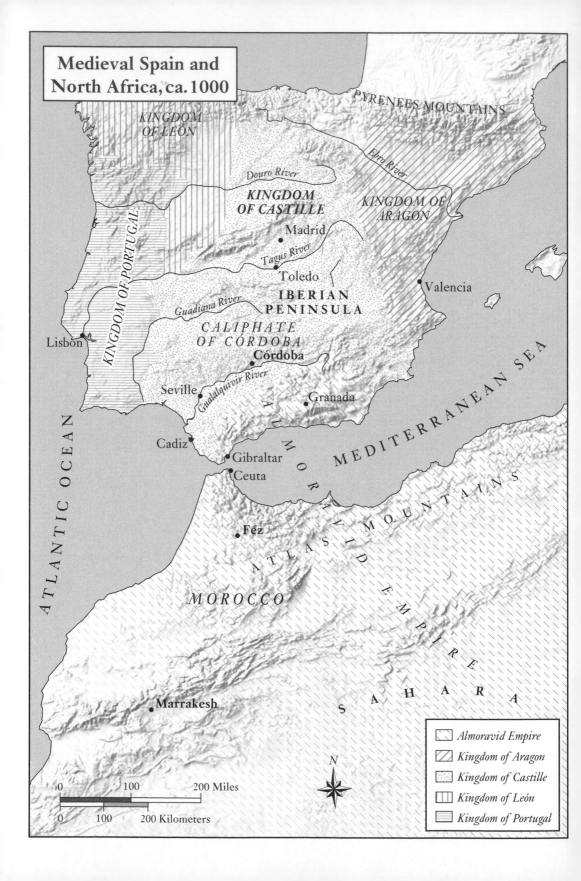

Medieval Spain and North Africa, ca. 1000

PYRENEES MOUNTAINS

KINGDOM OF LEÓN

Douro River

Ebro River

KINGDOM OF CASTILLE

KINGDOM OF ARAGON

KINGDOM OF PORTUGAL

• Madrid

Tagus River

IBERIAN PENINSULA

Toledo

• Valencia

Guadiana River

CALIPHATE OF CÓRDOBA

Lisbon •

Córdoba

Seville •

Guadalquivir River

• Granada

ATLANTIC OCEAN

Cadiz •

Gibraltar •

Ceuta •

MEDITERRANEAN SEA

ALMORAVID EMPIRE

• **Fez**

ATLAS MOUNTAINS

MOROCCO

S A H A R A

• **Marrakesh**

N

0   100   200 Miles

0   100   200 Kilometers

	Almoravid Empire
	Kingdom of Aragon
	Kingdom of Castille
	Kingdom of León
	Kingdom of Portugal

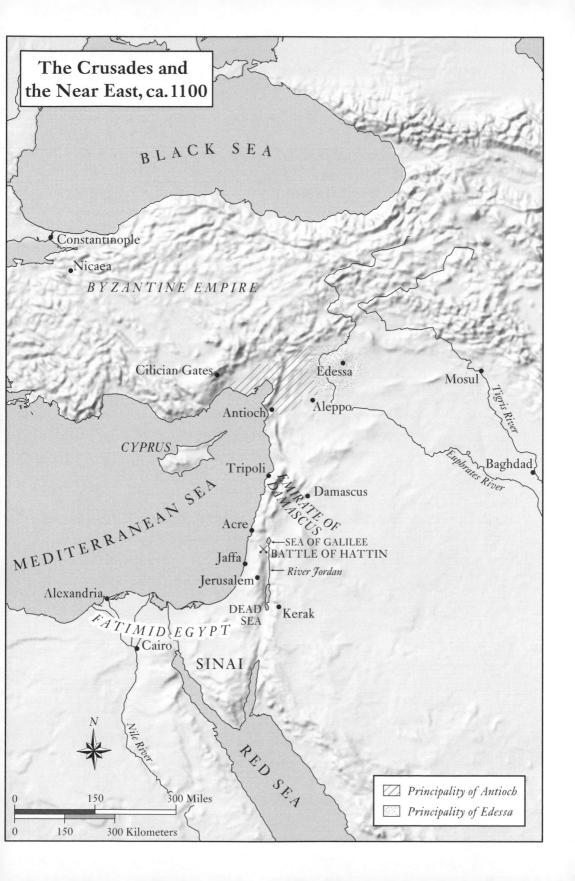

The Crusades and
the Near East, ca. 1100

BLACK SEA

Constantinople

Nicaea

BYZANTINE EMPIRE

Cilician Gates

Edessa

Mosul

Antioch

Aleppo

Tigris River

CYPRUS

Baghdad

Euphrates River

Tripoli

EMIRATE OF
DAMASCUS

Damascus

MEDITERRANEAN SEA

Acre

SEA OF GALILEE
BATTLE OF HATTIN

Jaffa

River Jordan

Jerusalem

Alexandria

DEAD
SEA

Kerak

FATIMID EGYPT

Cairo

SINAI

N

Nile River

RED SEA

| 0 | 150 | 300 Miles |
| 0 | 150 | 300 Kilometers |

Principality of Antioch

Principality of Edessa

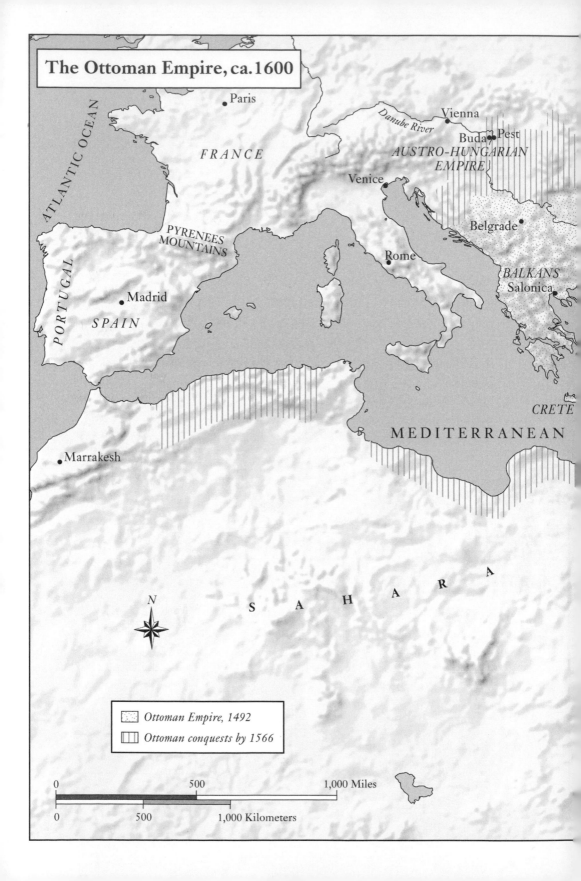

The Ottoman Empire, ca. 1600

ATLANTIC OCEAN

Paris

FRANCE

Danube River

Vienna

Buda Pest

AUSTRO-HUNGARIAN
EMPIRE

Venice

Belgrade

PYRENEES
MOUNTAINS

Rome

BALKANS
Salonica

PORTUGAL

Madrid

SPAIN

CRETE

MEDITERRANEAN

Marrakesh

S A H A R A

N

Ottoman Empire, 1492

Ottoman conquests by 1566

0		500		1,000 Miles

0		500		1,000 Kilometers

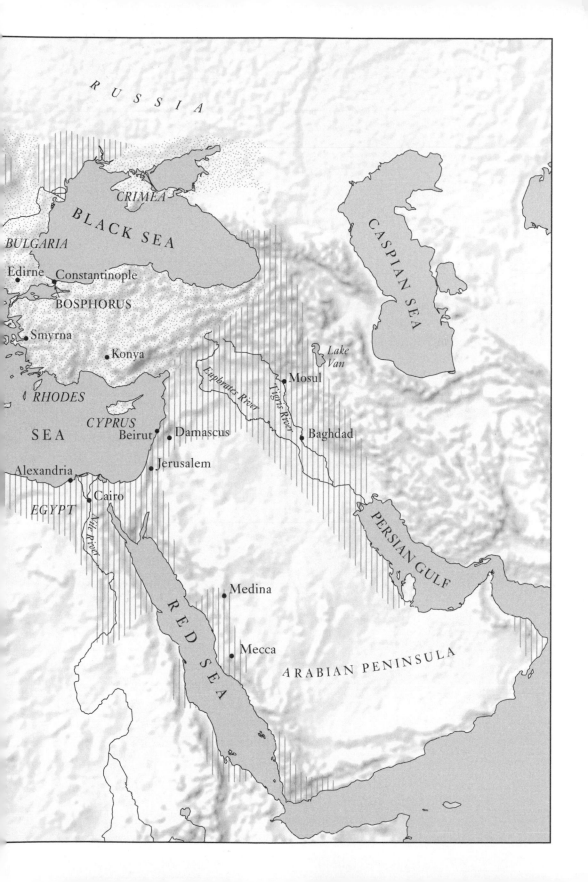

RUSSIA

CRIMEA

BLACK SEA

BULGARIA

Edirne   Constantinople

BOSPHORUS

Smyrna

Konya

RHODES

CYPRUS

SEA   Beirut   Damascus

Alexandria   Jerusalem

Cairo

EGYPT   *Nile River*

Euphrates River

Tigris River

Lake
Van

Mosul

Baghdad

CASPIAN SEA

PERSIAN GULF

Medina

RED SEA

Mecca   ARABIAN PENINSULA

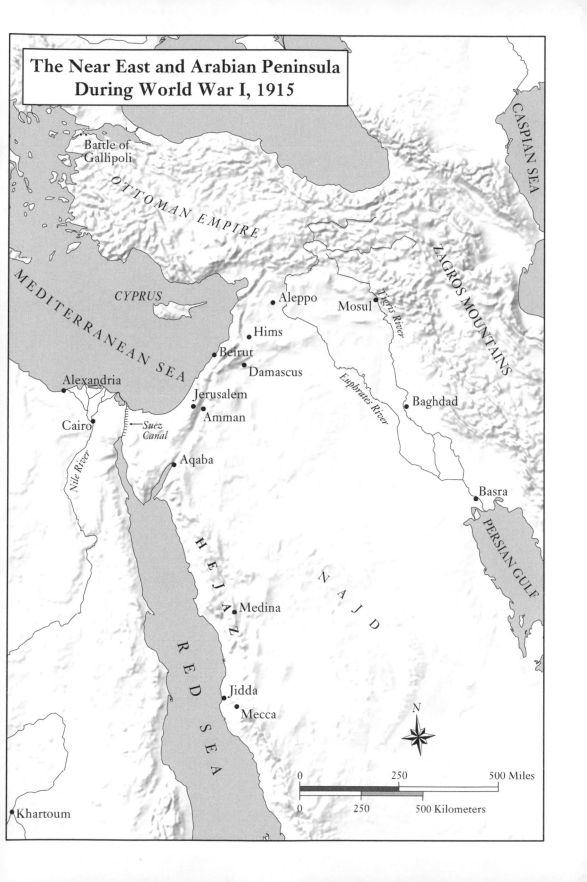

The Near East and Arabian Peninsula During World War I, 1915

CASPIAN SEA

Battle of Gallipoli

OTTOMAN EMPIRE

ZAGROS MOUNTAINS

MEDITERRANEAN SEA

CYPRUS

Aleppo

Mosul

Tigris River

Hims

Beirut

Damascus

Euphrates River

Baghdad

Alexandria

Jerusalem

Amman

Cairo

Suez Canal

Aqaba

Nile River

Basra

PERSIAN GULF

H E J A Z

N A J D

Medina

RED SEA

Jidda

Mecca

N

Khartoum

0   250   500 Miles

0   250   500 Kilometers

The Modern Middle East

N

ATLANTIC OCEAN

Paris

GERMANY

CZECH REP.

SLOVAKIA

Vienna

AUSTRIA

HUNGARY

SWITZ.

SLOVENIA

CROATIA

Danube River

FRANCE

ITALY

BOSNIA & HERZ.

SERBIA

MONT.

Rome

ALBANIA

MACE

SPAIN

GREECE

Madrid

Lisbon

PORTUGAL

Algiers

Tunis

MEDITERRANEAN

Casablanca

ATLAS MOUNTAINS

TUNISIA

MOROCCO

Tripoli

Marrakesh

ALGERIA

LIBYA

S A H A R A

MAURITANIA

MALI

NIGER

Niger River

CHAD

Lake Chad

BURKINA FASO

BENIN

NIGERIA

GUINEA

TOGO

SIERRA LEONE

CÔTE D'IVOIRE

GHANA

CENTRAL AFRICAN REPUBLIC

LIBERIA

CAMEROON

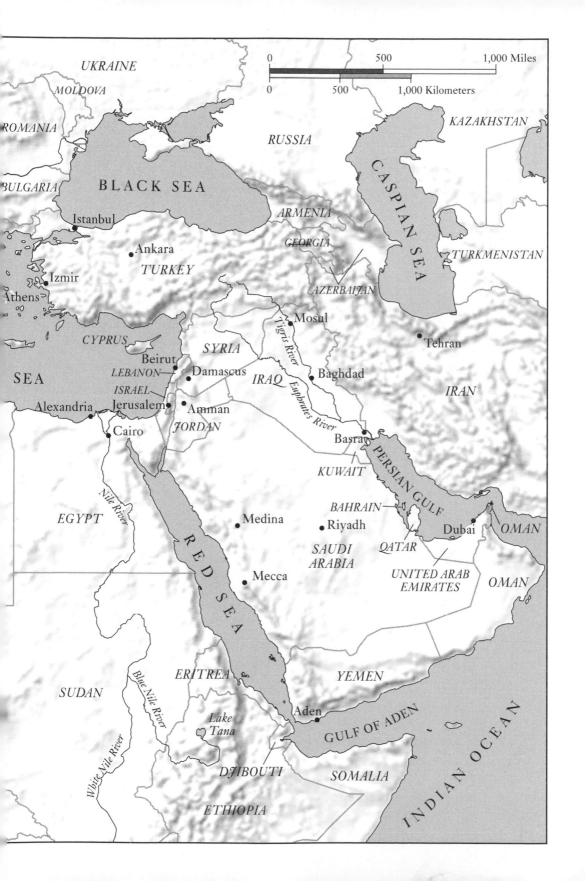

NOTES

CHAPTER ONE: IN THE NAME OF THE LORD

1. This description relies on Stephen Humphries, *Islamic History: A Framework for Inquiry* (Princeton, N.J.: Princeton University Press, 1991), 92–98, and W. Montgomery Watt, *Islamic Political Thought* (Edinburgh: University of Edinburgh Press, 1968), 4–9 and appendix. Watt relies on the account of Ibn Ishaq, one of the canonical biographers of the Prophet, who wrote in the eighth century. For pre-Islamic alliances, see Michael Cook, *Forbidding Wrong in Islam* (Cambridge: Cambridge University Press, 2003), 150ff. Some scholars question whether this agreement actually existed and believe that it was invented by chroniclers writing several hundred years after the fact. But to dismiss the notion entirely seems foolish. See John Wansbrough, *Quranic Studies: Sources and Methods of Scriptural Interpretation* (New York: Oxford University Press, 1977), and Patricia Crone and Michael Cook, *Hagarism: The Making of the Islamic World* (Cambridge: Cambridge University Press, 1976).
2. Abu-l Abbas Ahmad ibn Jabir al-Baladhuri, *The Origins of the Islamic State*, trans. Philip Khuri Hitti (Piscataway, N.J.: Gorgias Press, 2002), 33. This is a reprint of the original 1916 edition, published by Columbia University Press.
3. Passages from the Quran are taken from A. J. Arberry, *The Koran Interpreted* (New York: Touchstone, 1955, 1996).
4. The account was written by the Armenian historian Sebeos and is quoted in A. A. Vasiliev, *History of the Byzantine Empire*, vol. I (Madison: University of Wisconsin Press, 1952), 199. See also George Ostrogorsky, *History of the Byzantine State* (London: Blackwell, 1956), 110ff. For a unique take on the origin of the caliphate, see Patricia Crone, *God's Rule: Government and Islam* (New York: Columbia University Press, 2004).
5. See Claude Cahen, "Dhimma," in *The Encyclopedia of Islam* (Leiden: E. J. Brill, 1991); Bat Ye'or, *The Decline of Eastern Christianity: From Jihad to Dhimmitude* (London, 1996), 121ff.; Suhayl Qasha, *Al-Masihiyan fi al-Dawlah al-Islamiya* [Christians in the Muslim State] (Beirut: Dar al-Malak, 2002), 54ff.; C. E. Bosworth, "The Concept of Dhimma in Early Islam," in Bosworth, *The Arab, Byzantium, and Iran* (Burlington, Vt.: Ashgate Publishing, 1996), 285ff.

6. Quoted Khalid ibn al-Walid, and the inhabitants of Hims all quoted in al-Baladhuri, *The Origins of the Islamic State,* 187, 211. Though some of the depiction of Christians and Jews rushing to the side of the Arabs may be exaggerated by al-Baladhuri, he is far from the only early historian to record the widespread discontent with Byzantine rule.

7. See for instance Ibn Abd al-Hakam, *History of the Conquests of Egypt, North Africa, and Spain,* ed. Charles Torrey (Piscataway, N.J.: Gorgias Press, 2002), and Jamal al-Din Shayyal, *Tarikh Misr al-Islamiya* [The Islamic History of Egypt] (Alexandria: Dar al-Ma'arif, 1967).

8. Chase F. Robinson, *Empire and Elites After the Muslim Conquest: The Transformation of Northern Mesopotamia* (Cambridge: Cambridge University Press, 2000), 28ff.

9. For the best analysis of conversion to Islam, see Richard Bulliet, *Conversion to Islam in the Medieval Period* (Cambridge: Harvard University Press, 1979). For a detailed analysis of Quran 2:256, see Yohanan Friedmann, *Tolerance and Coercion in Islam: Interfaith Relations in Muslim Tradition* (New York: Cambridge University Press, 2003), 100ff.

10. A good account of the fall of Jerusalem and Umar's visit can be found in Karen Armstrong, *Jerusalem: One City, Three Faiths* (New York: Knopf, 1996), 226–34. For Sophronius, see Robert Hoyland, *Seeing Islam as Others Saw It: A Survey and Evaluation of Christian, Jewish and Zoroastrian Writings on Early Islam* (Princeton, N.J.: Darwin Press, 1997), 66–74.

11. Hoyland, *Seeing Islam as Others Saw It,* 480ff.; Hugh Goddard, *A History of Muslim-Christian Relations* (Chicago: New Amsterdam Books, 2000), 38–41.

CHAPTER TWO: AT THE COURT OF THE CALIPH

1. Dimitri Gutas, *Greek Thought, Arabic Culture: The Graeco-Arabic Translation Movement in Baghdad and Early Abbasid Society* (New York: Routledge, 1998), 28ff. Timothy quotation from Sydney Griffith, *Arabic Christianity in the Monasteries of Ninth-Century Palestine* (Burlington, Vt.: Ashgate Publishing, 1992), 140–45. See also Hugh Kennedy, *The Early Abbasid Caliphate* (London: Croom & Helm, 1981); Jacob Lassner, *The Shaping of Abbasid Rule* (Princeton, N.J.: Princeton University Press, 1980); al-Tabari, *The Early Abbasid Empire,* vol. 2, trans. John Alden Williams (New York: Cambridge University Press, 1989).

2. For the building of Baghdad, see Hugh Kennedy, *The Court of the Caliphs: The Rise and Fall of Islam's Greatest Dynasty* (London: Weidenfeld & Nicholson, 2005), 132ff.

3. Sydney Griffith, *The Beginnings of Christian Theology in Arabic: Muslim-Christian Encounters in the Early Islamic Period* (Burlington, Vt.: Ashgate, 2002), 155ff.; Majid Fakhry, *Islamic Philosophy, Theology, and Mysticism* (Oxford, England: Oneworld, 1997); Ignaz Goldziher, *Introduction to Islamic Theology and Law* (Princeton, N.J.: Princeton University Press, 1991); Hoyland, 454–56; Goddard, 52–54; Louis Cheikho, *Ulama' al-Nasraniyah fi al-Islam, 622–1300* [Christian Scholars Under Islam] (Juniyah, Lebanon: al-Maktabah al-Bulusiyah, 1983).

4. Qasha, 110; G. Stange, *Baghdad During the Abbasid Caliphate* (London: Oxford University Press, 1924), 202ff.

5. The best study, bar none, of this process is Richard Bulliet, *Conversion to Islam in the Medieval Period* (Cambridge: Harvard University Press, 1979).

6. Abu Nuwas quoted in Eric Schroeder, *Muhammad's People: An Anthology of Muslim Civilization* (Mineola, N.Y.: Dover Publications, 1955, 2002), 315. Also see Marshall C. S. Hodgson, *The Venture of Islam,* vol. 1 (Chicago: University of Chicago Press, 1974), 462–63.

7. See Dimitri Gutas, 58–60, for the argument that the *bayt al-hikma* was little more than a simple library.

8. Quoted in Schroeder, 366–67.

9. Al-Ma'mun quoted in al-Tabari, *The History of al-Tabari,* vol. 32, trans. C. E. Bosworth (Albany: State University of New York Press, 1987), 100–101. For al-Kindi, see Fakhry, 21–29, and Felix Klein-Franke, "Al-Kindi," in Seyyed Hossein Nasr and Oliver Leaman, eds., *History of Islamic Philosophy: Part 1* (London: Routledge, 1996), 165ff.

10. Both al-Jahiz and the chief judge quoted in Bernard Lewis, *The Jews of Islam* (Princeton, N.J.: Princeton University Press, 1984), 15, 59–60.

11. This exchange is frequently cited, and the translation here is from Hugh Kennedy, 80–81. See also J. J. Saunders, *A History of Medieval Islam* (London: Routledge and Kegan Paul, 1965), 114; C. E. Bosworth, *The Arab, Byzantium and Iran* (Burlington, Vt.: Ashgate Publishing, 1996).

12. See Alessandro Barbero, *Charlemagne: Father of a Continent* (Berkeley: University of California Press, 2004), 90–91; Richard Fletcher, *The Cross and the Crescent: Christianity and Islam from Muhammad to the Reformation* (New York: Viking, 2004), 50ff.

13. Al-Tabari, *The History of al-Tabari,* vol. 32, 195–97.

CHAPTER THREE: THE SACRIFICE OF ISAAC

1. There have been many accounts of the Córdoban martyrs. See Jessica Coope, *The Martyrs of Córdoba: Community and Family Conflict in an Age of Mass Conversion* (Lincoln: University of Nebraska Press, 1995); Norman Daniel, *The Arabs and Mediaeval Europe* (London: Longman, 1975), 230–48; Kenneth Baxter Wolf, *Christian Martyrs in Muslim Spain* (New York: Cambridge University Press, 1987). Also, Paul Alvarus, "The Life of Eulogius," in Olivia Remie Constable, ed., *Medieval Iberia: Readings from Christian, Muslim, and Jewish Sources* (Philadelphia: University of Pennsylvania Press, 1997), 48–51. For the text of the surrender of Murcia, see Constable, 37.

2. The phrase "ornament of the world" comes from the Saxon writer Hroswitha in the tenth century and is used as the title of Maria Rosa Menocal's superb study, *The Ornament of the World: How Muslims, Jews and Christians Created a Culture of Tolerance in Medieval Spain* (New York: Little Brown, 2002). Earlier Paul Alvarus quotation from Menocal, 66. The phrase "men who worship God and acknowl-

edge heavenly laws" is from John McManners, *The Oxford Illustrated History of Christianity.* (New York: Oxford University Press, 2001).

3. The excerpt from the life of John of Gorze and descriptions of tenth-century Córdoba come from Richard Fletcher, *Moorish Spain* (Berkeley: University of California Press, 1992), 66–70; see also Richard Reilly, *The Medieval Spains* (Cambridge: Cambridge University Press, 1993).

4. See S. D. Goitein, *A Mediterranean Society: An Abridgement in One Volume* (Berkeley: University of California Press, 1999). This is a condensed version of Goitein's lifetime study of the documents of the Cairo Geniza, charting the intricate commercial ties between Jews throughout the Mediterranean. See also Olivia Remie Constable, *Trade and Traders in Muslim Spain: The Commercial Realignment of the Iberian Peninsula* (New York: Cambridge University Press, 1994).

5. Translations of these letters can be found at the Web site www.fordham.edu/halsall/source/khazars1.html, which is part of the Internet Medieval Sourcebook compiled by the Fordham Center for Medieval Studies and edited by Paul Halsall. See also Douglas M. Dunlop, *A History of the Jewish Khazars* (Princeton, N.J.: Princeton University Press, 1954); Jane Gerber, *The Jews of Spain: A History of the Sephardic Experience* (New York: Free Press, 1992), 46–61; Vivian Mann et al., eds., *Convivencia: Jews, Muslims, and Christians in Medieval Spain* (New York: Braziller and the Jewish Museum, 1992), 40–44.

6. The description of Samuel as a lover of knowledge comes from Moses ibn Ezra, "Kitab al-Muarah," from Joseph Jacobs, "Samuel Ha-Nagid," in www.jewish encyclopedia.com. See also Jefim Schirmann, "Samuel Hannagid, the Man, the Soldier, the Politician," *Jewish Social Studies* 2 (April 1951), 107. The excerpted poem that begins "Man's wisdom..." is from David Goldstein, *Hebrew Poems from Spain* (New York: Schocken Books, 1996). For the Nagid's poem in which he calls himself "the David of his age," see Menocal, 102. For the poem describing the carnage of the battlefield, see Israel Zinberg, *History of Jewish Literature: Arabic-Spanish Period,* trans. Bernard Martin (Cleveland: Case Western Reserve University Press, 1972).

7. From Constable, ed., *Medieval Iberia,* 97–99.

8. Hugh Kennedy, *Muslim Spain and Portugal: A Political History of al-Andalus* (New York: Longman, 1996), 146.

9. Kennedy, 154ff.; Richard Fletcher, *Moorish Spain,* 105ff.; Bernard Reilly, 90–128; Andrew Wheatcroft, *Infidel: A History of the Conflict Between Christendom and Islam* (New York: Random House, 2003), 85ff.

CHAPTER FOUR: THE CRUSADES

1. Pope Urban II quoted in Thomas Asbridge, *The First Crusade: A New History: The Roots of Conflict Between Christianity and Islam* (New York: Oxford University Press, 2005), 32–33. Some scholars have questioned whether Jerusalem was indeed the stated goal of the First Crusade, but most have concluded that it was.

For these historiographical debates, see Andrew Jotischky, *Crusading and the Crusader States* (New York: Longman, 2004), chap. 1.

2. Al-Hakim's eccentricities are described in Marshall Hodgson, *The Venture of Islam,* vol. 2, 26–28. Some have said that Hakim was the victim of later polemicists and that he was not at all addled.

3. The literature on the origins of Christian holy war is immense. See Asbridge, *The First Crusades,* chap. 1; Christopher Tyerman, *Fighting for Christendom: Holy War and the Crusades* (New York: Oxford University Press, 2004); Jotischky, *Crusading and the Crusader States;* Claude Cahen, *Orient et Occident au temps des Croisades* (Paris: Editions Aubier, 1983), 54–80.

4. The first Urban quote is from the account written by Fulcher of Chartres, the second by Robert the Monk, both of which can be found in the Internet Medieval Sourcebook at www.fordham.edu/halsall/sbook1k.html.

5. The story about a possible alliance between the Fatimids and the Crusaders comes from a thirteenth-century chronicler named Ibn al-Athir, quoted in Carole Hillenbrand, *The Crusades: Islamic Perspectives* (New York: Routledge, 2000), 46.

6. Anna Comnena is the primary source on Alexius. Good secondary sources include John Julius Norwich, *Byzantium: The Decline and Fall* (New York: Knopf, 1995), 31–35; Ostrogorsky, *History of the Byzantine State,* 349–70. Anna Comnena on Bohemond quoted in Elizabeth Hallam, ed., *Chronicles of the Crusades: Eye-Witness Accounts of the Wars Between Christianity and Islam* (New York: Welcome Rain, 2000), 69–70.

7. For the phrase "armed pilgrims," see Georges Bordonove, *Les Croisades et le royaume de Jerusalem* (Paris: Editions Pygmalion, 2002).

8. See the accounts of Ibn al-Athir, quoted in Francesco Gabrielli, *Arab Historians of the Crusades* (Berkeley: University of California Press, 1969), 3–9; Ibn al-Qalanisi, *The Damascus Chronicle of the Crusades,* ed. and trans. H. A. R. Gibb (New York: Dover Publications, 1932, 2002), 43–46. See also the magisterial history of Steven Runciman: *A History of the Crusades,* vol. 1, *The First Crusades and the Foundation of the Kingdom of Jerusalem* (Cambridge: Cambridge University Press, 1951), 213ff.

9. The historian, Ibn al-Athir, is quoted at length in P. M. Holt, *The Crusader States and Their Neighbors* (New York: Longman, 2004), 18.

10. See Runciman, 279ff.; Hallam, *Chronicles of the Crusades,* 88–94; Hans Eberhard Meyer, *The Crusades* (New York: Oxford University Press, 1965, 1988), 54–57; Asbridge, *The First Crusaders,* 316–19; Amin Maalouf, *The Crusades Through Arab Eyes* (New York: Schocken Books, 1983, 1987), 48–52.

11. Ibn al-Athir quoted in Maalouf, 55.

12. Piers Paul Read, *The Templars* (London: Weidenfeld & Nicholson, 1999); Edith Clementine Bramhall, "The Origins of the Temporal Privileges of Crusaders," *American Journal of Theology* (April 1901), 279–92.

13. Quoted in Holt, 45.

14. The first quotation, about Frankish religious toleration, is from Imad al-Din

and is quoted in Benjamin Kedar, "The Subjected Muslims of Frankish Levant," in James M. Powell, ed., *Muslims Under Latin Rule, 1100–1300* (Princeton, N.J.: Princeton University Press, 1990), 161. The second, from Ibn Jubayr, is quoted in Kedar, 167. Ibn al-Qalanisi quoted in Hillenbrand, 396.

15. See Ronnie Ellenblum, *Frankish Settlement in the Latin Kingdom of Jerusalem* (Cambridge: Cambridge University Press, 1998).

16. Usama ibn Munqidh, *An Arab-Syrian Gentleman and Warrior in the Period of the Crusades,* trans. Philip Hitti (New York: Columbia University Press, 1929, 2000), 161–70.

CHAPTER FIVE: SALADIN'S JIHAD?

1. Imad ad-Din quoted in Gabrielli, *Arab Historians of the Crusades,* 160ff.; Saladin's response to the delegation from Jerusalem and the speech of the *qadi* of Aleppo in Al-Aqsa Mosque both quoted in Stanley Lane-Poole, *Saladin: All Powerful Sultan and the Uniter of Islam* (New York: Cooper Square Press, 1898, 2002), 224–25, 236ff., which in turn translates from Ibn Khallikan. Also see Runciman, *A History of the Crusades,* vol. 2, *The Kingdom of Jerusalem and the Frankish East, 1100–1187.*

2. The account of Saladin's character comes from Baha al-Din ibn Shaddad, quoted in Hallam, 155–56.

3. Quoted in Malcolm Cameron Lyons and D. E. P. Jackson, *Saladin: The Politics of Holy War* (New York: Cambridge University Press, 1982), 119–20.

4. Gibbon quoted in Hillenbrand, 185. See also Edward Gibbon, *The Decline and Fall of the Roman Empire,* vol. 3 (New York: Heritage Press, 1946), 2084–85.

5. Both quotations in Lyons and Jackson, 194 and 228, as are statistics about time spent fighting Christians versus time spent campaigning against Muslims. Also, for a skeptical portrait of Saladin, see Andrew Ehrenkreutz, *Saladin* (Albany: State University of New York Press, 1972).

6. See David Cook, *Understanding Jihad* (Berkeley: University of California Press, 2005); Sayyid Hossein Nasr, *Islam: Religion, History and Civilization* (San Francisco: HarperSanFrancisco, 2003), 91ff.

7. Frankish account by Ernoul, written c. 1197, trans. Peter Edbury and Paul Hayams, in Fordham's Medieval Sourcebook, www.fordham.edu/halsall/source/1187.ernoul.html. See also the account of Ibn al-Athir in Gabrielli, 122–25.

8. Runciman, *A History of the Crusades,* vol. 3, *The Kingdom of Acre and the Later Crusades,* 53. For the Christian chronicler see *Itinerarium Peregrinorum et Gesta Regis Ricardi,* ed. William Stubbs, Rolls Series (London: Longmans, 1864), IV, 2, 4 (pp. 240–41, 243), translated by James Brundage in *The Crusades: A Documentary History* (Milwaukee: Marquette University Press, 1962), 183–84.

9. Runciman, vol. 3, 27.

10. Most of this account of the marriage proposal is taken from Baha ad-Din, in Gabrielli, 225–31. Saladin's reluctance to agree to truce is in Imad ad-Din, also in Gabrielli, 236–37.

11. For an excellent recent account, see Jonathan Phillips, *The Fourth Crusade and the Sack of Constantinople* (New York: Penguin Group, 2004).

CHAPTER SIX: THE PHILOSOPHER'S DREAM

1. See for instance Mark Myerson, *A Jewish Renaissance in Fifteenth-Century Spain* (Princeton, N.J.: Princeton University Press, 2004), 12. Derogatory quotation about those who favored martyrdom from Jane Gerber, *The Jews of Spain,* 81. All Maimonides quotations from Isadore Twersky, ed., *A Maimonides Reader* (Springfield, N.J.: Behrman House, 1972). On Maimonides and philosophy, see Joel Kraemer, "Maimonides and the Spanish Aristotelian School," in Mark Myerson and Edward English, eds., *Christians, Muslims, and Jews in Medieval and Early Modern Spain* (Notre Dame, Ind.: University of Notre Dame Press, 2000). For al-Ghazali, see Fakhry, *Islamic Philosophy,* 69–106, as well as Marshall Hodgson, *The Venture of Islam,* vol. 2, 180–92. For Ibn Arabi, see Seyyid Hossein Nasr, *Three Muslim Sages* (Cambridge: Harvard University Press, 1964), chap. 3 (the Ibn Arabi quotation is on p. 116). Also on Ibn Arabi, al-Ghazali, and mysticism in general, see Annemarie Schimmel, *Mystical Dimensions of Islam* (Chapel Hill: University of North Carolina Press, 1975), and John Renard, *Seven Doors to Islam: Spirituality and the Religious Life* (Berkeley: University of California Press, 1996).
2. Almohad "Doctrine of Divine Unity" in Olivia Remie Constable, *Medieval Iberia,* 190ff.
3. Ibn Khaldun, *The Muqaddimah,* trans. Franz Rosenthal (Princeton, N.J.: Princeton University Press, 1967).
4. Abu al-Baqa al-Rundi, "Lament for the Fall of Seville," in Constable, 120–23.
5. Charter issued by King Jaime of Aragon in Constable, 214–15.
6. Mosen Diego de Valera quoted in Vivian Mann et al., *Convivencia,* 75.
7. The description of Fernando's tomb, as well as the relevant details about Alfonso's life, are taken from Robert Burns, ed., *Emperor of Culture: Alfonso X the Learned of Castile and His Thirteenth-Century Renaissance* (Philadelphia: University of Pennsylvania Press, 1990).
8. See Menocal, *Ornament of the World,* 225–226; quotation of Alfonso's nephew in Norman Roth, "Jewish Collaborators in Alfonso's Scientific Work," in Burns, *Emperor of Culture,* 59ff.

CHAPTER SEVEN: THE LORD OF TWO LANDS

1. The story of Mehmed and the soldier in Hagia Sophia is told in countless narratives. This version is from Lord Kinross, *The Ottoman Centuries: The Rise and Fall of the Turkish Empire* (New York: Morrow, 1977), 109. For the fall of the city, see David Nicol, *The Last Centuries of Byzantium, 1261–1453* (New York: Cambridge University Press, 1993), chap. 18; John Freely, *Istanbul: The Imperial City* (New York: Penguin Books, 1996), chap. 15. For the quotation "better the turban

of the Muslim," see David Talbot Rice, *The Byzantines* (New York: Praeger, 1962), 74. For a primary source on Mehmed, see the work of the fifteenth-century Ottoman chronicler Tursun Beg, *The History of Mehmed the Conqueror*, trans. Halil Inalcik and Rhoads Murphy (Minneapolis: Bibliotheca Islamica, 1978). On the appointment of Gennadius, see for instance Daniel Goffman, *The Ottoman Empire and Early Modern Europe* (New York: Cambridge University Press, 2002), 171–73; the contemporary chronicler was Kritovoulus and is quoted in Benjamin Braude, "Foundation Myths of the Miller System," in Benjamin Braude and Bernard Lewis, eds., *Christians and Jews in the Ottoman Empire: The Functioning of a Plural Society*, vol. 1 (New York: Holmes & Meier, 1982), 78; Kritovoulus, *History of Mehmed the Conqueror*, trans. Charles Riggs (Princeton, N.J.: Princeton University Press, 1954).

2. That is exactly what *The Oxford English Dictionary* suggests the word meant in the sixteenth and seventeenth centuries. See Roger Crowley, *1453: The Holy War for Constantinople and the Clash of Islam and the West* (New York: Hyperion, 2005), 243.

3. For good primers on the Ottomans, see Kinross, *The Ottoman Centuries;* Jason Goodwin, *Lords of the Horizon* (New York: 20004); Colin Imber, *The Ottoman Empire, 1300–1650: The Structure of Power* (New York: Palgrave, 2002). For skepticism on the so-called *ghazi* thesis, see Cemal Kafadar, *Between Two Worlds: The Construction of the Ottoman State* (Berkeley: University of California Press, 1995). On relations between the West and the Ottomans and the legacy of negative images, see Goffman, *The Ottoman Empire and Early Modern Europe.* See also Bruce Masters, *Christians and Jews in the Ottoman Arab World: The Roots of Secularism* (New York: Cambridge University Press, 2001). The best survey on the Mediterranean world in this period and into the seventeenth century is Ferdinand Braudel, *The Mediterranean World.*

4. Joseph Hacker, "Ottoman Policy Toward the Jews and Jewish Attitudes Toward the Ottomans During the Fifteenth Century," in Braude and Lewis, eds., *Christians and Jews in the Ottoman Empire*, 117–26; quotation about the Turks welcoming the Jews from Mark Mazower, *Salonica, City of Ghosts* (New York: Knopf, 2005), 48.

5. Bartolomeo Contarini quoted in Alan Fisher, "The Life and Family of Suleyman I," in Halil Inalcik and Cemal Kafadar, eds., *Suleyman the Second and His Time* (Istanbul: Isis Press, 1993), 2. Also, Antony Bridge, *Suleiman the Magnificent* (New York: Dorset Press, 1966). Busbecq quoted in Kinross, 202. Luther quotations and Bodin quotations (which I have put in contemporary English) both from Goffman, 109–111. The primary Turkish source is Sinan Chavush, *Suleymanname* (Istanbul: Historical Research Foundation, 1987).

6. For Suleyman and European Protestants, see Halil Inalcik, *The Ottoman Empire: The Classical Age, 1300–1600*, trans. Norman Itzkowitz and Colin Imber (New York: Praeger, 1973), 30–38. Also, Stephen Fischer-Galati, *Ottoman Imperialism and German Protestantism* (Cambridge: Harvard University Press, 1959); Eugene Rice and Anthony Grafton, *The Foundations of Early Modern Europe, 1460–1559* (New York: Norton, 1994), 135–45.

CHAPTER EIGHT: THE TIDE BEGINS TO TURN

1. On the *millet* system, see Bruce Masters, *Christians and Jews in the Ottoman Arab World*, 34ff. One of the best Turkish sources is Gulnihal Bozkurt, *Alman-Ingiliz ve siyasi gelismelerin isigi altinda gayriMuslim Osmanli vatandaslarinin hukuki durumu* (Ankara: Turk Tarik Kuruma Basimevi, 1989). Also, Carter Findley, *Ottoman Civil Officialdom* (Princeton, N.J.: Princeton University Press, 1989); Mark Epstein, "The Leadership of the Ottoman Jews in the Fifteenth and Sixteenth Centuries," and Joseph Hacker, "Ottoman Policy Toward the Jews and Jewish Attitudes Towards the Ottoman During the Fifteenth Century," in Braude and Lewis, 100–126. Quotation of the patriarch of Jerusalem from Benjamin Braude and Bernard Lewis, Introduction, in Braude and Lewis, 17. See also Caroline Finkel, *Osman's Dream: The Story of the Ottoman Empire* (London: John Murray, 2005).

2. For Ottoman rule on Crete, see Molly Greene, *A Shared World: Christians and Muslims in the Early Modern Mediterranean* (Princeton, N.J.: Princeton University Press, 2000).

3. Quotation from a Catholic chronicler in 1667, cited in John Freely, *The Lost Messiah: In Search of the Mystical Rabbi Sabbatai Sevi* (New York: Overlook Press, 2001), 99. The magisterial work in the field remains Gershom Scholem, *Sabbatai Sevi: The Mystical Messiah* (Princeton, N.J.: Princeton University Press, 1973).

4. Lady Montagu quotation from Goffman, 169; the French general was Count Maurice de Saxe, quoted in Bernard Lewis, ed., *A Middle East Mosaic*, 290–91.

5. Sir William Eaton, *A Survey of the Ottoman Empire* (London, 1799), excerpted in the Internet Modern History Sourcebook at www.fordham.edu/halsall. On the capitulations, see Caglor Keydar, Y. Eyup Ozverum, and Donald Quataert, "Port-Cities in the Ottoman Empire," *Fernand Braudel Center Review* 16 (fall 1995), 519–58.

CHAPTER NINE: BRAVE NEW WORLDS

1. Examples of trumpeting the period are Niall Ferguson, *Empire* (New York: Basic Books, 2004), and Paul Johnson, *The Birth of the Modern* (New York: HarperCollins, 1991). The negative stereotypes are too numerous to list, though one pure example might be the works of the English historian Eric Hobsbawm, or earlier in the century, J. A. Hobson, *Imperialism* (London: Allen & Unwin, 1948), originally published in 1902, which set the tone for much of what has been written subsequently.

2. See M. S. Anderson, *The Eastern Question* (London: Macmillan, 1966).

3. Napoleon quoted in J. M. Thompson, *Napoleon Bonaparte* (Oxford, England: Blackwell, 1952), 109. Al-Jabarti's observations found in Abd al-Rahman al-Jabarti, *Journal d'un notable du Cairo durant l'éxpedition française, 1798–1801*, trans. and annotated by Joseph Cuoq (Paris: Albin Michel, 1979), 90–95.

4. On Tahtawi, see Albert Hourani, *Arabic Thought in the Liberal Age, 1798–1939* (Cambridge: Cambridge University Press, 1983), 67–84. The quotation about

national welfare and human progress comes from Tahtawi himself, in Hourani, 82. Also, Lisa Pollard, "The Habits and Customs of Modernity: Egyptians in Europe and the Geography of Nineteenth-Century Nationalism," *Arab Studies Journal* (fall 1999), 51–60. On Muhammad Ali, see Afaf Lutfi al-Sayyid Marsot, *Egypt in the Reign of Muhammad Ali* (Cambridge, England: Cambridge University Press, 1984); Henry Dodwell, *The Founder of Modern Egypt* (1931; repr., New York: AMS Press, 1977); P. J. Vatikiotis, *The History of Egypt*, 3rd ed. (Baltimore: Johns Hopkins University Press, 1985); Khaled Fahmy, "The Era of Muhammad Ali Pasha," in *The Cambridge History of Egypt*, vol. 2, 139–180; Alain Silvera, "The First Egyptian Student Mission to France Under Muhammad Ali," *Middle Eastern Studies* 16 (May 1980), 1–19. I have also drawn on my own descriptions of Muhammad Ali in *Parting the Desert: The Creation of the Suez Canal* (New York: Knopf, 2003).

5. On the Ottoman reforms, see Roderic Davison, *Reform in the Ottoman Empire, 1856–1876* (New York: Gordian Press, 1973). Quotation about the Ottoman state being like a "block of flats" found in Kemal Karpat, "Millets and Nationality," in Braude and Lewis, eds., 141–69. See also Alan Palmer, *The Decline and Fall of the Ottoman Empire* (New York: Barnes & Noble, 1992), 105–43; Stanford Shaw and Ezel Kural Shaw, *History of the Ottoman Empire and Modern Turkey*, vol. 2, *Reform, Revolution and Republic* (New York: Cambridge University Press, 1977), 55ff.; Carter Findley, *Bureaucratic Reform in the Ottoman Empire: The Sublime Porte, 1789–1922* (Princeton, N.J.: Princeton University Press, 1980); Bernard Lewis, *The Emergence of Modern Turkey* (New York: Oxford University Press, 1961).

6. A. L. Tibawi, *A Modern History of Syria* (London, 1969), 138–40; Kamal Salibi, *The Modern History of Lebanon* (London: Weidenfeld and Nicholson, 1965), 139; Meir Zamir, *The Formation of Modern Lebanon* (Ithaca, N.Y.: Cornell University Press, 1985), chap. 1; Samir Khalaf, "Communal Conflict in Nineteenth-Century Lebanon," in Braude and Lewis, eds., *Christians and Jews in the Ottoman Empire*, vol. 2, *The Arabic-Speaking Lands* (New York: Holmes & Meier, 1982), 107–33.

7. For the failures of the *Tanzimat*, see Kemal Karpat, "Millets and Nationality," in Braude and Lewis, vol. 1, 141–69; Fatme Muge Goçek, "Ethnic Segmentation, Western Education, and Political Outcomes: Nineteenth Century Ottoman Society," *Politics Today* (1993); and Fatma Müge Göçek, *Rise of the Bourgeoisie, Demise of Empire: Ottoman Westernization and Social Change* (New York: Oxford University Press, 2002).

CHAPTER TEN: THE AGE OF REFORM

1. Abduh quotations come from Charles Adams, *Islam and Modernism in Egypt* (New York: Russell & Russell, 1933, 1968), 130, and from Malcolm Kerr, *Islamic Reformers* (Los Angeles: University of California Press, 1966), 149. On Abduh, also see Hourani, *Arabic Thought in the Liberal Age*, 131–60. On Afghani, see Hourani as well; also, Nikki Keddi, *An Islamic Response to Imperialism: The Writings*

and Teachings of Sayyid Jamal ad-Din Afghani (Berkeley: University of California Press, 1983). On the legacy of the *salafiyya*, see Nazib Ayubi, *Political Islam: Religion and Politics in the Arab World* (New York: Routledge, 1991); also, Olivier Roy, *The Failure of Political Islam*, trans. Carol Volk (Cambridge: Harvard University Press, 1994). For a look at how the ideas of Abduh and Afghani evolved in the twentieth century, see Jacob Landau, *The Politics of Pan-Islam* (New York: Oxford University Press, 1990).

2. Anne Blunt, *Bedouin Tribes of the Euphrates* (London: Frank Cass, 1968; originally published in 1879). The quotation about the eternal truth of Islam is from Wilfrid Scawen Blunt, *The Future of Islam* (London, 1882), 142. Also, see Elizabeth Longford, *A Pilgrimage of Passion* (London: Weidenfeld & Nicholson, 1979). On Egypt, see Jacques Berque, *Egypt: Imperialism and Revolution,* trans. Jean Stewart (New York: Praeger, 1972).

3. The seminal, and controversial, work describing this group is Edward Said, *Orientalism* (New York: Random House, 1978). The book also contains extensive references to Renan.

4. William Marmaduke Pickthall, *Meaning of the Glorious Koran: An Explanatory Translation* (New York: Knopf, 1930), and *Islam and Progress* (London: Muslim Book Society, 1920).

5. For a general survey of economic trends, see Roger Owen, *The Middle East in the World Economy 1800–1914* (London: I. B. Tauris, 1981). Also, Charles Issawi, *An Economic History of the Middle East and North Africa* (New York: Columbia University Press, 1982).

6. Elie Kedourie, "The American University in Beirut," *Middle Eastern Studies* (October 1966), 74–90; "The American University of Beirut," *Journal of World History* (fall 1967); Daniel Bliss, *The Reminiscence of Daniel Bliss* (New York: Revell, 1920).

7. See E. M. Forster, *Alexandria: A History and a Guide* (New York: Oxford University Press, 1922).

8. Lord Cromer, *Modern Egypt* (New York, 1908), 343; Roger Owen, *Lord Cromer* (New York: Oxford University Press, 2004); Afaf Lutfi al-Sayyid Marsot, *Egypt Under Cromer* (London: John Murray, 1968).

9. Benedict Anderson, *Imagined Communities* (New York: Verso, 1983), 15.

CHAPTER ELEVEN: HOPE AND DESPAIR

1. See, for instance, Robert Spencer, ed., *The Myth of Islamic Tolerance: How Islamic Law Treats Non-Muslims* (New York: Prometheus Books, 2005).

2. See David Fromkin, *A Peace to End All Peace: Creating the Modern Middle East* (New York: Holt, 1989); John Marlowe, *The Seat of Pilate: An Account of the Palestine Mandate* (London: Cresset, 1959)

3. T. E. Lawrence, *Seven Pillars of Wisdom* (New York: Penguin, 1935), 23; Jeremy Wilson, *Lawrence of Arabia: The Authorized Biography of T. E. Lawrence* (New York: Atheneum, 1989).

4. See Fromkin, *A Peace to End All Peace*, 273–300. For the complete text of the Husayn-McMahon correspondence, see George Antonius, *The Arab Awakening*; also, Marlowe, *The Seat of Pilate*, and Christopher Sykes, *Crossroads to Israel* (Bloomington: Indiana University Press, 1973).

5. Quincy Wright, *Mandates Under the League of Nations* (New York: Greenwood Press, 1930, 1968).

6. One of the more prominent of those who portray them as puppets is Elie Kedourie, *England and the Middle East, 1914–1921* (London: Bowes & Bowes, 1956). More nuanced is Elizabeth Monroe, *Britain's Moment in the Middle East, 1914–1956* (Baltimore: Johns Hopkins University Press, 1963).

7. Churchill to Sir Percy Cox, August 15, 1921, in Colonial Office records 730/4/40704, Public Records Office, Kew Gardens, England. On Iraq, see Peter Sluglett, *Britain in Iraq, 1914–1932* (London: Ithaca Press, 1976).

8. Quoted in Sylvia Haim, *Arab Nationalism* (Berkeley: University of California Press, 1976), 64. Also, Fred Lawson, "Westphalian Sovereignty and the Emergence of the Arab State System: The Case of Syria," *International History Review* (September 2000), 529–56.

9. Janice Terry, *The Wafd, 1919–1952: Cornerstone of Egyptian Political Power* (London: Third World Centre, 1982); Marius Deeb, *Party Politics in Egypt: The Wafd and Its Rivals, 1919–1939* (Oxford, England: Ithaca Press for St. Antony's College, 1979).

10. From the White Paper of 1922, quoted in Bernard Wasserstein, *The British in Palestine* (London: Royal Historical Society, 1978), 118.

11. The literature on the creation of Israel is vast. Here are a few select titles: Conor Cruise O'Brien, *The Siege: The Story of Israel and Zionism* (London: George Weidenfeld & Nicolson, 1986); Avi Shlaim, *The Iron Wall: Israel and the Arab World* (New York: Norton, 1999); Benny Morris, *1948 and After: Israel and the Palestinians* (New York: Oxford University Press, 1990); Philip Mattar, *The Mufti of Jerusalem* (New York: Columbia University Press, 1988); Tom Segev, *One Palestine, Complete: Jews and Arabs Under the British Mandate* (New York: Metropolitan Books, 2000); Charles Smith, *Palestine and the Arab-Israeli Conflict*, 3rd ed. (New York: St. Martin's Press, 1996); Howard Sachar, *A History of Israel: From the Rise of Zionism to Our Time* (New York: Knopf, 1996).

CHAPTER TWELVE: IN AN OTHERWISE TURBULENT WORLD

1. See for instance, Fawaz Gerges, *The Far Enemy: Why Jihad Went Global* (New York: Cambridge University Press, 2005); Malise Ruthven, *A Fury for God: The Islamist Attack on America* (London: Granta, 2002); Cook, *Understanding Jihad*; Mark Juergensmeyer, *Terror in the Mind of God: The Rise of Global Religious Violence* (Berkeley: University of California Press, 2003); Nazih Ayubi, *Political Islam* (New York: Routledge, 1993).

2. Here, too, there are of course notable exceptions, one of the most stunning of

which is Richard Bulliet, *The Case for Islamo-Christian Civilization* (New York: Columbia University Press, 2004).

3. Amos Elon, *The Israelis: Founders and Sons* (New York: Penguin, 1971), 106–76; Eyal Zisser, "The Maronites, Lebanon, and the State of Israel: Early Contacts," *Middle Eastern Studies* (October 1995), 889ff.

4. Abdullah quotations from Sachar, *A History of Israel*, 322–23. The "best of enemies" quotation is in Shlaim, *The Iron Wall*, 38. Also see Avi Shlaim, *Collusion Across the Jordan: King Abdullah, the Zionist Movement and the Partition of Palestine* (New York: Columbia University Press, 1988). The Moshe Dayan quotations are from his memoirs, and quoted in Conor Cruise O'Brien, *The Siege*, 368. On Hussein, see for instance Douglas Little, "A Puppet in Search of a Puppeteer: The United Sates, King Hussein, and Jordan," *International History Review* (August 1995), 512–44; Robert Satloff, *From Abdullah to Hussein: Jordan in Transition* (New York: Oxford University Press, 1994); Mary Wilson, ed., *King Abdullah, Britain, and the Making of Jordan* (New York: Cambridge University Press, 1988). See also King Abdullah, *Memoirs*, ed. Philip P. Graves (London: Cape, 1950); and Nadav Safran, *Israel: The Embattled Ally* (Cambridge: Belknap Press, 1981).

5. This was brought home to me most clearly in a speech that King Hussein gave at Oxford University in May 1990, and at a series of conversations I was part of at a World Economic Forum conference at one of Jordan's Dead Sea resorts, hosted by Abdullah and his wife, Queen Rania, in May 2004.

6. The quotation on the National Pact is from Bisharra al-Khuri, in Raghid Solh, *Lebanon and Arab Nationalism, 1936–1945* (unpublished Ph.D. dissertation, St. Antony's College, Oxford University, 1986), 289. On Lebanon and faded dreams, see Fouad Ajami, *The Dream Palace of the Arabs* (New York: Pantheon, 1998); Kamil Salibi, *A House of Many Mansions: The History of Lebanon Reconsidered* (Berkeley: University of California Press, 1989).

7. And the literature here is endless, beginning with V. S. Naipaul, *Among the Believers: An Islamic Journey* (New York: Knopf, 1981), and *Beyond Belief: Islamic Excursions Among the Converted Peoples* (New York: Random House, 1998); Robert Kaplan, *To the Ends of the Earth: A Journey at the Dawn of the 21th Century* (New York: Random House, 1996); Benjamin Barber, *Jihad v. McWorld* (New York: Times Books, 1995); Samuel Huntington, *The Clash of Civilizations and the Remaking of World Order* (New York: Simon & Schuster, 1996); Jeffrey Taylor, *Angry Wind: Through Muslim Black Africa by Truck, Bus, Boat, and Camel* (New York: Houghton Mifflin, 2005); Yaroslav Trofimov, *Faith at War: A Journey on the Frontlines of Islam from Baghdad to Timbuktu* (New York: Henry Holt, 2005); Andrew Wheatcroft, *Infidels: A History of the Conflict Between Christendom and Islam* (New York: Random House, 2004); Bernard Lewis, *What Went Wrong: The Clash Between Islam and Modernity in the Middle East* (New York: Oxford University Press, 2001), and *The Crisis in Islam: Holy War and Unholy Terror* (New York: Modern Library, 2003). There is also the highly regarded and sober work of Giles Kepel, most recently his *The War for Muslim Minds: Islam and the West* (Cambridge: Belknap Press of Harvard University Press, 2004). Then the polemics from the right

and from the left: Robert Spencer, *Islam Unveiled* (New York: Encounter Books, 2002); Tony Blankley, *The West's Last Chance: Will We Win the Clash of Civilizations?* (New York: Regnery, 2005); Irshad Manji, *The Trouble with Islam Today: A Muslim's Call for Reform in Her Faith* (New York: St. Martin's Press, 2004).

8. See once again Richard Bulliet, *The Case for Islamo-Christian Civilization*; also, Noah Feldman, *After Jihad: America and the Struggle for Islamic Democracy* (New York: FSG, 2003); Imam Faisal Abul Rauf, *What's Right with Islam: A New Vision for Muslims and the West* (New York, 2004); Reza Aslan, *No God but God* (New York: Random House, 2005); the many works of John Esposito, including *The Islamic Threat: Myth or Reality?* (New York: Oxford University Press, 1999).

9. Daniel Yergin, *The Prize: The Epic Quest for Oil, Money, and Power* (New York: Simon & Schuster, 1991); David Lamb, "Oil Company Is Heart of Confrontation," *Los Angeles Times*, December 16, 1990; "Discovery! The Story of Aramco Then," *Aramco World* (this multipart series ran in all six issues in 1968). Rachel Bronson, *Thicker Than Oil: America's Uneasy Partnership with Saudi Arabia* (New York: Oxford University Press, 2006).

10. Behcet Yesilbursa, "Turkey's Participation in the Middle East Command and Its Admission to NATO," *Middle Eastern Studies* (October 1999), 70–101; Birol Yesilada, "Turkey's Candidacy for EU Membership," *Middle East Journal* (winter 2002), 94–111; Andrew Mango, "Turkey and the Enlargement of the European Mind," *Middle Eastern Studies* (April 1998), 171–91.

BIBLIOGRAPHY

Abd Allah ibn Hussein. *Memoirs of King Abdullah of Transjordan.* New York: Philosophical Library, 1950.

Adams, Charles. *Islam and Modernism in Egypt.* New York: Russell & Russell, 1933, 1968.

Ajami, Fouad. *The Dream Palace of the Arabs.* New York: Pantheon, 1998.

Anderson, Benedict. *Imagined Communities.* New York: Verso, 1983.

Anderson, M. S. *The Eastern Question.* London: Macmillan, 1966.

Antonius, George. *The Arab Awakening: The Story of the Arab National Movement.* London: Kegan Paul, 2000.

Arberry, A. J. *The Koran Interpreted.* New York: Touchstone, 1955, 1996.

Armstrong, Karen. *Jerusalem: One City, Three Faiths.* New York: Knopf, 1996.

———. *The Battle for God.* New York: Knopf, 2000.

Asbridge, Thomas. *The First Crusade: A New History: The Roots of Conflict Between Christianity and Islam.* New York: Oxford University Press, 2005.

Aslan, Reza. *No God but God: The Origins, Evolution, and Future of Islam.* New York: Random House, 2005.

Ayubi, Nazib. *Political Islam: Religion and Politics in the Arab World.* New York: Routledge, 1991.

al-Baladhuri, Abu-l Abbas Ahmad ibn Jabir. *The Origins of the Islamic State.* Trans. Philip Khuri Hitti. Piscataway, N.J.: Gorgias Press, 2002. Reprint of original 1916 edition, Columbia University Press.

Barber, Benjamin. *Jihad v. McWorld.* New York: Times Books, 1995.

Barbero, Alessandro. *Charlemagne: Father of a Continent.* Berkeley: University of California Press, 2004.

Beg, Tursun. *The History of Mehmed the Conqueror.* Trans. by Halil Inalcik and Rhoads Murphy. Minneapolis: Bibliotheca Islamica, 1978.

Berque, Jacques. *Egypt: Imperialism and Revolution.* Trans. Jean Stewart. New York: Praeger, 1972.

Blankley, Tony. *The West's Last Chance: Will We Win the Clash of Civilizations?* New York: Regnery, 2005.

Bliss, Daniel. *The Reminiscence of Daniel Bliss.* New York: Revell, 1920.

Blunt, Anne. *Bedouin Tribes of the Euphrates.* London: Frank Cass, 1968; originally published 1879.

Blunt, Wilfrid Scawen. *The Future of Islam.* London, 1882.

Bordonove, Georges. *Les Croisades et le royaume de Jerusalem.* Paris: Editions Pygmalion, 2002.

Bosworth, C. E. *The Arabs, Byzantium, and Iran.* Burlington, Vt.: Ashgate Publishing, 1996.

Bozkurt, Gulnihal. *Alman-Ingiliz ve siyasi gelismelerin isigi altinda gayriMuslim Osmanli vatandaslarinin hukuki durumu.* Ankara: Turk Tarik Kuruma Basimevi, 1989.

Bramhall, Edith Clementine. "The Origins of the Temporal Privileges of Crusaders." *American Journal of Theology* (April 1901): 279–92.

Braude, Benjamin and Bernard Lewis, eds. *Christians and Jews in the Ottoman Empire.* Vol. 1, *The Central Lands.* New York: Holmes & Meier, 1982.

———. *Christians and Jews in the Ottoman Empire.* Vol. 2, *The Arabic-Speaking Lands.* New York: Holmes & Meier, 1982.

Braudel, Fernand. *The Mediterranean and the Mediterranean World in the Age of Philip II.* Vol. 1. Berkeley: University of California Press, 1996 (reprint edition).

Bridge, Antony. *Suleiman the Magnificent.* New York: Dorset Press, 1966.

Bronson, Rachel. *Thicker than Oil: America's Uneasy Partnership with Saudi Arabia.* New York: Oxford University Press, 2006.

Brundage, James *The Crusades: A Documentary History.* Milwaukee: Marquette University Press, 1962

Bulliet, Richard. *The Case for Islamo-Christian Civilization.* New York: Columbia University Press, 2004.

———. *Conversion to Islam in the Medieval Period.* Cambridge: Harvard University Press, 1979.

Burns, Robert, ed. *Emperor of Culture: Alfonso X the Learned of Castile and His Thirteenth-Century Renaissance.* Philadelphia: University of Pennsylvania Press, 1990.

Cahen, Claude. "Dhimma." In *The Encyclopedia of Islam.* Leiden: E. J. Brill, 1991.

———. *Orient et Occident au temps des Croisades.* Paris: Editions Aubier, 1983.

Chavush, Sinan. *Suleymanname.* Istanbul: Historical Research Foundation, 1987.

Cheikho, Louis. *Ulama' al-Nasraniyah fi al-Islam, 622–1300* [Christian Scholars Under Islam, 622–1300]. Juniyah, Lebanon: al-Maktabah al-Bulusiyah, 1983.

Constable, Olivia Remie. *Trade and Traders in Muslim Spain: The Commercial Realignment of the Iberian Peninsula.* Cambridge: Cambridge University Press, 1994.

Constable, Olivia Remie, ed. *Medieval Iberia: Readings from Christian, Muslim, and Jewish Sources.* Philadelphia: University of Pennsylvania Press, 1997.

Cook, David. *Understanding Jihad.* Berkeley: University of California Press, 2005.

Cook, Michael. *Forbidding Wrong in Islam.* Cambridge: Cambridge University Press, 2003.

Coope, Jessica A. *The Martyrs of Córdoba: Community and Family Conflict in an Age of Mass Conversion.* Lincoln: University of Nebraska Press, 1995.

Cromer, Lord. *Modern Egypt.* London: Macmillan, 1908.

Crone, Patricia. *God's Rule: Government and Islam.* New York: Columbia University Press, 2004.

Crone, Patricia, and Michael Cook. *Hagarism: The Making of the Islamic World.* Cambridge: Cambridge University Press, 1976.

Crowley, Roger. *1453: The Holy War for Constantinople and the Clash of Islam and the West.* New York: Hyperion, 2005.

Daniel, Norman. *The Arabs and Mediaeval Europe.* London: Longman, 1975.

Davison, Roderic. *Reform in the Ottoman Empire, 1856–1876.* New York: Gordian Press, 1973.

Deeb, Marius. *Party Politics in Egypt: The Wafd and Its Rivals, 1919–1939.* Oxford: Ithaca Press for St. Antony's College, 1979.

al-Din Shayyal, Jamal. *Tarikh Misr al-Islamiya* [The Islamic History of Egypt]. Alexandria: Dar al-Ma'arif, 1967.

Dodwell, Henry. *The Founder of Modern Egypt.* 1931. Reprint, New York: AMS Press, 1977.

Dunlop, Douglas M. *A History of the Jewish Khazars.* Princeton, N.J.: Princeton University Press, 1954.

Eaton, Sir William. *A Survey of the Ottoman Empire.* London, 1799. In Fordham Internet Modern History Sourcebook at www.fordham.edu/halsall.

Ehrenkreutz, Andrew. *Saladin.* Albany: State University of New York Press, 1972.

Ellenblum, Ronnie. *Frankish Settlement in the Latin Kingdom of Jerusalem.* Cambridge: Cambridge University Press, 1998.

Elon, Amos. *The Israelis: Founders and Sons.* New York: Penguin, 1971.

Esposito, John. *The Islamic Threat: Myth or Reality?* New York: Oxford University Press, 1999.

Fahmy, Khaled. "The Era of Muhammad Ali Pasha." Edited by M. W. Daly. Vol. 2 of *The Cambridge History of Egypt.* Cambridge, England: Cambridge University Press, 1998.

Fakhry, Majid. *Islamic Philosophy, Theology, and Mysticism.* Oxford, England: Oneworld, 1997.

Feldman, Noah. *After Jihad: America and the Struggle for Islamic Democracy.* New York: Farrar, Straus and Groux, 2003.

Ferguson, Niall. *Empire.* New York: Basic Books, 2004.

Findley, Carter. *Bureaucratic Reform in the Ottoman Empire: The Sublime Porte, 1789–1922.* Princeton, N.J.: Princeton University Press, 1980.

———. *Ottoman Civil Officialdom.* Princeton, N.J.: Princeton University Press, 1989.

Finkel, Caroline. *Osman's Dream: The Story of the Ottoman Empire.* London: John Murray, 2005.

Fischer-Galati, Stephen. *Ottoman Imperialism and German Protestantism.* Cambridge: Harvard University Press, 1959.

Fletcher, Richard. *The Cross and the Crescent: Christianity and Islam from Muhammad to the Reformation.* New York: Viking, 2004.

———. *Moorish Spain.* Berkeley: University of California Press, 1992.

Fordham Center for Medieval Studies. Internet Medieval Sourcebook, compiled by and edited by Paul Halsall. www.fordham.edu/halsall/source.

Forster, E. M. *Alexandria: A History and a Guide.* New York: Oxford University Press, 1922.

Freely, John. *Istanbul: The Imperial City.* New York: Penguin Books, 1996.

———. *The Lost Messiah: In Search of the Mystical Rabbi Sabbatai Sevi.* New York: Overlook Press, 2001.

Friedmann, Yohanan. *Tolerance and Coercion in Islam: Interfaith Relations in Muslim Tradition.* New York: Cambridge University Press, 2003.

Fromkin, David. *A Peace to End All Peace: Creating the Modern Middle East.* New York: Holt, 1989.

Gabrielli, Francesco. *Arab Historians of the Crusades.* Berkeley: University of California Press, 1969.

Gerber, Jane. *The Jews of Spain: A History of the Sephardic Experience.* New York: Free Press, 1992.

Gerges, Fawaz. *The Far Enemy: Why Jihad Went Global.* New York: Cambridge University Press, 2005.

Gibbon, Edward. *The Decline and Fall of the Roman Empire,* vol. 3. New York: Heritage Press, 1946.

Göçek, Fatma Müge. "Ethnic Segmentation, Western Education, and Political Outcomes: Nineteenth Century Ottoman Society." *Politics Today* (1993).

———. *Rise of the Bourgeoisie, Demise of Empire: Ottoman Westernization and Social Change.* New York: Oxford University Press, 2002.

Goddard, Hugh. *A History of Muslim-Christian Relations.* Chicago: New Amsterdam Books, 2000.

Goffman, Daniel. *The Ottoman Empire and Early Modern Europe.* New York: Cambridge University Press, 2002.

Goitein, S. D. *A Mediterranean Society: An Abridgement in One Volume.* Berkeley: University of California Press, 1999.

Goldstein, David. *Hebrew Poems from Spain.* New York: Schocken Books, 1996.

Goldziher, Ignaz. *Introduction to Islamic Theology and Law.* Princeton, N.J.: Princeton University Press, 1991.

Goodwin, Jason. *Lords of the Horizon: A History of the Ottoman Empire.* New York: Picador, 2003.

Greene, Molly. *A Shared World: Christians and Muslims in the Early Modern Mediterranean.* Princeton, N.J.: Princeton University Press, 2000.

Griffith, Sydney. *Arabic Christianity in the Monasteries of Ninth-Century Palestine.* Burlington, Vt.: Ashgate Publishing, 1992.

———. *The Beginnings of Christian Theology in Arabic: Muslim-Christian Encounters in the Early Islamic Period.* Burlington, Vt.: Ashgate Publishing, 2002.

Gutas, Dimitri. *Greek Thought, Arabic Culture: The Graeco-Arabic Translation Movement in Baghdad and Early Abbasid Society.* New York: Routledge, 1998.

Haim, Sylvia. *Arab Nationalism.* Berkeley: University of California Press, 1976.

Hallam, Elizabeth, ed. *Chronicles of the Crusades: Eye-Witness Accounts of the Wars Between Christianity and Islam.* New York: Welcome Rain, 2000.

Hillenbrand, Carole. *The Crusades: Islamic Perspectives.* New York: Routledge, 2000.

Hobson, J. A. *Imperialism.* London: Allen & Unwin, 1948; originally published 1902.

Hodgson, Marshall C. S. *The Venture of Islam,* vols. 1 and 2. Chicago: University of Chicago Press, 1974.

Holt, P. M. *The Crusader States and Their Neighbors.* New York: Longman, 2004.

Hourani, Albert. *Arabic Thought in the Liberal Age, 1798–1939.* Cambridge: Cambridge University Press, 1983.

Hoyland, Robert. *Seeing Islam as Others Saw It: A Survey and Evaluation of Christian, Jewish and Zoroastrian Writings on Early Islam.* Princeton: Darwin Press, 1997.

Humphries, Stephen. *Islamic History: A Framework for Inquiry.* Princeton, N.J.: Princeton University Press, 1991.

Huntington, Samuel. *The Clash of Civilizations and the Remaking of World Order.* New York: Simon & Schuster, 1996.

Ibn Abd al-Hakam. *History of the Conquests of Egypt, North Africa, and Spain.* Edited by Charles Torrey. Piscataway, N.J.: Gorgias Press, 2002.

Ibn Khaldun. *The Muqaddimah.* Trans. Franz Rosenthal. Princeton, N.J.: Princeton University Press, 1967.

Ibn Munqidh, Usama. *An Arab-Syrian Gentleman and Warrior in the Period of the Crusades.* Trans. Philip Hitti. New York: Columbia University Press, 1929, 2000.

Ibn al-Qalansi. *The Damascus Chronicle of the Crusades.* Ed. and trans. H. A. R. Gibb. New York: Dover Publications, 1932, 2002.

Imber, Colin. *The Ottoman Empire, 1300–1650: The Structure of Power.* New York: Palgrave, 2002.

Inalcik, Halil. *The Ottoman Empire: The Classical Age, 1300–1600.* Trans. Norman Itzkowitz and Colin Imber. New York: Praeger, 1973.

Inalcik, Halil and Cemal Kafadar, eds., *Suleyman the Second and His Time.* Istanbul: Isis Press, 1993.

Irwin, Robert. *For Lust of Knowing: The Orientalists and Their Enemies.* London: Allen Lane, 2006.

Issawi, Charles. *An Economic History of the Middle East and North Africa.* New York: Columbia University Press, 1982.

al-Jabarti, Abd al-Rahman. *Journal d'un notable du Cairo durant l'expédition française, 1798–1801.* Trans. and annotated by Joseph Cuoq. Paris: Albin Michel, 1979.

Jacobs, Joseph. "Samuel Ha-Nagid." www.jewishencyclopedia.com.

Johnson, Paul. *The Birth of the Modern.* New York: HarperCollins, 1991.

Jotischky, Andrew. *Crusading and the Crusader States.* New York: Longman, 2004.

Juergensmeyer, Mark. *Terror in the Mind of God: The Rise of Global Religious Violence.* Berkeley: University of California Press, 2003.

Kafadar, Cemal. *Between Two Worlds: The Construction of the Ottoman State.* Berkeley: University of California Press, 1995.

Kaplan, Robert. *To the Ends of the Earth: A Journey at the Dawn of the 21th Century.* New York: Random House, 1996.

Karabell, Zachary. *Parting the Desert: The Creation of the Suez Canal.* New York: Knopf, 2003.

Keddi, Nikki. *An Islamic Response to Imperialism: The Writings and Teachings of Sayyid Jamal ad-Din Afghani.* Berkeley: University of California Press, 1983.

Kedourie, Elie. "The American University in Beirut." *Middle Eastern Studies* (October 1966): 74–90.

———. *England and the Middle East, 1914–1921.* London: Bowes & Bowes, 1956.

Kennedy, Hugh. *The Court of the Caliphs: The Rise and Fall of Islam's Greatest Dynasty.* London: Weidenfeld & Nicholson, 2005.

———. *The Early Abbasid Caliphate.* London: Croom & Helm, 1981.

———. *Muslim Spain and Portugal: A Political History of al-Andalus.* New York: Longman, 1996.

Kepel, Giles. *The War for Muslim Minds: Islam and the West.* Cambridge: Belknap Press of Harvard University Press, 2004.

Kerr, Malcolm. *Islamic Reformers.* Los Angeles: University of California Press, 1966.

Keydar, Caglor, Y. Eyup Ozverum, and Donald Quataert. "Port-Cities in the Ottoman Empire." *Fernand Braudel Center Review* 16 (Fall 1995): 519–58.

Kinross, Lord. *The Ottoman Centuries: The Rise and Fall of the Turkish Empire.* New York: Morrow, 1977.

Kritovoulus. *History of Mehmed the Conqueror.* Trans. Charles Riggs. Princeton, N.J.: Princeton University Press, 1954.

Landau, Jacob. *The Politics of Pan-Islam.* New York: Oxford University Press, 1990.

Lane-Poole, Stanley. *Saladin: All Powerful Sultan and the Uniter of Islam.* 1898. Reprint, New York: Cooper Square Press, 2002.

Lassner, Jacob. *The Shaping of Abbasid Rule.* Princeton, N.J.: Princeton University Press, 1980.

Lawrence, T. E. *Seven Pillars of Wisdom.* New York: Penguin, 1935.

Lawson, Fred. "Westphalian Sovereignty and the Emergence of the Arab State System: The Case of Syria." *International History Review* (September 2000): 529–56.

Lewis, Bernard. *The Crisis in Islam: Holy War and Unholy Terror.* New York: Modern Library, 2003.

———. *The Emergence of Modern Turkey.* New York: Oxford University Press, 1961.

———. *The Jews of Islam.* Princeton, N.J.: Princeton University Press, 1984.

———. *What Went Wrong: The Clash Between Islam and Modernity in the Middle East.* New York: Oxford University Press, 2001.

———, ed. *A Middle East Mosaic: Fragments of Life, Letters, and History.* New York: Random House, 2000.

Little, Douglas. "A Puppet in Search of a Puppeteer: The United States, King Hussein, and Jordan." *International History Review* (August 1995): 512–44.

Lockman, Zachary. *Contending Visions of the Middle East: The History and Politics of Orientalism.* Cambridge: Cambridge University Press, 2004.

Longford, Elizabeth. *A Pilgrimage of Passion.* London: Weidenfeld & Nicholson, 1979.

Lyons, Malcolm Cameron, and D. E. P. Jackson. *Saladin: The Politics of Holy War.* New York: Cambridge University Press, 1982.

Maalouf, Amin. *The Crusades Through Arab Eyes.* New York: Schocken Books, 1983, 1987.

Mango, Andrew. "Turkey and the Enlargement of the European Mind." *Middle Eastern Studies* (April 1998): 171–91.

Manji, Irshad. *The Trouble with Islam Today: A Muslim's Call for Reform in Her Faith.* New York: St. Martin's Press, 2004.

Mann, Vivian B., Thomas F. Glick, and Jerrilynn D. Dodds, eds. *Convivencia: Jews, Muslims, and Christians in Medieval Spain.* New York: Braziller and the Jewish Museum, 1992.

Marlowe, John. *The Seat of Pilate: An Account of the Palestine Mandate.* London: Cresset, 1959.

Masters, Bruce. *Christians and Jews in Ottoman Arab World: The Roots of Secularism.* New York: Cambridge University Press, 2001.

Mattar, Philip. *The Mufti of Jerusalem.* New York: Columbia University Press, 1988.

Mazower, Mark. *Salonica, City of Ghosts: Christians, Muslims and Jews, 1430–1950.* New York: Knopf, 2005.

McManners, John. *The Oxford Illustrated History of Christianity.* New York: Oxford University Press, 2001.

Menocal, Maria Rosa. *The Ornament of the World: How Muslims, Jews and Christians Created a Culture of Tolerance in Medieval Spain.* New York: Little Brown, 2002.

Meyer, Hans Eberhard. *The Crusades.* New York: Oxford University Press, 1965, 1988.

Monroe, Elizabeth. *Britain's Moment in the Middle East, 1914–1956.* Baltimore: Johns Hopkins University Press, 1963.

Morris, Benny. *1948 and After: Israel and the Palestinians.* New York: Oxford University Press, 1990.

Myerson, Mark. *A Jewish Renaissance in Fifteenth-Century Spain.* Princeton, N.J.: Princeton University Press, 2004.

Myerson, Mark and Edward English, eds., *Christians, Muslims, and Jews in Medieval and Early Modern Spain.* Notre Dame, Ind.: University of Notre Dame Press, 2000.

Naipaul, V. S. *Among the Believers: An Islamic Journey.* New York: Knopf, 1981.

———. *Beyond Belief: Islamic Excursions Among the Converted Peoples.* New York: Random House, 1998.

Nasr, Seyyed Hossein. *Islam: Religion, History, and Civilization.* San Francisco: HarperSanFrancisco, 2002.

———. *Three Muslim Sages.* Cambridge: Harvard University Press, 1964.

Nasr, Seyyed Hossein, and Oliver Leaman, eds., *History of Islamic Philosophy: Part 1.* London: Routledge, 1996.

Nicol, David. *The Last Centuries of Byzantium, 1261–1453.* New York: Cambridge University Press, 1993.

Norwich, John Julius. *Byzantium: The Decline and Fall.* New York: Knopf, 1995.

O'Brien, Conor Cruise. *The Siege: The Story of Israel and Zionism.* London: George Weidenfeld & Nicolson, 1986.

Ostrogorsky, George. *History of the Byzantine State.* London: Blackwell, 1956.

Owen, Roger. *Lord Cromer.* New York: Oxford University Press, 2004.

———. *The Middle East in the World Economy, 1800–1914*. London: I. B. Tauris, 1981.

Palmer, Alan. *The Decline and Fall of the Ottoman Empire*. New York: Barnes & Noble, 1992.

Phillips, Jonathan. *The Fourth Crusade and the Sack of Constantinople*. New York: Penguin Group, 2004.

Pickthall, William Marmeduke. *Islam and Progress*. London: Muslim Book Society, 1920.

———. *Meaning of the Glorious Koran: An Explanatory Translation*. New York: Knopf, 1930.

Pollard, Lisa. "The Habits and Customs of Modernity: Egyptians in Europe and the Geography of Nineteenth-Century Nationalism." *Arab Studies Journal* (Fall 1999): 51–60.

Powell, James M., ed., *Muslims Under Latin Rule, 1100–1300*. Princeton, N.J.: Princeton University Press, 1990.

Qasha, Suhayl. *Al-Masihiyan fi al-Dawlah al-Islamiya* [Christians in the Muslim State]. Beirut: Dar al-Malak, 2002.

Rauf, Imam Feisal Abdul. *What's Right with Islam: A New Vision for Muslims and the West*. San Francisco: HarperSanFrancisco, 2004.

Read, Piers Paul. *The Templars*. London: Weidenfeld & Nicholson, 1999.

Reilly, Richard. *The Medieval Spains*. Cambridge: Cambridge University Press, 1993.

Renard, John. *Seven Doors to Islam: Spirituality and the Religious Life*. Berkeley: University of California Press, 1996.

Rice, David Talbot. *The Byzantines*. New York: Praeger, 1962.

Rice, Eugene, and Anthony Grafton. *The Foundations of Early Modern Europe, 1460–1559*. New York: Norton, 1994.

Robinson, Chase F. *Empire and Elites After the Muslim Conquest: The Transformation of Northern Mesopotamia*. Cambridge: Cambridge University Press, 2000.

Roy, Olivier. *The Failure of Political Islam*. Trans. Carol Volk. Cambridge: Harvard University Press, 1994.

Runciman, Steven. *A History of the Crusades*. 3 vols. Cambridge: Cambridge University Press, 1951–54.

Ruthven, Malise. *A Fury for God: The Islamist Attack on America*. London: Granta, 2002.

Sachar, Howard. *A History of Israel: From the Rise of Zionism to Our Time*. New York: Knopf, 1996.

Safran, Nadav. *Israel: The Embattled Ally*. Cambridge, Mass.: Belknap Press, 1981.

Said, Edward. *Orientalism*. New York: Random House, 1978.

Salibi, Kamil. *A House of Many Mansions: The History of Lebanon Reconsidered*. Berkeley: University of California Press, 1989.

———. *The Modern History of Lebanon*. London: Weidenfeld and Nicholson, 1965.

Satloff, Robert. *From Abdullah to Hussein: Jordan in Transition*. New York: Oxford University Press, 1994.

Saunders, J. J. *A History of Medieval Islam*. London: Routledge and Kegan Paul, 1965.

al-Sayyid Marsot, Afaf Lutfi. *Egypt in the Reign of Muhammad Ali*. Cambridge: Cambridge University Press, 1984.

———. *Egypt Under Cromer.* London: John Murray, 1968.

Schimmel, Annemarie. *Mystical Dimensions of Islam.* Chapel Hill: University of North Carolina Press, 1975.

Schirmann, Jefim. "Samuel Hannagid, the Man, the Soldier, the Politician." *Jewish Social Studies* 2 (April 1951).

Scholem, Gershom. *Sabbatai Sevi: The Mystical Messiah.* Princeton, N.J.: Princeton University Press, 1973.

Schroeder, Eric. *Muhammad's People: An Anthology of Muslim Civilization.* Mineola, N.Y.: Dover Publications, 1955, 2002.

Segev, Tom. *One Palestine, Complete: Jews and Arabs Under the British Mandate.* New York: Metropolitan Books, 2000.

Shaw, Stanford, and Ezel Kural Shaw. *History of the Ottoman Empire and Modern Turkey.* Vol. 2, *Reform, Revolution, and Republic.* New York: Cambridge University Press, 1977.

Shlaim, Avi. *Collusion Across the Jordan: King Abdullah, the Zionist Movement, and the Partition of Palestine.* New York: Columbia University Press, 1988.

———. *The Iron Wall: Israel and the Arab World.* New York: Norton, 1999.

Sluglett, Peter. *Britain in Iraq, 1914–1932.* London: Ithaca Press, 1976.

Silvera, Alain. "The First Egyptian Student Mission to France Under Muhammad Ali." *Middle Eastern Studies* 16 (May 1980): 1–19.

Smith, Charles. *Palestine and the Arab-Israeli Conflict.* 3rd ed. New York: St. Martin's Press, 1996.

Spencer, Robert. *Islam Unveiled.* New York: Encounter Books, 2002.

———, ed. *The Myth of Islamic Tolerance: How Islamic Law Treats Non-Muslims.* New York: Prometheus Books, 2005.

Stange, G. *Baghdad During the Abbasid Caliphate.* London: Oxford University Press, 1924.

Sykes, Christopher. *Crossroads to Israel.* Bloomington: Indiana University Press, 1973.

al-Tabari. *The Early Abbasid Empire,* vol. 2. Trans. John Alden Williams. New York: Cambridge University Press, 1989.

———. *The History of al-Tabari,* vol. 32. Trans. C. E. Bosworth. Albany: State University of New York Press, 1987.

Taylor, Jeffrey. *Angry Wind: Through Muslim Black Africa by Truck, Bus, Boat, and Camel.* New York: Houghton Mifflin, 2005.

Terry, Janice. *The Wafd, 1919–1952: Cornerstone of Egyptian Political Power.* London: Third World Centre, 1982.

Thompson, J. M. *Napoleon Bonaparte.* Oxford, England: Blackwell, 1952.

Tibawi, A. L. *A Modern History of Syria.* London, 1969.

Trofimov, Yaroslav. *Faith at War: A Journey on the Frontlines of Islam from Baghdad to Timbuktu.* New York: Henry Holt, 2005.

Twersky, Isadore, ed. *A Maimonides Reader.* Springfield, N.J.: Behrman House, 1972.

Tyerman, Christopher. *Fighting for Christendom: Holy War and the Crusades.* New York: Oxford University Press, 2004.

Vasiliev, A. A. *History of the Byzantine Empire*, vol. 1. Madison: University of Wisconsin Press, 1952.

Vatikiotis, J. *The History of Egypt.* 3rd ed. Baltimore: Johns Hopkins University Press, 1985.

Wansbrough, John. *Quranic Studies: Sources and Methods of Scriptural Interpretation.* New York: Oxford University Press, 1977.

Wasserstein, Bernard. *The British in Palestine: The Mandatory Government and the Arab-Jewish Conflict 1917–1929.* London: Royal Historical Society, 1978.

Watt, W. Montgomery. *Islamic Political Thought.* Edinburgh: University of Edinburgh, 1968.

Wheatcroft, Andrew. *Infidels: A History of the Conflict Between Christendom and Islam.* New York: Random House, 2004.

Wilson, Jeremy. *Lawrence of Arabia: The Authorized Biography of T. E. Lawrence.* New York: Atheneum, 1989.

Wilson, Mary, ed. *King Abdullah, Britain, and the Making of Jordan.* New York: Cambridge University Press, 1988.

Wolf, Kenneth Baxter. *Christian Martyrs in Muslim Spain.* Cambridge: Cambridge University Press, 1987.

Wright, Quincy. *Mandates Under the League of Nations.* New York: Greenwood Press, 1930, 1968.

Ye'or, Bat. *The Decline of Eastern Christianity Under Islam: From Jihad to Dhimmitude: 7th–20th Century.* Trans. Miriam Kochan and David Littman. Cranbury, N.J.: Fairleigh Dickinson University Press, 1996.

Yergin, Daniel. *The Prize: The Epic Quest for Oil, Money, and Power.* New York: Simon & Schuster, 1991.

Yesilada, Birol. "Turkey's Candidacy for EU Membership." *Middle East Journal* (Winter 2002): 94–111.

Yesilbursa, Behcet. "Turkey's Participation in the Middle East Command and Its Admission to NATO." *Middle Eastern Studies* (October 1999): 70–101.

Zamir, Meir. *The Formation of Modern Lebanon.* Ithaca, N.Y.: Cornell University Press, 1985.

Zinberg, Israel. *History of Jewish Literature: Arabic-Spanish Period.* Trans. Bernard Martin. Cleveland: Case Western Reserve University Press, 1972.

Zisser, Eyal. "The Maronites, Lebanon, and the State of Israel: Early Contacts." *Middle Eastern Studies* (October 1995): 889ff.

ACKNOWLEDGMENTS

Like all books, this one would not have existed without the help and support of friends, colleagues, spouses, and children (though in this particular case, the children in question were either preverbal or not yet born). I also benefitted enormously from that newfangled creation, the Internet and its attendant features, such as the comprehensive used-book network created by Amazon.com and B&N.com that allowed me to assemble a considerable library delivered to my door overnight.

My passion for this subject goes back almost as long as I can remember, but not until my freshman year in college was I introduced to the early history of Islam and the West, in a class taught by Richard Bulliet of Columbia. Not only was he an astonishing lecturer with acute and quirky insights into a long and complex history, but he became a friend and mentor for the next decade and a half, and he has remained a central inspiration. He also offered invaluable advice on the manuscript for this book. Subsequent teachers and colleagues were equally vital, especially the late Albert Hourani of St. Antony's College, Oxford, who guided me gently but firmly toward a more rigorous approach to the past. I owe a debt as well to Derek Hopwood, Rashid Khalidi, Roy Mottahedeh, Roger Owen, and Avi Shlaim.

Though I once knew Arabic, working knowledge has faded, and I benefitted from the assistance of Ja'far Muhibullah in tracking down both old and new Arabic texts and translating select passages. In a related vein, Koray Caliskan provided Ottoman-era documents and contemporary Turkish scholarship to broaden my perspective of the empire and its governance. And LeeAnna Keith once again came to the rescue and did the arduous work of culling through twentieth-century articles on the contemporary Middle East.

Perspective on one's own writing is always difficult, and a number of people generously spent time critiquing and correcting my prose, my interpretations, and my facts. Though I doubt the final text is free from problems in any of these areas, their input can only have improved it. Bruce Feiler, Fareed Zakaria, Gideon Rose, Steven Cook, and Timothy Naftali, dear friends all, and my father, David Karabell (who remains my Platonic ideal of the perfect reader), made me rethink the framework and the tone. Both Zachary Lockman and Rashid Khalidi then went through the later sections line-by-line and forced me to hone my earlier drafts. I cannot thank all of them enough.

It has been more than ten years since John Hawkins agreed to represent me, and I do not know what I would have done without him. As an agent, he has done what any great agent does, but as a friend, he has been more supportive and generous with his time than I ever could have asked. And along with John, Moses Cardona has again made sure that the trains ran on time.

For this work as for others, I have been blessed with an editor whose acumen and pitch-perfect sense for what works and what doesn't makes all of his authors better writers. Ash Green has taught me more about books and writing than I could have imagined, and has done so with fewer words than I might have thought possible. His assistants Luba Ostashevsky and Sara Sherbill have also been invaluable. In England, I owe thanks to Caroline Knox, Gordon Wise, and Eleanor Birne of John Murray in its several incarnations, and each has also added to the manuscript and made possible its final publication.

At Knopf, I have once again been in the capable and astute hands of a marketing and publicity team that includes Sarah Gelman, Nicholas Latimer, and Kathy Zuckerman, all of whom have done their utmost to see that the book gets heard in a noisy, busy world; at John Murray in London, the effervescent Lucy Dixon has done the same. And to Sonny Mehta, thank you for once again gracing this book with your support.

Finally, my wife and companion Nicole Alger read and reread and through it all (and it was a long haul for this one) made her adamant, unwavering support unequivocally clear—even with a toddler in tow and one on the way, with Griffin and then Jasper filling the house with tumult and love. I hope this book makes a contribution to our sometimes-wrenching present, but they are what matters.

INDEX

A NOTE ABOUT THE AUTHOR

Zachary Karabell was educated at Columbia; at Oxford, where he received a master's degree in modern Middle Eastern studies; and at Harvard, where he earned his Ph.D. in 1996. He has taught at Harvard, the University of Massachusetts at Boston, and Dartmouth. He is the author of several books, including *Parting the Desert: The Creation of the Suez Canal* and *The Last Campaign: How Harry Truman Won the 1948 Election,* which won the *Chicago Tribune*'s Heartland Prize. His essays and reviews have appeared in various publications, including *The New York Times, The Wall Street Journal,* the *Los Angeles Times, Newsweek,* and *Foreign Affairs.* He lives in New York City.

A NOTE ON THE TYPE

This book was set in Janson, a typeface long thought to have been made by the Dutchman Anton Janson, who was a practicing typefounder in Leipzig during the years 1668–1687. However, it has been conclusively demonstrated that these types are actually the work of Nicholas Kis (1650–1702), a Hungarian, who most probably learned his trade from the master Dutch typefounder Dirk Voskens. The type is an excellent example of the influential and sturdy Dutch types that prevailed in England up to the time William Caslon (1692–1766) developed his own incomparable designs from them.

Composed by North Market Street Graphics, Lancaster, Pennsylvania

Printed and bound by Berryville Graphics, Berryville, Virginia

Maps by Mapping Specialists

Book design by Robert C. Olsson